P9-EKS-539

WITHDRAWN

MILITARY PERSUASION

STEPHEN J. CIMBALA

MILITARY PERSUASION

DETERRENCE AND PROVOCATION IN CRISIS AND WAR

THE PENNSYLVANIA STATE UNIVERSITY PRESS
UNIVERSITY PARK, PENNSYLVANIA

Library of Congress Cataloging-in-Publication Data

Cimbala, Stephen J.
    Military persuasion: deterrence and provocation in crisis and war / Stephen J.
Cimbala.
        p.   cm.
    Includes bibliographical references and index.
    ISBN 0-271-01005-3. — ISBN 0-271-01006-1 (paper)
    1. Deterrence (Strategy)   2. Nuclear crisis stability.   I. Title.
U162.6.C57   1994
355.02′17—dc20   93-1202
                                                                                   CIP

Published by The Pennsylvania State University Press,
Barbara Building, Suite C, University Park, PA 16802-1003

It is the policy of The Pennsylvania State University Press to use acid-free paper for the
first printing of all clothbound books. Publications on uncoated stock satisfy the minimum requirements of American National Standard for Information Sciences—Perma-
nence of Paper for Printed Library Materials, ANSI Z39.48—1984.

To Father, Whom I Missed

CONTENTS

ACKNOWLEDGMENTS

The author gratefully acknowledges Richard Ned Lebow for reading the entire manuscript in draft and for making many helpful suggestions for revision. Ned's uncommon insights into the problem of crisis management in historical perspective were of much value. I also acknowledge with gratitude colleagues at the Foreign Military Studies Office, Fort Leavenworth, Kansas, especially Jacob Kipp, David Glantz, Timothy Sanz, and Graham Turbiville, Jr., for useful references. I am also in debt to Charles Dick, Director, Soviet Studies Research Centre, Royal Military Academy, Sandhurst, for his kind assistance in updating my knowledge of post-Soviet Russian military doctrine and personnel policy. David Tarr, University of Wisconsin, Madison, and George Quester, University of Maryland, College Park, have taught me a great deal about nuclear strategy pertinent to this study. My awareness of NATO past and present owes much to Gregory Treverton, Council on Foreign Relations, and to Keith Dunn, presently assigned to the U.S. NATO mission. Raymond Garthoff and Bruce Blair of the Brookings Institution have responded to numerous inquiries of mine with unfailing insight and good humor.

For the chapter on World War I mobilization I am especially grateful to Todd Christensen and Jack Snyder, both of Columbia University, for helpful references and shared insights. Jack Levy, Rutgers University, pointed me toward very important references on the subject of system polarity and war. Desmond Ball has provided many helpful sources, including his own definitive writings, on the evolution of U.S. nuclear strategy. Colin Gray and Keith Payne of National Security Research, Inc. and James Tritten, U.S. Naval Postgraduate School, have generously shared their work and insights on nuclear strategic doctrine. Commander Michael N. Pocalyko, USN, Fellow of the Atlantic Council of the United States, has offered stimulating critiques and vital encouragement for my work, as has William Martel of Harvard University. Patrick M. Morgan, University of California, Irvine, has reviewed draft manuscripts for me and called to my attention with great tact and erudition omissions and potential misconstructions. None of the persons named above shares any responsibility for arguments or viewpoints expressed here, nor does the Pennsylvania State University.

Special thanks are owed to Madlyn Hanes and Edward Tomezsko of the Penn State Delaware County Campus for institutional support. At Penn State Press, Peter Potter, editor, provided important encouragement to complete this study, and Cherene Holland, managing editor, supervised the editing and production process. Charles Purrenhage's careful eye caught errors of commission and omission. Diane Wolf of the Delaware County Campus provided clerical support, and my family accepted another academic excursion with good grace.

INTRODUCTION

This book was prompted by years of work in the field of nuclear strategy and deterrence theory as applied to crisis management. I became increasingly aware of the disparity between the kinds of threats that nuclear armed states would have to make in order to use nuclear weapons as a means of war prevention, on one hand, and the extent to which history supported confidence in the crisis management skills of political leaders, on the other. The history of prenuclear crisis management and deterrence failure was considerable. Some of the more important twentieth-century cases are discussed in the chapters that follow. Nevertheless, U.S., Soviet, and other political leaders and academics during the Cold War years expressed great confidence in the durability of nuclear deterrence and in the stability of crisis management based on nuclear brinkmanship. The absence of any war, nuclear or otherwise, between the U.S. and Soviet superpowers from 1945 to 1991 provides compelling evidence for some observers that the *pax atomica* prevented wars which otherwise might have propelled Washington, Moscow, and their allies into a war of unprecedented destructiveness.

Believers in the efficacy of nuclear deterrence were the inheritors of the Western tradition founded by Clausewitz which encouraged optimism about the ability of prudently used force to support policy objectives. Although an actual nuclear war would be too destructive to serve any useful policy aim, nuclear-crisis management could be choreographed along the same lines that prenuclear systems of threat and coercion had been. The difference was that prenuclear threateners were provided with no crystal ball to determine what might happen if deterrence actually failed, whereas policymakers and military planners in the nuclear age thought they knew only too well. Therefore, pessimism about the actual conduct of a nuclear war developed hand in hand with optimism about using the tools of crisis management for nuclear coercion.

I argue that both prenuclear and nuclear threatmaking were dependent for their success on the ability of political leaders and military planners to make specific and limited threats, backed by implicit or explicit reassurances against further crisis deterioration or military escalation. In contrast to much writing in the field of military studies and political science, to the effect that the most imposing threats of the most dire punishment make for successful military persuasion, I argue that sticks unaccompanied by carrots almost always prove to be self-destructive. Threats to impose military costs on a prospective attacker during a crisis, or threats to escalate an ongoing conflict, are more likely to be persuasive if they also include clear signals that the threatener intends to avoid military provocation unrelated to the initial demand.

In contrast to the roseate appraisal of nuclear deterrence stability offered by policymakers and by many analysts, I suggest that many Cold War deterrent threats were dangerously one-sided. They sufficed to raise the anxieties of political leaders and military planners on the other side, but they did not provide an equally important component for peacetime and crisis stability: the avoidance of undesired and unnecessary provocation of potential adversaries. What appeared to be very simple threats of nuclear first strike, first use, or retaliation actually relied upon political and military-technical factors that complicated the process of threatmaking. What was intended by one side as a message for the other was not always the message that was received. Threats were not unconditional if they were to be persuasive; they had to be very specific as to the behavior required of one state by another, and they had to convince the compliant state that its compliance would leave it better off than noncompliance would.

In a classroom experiment it might be easy to communicate precisely the specific actions demanded by the threatener and the precise nature of the consequences that would follow for the recipient of the threat in the event of noncompliance. In actual situations of crisis management, leaders are under stress and engaged in a hot-headed activity. Their information comes from partial and distorted sources, filtered through layers of bureaucratic residue and coded by means of perceptual frameworks that give subjective and arbitrary meaning to events. Leaders during a crisis are concerned not only about the foreign policy and strategic outcomes of their choices, but also about the domestic policy implications of their decisions. Some crisis man-

agement decisions that were wrongly taken have forced leaders into resignation or other political disgrace; other wrong decisions have, as we shall see
in the chapters that follow, destroyed empires and remade the map of Europe.

In Chapter 1 I attempt to bring together some of the more important
streams of policy theory and strategic analysis relevant to crisis management
during July 1914, at the start of World War I. There is a significant controversy in the academic literature concerning the extent to which the Great
War was accidental or inadvertent: that is to say, in what measure the powers
of Europe stumbled into war rather than having intended it. One side of the
argument points to the ominous signs during the years before the crisis: the
increasing rigidity of alliance systems in the decades immediately preceding
the outbreak of war; the false expectation by political leaders that they could
contain or surmount crises as they had in the second Moroccan crisis and in
the Balkan crisis of 1912; the naive belief that any war, if it should break out
in one region, say the Balkans, could be localized and need not spread beyond the confines of that region.

Another side of the argument acknowledges important factors external to
the mind-sets of Europe's political leaders and military planners in July and
August. Yet such factors, in this view, constitute a necessary but not a sufficient explanation for the onset of the July crisis and its spiral into war. The
perceptions and expectations of policymakers and military planners prior to
the outbreak of war, and even before the July crisis itself, must also be taken
into account. There are two ways in which these perceptions and expectations (i.e., perceptions about the future, expectations of certain states of
affairs) are relevant to 1914 crisis management. First, and the more obvious,
is that decisions in July 1914 were being made by leaders with certain mental
predispositions and on the basis of what was known at the moment. Second,
and more subtle, the available choices in July 1914 had been conditioned by
previous decisions taken by foreign offices and military planners. Those decisions had established organizational and military-doctrinal precedents
which proved to influence the subsequent choices made by political leaders
to escalate the crisis of July 1914 and to engage in war.

Among these precedents were the mobilization systems of the great powers
of Europe. Not only did these systems determine how many men were put
into the colors and saddled up for war, and at what speed, but they embodied
a theory of war. The German system of mobilization went hand in hand with
a strategy for a rapid campaign of annihilation against France, after which
Germany would strike at the slower-to-mobilize Russians. The German strat-

egy, based on the various versions of the Schlieffen Plan and modeled on a classical "Cannae," or envelopment of the defender's forces by the attacker, depended on getting in the first decisive blow against opponents to the east or to the west. Germany's offensive grand strategy, left largely to the General Staff to devise in the years preceding the outbreak of war, admitted of no partial victory or mobilization for the purpose of deterrence only.

Germany's strategy, therefore, depended upon the Russians' inability to rapidly deploy forces capable of launching offensives into East Prussia before Germany could defeat France, in a campaign estimated to last about six weeks. As Russia improved its capabilities for mobilization after 1912, German military planners faced the unpleasant prospect of fighting on two fronts simultaneously. This might have suggested to the German General Staff and to Germany's political leadership the need to reconsider the basic premises of its strategy. Instead, it caused leaders to grasp even more tightly the preconceived campaign plan based on rapid mobilization. Since any lag in German mobilization behind that of its potential enemies was judged by the German high command to be fatal, mobilization became tantamount to war for the German political leadership as well as for the military.

It was all the more unfortunate that Germany's reasoning entered this cul-de-sac, since not everyone in Russia's political and military leadership considered mobilization to be tantamount to war. In July 1914 the Russian foreign minister attempted a scheme of partial mobilization limited to those military districts facing Austria-Hungary, avoiding for the moment the mobilization of military districts facing Germany. The Russian General Staff could not implement this plan, however, owing to the objections of the quartermaster general and others that a partial mobilization was both technically impossible and potentially disruptive of general mobilization should that become necessary. The first objection had merit, but the second was undemonstrated and offered a convenient rationale for filibustering to death the option of partial mobilization. Even had Russia stuck to partial mobilization, rather than moving rapidly into general mobilization shortly thereafter, partial mobilization alone was sufficiently threatening to Germany's strategy. For Germany's planning assumptions did not allow for any slippage in the timetable by which Germany's mobilization was to outpace Russia's.

Russian mobilization was complicated by diverse theories of war and of the relative importance of various theaters of operation, should Germany attack in alliance with Austria-Hungary. Two variants of a preferred war plan were laid down in the 1912 revisions: one variant assumed (correctly) that Germany's main thrust would be directed westward against France; the other provided for the less likely contingency that Germany would unleash the larger share of its fighting power against Russia immediately upon the outbreak of war. Unfortunately for the Russians, their strategy and mobilization plans were just sufficient to provoke worries in Berlin about the viability of German strategy, but insufficient to guarantee reliable performance in the event of deterrence failure. Within weeks of the outbreak of war, Russia committed its forces to a prompt offensive in two directions: against Austria-Hungary Russia attained considerable success, but against Germany its forces met with military disaster.

The irony is that Germany and Russia were both practicing crisis management without a license. Each had paper plans for a two-front war, but neither had the capability to fight even a short war on two fronts, let alone an extended one. Germany and Russia attempted to bluff their way through the July crisis with threats but did nothing to avoid unnecessary provocations. Thus, both sides' military planning assumptions helped create a crisis security dilemma. Each side viewed the other's moves to resolve the crisis as devious positioning for an inevitable war. This judgment then became a self-fulfilling prophecy: efforts to resolve the crisis diplomatically were disregarded as leaders on both sides focused on the military mobilizations taking place. Eventually, leaders in Berlin and St. Petersburg concluded that the crisis was no longer amenable to resolution by peaceful means. Through a complex maze of mutual recrimination, faulty communications, and mismatched expectations, preparedness for war had led to war itself.

In Chapter 2 I ask whether U.S. nuclear war plans during the Cold War resembled the Schlieffen Plan by which Germany prepared for the eventuality of World War I. They certainly resembled the Schlieffen Plan in one respect: whether dictated by technology or improvised by the creativity of military planners and military leaders, U.S. nuclear war plans offered little flexibility for crisis-bound presidents on the brink of nuclear war. Some would lay the blame for this condition on the technology itself. In this admittedly compelling view, nuclear weapons were so destructive even in small numbers that the idea of nuclear flexibility was mischievously misleading to policymakers who might mistakenly believe nuclear war to be politically feasible. However logical this argument was, policymakers and military planners resisted it. Presidents, defense secretaries, and their principal military advisers wanted options other than the option of massive retaliatory nuclear strikes, on the reasonable grounds that unlimited retaliation might not be appropriate in response to limited aggression.

Allowing for the possibility that limited nuclear options did exist which were feasible in the context of planning scenarios, the implementation of such options in fielded forces must have proved discouraging to proponents of flexibility. The problem was that war plans had to be laid down far in advance and executed with rigid precision, much as the Schlieffen Plan had to be, in order for traditional military objectives to be accomplished after deterrence had failed. Knowing this, the Americans and the Soviets alike built retaliatory forces, certain components of which were primed for prompt retaliatory launch or even preemptive attack. Further, the establishment of secure command and control over nuclear weapons in peacetime disallowed a plenitude of limited options for a multitude of scenarios for actual warfighting. The U.S. strategic nuclear command-and-control system could under the best of conditions provide for a responsive launch against a comprehensive target set following surprise attack. Limited strikes for the purpose of demonstrating resolve, in the face of Soviet political intimidation supported by selective attacks, were of little interest to military operators of the command system and were judged to be equally irrelevant by the unified and specified commanders whose nuclear forces would be sent into battle.

With regard to nuclear crisis management, U.S. and Soviet nuclear command-and-control systems were required to optimize between two admittedly desirable, but not fully reconcilable, objectives. They were tasked to respond promptly to authorized launch commands, and they were tasked equally to guarantee against accidental or unauthorized launch. In time of peace the second objective, sometimes referred to as "negative control," took precedence. During a crisis, more attention had to be paid to the first objective, often described as "positive control." At the margin, an escalating crisis would of necessity pass a point at which positive control became relatively more important than negative control. This point would be reached when U.S. and Soviet forces were both poised to retaliate in case the other struck first, a condition that very competent Western analysts contend never actually came about during the nuclear age.

During several Cold War crises U.S. and Soviet leaders learned a good deal about how their command-and-control systems really worked. It turned out in several important cases that options which had been preplanned for crisis management, using nuclear or conventional forces to support diplomacy, proved insufficient for presidential taste. The Berlin crisis of 1948 and the Cuban missile crisis of 1962 required that leaders order à la carte: the Berlin airlift and the U.S. "quarantine" of Soviet shipments into Cuba. Nuclear weapons in these and other instances, at best backed up a position that was already strong on the basis of one side's conventional force capabilities.

By dint of conventional force strength, the Soviets were in a relatively favorable position in Berlin, as was the United States in Cuba. In both instances,
too, U.S. and Soviet leaders discovered that brinkmanship strategies have
their delayed risks, and that those risks are not necessarily controllable to
unilateral advantage.

Chapter 3 takes up the problem of war's opening phase and how visions of
the initial period of war are reflected in a state's crisis management techniques and mobilization plans. Soviet strategy in the years immediately preceding World War II offered a conciliatory diplomatic stance, including the
ultimate concession of a temporary alliance with Hitler, in order to buy time
for the sorting out of Soviet military preparedness. Some of the shortfall in
equipment and training was made good by June 22, 1941, but not the lack
of adequate intelligence on the German style of warfare. Nor did the 1939–
41 period allow a decimated Soviet General Staff and subordinate commands
sufficient time to replace highly skilled officers killed in the purge. Stalin
emphasized nonprovocation of Hitler until the Soviet armed forces could be
fully readied for battle, which Stalin hoped to accomplish by 1942. Hitler
pushed the button sooner, aware that the socialist Soviet Union could not
be counted on as a perpetual ally for a fascist Germany.

Stalin's failure was not the mistake of appeasement, but a flawed grand
strategy which sought to compensate for the void left by his potential allies
in the west. By the time the British and French were convinced that something had to be done to resist Hitler, Stalin was persuaded that they might
never move at all. Accordingly, he jiggered the odds in his favor by accepting
the Ribbentrop-Molotov Pact's guaranty of eastern Poland as a buffer zone.
In the event, in June 1941, it buffered very little as Hitler's legions streamed
across on their way to the gates of Moscow. Subsequent to Stalin's death,
Soviet historians treated his grand strategy with rude hostility. Stalin is assumed to have overlooked repeated and validated warnings of Hitler's intentions prior to the actual start of Operation Barbarossa. However, Stalin had
reason to distrust reports from his Western "allies," including their earlier
failure to stand against Hitler when the cost would have been less. Stalin
also had little naiveté concerning Hitler's long-range ambitions: these were
plainly spelled out in the führer's much ballyhooed diatribe of the 1920s,
Mein Kampf. The Soviet leader saw in the international system a special
security problem: the naturally untrustworthy character of capitalist states in
general, supplemented by their perfidious efforts, as he saw it, to turn Hitler
against him.

If the Soviet grand strategy in the first years of World War II placed too many bets on nonprovocation and too few on deterrence, the experience of World War II chastened postwar Soviet military planners and political leaders. After 1945 they understood the importance of surprise in the initial period of a modern war: the attacker could, with adequate surprise followed by sufficient military weight, place the defender in a hopeless position. Modern weapon technologies, even without nuclear weapons, made possible the infliction of devastating surprise strikes and stunning blows on unprepared defenders. The Japanese attack on U.S. naval forces at Pearl Harbor had shown, too, that important tactical success could be achieved by means of sufficient surprise as to the precise time and place of attack.

The problem for the Japanese and the Germans in 1941 was that operational and tactical successes could not be compounded into strategic victories. Their American and Soviet opponents had the time and resources to mobilize for an extended war of attrition, which neither the Japanese nor the Germans could win. Thus, brilliant strategies for the initial period of a war of destruction proved insufficient to resolve the test of total war, in which the productive capacities of entire societies and their ability to mobilize for war were tested to the limit. World War I had rather unexpectedly provided for the combatants a preview of what a total and protracted global conflict might be like. This had two effects on grand strategic and mobilization planning by the powers between the world wars. On one hand, recent memory of the scope and destructiveness of World War I made leaders conscious of the benefits of conciliation and nonprovocation. The door was open to diplomatic approaches of all sorts, and the 1920s and 1930s saw a movable feast of proposals for multilateral peacekeeping, arms control, and disarmament, including a declaration by major powers outlawing war itself.

On the other hand, memories of World War I played tricks on the leaders, who misremembered and imagined that airplanes used for the purpose of direct attacks on populations might circumvent the necessity for prolonged and sluggish fighting on the ground. Military theorists in Britain, France, and Germany struggled to devise prewar strategies that would avoid the protracted stalemate of World War I. Germany came closest to getting it right: operational and tactical innovations which came to be known as blitzkrieg gave the Wehrmacht an impressive victory over France in the spring of 1940. But such victories left Germany encircled by potentially hostile states and actual enemies against which operational and tactical creativity could not compensate. Hitler was not content with a war of limited liability, and he knew nothing of war termination short of final victory or defeat. As his retreating forces in the east and west gave way to the Soviets and to the

U.S., British, and Canadian invaders of Fortress Europe, a new world order had been established.

The post-1945 world order would be based on bipolarity, nuclear weapons technology, and U.S.-Soviet ideological rivalry. In time this settled into a predictable opposition between U.S. "containment" strategy and a two-sided Soviet foreign and defense policy. The first side of Soviet Cold War policy was the official side: the Soviet Union would take its place as a status quo power and as a member of the U.N. Security Council charged with the collective promotion of international peace and security. The second side was the ideological side, which insisted upon the waging of a perpetual struggle against capitalist democracy, although during the 1950s Soviet Premier Khrushchev allowed that this struggle need not result inevitably in world war. A competitive "peaceful coexistence" required that both sides adjust to bipolarity, to nuclear weapons, and to the need for developing rules for crisis management as well as for the conduct of day-to-day business.

Soviet military planners were required to serve both sides of the policy requirement. Weapons of mass destruction provided a deterrent in support of the politico-military status quo against U.S. and NATO nuclear first use, and those same weapons conferred upon Soviet diplomacy the favorable aura of nuclear superpower status. At the same time, because the Soviet Union during the Cold War remained, in its view, a socialist vanguard vulnerable to encirclement by capitalist states, military vigilance could not be relaxed. A high standard of vigilance was required because of the speed and destructiveness of nuclear weapons in the hands of the Soviet Union's mortal enemies.

As a result, the sociopolitical level of Soviet military doctrine and the military-technical level, insofar as it applied to expectancy of and preparedness for total war, existed in separate compartments for much of the Cold War. The social and political level of doctrine emphasized that war between capitalism and socialism was not inevitable and, eventually, that any such conflict would be downright foolish. The move toward U.S.-Soviet détente in the 1970s was one for which the sociopolitical level of doctrine was reasonably well prepared. The military-technical level of doctrine, on the other hand, was less congruent with the flow of diplomacy, high politics, and arms control. At the military-technical level, Soviet military theorists of the 1970s and first half of the 1980s continued to emphasize the need to prepare for war and to respond to surprise attack, whether conventional or nuclear, by inflicting a decisive retaliatory strike or counteroffensive.

Mikhail Gorbachev's revolutionary years influenced Soviet military strategy in profound ways, but the reforms turned to the experience of the Second World War for some of their more important insights. Analyses by Soviet "new thinkers" of a possible realignment of Soviet military strategy toward the strategic, operational, or tactical defensive were encouraged by West European counterparts who studied "nonoffensive defense." Gorbachev's dramatic 1988 announcement, concerning his plan for major unilateral reductions in Soviet ground and tactical air forces stationed in Eastern Europe and in the western military districts of the Soviet Union, meant that the USSR had adopted military defensivism as its official grand strategy, although it took some time for Western observers to become believers. Once the West was convinced, the door was open to the conclusion of far-reaching arms control agreements on disarmament in Central Europe, including the important Conventional Forces in Europe (CFE) agreement of November 1990.

If the CFE reductions were carried out as it appeared they would be, then the Commonwealth republics of the former Soviet Union, especially Russia, could pursue "operational arms control" as a complement to structural arms reductions in the 1990s. Operational arms control is intended to render military forces, doctrines, and strategies more transparent to observers. This transparency reassures all sides that no one intends a surprise attack, and the monitoring and limitation of military exercises further increases the likelihood of deterrence and crisis stability. Operational arms control is a test of states' ability to combine the value of a nonprovocative military posture with the capability for deterring any aggression that might be contemplated by political or military leaders in times of stress.

Structural arms control (force reductions) and operational arms control (force operations) are way stations toward an improved security community, one in which war between the constituent members becomes, literally, unthinkable. It will be some time (if ever) before Europe reaches so benign a condition, even if civil wars such as the one in Yugoslavia during 1991 are not counted in the tally of wars. U.N. sanctions against Iraq in 1990 and the U.S.-led coalition war against that country in 1991 persuaded some observers that a security community at the international level was no longer a will-o'-the-wisp. The "new world order" was once again an acceptable phrase in polite conversation, and the unprecedented success of U.S.-led multilateral diplomacy and coalition warfare was judged by many observers as a favorable omen for future international stability.

In Chapter 4 I discuss the Gulf War of 1991 as an exercise in coercive diplomacy comprising two stages. The first stage was an effort by the United

States and its allies, through diplomatic pressures and economic sanctions, to induce Iraq to quit Kuwait. This effort having failed, the second stage involved the waging of a coercive air war in order to get Saddam Hussein to cry uncle and surrender before engaging in ground warfare. One might add that this last notion was more appealing to George Bush and other heads of state, and to those who wore air force uniforms, than it was to the ground commanders of the coalition states and to their Pentagon colleagues who wanted in on the action. In any event, both stages of "coercive diplomacy" failed to terminate the conflict (the significance of coercive diplomacy in war termination is expanded upon in Chapter 5).

From the standpoint of Western models of deterrence theory, it was difficult to understand what kept Saddam hanging in. He apparently counted on breaking up the coalition, prior to war or during it, by creating rifts between the Arab members of the Bush entente and the others. His attacks on Israeli cities with Scud surface-to-surface missiles were designed to bring Israel into the war as a coalition-buster. Many Western and other experts in war and diplomacy were surprised at Israel's apparent restraint, no doubt related to the efficiency with which the Iraqi air force and command-and-control infrastructure were destroyed or immobilized without Israel's help. Also relevant was the U.S. willingness to provide Patriot air-defense missiles as a symbol of commitment to the principle that Israeli citizens at large should not pay the price for their government's perceived self-restraint. (Whether the Patriots actually reduced or increased casualties from Iraqi attacks was a matter of some debate among military experts, but not germane to the political issue being noted here.)

Saddam's strategy had three basic components which had to be influenced by U.S. and allied pressure short of war or by actual use of force. First, he sought to pose to the United States and its allies the plausible threat of a war of attrition on the ground, conveying with little subtlety an image of massive casualties which Saddam assumed would restrain Western publics and their governments. A second component, already discussed with regard to possible Israeli involvement in the war, was horizontal escalation: if war there must be, then shatter the opposed coalition with a knight's move that divides the opposed entente along painful lines of cultural and political cleavage. A third component of Saddam's grand strategy was to preserve his personal political-military command and control over the armed forces and society of Iraq even after any military phase of the conflict had been concluded. In this he has succeeded thus far, having survived into 1993 as head of state, party, government, and everything else.

The Bush administration was criticized in some quarters for stopping coalition military operations short of Saddam's capture and overthrow. Such hindsight wisdom failed to take into account the constraints under which Bush had to operate in order to hold together a disparate coalition, whose Arab members could not be counted on to support the overthrow of Saddam's regime. In the event, the coalition held together, and the United Nations granted approval for the use of force in a very limited and specific war aim: the expulsion of Iraq from Kuwait. That having been accomplished, any more ambitious political objective improvised after the fact would complicate future efforts to bring together status quo states against rejectionists.

Whether Iraq's decision to attack Kuwait was a failure of deterrence can be debated. Saddam was desperate for oil revenues, and the United States and other oil-consuming powers were less than totally clear in their messages prior to August 2, 1991, about what they would and would not accept. Had Iraq known that Gorbachev's Soviet Union was going to side with the United Nations and against its former military client in Baghdad, it might have made calculations by Saddam's military advisers more pessimistic with regard to the probable outcome of an invasion. Then, too, Saddam was economically desperate, having brought his economy close to bankruptcy with the Iran-Iraq War in the 1980s. On the other hand, the occupation of Kuwait would not yield additional revenues for Iraq unless the invasion met with no international resistance or only token resistance. Perhaps the latter was what Saddam expected; but, even so, the seizure of Kuwait alone would not rescue his entire portfolio. Iraqi leaders must have counted on the seizure of Kuwait being followed by the coercion of Saudi Arabia through threat of invasion, for Saudi Arabia was the key to global prices for crude oil.

Although Saddam's scheme was momentarily derailed and the United Nations gave an unprecedented demonstration of international security and peacekeeping in action, the outcomes of the Gulf crisis and the war were not entirely positive. U.S. and allied crisis management, including coercive diplomacy backed by overwhelming strategic military capabilities, failed to dislodge Iraq from Kuwait without resort to war. Iraq was not deterred from attacking Kuwait. Once war had begun, the most devastating conventional air bombardment since World War II failed to coerce Iraq to surrender. Saddam hoped that fear of a costly ground war would act as an intrawar deterrent for democratic governments accountable to their publics. This was an Arab post-Vietnam analysis of U.S. strategic culture and public policy which proved fatal to Iraq's military strategy, though not to Saddam's regime. Finally, by surviving with a crippled armed force but with absolute political power, Saddam had obtained a personal victory of sorts, regardless of the losses his countrymen suffered as a result.

Those losses, incidentally, told a story about the strategy of coercive air warfare. The concept of a "surgical" air campaign or of precision bombing of military targets only, whether in World War II or in Iraq in 1991, was more theory than practice. The great majority of the bombs dropped on Iraq were not laser-designated "smart bombs" which flew into open chimneys, but "dumb bombs" which were dropped en masse over the dug-in positions of Iraqi defenders (and far from the prying eyes of U.S. news media). The air war against Iraq was intentionally both coercive, or compellent, and destructive. In conventional war, as opposed to nuclear war, the retaliatory punishment is part of the bargaining and negotiation being conducted between adversaries. The destruction visited on Iraq by coalition air power, bombing almost at will from the first days of the war, could not be separated analytically (or in the daily experience of Iraqi noncombatants and soldiers) from the message that those sorties were intended to convey. Coercive air power in the Persian Gulf was used both massively and selectively. Civilians were not targeted indiscriminately, but neither were they spared if they got in the way of destruction that military planners considered essential to successful prosecution of the war. In conventional war, the coercive and destructive aspects of fighting are products of the same forces; in nuclear deterrence strategy, the two effects are separated, and the coercive power of nuclear weapons is thought to reside in their skillful nonuse.

Chapter 5 engages a question that is raised indirectly in the chapter that precedes it: namely, bringing wars to conclusion, and the relationship between deterrence and nonprovocation in doing so. I argue that there are three principal components to the problem of war termination: an agreed battle, escalation control, and coercive diplomacy. These are not the traditional categories within which people have discussed how to end wars. Understandably, policymakers and many academic theorists have emphasized the division of spoils at the conclusion of a war: who won and who lost, and by how much? Obviously these are important issues, but I want to consider them in a special way. Instead of looking backward from the *outcomes* of crisis management or war and inferring what the motives for continued fighting "must have been," I emphasize the *process* of decisionmaking by which leaders and military planners establish a calculus of victory or defeat.

A process-oriented focus on war termination does not exclude awareness of relative stakes and interests held by the warring parties. Nor does it imply that outcome-oriented analysis is not valuable; to the contrary, analysis that is focused on crisis or wartime outcomes is indispensable for progress in the fields of peace and defense studies. My emphasis in the present discussion treats outcomes as components of a process. Actors' expectations about possible outcomes, their subjective estimates of consequences attached to possible outcomes, and their preference orderings among those consequences are "inputs" into a larger matrix of objective and subjective variables leading to decision. For example, it mattered very much to President Kennedy and his advisers during the Cuban missile crisis that the principal U.S. objective of crisis management remain clear to Khrushchev *and* to the various presidential advisers and other U.S. governmental players in decisionmaking. That objective was specified by the president early on: the removal of Soviet missiles from Cuba.

In the course of U.S. crisis deliberations about the Cuban missiles in October 1962, objectives in addition to the objective of missile removal were introduced by one or more participants in the decisionmaking process. And once the crisis became public, persons outside the circle of Kennedy's advisers offered menus of their own. It was also important that although the president had established a clearly predominant political objective for crisis management, the hierarchy of the objectives below missile removal was less clear. The United States wanted to see the missiles removed without a war between American and Soviet forces. In order to convince Khrushchev that he meant business, though, Kennedy judged that it was necessary to commit the United States to an air strike against Soviet missile sites in Cuba and other targets, or to an invasion of Cuba with U.S. forces, in the event that Khrushchev refused to back down. Thus, although the United States preferred to avoid war, it was not prepared to avoid war at any price. It was willing to risk war, even nuclear war, in order to cause the missiles to be removed.

It might be objected to the last assertion that the United States knew, as a result of its airborne and newly available satellite reconnaissance, that it had strategic nuclear superiority over the Soviet Union. Therefore, Kennedy could afford to press Khrushchev to the limit. That Kennedy chose not to do so demonstrated an innate shrewdness on his part plus an intellectual comprehension of the problem of inadvertent escalation. Kennedy assessed correctly, undoubtedly with the assistance of advisers such as Robert McNamara, that a *relatively favorable* outcome of any U.S.-Soviet nuclear exchange would represent an *absolute* disaster. Khrushchev was also smart enough to recognize this. Thus, Kennedy's bargaining position was not as strong as it might have seemed on the basis of comparative force ratios, including the poststrike ratios of Soviet forces compared to U.S. forces.

Khrushchev had gambled that he could get away with his bold move undetected, thus presenting the United States with a fait accompli. When this plan miscarried, his main bargaining chip was the danger (which he and Kennedy shared) of inadvertent escalation and nuclear war. Khrushchev played this weak hand very skillfully. In fact, from the standpoint of a process-oriented approach to decisionmaking, he played it brilliantly. The United States used coercive diplomacy backed by superior conventional military power to force the missiles out of Cuba. But Kennedy could not force the removal of the missiles without war unless Khrushchev cooperated in reversing his intended course of action. In addition, since some missiles had already been deployed at the time U.S. photographic reconnaissance discovered them, Kennedy had to *compel* the Soviets to undo actions already taken, a more difficult assignment than to *deter* them from actions not yet under way.

The Cuban missile crisis, then, was very similar to a limited war between two very powerful states that hold back some of their military strength because they want to limit the costs of fighting or reduce the risks of escalation. Limited wars in which leaders seek consciously to control the risks of escalation offer decisionmaking problems very similar to those which face statesmen in situations of crisis management. The analogy is more specific than it may appear at first. All wars are "limited" in some sense: Carthaginian peaces imposed on losers by victors are more the historical exception than the rule. But the reasons why wars are limited vary. Sometimes they are limited because states lack the means for escalation. At other times, one side's escalation cancels another's, and after repeated "trials" of this "experiment" both combatants agree that future escalation serves no point. These are valid reasons for war limitation, but they have less in common with crisis management decisionmaking than do other instances of war limitation.

In some instances leaders attempt to limit the scope and destructiveness of warfare because the imposed limits are consistent with the leaders' political objectives. In these cases war is intentionally limited, even though the states could fight harder. Such limited war situations are analogous to the unwillingness of nuclear age crisis managers to go too far toward the brink. Political leaders in situations of crisis management or in limited wars want to obtain as many of their preferred political objectives as possible, but they do not want to leave the process of escalation open-ended. The ability to obtain some or all of one's major objectives is interdependent with the ability of the other side to do likewise, and "games" of interdependent decision are the result (I use the quotation marks by way of alluding to the discipline of game theory, a formalized way of summarizing the decisionmaking properties of actors in a crisis management situation or during limited war).

Game theory depictions of crises or limited wars can be very useful, provided they are not substituted for the broader and richer descriptive accounts of decisionmaking that must form the basis of historical reference. From a larger reality, game theory abstracts core propositions about the strategies policymakers can use most successfully under certain conditions, *given* their objectives. But neither game theory nor any other rational model of decisionmaking can explain why leaders choose the objectives they choose. I do not use mathematical or very abstract models of game theory in Chapter 5. Rather, my approach emphasizes those aspects of the process of war termination which are important for leaders who want to come as close as they can to a rational decision (i.e., one that is logically consistent with their own preferred policy objectives). In order to do so, they must adopt the standards of an agreed battle, seek to control escalation, and use coercive diplomacy to accomplish their objectives through interdependent bargaining games.

There is one important difference, though, between the game theory approach or my own, more process-oriented discussion of war termination and the *essentialist* approach, which is equally valid. An essentialist would ask whether there is any "rational" outcome to limited war or to nuclear-crisis management: in all likelihood, he or she would deny that there is one. Therefore, the philosophical essentialist would argue against a rational choice or process-oriented focus on the problem of strategic decisionmaking in crisis or limited war. He or she would find my analysis of conflict termination to be confined within orthodox social science parameters, thereby excluding such foci as the effects of crisis management and conflict termination experiences on basic individual and social values. Ironically, one form of anti–crisis management essentialism characterized Soviet views of nuclear-crisis management during the Cold War. Whereas U.S. policymakers and many academic strategists had high confidence in the tools of nuclear-crisis management or even conflict termination, Soviet leaders and scholars were more inclined to stress the avoidance of crisis as a means of preventing war. Once a dangerous political crisis had broken out, Soviet leaders were apt to be more pessimistic or fatalistic about managing the crisis successfully and avoiding war.

There were many good reasons to agree with this Soviet skepticism about crisis management, but my usage of the term "essentialist" differs from that of a Marxist-Leninist. At least it differs from that of the traditional Marxist, but former Soviet President Gorbachev offered a perspective similar to my view of essentialism when he argued that the values of humankind must take priority over the values of class. This heresy was even published in his book *Perestroika*, which was translated into English and made widely available in the West in 1987. Gorbachev's declaration of an end to the "class struggle" was not just an excursion in Marxist theology; it was a statement to the West about the form in which future competition between capitalism and socialism should take place, in his view. If there was no class struggle, it followed that there was no irreconcilable political difference between the world's leading capitalist and socialist states that required war, threat of war, or resolution of crisis by other than political means exclusive of military threats. This new version of a Soviet leadership paradigm for conflict resolution was one component of Gorbachev's recipe for general conflict *termination* between the Soviet Union and the socialist community, on one side, and the United States and its Cold War allies on the other.

Gorbachev's restructuring of Marxism-Leninism on this point was a noteworthy shift in frame of reference, for it offered the West a conceptual framework for conflict termination which superceded the previously dominant model of two-sided containment and ubiquitous bipolar confrontation. At first, U.S. officials could not believe it. Later they cautiously moved toward Gorbachev's new model. During the Gulf War of 1991, Soviet cooperation with U.N. sanctions against Iraq gave tangible evidence that a restructuring of Soviet global objectives had taken place, and that this restructuring included putting an end to the Cold War. Although in the aftermath of the Soviet state's demise Gorbachev's restructuring of the terms for conflict termination might seem insignificant, in fact it was—and remains—of vital significance. The decision to terminate the Cold War was a necessary prelude to the restructuring of the Soviet economy and to the realignment of other Soviet foreign policy objectives, and these processes continued even after the Cold War became history and Gorbachev joined his predecessors in official retirement.

1

MOBILIZATION, DETERRENCE, AND CONCILIATION

Lessons from the First World War

The powers of Europe on the eve of World War I were confident that their system of alliance diplomacy and military deterrence was shock-resistant. These optimistic expectations of continued peace were shattered at the end of July and the beginning of August 1914, when Europe plunged into war. In this chapter I argue that one cause for the failure of the great powers to prevent war in 1914 was their inability to balance a strategy of deterrence with a strategy for nonprovocation. Without a component of nonprovocation, deterrent messages are liable to be misread by potential opponents, as imminent threats to their military viability instead of proposals for bargaining over the terms by which war might be avoided. Establishing the correct balance between deterrence and nonprovocation during crisis management

This chapter draws upon material included in the author's *Nuclear Weapons and the New World Order* (New York: Paragon House, 1993).

requires a feel for the shifting sands of decisionmaking context. As the context changes, so too will the most desirable balance of deterrence and conciliation.

This general argument has additional implications. First, the balance between leaders' needs to communicate signals of deterrence, compared with
signals of nonprovocation, changes as states pass from a situation of generalized security dilemma to one of immediate threat. Second, leaders frequently fail to perceive that this is so. Third, the most appropriate way to
understand how mobilization systems contribute to the likelihood of war is
to trace the effects of leaders' expectations about mobilization on their perception of the trade-off between deterrence and nonprovocation. Mobilizations which restrict leaders' freedom of action during a crisis and which suggest to potential opponents that the slide of crisis into war has become
irreversible contribute to a crisis security dilemma that defies resolution without military force.[1]

In order to make these points and to set the stage for related arguments in
later chapters about the trade-offs between deterrence and provocation, the
present chapter proceeds as follows. I discuss the problem of mobilization
and its relationship to the deterrence dilemmas of July 1914, with emphasis
on Russian decisionmaking. The mobilization plans of the powers just before
the outbreak of World War I have been analyzed extensively by historians.
My addition to those discussions is one of perspective, not new data. I argue
that the strategic difficulties facing Germany, Russia, and other members of
the two major alliances that moved toward war in July 1914 were real. Germany and Russia, therefore, were confronted with hard choices to which
their policy- and strategymaking systems were maladapted. Specifically,
these powers required systems that could guarantee careful manipulation of
the signals of belligerence and conciliation, depending on the actual circumstances of a crisis.

1. A "crisis security dilemma" results when the military doctrines, strategies, and operations of potential opponents adversely affect three dimensions of crisis stability. Actions that
states take to increase security, deter escalation, or improve bargaining positions during a crisis
can unexpectedly prompt the opponent 1) to launch a preemptive attack, or 2) to perceive
that efforts to resolve the crisis by means other than force are irrevocably lost, or 3) can result
in the use of force not controlled by state leaders. For an expansion of this concept, see Joseph
F. Bouchard, *Command in Crisis: Four Case Studies* (New York: Columbia University Press,
1991), 20 et pass. The concept of a security dilemma has been developed most fully in the
literature of international security policy by Robert Jervis. See Jervis, "Cooperation Under the
Security Dilemma," *World Politics* (January 1978): 167–86, in Robert J. Art and Robert Jervis,
International Politics: Anarchy, Force, Political Economy and Decision Making (New York: Harper
Collins, 1985), 86–100.

GENERALIZED AND IMMEDIATE
THREAT PERCEPTIONS

"Deterrence" is a term applied to a variety of influence strategies. It has often been used in the political science literature to describe the process of influence by threatmaking. Deterrence has both active and passive forms. Passive deterrence is the ability of state A to dissuade state B from taking an action which has not yet begun, but which A has reason to believe B is considering. Active deterrence, sometimes called "compellence," involves the use of threats by A to get B to stop and undo an action already in progress. According to these distinctions, John F. Kennedy's threats during the Cuban missile crisis to respond to any nuclear launch from Cuba against any Western Hemisphere target with a full retaliatory strike on the Soviet Union was a deterrent threat. On the other hand, Kennedy's demand for the removal of Soviet missiles already deployed in Cuba was supported by the compellent threats of blockade and a possible invasion or air strike.

A condition of potential deterrence exists in the structure of legal and institutional anarchy of the international state system. States are reliant on their own uses of persuasion or coercion in order to obtain their objectives. On account of this security dilemma, a situation of *generalized threat perception* exists in the potential of states to use force against one another.[2] In deterrence situations related to generalized threat perceptions, states acknowledge the possibility that war may occur and therefore maintain armed forces to dissuade potential attackers from aggression. But the latent potential for aggression is not yet manifest in the form of specific war plans for aggression by one or more states against particular enemies.

In contrast to a situation of deterrence related to a generalized threat perception, states with an *immediate threat perception* are actively contemplating war and are, or probably ought to be, preparing for it. Patrick Morgan has identified four features that characterize a condition of immediate deterrence. First, assuming a hostile relationship between two states, leaders in at least one state are giving serious consideration to attacking the other state or to attacking the second state's vital interests outside its home territory. Second, leaders of the second state are aware of the consideration being given to war by the first state. Third, leaders of the second state make an

---

2. Patrick M. Morgan, *Deterrence: A Conceptual Analysis*, 2d ed. (Beverly Hills, Calif.: Sage, 1983), 27–48.

explicit threat to use retaliatory force in order to prevent the attack. Fourth, according to Morgan, leaders of the first state (the potential attacker) decide not to attack, *primarily* because of the threat of retaliation.[3] Unless the first three conditions exist, deterrence has not really been attempted. In the absence of the fourth condition, deterrence has not succeeded.

The development of a crisis in the relations between two states indicates that general deterrence has failed. The further deterioration of crisis into war is a failure of immediate deterrence. Although the hypothetical possibility of moving directly from a state of general deterrence to war cannot be excluded, few examples are available of major wars that began suddenly without a preceding period of growing hostility and threat.[4] Crises are characterized by a high degree of threat to important values, by short decision times, and by unanticipated surprises in the development of events abroad or in the outcomes of national decisionmaking.[5] It would seem obvious that political leaders, commanders, and military organizations ought to behave differently in crises, compared to their behavior in noncrisis situations. However, what is apparently obvious is not so easily documented, and what is documented is not done without controversy.

Consider, for example, the contrasting images provided by scholars with respect to two crises: the July 1914 crisis, preceding the outbreak of World War I, and the Cuban missile crisis of October 1962. The July crisis has produced two images in the literature: inadvertent or accidental war which overtook the very powers that so desperately sought to avoid it; and, in contrast, a war which at least some of the powers had anticipated and welcomed in order to provide the means for their foreign policy expansion.[6] The Cuban missile crisis has served up the same sort of contrasting images to research scholars and policy analysts. Some accounts of the crisis have created the impression of a flawlessly executed set of decisions by President Kennedy and his advisers that obtained the removal of the Soviet missiles from Cuba while

3. Ibid., 38.
4. Low-intensity conflicts pitting revolutionary groups and guerrilla factions against governments do not fit most deterrence models, which have been developed to explain conventional or nuclear deterrence relationships among relatively developed states.
5. For an overview of contemporary social science research contributions to the study of crisis management, see Ole R. Holsti, "Crisis Decision Making," ch. 1 in *Behavior, Society, and Nuclear War*, ed. Philip E. Tetlock, Jo L. Husbands, Robert Jervis, Paul C. Stern, and Charles Tilly (New York: Oxford University Press, 1989), 1:8–84.
6. A review of the literature on the causes of World War I and the July crisis appears in Jack S. Levy, "Preferences, Constraints and Choices in July 1914," *International Security* (Winter 1990–91): 151–86. See also citations in notes, below.

successfully controlling the risks of escalation. Other accounts have described a policymaking process full of pitfalls and potholes, causing the reader to wonder how the two sides ever succeeded in resolving the crisis without war.[7]

Crisis involves many stimuli and responses on the part of military and other organizations, which may account for the diverse images experienced by participants and for the different emphases in academic research studies. One thing that military organizations frequently must do in a crisis is mobilize. Mobilization means that a state deliberately increases the *war-readiness* of its military organizations and of the political leadership to which those military organizations are accountable. However, mobilization is not always of a piece. States differ in their approach to mobilization, depending on their domestic political priorities, economic systems, civil-military relations, and other variables. Besides variation in approaches to mobilization caused by domestic forces, states perceive threats to their security differently. Some have sensitive antennae that interpret almost any moving object on the horizon as a potential threat; others are content to wait until their fundamental values are at risk.

Because of the assumption that a crisis must be conducted during a short time period, the relationship between crisis and mobilization is not always perceived. A short time for decision is usually a characteristic feature of crises, but one mission of intelligence agencies is to provide earlier advance warning of impending crisis. Thus, the term "crisis mobilization" is not necessarily an oxymoron: U.S. official planners for crisis management sought in 1988 to increase their options for handling crises by improving their ability to anticipate crises and to preplan measures of graduated response.[8] A pro-

7. The literature on the Cuban missile crisis is enormous. For recent and authoritative accounts, see James G. Blight and David A. Welch, *On the Brink: Americans and Soviets Reexamine the Cuban Missile Crisis* (New York: Hill & Wang, 1989), and Raymond L. Garthoff, *Reflections on the Cuban Missile Crisis*, rev. ed. (Washington, D.C.: Brookings Institution, 1989). Both these sources take into account the results of meetings in 1987 between U.S. and Soviet crisis participants which produced important new insights about both sides' crisis management behavior.

8. A U.S. government interagency conference at Emmitsburg, Maryland, in 1988 adopted a formal definition of "graduated mobilization response" (GMR). According to published guidance pursuant to those discussions, GMR was to place "emphasis on low cost preparatory actions during the early stages of a crisis to materially reduce lead times in the event that the crisis were to worsen" and to produce a "well-defined, incremental menu of graduated, increasing readiness measures." Paul E. Taibl, *Graduated Mobilization Response: A Key Element in National Deterrent Strategy* (Washington, D.C.: Mobilization Concepts Development Center, Institute for National Strategic Studies, April 1988), 2–3.

tracted war fought by highly industrialized states almost demands by definition an extended period of prewar economic mobilization. Graduated mobilization for protracted conventional war was of little interest to many U.S.
defense officials for much of the Cold War, when planning was dominated
by a fixation on short warning, nuclear scenarios, or sudden Soviet thrusts
against Western Europe. The 1991 Gulf War stimulated some renewed interest in the relationship between mobilization and crisis, for an extended crisis
period (from August 2, 1990, through mid-January 1991) had created the
opportunity for extensive U.S. and allied mobilization planning for war.

The relationship between crisis management and mobilization for war is
also mediated by the structure of the international system. The structure of
the system includes the polarity of power within the system (unipolar, bipolar, or multipolar) and the ideological homogeneity or heterogeneity of the
most important actors. Kenneth Waltz's structural theory of international
system stability suggested that bipolar systems might be more stable than
multipolar ones.[9] Scholars have deduced from Waltz's theory that multipolar
systems are prone to instability for two important, but opposite, reasons.
First, states may mistakenly ally themselves with others that drag them into
wars against their best interests. Second, and opposite, states in a multipolar
system are also tempted to shirk their responsibility for standing firm against
a rising hegemon by shifting the burden of wars to others. The first pattern
has been termed "chain ganging" and the second "buck passing" by Thomas
Christensen and Jack Snyder.[10] The chain-ganging pattern was observed by
members of the Triple Alliance and Triple Entente prior to the outbreak of
World War I; the second, or buck-passing, pattern was evident in the 1930s

9. Kenneth Waltz, *Theory of International Politics* (Reading, Mass.: Addison-Wesley,
1979).
10. Thomas J. Christensen and Jack Snyder, "Chain Gangs and Passed Bucks: Predicting
Alliance Patterns in Multipolarity," *International Organization* (Spring 1990): 137–68. Waltz
argues that neither chain ganging nor buck passing is likely in a bipolar system, thus enhancing
its stability. This may be true of U.S.-Soviet behavior from 1945 to 1985, but it was certainly
not true of other major powers in the same time period. The entire notion of "extended
deterrence," meaning a U.S. nuclear guarantee against a Soviet conventional attack on Western Europe, was in part an exercise in both chain ganging and buck passing. European members of NATO chained themselves to the U.S. nuclear deterrent and to U.S. political leadership in peacetime military planning. But they also passed the buck of preparedness for
conventional war, forgoing NATO's original conventional force goals of ninety-six active and
reserve divisions in Europe. There is also the question of whether all bipolar systems behaved
with the same degree of stability as the U.S.-Soviet Cold War system; the Peloponnesian War
speaks very softly in favor of the stability of bipolarity.

as Hitler challenged peace and stability in Europe. Stephen Walt has noted that states faced with challenges to their security from an aspiring or actually dominant power may "bandwagon" with the leader or seek to thwart the leader by "balancing" in alignment with opponents to the aspiring hegemon.[11]

U.S. officials during the Cold War were motivated by concerns that non-aligned states would bandwagon to the side of the Soviet Union if Soviet military power and prestige were seen to be growing at a faster rate than that of the United States.[12] Thus, states which do not necessarily aspire to hegemonial status can perceive themselves as the potential victims of a "domino theory" that will eventually align decisive forces against them regionally or globally. U.S. military intervention in South Vietnam and U.S. concern with the potentially disruptive effects of "wars of national liberation" illustrate the power of the perception that others might bandwagon with an opposed bipolar state at a significant cost to U.S. security. It is also the case that the same state can bandwagon or balance at different times, depending on the circumstances. If a state defines its balancing and bandwagoning options in terms of opposing any regional hegemon instead of blocking the growth of a particular state, as did England with regard to the domination of Western Europe, then alternation of balancing and bandwagoning may be supportive of system stability.[13]

System polarity, as related to the propensity for crisis and mobilization, must not be defined only in terms of the unitary territorial state. Alliances are often very important actors on security and defense issues. Thus Waltz's argument that bipolar systems are more stable than multipolar ones may work when the units of analysis are individual states, but not when the units of analysis are alliance systems. A contributing cause for World War I, it can be argued, was the collapse of a multipolar system of territorial unitary states into a bipolar system of opposed alliances. Another important aspect of the relationship between system stability and polarity is whether states have offensive or defensive military doctrines and force structures. The issue is complicated (and various aspects of it will be considered throughout this book) both in historical compass and in reference to possible political and military

11. Stephen M. Walt, *The Origins of Alliances* (Ithaca, N.Y.: Cornell University Press, 1987), esp. ch. 2.

12. Ibid., 20.

13. This argument works whether actor objectives are entirely self-interested or whether the actor is conscious of some "system interest" also.

futures. Some scholars have suggested that offensive military doctrines were important contributory causes to the development of the crisis of July 1914 and to the subsequent outbreak of World War I.[14]

Military doctrines and military strategies may be best treated as "intervening" variables between system polarity and such outcomes as crisis, peace, or war. Mobilization is a component of both a state's political strategy (grand strategy) and its national military strategy. Mobilization by one state sends signals to others that the first state is readying its forces, command-and-control systems, and other means for possible war. The states receiving this signal must then determine how to respond: they can ignore the stimulus, or they can respond with feedback. Two types of feedback can be projected by the receiving state back to the sender: amplifying feedback or nullifying feedback. Amplifying feedback repeats the sender's message back to its origin: a message interpreted as one of hostility is responded to by sending one equally or more hostile. Nullifying feedback, on the other hand, calls for the sending of a message that is opposite in meaning to the message received. Thus, if state A sends a message warning of a possible attack on B, amplifying feedback would result in a threatened retaliation by B, but nullifying feedback would emphasize conciliation and a declared interest in reaching agreement without war.

It might seem that states facing threats to their security should always give peace additional time, sending nullifying responses to mobilizations or declaratory threats. But this course of action is sometimes unwise. Amplifying feedback was a problem that contributed to turning the July crisis into war, but nullifying feedback would not necessarily have avoided that war. Hitler might have been deterred by amplifying feedback in response to his early diplomatic demarches backed by military threats, but this "counterfactual" is not testable. We do know, on the other hand, that nullifying (in this case, conciliatory) feedback did not dissuade the German dictator from his larger agenda of attack and conquest. In this book, in the context of mobilization, amplifying feedback in response to another side's threats or mobilization is termed "deterrence"; nullifying feedback, in response to the same stimulus, is denoted as "nonprovocation."

14. Stephen Van Evera, "The Cult of the Offensive and the Origins of the First World War," in *Military Strategy and the Origins of the First World War*, ed. Stephen E. Miller (Princeton, N.J.: Princeton University Press, 1985), 58–107, and Jack Snyder, *The Ideology of the Offensive: Military Decision Making and the Disasters of 1914* (Ithaca, N.Y.: Cornell University Press, 1984). On the character of alliances as contributory factors to war in 1914, see Scott Sagan, "1914 Revisited: Allies, Offense and Instability," *International Security* (Fall 1986): 151–76.

Any mobilization must balance elements of deterrence, or dissuasion of aggressors by military threat of retaliation, with nonprovocation, or the avoidance of unnecessary amplifying feedback leading to undesired war or escalation. During the crisis of July 1914 the leading states of Europe attempted without success to find this balance. They depended almost entirely on the signals of deterrence sent by mobilization, and they mostly ignored the equally important need to send clear messages of nonprovocation. Although some of this behavior can be explained by system structure and alliance commitments, much of it cannot. The character of war plans as perceived by their makers and their potential opponents contributed importantly to the events of July and August 1914.[15]

MILITARY-STRATEGIC PLANNING AND THE PRELUDE TO WORLD WAR I

It became obvious to the powers of Europe well before the turn of the twentieth century that mobilization planning for future war would become more administratively complex, more strategically significant, and more closely tied to deterrence than in past wars. There were many reasons for this, but four explain most generally the changed assumptions about the character of future war which motivated general staffs, foreign offices, and their civilian political leaders from 1870 to 1914. First, the scientific spirit of the age led people to believe that war, both its operational and its logistical aspects, could be reduced to a science and denuded of all indeterminacy. Second, larger armies, made possible by the Industrial Revolution and the beginnings of mass politicization, included many reservists. Unprecedented numbers of civilians would have to be trained and deployed rapidly during a threatening period preceding war, and this training and deployment would have to proceed on the basis of standard operating procedures and programs. Third, the importance of railroads for strategic deployment increased emphasis on the observance of strict timetables for mobilization and concentration of forces. Fourth, a generalized peace in Europe from the end of the Franco-Prussian War until the outbreak of the Balkan Wars in 1912–13 contributed to opti-

15. Also on this point, see Richard Ned Lebow, *Between Peace and War: The Nature of International Crisis* (Baltimore, Md.: Johns Hopkins University Press, 1981).

mism about the controllability of local wars and the containment of escalation.[16]

Imperial Germany's Schlieffen Plan—though subsequently modified in application by Alfred von Schlieffen's successor as head of the German General Staff, Helmuth von Moltke (the younger)—called for a massive battle of annihilation against the French in a campaign of six weeks or so.[17] The Germans would fight a holding action against Russia in the east until the French were rapidly defeated; then the bulk of the German armed forces would swing eastward to dispose of the Russian armies, presumably held in check in the meantime by fighting against Austro-Hungarian forces. The Schlieffen Plan has probably absorbed more historical criticism than it deserves as a result of the emphasis placed by the "Fischer school" on Germany's responsibility for the outbreak of World War I.[18] The responsibility for the causation of World War I is complex, and by no means are historians agreed on a principal culprit. The Schlieffen Plan has also been faulted by historians, and with justification, on the grounds that it required the violation of Belgian neutrality in the initial period of war, ensuring Britain's immediate commitment to a European war on the side of the Entente powers.

However, neither alleged German responsibility for the outbreak of war nor the violation of Belgian neutrality embodied in the Schlieffen Plan is my major concern here. The aspect of the Schlieffen Plan that is of most interest for the present discussion is its assumption that a rapid campaign of annihilation in the west was Germany's only feasible war plan.[19] The as-

16. The trends are summarized in Martin Van Creveld, *Command in War* (Cambridge, Mass.: Harvard University Press, 1985), ch. 5, esp. 150–51.

17. There is a large body of literature on the Schlieffen Plan. See Gerhard Ritter, *The Schlieffen Plan: Critique of a Myth* (London: Oswald Wolff Publishers, 1958), esp. 134–48, for the text of Schlieffen's "great memorandum" of December 1905; L.C.F. Turner, "The Significance of the Schlieffen Plan," ch. 9 in *The War Plans of the Great Powers, 1880–1914*, ed. Paul M. Kennedy (London: Allen & Unwin, 1979), 199–221; and Holger M. Herwig, "The Dynamics of Necessity: German Military Policy During the First World War," ch. 3 in *Military Effectiveness. Vol. I: The First World War*, ed. Allan R. Millett and Williamson Murray (Boston: Unwin Hyman, 1988), 80–115.

18. See, for example, Fritz Fischer, *War of Illusions: German Policies from 1911 to 1914*, trans. Marian Jackson (New York: W. W. Norton, 1975), esp. 389–92 on the Schlieffen Plan; published in German as *Krieg der Illusionen* (Düsseldorf: Droste Verlag und Druckerei, 1969).

19. Historian Dennis Showalter argues that Germany's strategy, based on traditions dating from Prussia's military-strategic predicament in the seventeenth century, was one of "total war for limited objectives." By this he means that German military thinking emphasized prompt and significant battlefield victories followed by a negotiated peace. See Showalter, "Total War for Limited Objectives: An Interpretation of German Grand Strategy," in *Grand Strategies in War and Peace*, ed. Paul Kennedy (New Haven, Conn.: Yale University Press, 1991).

sumption may be regarded as a strong or as a weak one: it depended for its success on the quickness of the knockout blow against the French, on the slowness of Russian mobilization in the east, and on the ability of Austria-Hungary to keep the Russians at bay to forestall an invasion of East Prussia. The assumption of a *rapid* campaign of annihilation against France was very important.[20] In theory, Germany might have tried to defeat France in a slow campaign, withholding more forces for defensive actions on the eastern front against Russia. Germany might also have chosen, along the lines of planning guidance laid down by the elder Helmuth von Moltke in the Bismarckian era, to fight an offensive war in the east and a defensive war in the west.

But Germany chose the modified Schlieffen Plan; and pursuant to this the General Staff committed itself to a prompt and massive strategic Cannae in which French and allied defenders would be enveloped by the strong right wing of the German armies. The implications of this plan for the timing of mobilization prior to war were very significant. The powers had surmounted various crises before 1914 on the assumption that mobilization, while threatening, was not necessarily tantamount to war. The Balkan crisis of 1912 had been a virtual warm-up for the eventual outbreak of war that did occur in 1914. The assumption that armies could mobilize for the purpose of crisis bargaining and threat was shared by most of the powers, but for Germany such an assumption was a luxury. Faced with the prospect of a two-front war if French and Russian prewar commitments held firm, Germany had to beat Russian mobilization to the punch by a number of weeks sufficient to allow for the rapid defeat of France.[21]

Germany's assumption that mobilization was tantamount to war had grave consequences in view of the closer association between Russian and French

20. Schlieffen's plan is related to precedent and to subsequent developments in German military theory in Jehuda L. Wallach, *The Doctrine of the Battle of Annihilation: The Theories of Clausewitz and Schlieffen and Their Impact on the German Conduct of Two World Wars* (Westport, Conn.: Greenwood Press, 1986).

21. The case that German mobilization was unique and tantamount to war is argued by Paul Kennedy in his introduction to *The War Plans of the Great Powers*, 15–16. German planning for World War I might fit very well Graham T. Allison's Model II ("organizational process") on account of the wide latitude that was given to the General Staff to work out war plans, almost entirely independent of outside influence. In such cases, organizational ethos and standard operating procedures will be highly resistant to any change in the surrounding political and military environment. Bismarck, who had run into this with the elder Moltke, succeeded in forcing his policies on sometimes reluctant military leaders by force of personality and perseverance. Bismarck's successors were unable to do so. On the "organizational process" model of decisionmaking, see Graham T. Allison, *Essence of Decision: Explaining the Cuban Missile Crisis* (Boston: Little, Brown, 1971), 78–96. I gratefully acknowledge Jack Levy for suggesting this comparison.

military plans that developed after 1912. Prior to 1912, Russian plans for mobilization and concentration of forces were in a state of considerable flux, as explained below. After 1912, rethinking of Russia's geostrategic threat perception and pressure from their French allies led the tsar and his advisers to develop plans that were much more dependent on early offensives against Germany.[22] Russia would not have the option, as officials such as Foreign Minister Sergei Sazonov might have hoped, to announce a partial mobilization in the military districts facing Austria-Hungary but not in those districts most relevant to a war against Germany.[23] Sazonov and other civilian leaders of Russia failed to appreciate how constrained military options were in July 1914, as a result of previously taken decisions as well as uncertainty within the high command from 1906 to 1912 about whether the main threat to Russia lay in the east or in the west. Too, military and civilian leaders alike failed to consider the potential contribution of a Russian partial mobilization to crisis instability. From the standpoint of Russia's potential adversaries, especially the Germans, there was little difference between a Russian partial mobilization and a general one, since the Schlieffen Plan dictated that German mobilization must beat Russian mobilization by a large lead time.[24]

22. Thomas Christensen and Jack Snyder suggest that the phenomenon of "chain ganging," or chaining a state's fate to its allies in order to preserve the balance of power, was characteristic of the powers' behavior in the years immediately preceding the outbreak of World War I. They also note that, in a multipolar system, this phenomenon is more likely to occur when states perceive offensive doctrines and military technologies to be more advantageous than defensive ones. See Christensen and Snyder, "Chain Gangs and Passed Bucks," esp. p. 155 with regard to France and Russia.

23. For a discussion of Sazonov's role in Russian deliberations about partial and general mobilization during the July crisis, see Sidney Bradshaw Fay, The Origins of the World War, 2d ed., rev. (New York: Free Press, 1966), 2:446–81. Fay contends that the Russian decision to order general mobilization on July 30 was tantamount to war (2:479). He is also doubtful that Sazonov really expected anything to come of partial mobilization, other than protective diplomatic cover so that England would be certain to place the blame for general mobilization and war on Germany. On the other hand, the Russian decisionmaking system required that the tsar resolve all matters in dispute among his civilian and military advisers, and this system produced a great deal of wigwagging in Russian decisions on mobilization between July 25 and 30. On July 28 Russia ordered partial mobilization of the military districts of Kiev, Odessa, Moscow, and Kazan along with increased readiness for war in the Baltic and Black Sea fleets. On July 29, the tsar ordered general mobilization, but he later revoked it and insisted upon a reversion to partial mobilization (which, according to War Minister Vladimir Sukhomlinov, Chief of the General Staff Ianushkevich, and Quartermaster General Iukii Danilov, was not militarily feasible anyway). See D.C.B. Lieven, Russia and the Origins of the First World War (New York: St. Martin's Press, 1983), 144ff. and 155–62 (chronology).

24. L.C.F. Turner, "The Russian Mobilisation in 1914," ch. 11 in The War Plans of the Great Powers, 252–68, argues that the distinction between Russian partial and general mobilization was essentially meaningless in view of the interpretation Germany would place on ei-

From the conclusion of the Russo-Japanese War until the approval of war plans in 1912 that would carry Russia over the threshold to war in August 1914, Russia's foreign policy left open the question as to the identity of the chief threat to Russian security. Divided into "Easterners," who thought that a future war against Japan was most likely, and "Westerners," who considered that the Dual Alliance of Austria-Hungary represented the major threat, Russian military planners were caught on the horns of a dilemma. In December 1909 War Minister Sukhomlinov, whose sympathies lay with the Eastern view, proposed a series of military reforms. These included shifting large numbers of forces eastward, away from the western military districts and toward the center of the empire. His plan was influenced by a proposal put forward the previous year by Colonel Iurii N. Danilov of the General Staff. Impressed by the speed with which Germany and Austria could probably mobilize their forces compared to Russia, Danilov recommended that Russia concede large tracts of territory to the Austrians and Germans in the initial period of war while Russian forces safely mobilized and concentrated in the center of the country. Once Russian forces had been readied they would launch a decisive strategic counteroffensive to defeat their opponents.[25]

The mobilization plan approved by the tsar in 1910, Plan 19, was based on a plan first devised by Danilov in 1908. Danilov's plan was based on assumptions very appealing to Sukhomlinov, who became war minister in 1909. Danilov doubted that Russia could conduct a very successful defense of its western border districts in the initial period of war against a determined

---

ther. According to Turner, Sazonov sought to use partial mobilization against Austria-Hungary as a coercive measure short of war, but "he did not understand that a partial mobilisation involving thirteen Russian army corps along her northern border would compel Austria to order general mobilisation, which in turn would invoke the Austro-German alliance and require general mobilisation by Germany" (p. 260). Turner also doubts that Russian partial mobilization would have caused confusion, making later general mobilization impossible. See Turner, *Origins of the First World War* (New York: W. W. Norton, 1970), 104; he does acknowledge, though, that it would have caused some delay. Interesting arguments about Russian partial mobilization and its impact on Germany appear in Marc Trachtenberg, *History and Strategy* (Princeton, N.J.: Princeton University Press, 1991), 80–87 and 94–95. Trachtenberg suggests that Russian partial mobilization softened the stance of German Chancellor Theobald von Bethmann-Hollweg on the evening of July 29/30, prior to the adoption by Bethmann-Hollweg of a more fatalistic attitude toward war later that same day. Luigi Albertini refers to the plan for partial mobilization as "this bright idea of Sazonov's" and comments that the Russian General Staff had never worked up a plan for mobilization against Austria alone. Albertini, *The Origins of the War of 1914*, trans. and ed. Isabella M. Massey (London: Oxford University Press, 1953), 2:292–93.

25. I am grateful to William C. Fuller, Jr., for clarification of issues pertinent to this section and for the opportunity to read a draft chapter of his manuscript-in-progress on Russian war planning and mobilization. He is not, however, responsible for any arguments made here.

German offensive, and Sukhomlinov fretted a great deal about the weakness of Russian defenses in the east against a renewal of Japanese aggression.[26] Plan 19 in its 1910 version provided that large territories in Russian Poland would be conceded to Germany and Austria while Russian forces mobilized and concentrated in safety. The plan thus provided for reassurance against the possibility of a two-front war, should Japan take advantage of Russia's difficulties in the west to attack in the east. The 1910 version of Plan 19 also allowed for the possibility that Germany or Austria-Hungary might not immediately assume the offensive against Russia once war began. Germany in particular might launch the bulk of its forces against enemies in the west and fight a strategically defensive action in the east, at least initially. Thus, if the first stages of war proceeded according to the guidelines of Plan 19 and if the Germans and Austrians were limited by their entanglements on other fronts, Russia would have time to mobilize and to concentrate superior numbers against its western enemies.[27]

By 1912 this version of Plan 19 was obviously out of date, for several reasons. First, the military leadership now acknowledged that the probability of war with Japan was virtually nonexistent. Second, the Bosnian crisis of 1908–9 and more recent turbulence in the Balkans meant that a future war would take place mainly on Russia's western and southern fronts. Third, the French leadership wanted reassurance that Russian armies would invade East Prussia at the earliest possible moment in order to draw off German forces that otherwise might promptly crush French defenses in the west.[28] However,

26. Nonetheless, Sukhomlinov would fail to spend credits made available by the Finance Ministry to improve the eastern fortifications. General Unterberger, governor general of the Amur region, feared that the Japanese would soon attack Russia along its Vladivostok front, and in 1909 he sent numerous warning telegrams to that effect to the minister of war, the foreign minister, and others. Sukhomlinov agreed with Unterberger and blamed the Finance Ministry for not appropriating the necessary credits for improving the Vladivostok fortifications. Fortunately, Japanese policy called for friendly relations with Russia: Russia's defenses in the Far East were in deplorable shape, and the tsar was not amused to be informed of this state of unpreparedness in 1909 by the *Japanese* ambassador. Kokovtsov, *Out of My Past: The Memoirs of Count Kokovtsov*, ed. H. H. Fisher; trans. Laura Matveev (Stanford, Calif.: Stanford University Press, 1935), 229–33.

27. Fuller, draft manuscript (see note 25, above).

28. In addition to sources cited below, see Christensen and Snyder, "Chain Gangs and Passed Bucks," 151, for the argument that after the Moroccan crisis of 1911 France concluded that the risk of entrapment in any Russian war in the Balkans was less than the risk of Russian abandonment of France in a future crisis between France and Germany. The Christensen-Snyder argument in favor of French fear of abandonment receives support from the related argument that it was fear of alliance commitments not being honored that drove the powers toward war in 1914, not fear of being entangled in unnecessary commitments (i.e., fear of "buck passing" more than "chain ganging"). See Charles S. Maier, "Wargames: 1914, 1919,"

this French demand presented a dilemma to Russian military planners: they could not ignore their front with Austria, for an Austrian attack into Poland might stir Polish nationalism and lead to a breaking apart of the western empire. Therefore, to relieve the potentially beleaguered French and to contain the possibility of Austrian invasion, Russian military planning had to provide for prompt offensives in two directions: against Austria-Hungary into Galicia, and against Germany into East Prussia.[29]

As a result of these contrasting strategic appreciations, the Russians in 1912 developed two variations of Plan 19, revised, and the two were permitted to coexist. Variant A was the main variant, for the case in which Germany directed its main blow westward against France (see Table 1). In variant A, the Russian First and Second armies deployed against Germany formed the northwestern front. The First Army, commanded by General Paul Rennenkampf, included 6.5 infantry divisions and 5.5 cavalry divisions. The Second Army under General Alexander Samsonov included 11.5 infantry and 3 cavalry divisions. Altogether, the northwestern front under variant A disposed of 18 infantry and 8.5 cavalry divisions at the beginning of war, including 1,104 field guns and some 250,000 troops.[30] On the southwestern front, for a major offensive planned according to variant A against Austria-Hungary in Galicia, Russia deployed four armies (the Fourth, Fifth, Third, and Eighth) for a total at the outset of war of 34.5 infantry and 12.5 cavalry divisions, roughly 600,000 troops.[31] However, only about 75 percent of these forces were successfully mobilized according to the time schedule laid down in General Staff plans.[32]

Variant G was the backup plan, for the case in which Germany chose to throw the bulk of its offensive forces eastward against Russia. General Dani-

---

in *The Origin and Prevention of Major Wars*, ed. Robert I. Rotberg and Theodore K. Rabb (Cambridge: Cambridge University Press, 1988), 249–80.

29. See Norman Stone, *The Eastern Front* (New York: Charles Scribner's Sons, 1975), 33–36, and Snyder, *The Ideology of the Offensive*, chs. 6 and 7, for pertinent background.

30. *Istoriya pervoi mirovoi voiny*, ed. I. I. Rostunov (Moscow: "Nauka," 1975), 196–97, 251–52. See also I. I. Rostunov, *Russkii front pervoi mirovoi voiny* [The Russian Front in World War I] (Moscow: "Nauka," 1976), 92–94; Iu. Danilov, *La Russie dans la Guerre Mondiale (1914–1917)* [Russia in the World War], 134–36; and A. M. Zaionchkovskii, *Podgotovka Rossii k imperialisticheskoi voine* [Preparation of Russia for Imperialist War] (Moscow: 1926), 257 et pass. Implications of the reorganization of 1910 are noted in Rostunov, *Russkii front pervoi mirovoi voiny*, 58 (table 6), and the same source discusses the evolution of army organization in the context of developing war plans (pp. 42–59); on the correlation of forces in the East European theater of operations at the beginning of military operations, see p. 110 (table 13) and Rostunov, *Istoriya pervoi mirovoi voiny*, 254.

31. Rostunov, *Istoriya pervoi mirovoi voiny*, 252.

32. Ibid., 253.

Table 1.   Correlation of Forces, East European Theater, at Beginning
of Military Operations

	Russia		
	Infantry Divs.	Cavalry Divs.	Field Guns
Northwestern front			
First Army	6.5	5.5	402
Second Army	11.5	3	702
SUBTOTAL	18	8.5	1,104
Southwestern front			
Fourth Army	6.5	3.5	426
Fifth Army	8	3	516
Third Army	12	3	685
Eighth Army	8	3	472
SUBTOTAL	34.5	12.5	2,099
TOTAL	52.5	21	3,203

	Germany and Austria-Hungary		
	Infantry Divs.	Cavalry Divs.	Field Guns
Northwestern front			
German Eighth Army	15	1	1,044
SUBTOTAL	15	1	1,044
Southwestern front			
Voirsha Corps	2	0	72
Kummer Corps	3	1	144
Austrian First Army	9	2	480
Austrian Fourth Army	9	2	474
Austrian Third Army	6	3	318
Keves Group	8	3	366
SUBTOTAL	37	11	1,854
TOTAL	52.5	12	2,898

SOURCE: I. I. Rostunov, *Russkii front pervoi mirovoi voiny* (Moscow: "Nauka," 1976), 110.

lov indicates quite clearly that variant A was to be activated automatically
once the order for mobilization was received; variant G required the receipt
of a special order.[33] In this case the First, Fourth, and Second armies were to
be deployed against the front with Germany, while the Fifth and Third armies were to bear the brunt of first action against Austria.[34] Variant G called

33. Danilov, *La Russie dans la Guerre Mondiale*, 147.
34. Rostunov, *Russkii front pervoi mirovoi voiny*, 94.

for a larger proportion of Russian forces, fighting against both Austria and Germany on the defensive, to complete their deployment and concentration toward the interior of the country. The assumption by Danilov with regard to variant G was that Germany and Austria could easily envelop the Russian forces forward-deployed in the Polish salient. Russian strategy against variant G, therefore, had to have a defensive character initially, awaiting the arrival of fresh troops rushed to the front from Siberia, Turkestan, and the Transcaucasus.[35]

During staff conversations in 1912 and 1913, the Russians had attempted to assuage French fears by promising an offensive against Germany by the fifteenth day of mobilization with some 800,000 troops.[36] However, the revised war plans of 1910 had created a gap between capabilities and expectations with which Russia would be crippled when war did break out in 1914. The eastward shifting of forces in 1910 and the neglect of funding for railway modernization in the western military districts meant that neither the smooth operating procedures nor the infrastructure for a rapid mobilization westward could be counted on in 1914 to the extent that French military planners had hoped for.[37] The inability of Russian planners to shift rapidly from a strategically defensive to a strategically offensive footing was ironic in the light of Germany's conclusion that an early Russian offensive into East Prussia was almost certain. Germany expected to hold off any Russian offensive with a small fixing force until the decisive battles in the west had been fought, after which German troops would be transferred from the west to the east for a decisive counteroffensive. Ironically, Germany's actual mobilization planning for war with Russia in 1914 was thus very similar to Russia's mobilization planning of 1910 for war with Germany: initial defensive operations followed by a decisive counteroffensive.

Partial and General Mobilization

Political leaders in Germany and Russia during the crisis months of June and July 1914 did not know or fully appreciate the extent to which existing war plans, and military expectations based on those plans, would constrain the crisis management options of kaiser and tsar alike. I do not mean this in a literal or simplistic sense. Political leaders were aware of hostile alliances, of offensively oriented military doctrines, and of the expectations held by their

35. Danilov, *La Russie dans la Guerre Mondiale*, 145.
36. Fuller, draft manuscript (see note 25, above).
37. Ibid.

general staffs that the speed of mobilization might make the difference between victory and defeat in a short war.[38] In short, political leaders were not kept in the dark about the significance of war plans in general.[39] However, neither political leaders nor military advisers in Germany and Russia sufficiently appreciated the significance of a change in context, from general to immediate deterrence, as early as June 28. The condition of immediate deterrence that obtained from June 28 to July 23 (Austria's ultimatum to Serbia) was muted by complacency about Austria's willingness to push a local crisis into war. After July 23, priorities and expectations shifted: the avoidance of war became less important for policymakers and military planners than the prevention of defeat in the early stages of a war, should it occur. War plans and signals of diplomatic resolve that had appeared merely necessary and expedient prior to the last eight days of July took on entirely different meanings. Instead of deterring an outbreak of war, mobilizations and signals of resolve provoked escalation and war.

What is most significant about the primary source documents that political leaders and military planners of the time have left historians and political scientists is the subtle change of tone that occurs between July 23 and August 1. Leaders more and more frequently use the term "inevitability" to refer to the likelihood that war will erupt. This fatalistic attitude is not something that the heads of state or their principal advisers entered the July crisis with. Instead, it develops out of their interactions in a hothouse environment which is first created by the tension between Austria and Serbia over the assassination of Archduke Ferdinand and his spouse, and then exacerbated by the ultimatum and declaration of war against Serbia by Austria (July 23 and 28, respectively). Leaders' references to the "inevitability" of war in July

---

38. Oddly, few if any political leaders or military planners at the time seemed to appreciate that mobilization capacity for a long war would be even more critical than the speed of "surge mobilization" for a short war. Demonstrating to a prospective attacker that, even if he is successful in the initial period of war, he faces a prolonged and destructive war of attrition thereafter is an effective way to contribute to deterrence without raising the risk of crisis instability and provocation. The Russians could certainly have followed this strategy in July 1914, refusing the option of partial mobilization against Austria and emphasizing their staying power for a long war in diplomatic exchanges between July 24 and 30. Such a stance would have abandoned Serbia to Austrian coercion, which Russia was reluctant to do. Russian management of the tension between deterrence and provocation was complicated by the tension between the requirements for localizing the Austro-Serbian conflict and those for deterring its escalation into a wider war. The risks of the strategy I am recommending here for Russia prior to World War I were acceptable so long as the Schlieffen Plan hurled Germany's main forces westward against France, not eastward against Russia.

39. This is effectively demonstrated in Trachtenberg, History and Strategy, ch. 2.

1914 sound like expressions that rationalize their own responsibility for breaking the peace. A fairer appreciation is that statements of inevitable war reflect leaders' genuine frustration when additional measures of deterrence not only fail to prevent escalation but even provoke it. One could, with justification, divide the period of immediate deterrence preceding the outbreak of World War I into two separate phases: an earlier and relatively more stable phase; and a later, less stable one. The earlier phase began with the assassination of Archduke Ferdinand on the 28th of June and ended with the Austrian ultimatum to Serbia on July 23. The second phase began with the Austrian ultimatum and ended with the outbreak of war. Measures designed to preserve the peace through deterrence were especially likely to be construed as provocative challenges during this second and less stable phase of the crisis. Table 2 provides a chronology of the steps taken by the major powers during this crucial second phase of the July crisis.

German political leaders, including three successive chancellors, were familiar with the Schlieffen Plan in general, but they were largely unaware of how its precision and detail could limit leaders' viable political options during the later stages of a crisis.[40] The Russian military leadership was more concerned with avoiding delayed mobilization in case of war than it was with providing bargaining ballast to the tsar or to Foreign Minister Sazonov during the July crisis. On July 25, a meeting of the Russian Imperial Council presided over by the tsar decided to introduce at once the "Period Preparatory to War" throughout European Russia, taking all the steps necessary for an immediate mobilization should the tsar authorize such a step.[41] There is significant evidence that some Russian military leaders regarded this step not as a way to buy additional time for negotiation or for coercive diplomacy to influence Austro-Hungarian decisionmaking, but, instead, as a green light for war.

The meeting of the Imperial Council on the 25th had approved in principle a proposal presented to the council on the preceding day by Sazonov and Ianushkevich for partial mobilization of the Odessa, Kiev, Moscow, and Kazan military districts, although implementation of mobilization measures was suspended pending further review.[42] Several important Russian military

40. Turner, "The Significance of the Schlieffen Plan," 205, emphasizes this point. The German government also apparently understood that the Schlieffen Plan would probably entail the violation of Belgian and Dutch neutrality. The governments in question were headed by Chancellors Hohenlohe-Schillingsfurst, Bernhard von Bülow, and Bethmann-Hollweg, respectively. Logistical weakness inherent in the Schlieffen Plan may have been its undoing; see Theodore Ropp, *War in the Modern World* (Durham, N.C.: Duke University Press, 1959), 208.
41. Turner, "The Russian Mobilisation in 1914," 262.
42. Turner suggests that the partial mobilization proposed in July 1914 was not originally

Table 2.   Second Phase of the July 1914 Crisis and Opening States of the War

	Russia, Serbia	France	England	Germany	Austria-Hungary
July 24			First Lord of the Admiralty orders navy to remain mobilized after maneuvers		
July 25	Mobilization in Serbia; Russian troops return to permanent duty stations	French forces in Morocco receive changed plans, alerting them for possible use in Europe; general railway alert in metro France	Change of naval command	Squadron of battleships is called back from Norway	21:30 Partial mobilization against Serbia
July 26	Beginning of premobilization in all of Russia; fortresses on war footing	Leaves canceled; persons on leave recalled; civilians provide railroad security	Naval maneuvers end; navy remains mobilized		Corps on Serbian border is placed on war footing
July 27		All military units return to permanent duty stations; security for railroads	Replenishment of navy stockpiles	Sixteenth Army Corps cancels leaves to Bavaria on local orders; some soldiers given harvest leave, return to Metz	
July 28		Measures "in time of tension"		Some units return to permanent duty stations	First day of mobilization against Serbia

	Russia, Serbia	France	England	Germany	Austria-Hungary
July 29	Daytime: partial mobilization		First-line fleet to Scapa Flow; warning telegrams to army and navy as signal of threat of war	Evening: all units return to permanent duty stations; all return from leave; order to build positions for mobilization period	Evening: corps begin movement to Serbian front
July 30	18:00 General mobilization ordered	Establishment of border security by mobilization of 11 infantry divisions and 10 cavalry divisions		Partial border security in east by discretion of local command; mobilization of forts on eastern border; navy on war footing	
July 31	First day of mobilization	Various additional measures of mobilization according to schedule (Carnet B)		13:00 Threat of war issued; rail and telegraph links cut at French border by 15:00	11:30 General mobilization; war footing on Russian front
August 1		16:40 Mobilization of army and navy	14:15 Mobilization of navy	17:00 Mobilization of army and navy; declaration of war on Russia	First day of war footing on Russian front
August 2	Russian Fourth Cavalry Division crosses German border	First day of mobilization	02:15 Order to mobilize reserve navy	First day of mobilization	

Table 2. (continued)

	Russia, Serbia	France	England	Germany	Austria-Hungary
August 3		Morning: cover transports completed	12:00 Decision to mobilize ground forces; Aug. 5 designated as first day of mobilization	Declaration of war on France; German cavalry crosses border into Belgium	Units begin to reinforce covering forces in Galicia
August 4		Mobilization transports conclude		Six infantry brigades cross Belgian border opposite Liège	First day of mobilization against Russia
August 5		Beginning of concentration transport		Evening: main assault on Liège begins	
August 6	First actions on Austrian border				Austro-Hungarian declaration of war on Russia

SOURCE: A. Svechin, *Strategiya* [Strategy], 2d ed. (Moscow: Voennyi Vestnik, 1927); published in English and edited by Kent D. Lee (Minneapolis: East View Publications, 1991), 202–3.

leaders, especially General Dobrorolsky (responsible for mobilization) and Quartermaster General Danilov, sought to have general mobilization ordered instead. Both of these key leaders (Danilov, despite his innocuous-sounding title, was the principal Russian war planner and a prominent commander of forces on the eastern front in World War I) thought that partial mobilization would endanger general mobilization.[43] This was to some extent a fair cri-

---

or necessarily Sazonov's own idea, but was based on partial mobilization plans laid down during the autumn of 1912, pursuant to the events of the First Balkan War and a deterioration of relations between Austria and Russia. Ibid., 260. However, the point remains that Sazonov had different expectations about the contribution of this measure to crisis management than military leaders did.

43. Fay, *The Origins of the World War*, 2:450–51.

tique of Sazonov's plan, but from a different perspective: that of fighting an all-out war against the Central Powers, not of using military force for bargaining purposes.

Professional military skepticism toward partial mobilization had to do with how Russian personnel were mobilized for the various military districts into which the country was divided. Each military district drew personnel from regions outside its own territory. The multiracial nature of the Russian Empire required sensitivity to nationality distributions within military units and regions: rules existed that military units should be three-fourths Slav and, wherever possible, one-half Great Russian.[44] Skilled cadres were not randomly distributed throughout Russian territory but were concentrated in a few urban centers.[45] Therefore, under partial mobilization many reservists from the Moscow and Kazan military districts would eventually be assigned to units deployed against Germany, not Austria-Hungary. And the Kiev and Odessa military districts drew some of their reserve personnel from areas outside the four regions included in partial mobilization. Most crucial and problematic in a partial mobilization scenario was the Warsaw Military District, facing both Austria-Hungary and Germany. A bogging down of troop trains or other mobilization measures in this crucial district would, according to Russian General Staff appreciations, jeopardize Russian defenses against the expected Austrian attack from Galicia.[46]

For no apparent reason other than inexperience and deference to superior authority, Russian Chief of Staff Ianushkevich had not objected to Sazonov's plan for partial mobilization proposed on the 24th and approved in principle by the tsar on the 25th.[47] However, the plan was not immediately implemented, for Quartermaster General Danilov and other members of the Gen-

44. Lieven, *Russia and the Origins of the First World War*, 150.
45. Ibid.
46. Ibid.
47. Interservice, intraservice, and other political rivalries surrounding the high command resulted in the development of factional struggles for the control of military policy in prewar Russia. Grand Duke Nikolai Nikolaevich and future War Minister Sukhomlinov, for example, served as magnets for the expression of views by contending officers who were sympathetic to one or the other's perspectives. In 1908 the tsar appointed Sukhomlinov as chief of the General Staff, and in 1909 he made him minister of war. The War Ministry was charged by the tsar with establishing an independent perspective from the General Staff, and Sukhomlinov sought to ensure that no rival would emerge from the General Staff in the future. One result was that, from 1909 to 1914, the Russian General Staff had four chiefs of staff; Germany (including Prussia) had had four chiefs in the preceding fifty-three years. See David R. Jones, "Imperial Russia's Forces at War," ch. 8 in *Military Effectiveness*, ed. Millett and Murray, 249–328, esp. 255–56.

eral Staff objected to it. Ianushkevich, who had gone along with Sazonov's idea of partial mobilization on the 25th and 26th, was persuaded by Danilov and others to support general mobilization on the grounds that partial mobilization now would complicate any attempt later to institute general mobilization.[48] The extent to which this assessment was a genuine strategic appreciation as well as the result of bureaucratic politics is open to debate. Ianushkevich, notwithstanding the complaints of his staff, had prepared a plan for partial mobilization in response to the Imperial Council's decision of the 24th and the approval of the tsar on the 25th.

Regardless of the grounds for General Staff objection, it carried the day, and by July 27 Ianushkevich, now converted to the predominant view of his staff that partial mobilization would make an effective general mobilization impossible, began to urge Sazonov toward general mobilization.[49] Danilov contended that any partial mobilization was "nothing more than an improvisation" and could only introduce "germs of hesitation and disorder in a domain in which all must be based on preestablished calculations of the greatest precision."[50] In his memoirs published in 1927, Danilov maintained his position that partial mobilization was not possible against Russia's likely enemies in the west without compromising the ability to move to general mobilization.[51] He bases this claim on two technical points and one political argument. The technical points are 1) the limitations of Russian railways in moving troops from interior districts to the frontiers in time of war and 2) the absence of a territorial district system for mobilizing manpower. One could not mobilize an army corps or other large formation merely by drawing on manpower in the local region, leaving other regions undisturbed.[52] The political reason was the indissoluble linkage (as Danilov saw it) between Germany and Austria, such that the option of taking them on separately was

48. Danilov, La Russie dans la Guerre Mondiale, 32–33.
49. Albertini, The Origins of the War of 1914, 2:542, contends that additional pressure in favor of general mobilization and against partial mobilization came from the Grand Duke Nikolai Nikolaevich, Russian commander-in-chief and a political opponent of War Minister Sukhomlinov.
50. Danilov, La Russie dans la Guerre Mondiale, 33.
51. He acknowledges that plans for partial mobilization in the Far East had been developed, for in that theater one could foresee situations where it was necessary "to mobilize only a small number of troops and that without great haste." Ibid., 35.
52. According to Danilov, the "immensity of [our] territory and the insufficient development of our railroads obligated us to concentrate our troops principally on the western frontier, whereas the most important sources for completion [of mobilization]—in men as in horses— were located, to the contrary, in the provinces of the east and the south." Ibid., 34.

effectively ruled out. Moreover, according to Danilov and presumably reflecting the judgments of most General Staff planners, "each of these two countries represented by itself such a considerable military power that our security interests required, in case of conflict with one of them, a concentrated effort of the totality of our armed forces."[53]

Danilov's arguments about the dysfunctional relationship between partial and general mobilization, as the Russian General Staff understood both options at the time, has face validity. However, it leaves unanswered the larger question of whether, if the Russians had planned with more concern for the relationship between crisis management or deterrence and options for mobilization, Sazonov and Ianushkevich would have had additional options below the level of general mobilization. As the highly regarded Russian military theorist A. A. Svechin, who chaired the Soviet military-historical commission following World War I which investigated Russian performance in that conflict, noted:

> The need for mobilization plans to be flexible stems from the need to subordinate mobilization to the political situation at the time of mobilization. In 1914 Russia had a general mobilization plan, but the political situation required only a mobilization directed against Austria. . . . [T]he mobilization of some military districts proved to be technically careless: the districts were tied together by extensive transfers of reserves and so forth, and the avoidance of a general mobilization planned out in all its details forced the Russian army to improvise. Hence the *military command used all means possible to obtain an order for general mobilization*, which they succeeded in getting. Politics was subordinated to a clumsy inflexible mobilization. The means triumphed over the end.[54]

Faced with General Staff skepticism and angered by Austria's declaration of war against Serbia on the 28th of July, Sazonov ordered Ianushkevich that same day to prepare two ukases for the tsar's signature: one for partial and one for general mobilization.[55] When the tsar vacillated on July 29 by first

53. Ibid., 33.
54. A. A. Svechin, *Strategiya* [Strategy], 2d ed. (Moscow: Voennyi Vestnik, 1927); published in English and edited by Kent D. Lee (Minneapolis: East View Publications, 1991), 200. Emphasis added.
55. Albertini, *The Origins of the War of 1914*, 2:544.

ordering general mobilization and then canceling it, the cancellation was decided upon by his own initiative and after receiving a telegram from the kaiser urging restraint.[56] As their military organizations put into motion the very procedures that (albeit with some ambivalence) had been authorized earlier, the German and Russian heads of state and *chefs de cabinet* now sought to draw back from the brink of catastrophe. Russian military advisers maneuvered to reinstate the order for general mobilization, and the chief of staff asked Sazonov on the morning of July 30 to see the tsar, in order to persuade him to reverse his decision. Ianushkevich urged that Sazonov telephone him immediately with news of the tsar's consent. "After this," said Ianushkevich, "I will retire from sight, smash my telephone, and generally take all measures so that I cannot be found to give any contrary orders for a new postponement of general mobilization."[57] Ianushkevich was not to be disappointed. At 1:00 P.M. on the same day, Ianushkevich was called to the telephone by Sazonov, who declared that the tsar, after receiving the latest news from Berlin, had decided to decree general mobilization of the army and the fleet.[58] According to Dobrorolsky, Sazonov then told the Russian chief of staff: "Give your orders, my general, and then . . . disappear for the rest of the day."[59]

Rationality, Motivation, and Doctrine

German, French, and Russian military planning prior to World War I, according to Jack Snyder, was influenced by an organizational ideology based on three components: rational calculation, motivational biases, and doctrinal simplification.[60] Although the domestic conditions under which French military planning took place were different from those in Germany in the decade or so before 1914, the two countries shared some characteristic military and political decisionmaking behavior. In both cases, military planners had strong motivational biases to discount the risks of offensive operations, despite substantial evidence that technology and tactics would favor the defense in a future European war. The experiences of the American Civil War,

56. Fay, *The Origins of the World War*, 2:465; Albertini, *The Origins of the War of 1914*, 2:555–61.
57. Quoted in Fay, *The Origins of the World War*, 2:470.
58. S. Dobrorolsky, "La Mobilisation de l'armée russe en 1914," *Revue d'Histoire de la Guerre Mondiale* 1 (1923): 150.
59. Ibid.
60. Snyder, *The Ideology of the Offensive*, 200 et pass.

the Russo-Japanese War, and the Boer War had shown the difficulty of frontal attacks on fixed and fortified positions. Such fortifications could not be breached by frontal assaults in good time; attackers would wear out their best forces, allowing the defender to hold back until the culminating point of the attacker's offensive had been reached. Then, the defender's counteroffensive would strike a decisive blow against the retreating attacker; or, equally as bad, the war would be prolonged into an inconclusive war of attrition.

As alliances solidified and leaders began to take more seriously the possibility of war between 1910 and 1914, their fears of a disrupted offensive spent against formidable defensive barriers and entrenched firepower did not suggest to them the abandonment of offensive military strategies. Instead, French and German planners moved still more insistently toward an emphasis on the offensive as the key to victory. In the French case, doctrines supported by such leading theorists as Colonel de Grandmaison and commanders such as Ferdinand Foch and Joseph Joffre argued for the ability of élan and offensive spirit to compensate for any technology or tactics apparently favorable to the defense.[61] French military planners also assumed that any delay in mobilization would be fatal to their efforts to establish a coherent defense against German attackers. Every twenty-four hours of delay would, according to French prewar estimates, allow the Germans to advance an additional fifteen to twenty kilometers.[62] The professional officer corps of France also had a motivational bias against the ideas of "outsiders," including military critics in parlement, who had attempted to impose their own notions of doctrine and recruitment policy on the armed forces' leadership. Attempts to "civilianize" the French armed forces in order to break the hold of professional military ethnocentrism became especially intense after the Dreyfus affair, and professional resistance against perceived threats to organizational autonomy marked the behavior of the French armed forces' leadership down to 1914. One way of keeping external critics at bay was to establish a doctrine based on assertions of military principle that were not falsifiable by external standards (e.g., those asserting the importance of

61. Stefan T. Possony and Etienne Mantoux, "Du Picq and Foch: The French School," ch. 9 in Makers of Modern Strategy: Military Thought from Machiavelli to Hitler, ed. Edward Mead Earle (Princeton, N.J.: Princeton University Press, 1943), 206–33; S. R. Williamson, "Joffre Reshapes French Strategy, 1911–1913," ch. 6 in The War Plans of the Great Powers, 133–54; Michael Howard, "Men Against Fire: The Doctrine of the Offensive in 1914," ch. 18 in Makers of Modern Strategy: From Machiavelli to the Nuclear Age, ed. Peter Paret (Princeton, N.J.: Princeton University Press, 1986), 510–26.

62. Barry R. Posen, The Sources of Military Doctrine: France, Britain, and Germany Between the World Wars (Ithaca, N.Y.: Cornell University Press, 1984), 22.

moral qualities and offensive spirit). Another way was to espouse offensive military doctrines that required well-trained regular forces and de-emphasized the role of short-term reservists, along with the civilianized perspectives such new recruits might bring with them.[63]

Following the Prussian victory over France which established the German Reich in 1871, the German General Staff under the leadership of Helmuth von Moltke (the elder) undertook to plan for future wars Germany might have to fight. The revenge-minded French were obvious candidates (owing to the annexation of Alsace and Lorraine) and so were the Russians. Moltke took little comfort from Prussia's rapid victory over the French main forces in 1870: the heady battlefield victories were followed by a period of protracted insurrection by Frenchmen under the direction of Léon-Michel Gambetta which ended only in January 1871 after two weeks' bombardment of Paris.[64] Moltke had also observed the growing importance of firepower and the likelihood that future attacks on frontal positions could be far more expensive for the attacker.

Partly for these reasons, the elder Moltke gradually became less enchanted with the potential of strategic offensive operations. A new French fortification system had been developed sufficiently by 1879 to add to Moltke's doubts about the chances for any quick German victory based on an attack westward, and the same fortification system might have provided a suitable base for early French offensives against Germany. Moltke therefore urged Bismarck toward an alliance with Austria, which was signed in 1879 and depended on plans for an initial concentration of German and Austrian forces to the east against Russia.[65] An alternative plan was prepared, however, in which the major concentration and deployment of German forces would be against France, in case of changes in the political environment for military planning.

The flexible planning of Helmuth von Moltke and the diplomatic skills of Chancellor Otto von Bismarck were both missing, however, once the kaiser had dismissed Bismarck and Schlieffen had taken over as chief of the German General Staff. Germany planned for one war and one war only. Nor was this at all illogical. German planners assumed that their first objective was to defeat France in a short campaign and that their subsequent objective was to turn east and defeat Russia. There was some vagueness about the

63. For further discussion, see Snyder, The Ideology of the Offensive, ch. 3, esp. 70–97.

64. Col. T. N. Dupuy, USA, Ret., A Genius for War: The German Army and General Staff, 1807–1945 (Englewood Cliffs, N.J.: Prentice-Hall, 1977), 107–8.

65. Ibid., 120.

postwar political situation once Russia's military forces were defeated or stalemated. Moltke recognized that any attempt to pursue Russian forces far into the interior would probably use up too much of the German army, and his successors concurred to the extent that an initial offensive against France, not Russia, was deemed advisable.

German war planning was based on some confusion between the conduct of a war and the fighting of a campaign. A military campaign is a series of battlefield engagements taking place within a certain geographic theater of operations. Campaigns are intended to defeat the armed forces of the opponent. A war includes not only the results of campaigns, but the policy objectives for which those campaigns are being fought. Germany's war objectives in the First World War were formulated much less clearly than those of Russia or France. The kaiser and his military planners somehow supposed that they could wage a war for the occupation or conquest of France without the participation of England, and they further supposed that France having been subdued and England uninvolved, Germany could go on to crush the armies of Russia and to occupy part of Russian territory. The clarity and single-mindedness of German military planning was in drastic contrast to the plural confusion of Germany's political objectives for war.

In Russia and in France, the reverse was true. Russia and France knew with much greater precision than Germany what they wanted to get out of this war. France wanted to expel any German invader from its territory, to recover the lost provinces of Alsace and Lorraine, and to inflict on Germany a military defeat that would preclude future aggression against France. Russia wanted to accomplish analogous objectives: expulsion of the invader and his ultimate defeat by virtue of a decisive counteroffensive. However, neither Russia nor France gave sufficient consideration to the stability of a postwar power structure in Europe if Germany's regime should change its character from autocracy to something else. Nor did they give adequate consideration to the probable instabilities in postwar Europe if military technology should begin to favor offensive instead of defensive warfare, as it did during the 1920s and 1930s. Finally, like the Germans, they failed to think through the consequences of dissolving the Austro-Hungarian and Ottoman empires simultaneously. One can understand the reluctance of German and Russian planners to act on the assumption of their own demise, and one can also appreciate the difficulty they had in foreseeing the relationship between war and the end of their empires. But both Russia and Germany, with strong interests in the Balkans and in Turkey's political and military status from the onset of the twentieth century, should have considered what would happen if Turkey and Austria left the chessboard as major players.

Had they applied such geostrategic logic to the forecasting of war outcomes and their implications, the leaders of Germany and Russia in 1914 might have concluded that the logical winner of World War I was England. Notwithstanding the upheavals in British domestic politics following the war and the incredible losses suffered on the battlefields from Flanders to Gallipoli, Britain's imperial reach throughout the Middle East and Southwest Asia expanded enormously between 1914 and 1922.[66] The kaiser's personality occasionally drove him to fitful remonstrances against English duplicity, and Germany's military planners prior to World War I worried for obvious reasons about the status of the naval arms race between England and Germany. But German planning for World War I remained largely fixated on the military-operational campaign or theater strategy of conquering France, ignoring for the present the problem of what to do if the French could not be defeated in a shorter campaign and Germany were forced into a protracted conflict.

What do these historical cases suggest for current and recent U.S. war planning, especially given the dramatic changes in military technology since World War II? The Schlieffen Plan offered a prescription for operational elegance marching toward a political void. Russian military planning prior to World War I (of which more later) resulted in military-operational vacillation, but with a clearer sense of appropriateness and proportionality concerning the accomplishment of political aims. But one problem in prewar crisis management was that Germany's strategy for a short war, based on a militarily coherent but politically incoherent planning guidance, interacted with Russia's planning guidance, which was militarily incoherent but politically coherent. That is: Russia had a more-or-less consistent grand strategy after 1910 but a complicated, confusing, and scenario-driven system for operational war planning. Germany had the world's best system for operational war planning, but a confused notion of its wartime and postwar political objectives. Each of the two states most crucial for preventing or unleashing European war in July 1914 was unable to resolve the trade-off between deterrence and nonprovocation of potential opponents. As a result, they got less deterrence and more provocation than they expected.

Only England among the major powers had the flexibility to shift plans sufficiently when the situation in Europe changed rapidly after June 28,

---

66. See David Fromkin, *A Peace to End All Peace: Creating the Modern Middle East, 1914–1922* (London: André Deutsch, 1989).

1914, from one of general deterrence into one of immediate deterrence. Prior to the assassination of the Austrian archduke, deterrent threats without equally loud signals of nonprovocation cost leaders very little. This ambience carried over into early July, when the kaiser gave commitments to Austria which the latter would later use to involve Germany as its guarantor, during a process of escalation over which all the powers would subsequently lose control. When the shift from general to immediate deterrence became too obvious to be ignored (i.e., after the Austrian ultimatum to Serbia), signals of nonprovocation were drowned out by perceptions of hostile intent, by reciprocal mobilizations, and by the inability of political leaders to empathize with the decision dilemmas of their counterparts in other capitals.

U.S.-Soviet strategic nuclear bipolarity and the clear dividing lines of the Cold War contributed to the prevention of an outbreak of war in Europe of the kind witnessed in August 1914. Nevertheless, U.S. nuclear war plans from the 1940s through the 1980s were limited by some of the same constraints as the great powers shared in the years immediately preceding World War I. There were few risks to general deterrence between the nuclear superpowers, but on those occasions when crisis did erupt, it became more apparent that nuclear war plans were grossly inappropriate to crisis management. Designed for circumstances of large-scale, premeditated, and surprise attack, U.S. nuclear war plans offered no usable military options for other contingencies and served only to cast the shadow of inadvertent escalation over crisis bargaining. Designed for deterrence, the plans and options they provided to U.S. policymakers were equally or more suitable for provocation.

GERMAN AND RUSSIAN WAR PLANNING

If the Schlieffen Plan is understood as a plan for launching a first strike "in the last resort," as I believe is justified by the historical evidence, then it has certain commonalities with U.S. nuclear strategic planning, especially during the Eisenhower years. Just as the prospect of a two-front war presented Germany with no solution to its security dilemma without running very high risks, so too did the prospect of nuclear war (including limited nuclear war) present no risk-free option to American planners after 1945. However, the German mobilization plans were not the only ones of significance in 1914; Russian plans were equally important, if not more so. The problem in Russia was not a single concept around which all strategic planning was narrowly based, but a plurality of concepts which were invoked between 1910 and 1914, to the detriment of lucid crisis control in the face of rapidly moving events.[67] If to some extent Germany was trapped in 1914 by fixity of plans, Russia was encumbered by diversity. German fixity and Russian uncertainty about dominant strategic concepts, including the objectives of mobilization, were tragically and ironically blended together, adding to the likelihood of war. Germany prior to 1914 sought to solve the deterrence/nonprovocation trade-off with a strategy of massive retaliation, or even massive preemption; Russia, more uncertain of the way in which war might develop, sought a concept of mobilization that allowed for flexible response.

As noted, there was not "a" single unifying concept of mobilization shared by the various civilian and military organizations in tsarist Russia during the years immediately preceding the outbreak of war. Even within the military there were divergent views concerning the political and military implications of mobilization. The Foreign Office represented by Sazonov sought to use "partial" mobilization as a measure of coercive diplomacy against Austria-Hungary, in order to induce Austria-Hungary to moderate its demands against Serbia. However, the significance of any "partial" mobilization for demonstrative purposes was offset by its very different implications for the Russian military leadership. For War Minister Sukhomlinov, Chief of the General Staff Ianushkevich, and Quartermaster General Danilov it was inconceivable that a war between Austria-Hungary and Russia would not also involve Russia's main enemy, Germany. Sazonov's efforts to use brinkmanship on behalf of Russian foreign policy were used by the tsar's highest military advisers to prepare for a war they now judged to be inevitable. The military was not alone in offering mixed or inappropriate signals. Sazonov corrupted his own effort at coercive diplomacy by misreading his military options and by poorly estimating how the exercise of those options would be perceived in Germany and in Austria-Hungary.[68]

Much of Russia's ability to mobilize depended upon the quality of leadership at the level of its War Ministry, General Staff, and military district

67. According to I. I. Rostunov, the Russian General Staff in 1914 had already begun a detailed reworking of Plan 19 with the intention of producing a Plan 20, but they did not succeed in completing the work before war broke out. See Rostunov, *Russkii front pervoi mirovoi voiny*, 95.
68. In addition to sources cited above, one should consult Sazonov's views of these events in his first-person account, *Fateful Years, 1909–1916: The Reminiscences of Serge Sazonov* (London: Jonathan Cape, 1971), esp. 149–216.

commanders. War Minister Sukhomlinov made certain that no one served for very long under his jurisdiction as chief of the General Staff, perhaps because of the factionalism within the foreign policy and security establishment at that time and because of Sukhomlinov's desire to preserve his freedom of action against second-guessers. Ianushkevich as chief of the General Staff was inexperienced and lacked considerable knowledge about the details of mobilization planning, which were left to the Director of Mobilization, General Dobrorolsky. Sazonov, seeking limited mobilization options that would not convey a desire for war against both Germany and Austria-Hungary, but only for deterrence of Austria-Hungary, did not appreciate that "partial" mobilization could be the worst of both worlds, inside and outside Russia. Inside Russia it caused the military to panic, fearful that they would be left behind in a race to win the war in its initial period. Outside Russia, hostile states evaluated even those measures preparatory to mobilization, which Russia began to take on the 25th and 26th of July, as tantamount to mobilization and war. Finally, with regard to Russian confusion about the relationship of mobilization to deterrence and crisis management, the tsar had to resolve all interagency disputes personally, and he tended to defer to the most recent argument made to him, notwithstanding that earlier arguments might still be the convincing ones.

Crisis Management Precedents

These judgments are confirmed by the experience of the Russian leadership in dealing with the Balkan war of late autumn 1912. Bulgaria and Serbia inflicted defeats on Turkey, after which the two former allies fought one another. The war threatened to spread outside the Balkans and to engulf the great powers, as a similar crisis did in July 1914. On November 23, 1912, having been prompted by War Minister Sukhomlinov, the tsar called a meeting of political and military leaders to discuss the war in the Balkans. The tsar informed Foreign Minister Sazonov and Vladimir Nikolaevich Kokovtsov, chairman of the Council of Ministers, that the day before, at a conference of commanders of the Warsaw and Kiev military districts, "it was decided to mobilize the entire Kiev district and part of the Warsaw district, and to prepare to mobilize the Odessa district."[69] The tsar added that he wished

---

69. Kokovtsov, *Out of My Past,* 345; published in Russian as *Iz moego proshlago: Vospominaniya* [From My Past: Reminiscences] (Paris: Izdaniye Zhumala Illiustrirovannaya Rossya, 1933).

to stress particularly "the fact that this refers exclusively to our Austrian frontier and that we have no intention whatever of taking any steps against Germany."[70]

Others in the room had barely digested this news when the tsar offered Sukhomlinov the opportunity to elaborate. Sukhomlinov said he could not add anything, other than to inform those in attendance that "all telegrams pertaining to the mobilization *had been already prepared* and would be sent as soon as this conference had ended."[71] The tsar turned to Kokovtsov and added that "the Minister of War wanted to dispatch these orders yesterday" but the tsar asked Sukhomlinov to wait another day for consultation with other ministers who ought to know. Kokovtsov, holding back his amazement and fury, stated that the minister of war and the military district commanders "did not perceive the danger they were preparing for Russia in planning this mobilization — a danger of war with Austria and Germany, and at a time when in consideration of the state of our national defense, every effort should be made to avert this catastrophe."[72] The tsar responded to Kokovtsov's agitated presentation by stating that he, too, did not want war; the tsar agreed that Russia was not ready for war. What was being proposed was not war, he continued, but "a simple measure of precaution" by increasing the ranks of the Russian frontier army and by moving some troops forward from rear to front.[73]

Kokovtsov argued in response that, no matter how Russia explained what it was intending to do, "a mobilization remained a mobilization" and would "be countered by our adversaries with actual war, for which Germany was ready and only watching for a chance to begin."[74] The tsar resisted this argument on behalf of crisis instability, but he acquiesced in Kokovtsov's view on another, and ultimately decisive, argument: the war minister and the government had not consulted Russia's French allies, who might therefore stand aside from any outbreak of war. This argument proved to be dissuasive to the tsar, who then ordered that mobilization not be implemented.[75] The war minister then asked permission to send telegrams to the

70. Ibid.
71. Ibid.
72. Ibid. Note Kokovtsov's pessimistic reference to the "state of our national defense." As chairman of the Council of Ministers, he battled against waste in the War Ministry, often having to yield to the tsar's unwillingness to rein in the military despite Nicholas's acknowledgment that Sukhomlinov wasted a great deal of money. See esp. Kokovtsov's discussion of this (pp. 339–40).
73. Ibid., 345.
74. Ibid., 346.
75. For the status of French-Russian relations at this time, see V. I. Bovykin, *Iz istorii*

appropriate district commanders to the effect that no mobilization should be undertaken.[76] After the meeting, Foreign Minister Sazonov confronted Sukhomlinov, accusing the latter of nearly pushing Russia into war and of making a game of the country's fate. The war minister responded that *he* had suggested that the tsar call the others together; had he not done so, mobilization would have gone ahead and "no harm would have been done."[77] Advancing his own version of a preventive war theory, Sukhomlinov added that "we shall have a war anyway; we cannot avoid it, and it would be more profitable for us to begin it as soon as possible."[78]

Sukhomlinov can be cast as the demon if this episode is made into a morality play, but it would be fairer perhaps to evaluate his performance as motivated by a pessimistic threat assessment and an all-too-typical case of military-strategic realism. Realism here is not used as an opposite to unreality or idealism, but as a complex of ideas based on the inevitability of force in world affairs and on the necessity for preparedness by states. Sukhomlinov's strategic realism probably suggested to him, as indeed it had to others, that the powers might not survive *repeated* trials at crisis management in the Balkans without at least once breaking the peace. Errors for which the war minister can certainly be faulted, though, are 1) his bypassing of civilian channels for communicating his intentions and 2) his inflating of the capabilities of his forces, which everyone else in St. Petersburg (and Paris) real-

---

vozniknoveniya pervoi mirovoi voiny: Otnosheniya rossii i frantsii v 1912–1914 gg. [On the History of the Origins of World War I: Relations Between Russia and France from 1912 to 1914] (Moscow: Moscow University Publishing House, 1961), 150–53.

76. Presumably, no order for mobilization should yet have been issued. It is not explained by Kokovtsov why Sukhomlinov surmised that orders would now have to be sent instructing commanders *not* to mobilize.

77. Kokovtsov, *Out of My Past,* 348.

78. Ibid. Sukhomlinov added that "it is your [Sazonov's] opinion and that of the Chairman of the Council of Ministers [Kokovtsov] that we are not ready, while the Tsar and I with him believe in our army and know that a war would bring us nothing but good" (p. 348). Two cautions are in order in accepting this account. First, Kokovtsov and Sukhomlinov were enemies, and this undoubtedly gave a one-sided character to the former's description of events. Second, the War Ministry and the General Staff were separate entities: the War Ministry was responsible for administrative matters, and the General Staff for war planning and strategy. After his 1908 appointment by the tsar as war minister, Sukhomlinov sought to subordinate the General Staff to the War Ministry, and in so doing he both improved its performance and set the stage for additional institutional rivalry. Besides this institutional difference in responsibility, there were personal and political rivalries throughout the Russian military establishment. Though regarded as part of the old army establishment, Sukhomlinov from 1908 until the outbreak of war was actually a modernizer, which brought him into conflict with traditionalists in the artillery and cavalry, not to mention those commanders who advocated strengthening fortresses in the west. See Stone, *The Eastern Front,* 24–28.

ized was a bluff. In effect, *his* mobilization plan was preemption, and the war minister did not move away from this view in the more disastrous crisis of July 1914 until Director of Mobilization for the General Staff Dobrorolsky placed the actual directive for general mobilization in front of him for signature on July 29. One might argue that the Balkan war of 1912–13 set in motion a train of thinking that resulted in Russia's early decision to take those measures preparatory to mobilization on July 25 and 26, 1914, which so alarmed her adversaries, especially in Berlin.

Sazonov's outburst at Sukhomlinov during the mobilization crisis of 1912 was not entirely fair to the war minister. Although Sukhomlinov unduly discounted Austrian connections with Germany that could have turned any Russian mobilization against Austria into a wider war, Sazonov reintroduces the same assumption of crisis localization into his own calculations during the crisis of July 1914. When his assumption—that diplomacy, supported by partial mobilization against Austria, can localize and contain the crisis—is proved incorrect, he reverses himself and decides that war is inevitable. Thereafter, he joins with military colleagues in urging the tsar toward general mobilization. By this time, even Sazonov has given up on the idea of partial mobilization for deterrence; some historians doubt that he ever really meant it to succeed.[79] Dobrorolsky contends that "on July 28, the day of the Austrian declaration of war on Serbia, Sazonov's optimism vanishes at a stroke. He is filled with the idea that a general war is inevitable, and informs Ianushkevich that one must no longer delay with the mobilization of our army, . . . that he was even astonished that it had not begun sooner."[80] This sudden shift from optimism to pessimism on Sazonov's part has confused historians, as it confused not a few of his contemporaries.

Such an abrupt change of perspective by the Russian foreign minister reflected the failure of an improvised strategy for the "manipulation of risk." A manipulation-of-risk strategy is an approach to bargaining which emphasizes the contest of wills or nerve between opponents.[81] A side that uses a

79. Fay, *The Origins of the World War*, 2:446–47 et pass.

80. Dobrorolsky, quoted ibid., 448. Fay is among those sources highly critical of Sazonov, partly on the grounds of his allegedly mercurial temperament. See also the judgments of Baron M. de Taube, *La Politique russe d'avant-guerre et la fin de l'empire des tsars, 1904–1917* (Paris: Librairie Ernest Leroux, 1928). De Taube places a great deal of blame on Sazonov for contributing to the pressure on the tsar for general mobilization, despite some last-minute opportunities for diplomatic containment of the Austro-Serbian war (pp. 362–63). He cites, among extenuating circumstances, Sazonov's "nervosité maladive de sa nature" (the sickly nervousness of his nature), p. 363.

81. See Thomas C. Schelling, *Arms and Influence* (New Haven, Conn.: Yale University Press, 1966), 92–109.

manipulation-of-risk strategy exploits the uncertainty it shares with its opponent about the course of future events. As Thomas Schelling notes, one threatens not so much the deliberate decision to make war, but rather a decision to initiate a process over which both sides might subsequently lose control. There is a shared danger that each side might take a series of steps that will gradually convince both sides that war has, for all practical purposes, already begun. The decision environment within which such a process can take place is an important influence on the probable success or failure of a manipulation-of-risk strategy: "The process would have had to be unforeseeable and unpredictable. If there were some clearly recognizable final critical steps that converted the situation from one in which war was unnecessary to one in which war was inevitable, the step would not have been taken. Alternatives would have been found. Any transition from peace to war would have had to traverse a region of uncertainty—of misunderstandings or miscalculations or misinterpretations, or actions with unforeseen consequences, in which things got out of hand."[82]

In order to play this strategy successfully in the context of July 1914, Sazonov required a situation in which other governments and his own military understood the difference between this version of a coercive *bargaining* strategy and a strategy designed to intimidate the opponent by superior force. A manipulation-of-risk strategy can backfire if a state decides that it is not being negotiated with, but is being asked for unilateral concessions on the basis of another state's force superiority. The choice between a manipulation-of-risk strategy and a strategy of intimidation through force superiority (or "escalation dominance") is a matter of relative emphasis, but an important one. The size of Russia's forces in 1914 was obviously pertinent to Russia's ability to play successfully at either a manipulation-of-risk or an escalation dominance strategy. The major difference between the risk-manipulating and the force-intimidating approaches to crisis management is the greater dependency of the risk-manipulating approach on indeterminacy and uncertainty.[83]

Models of Mobilization

One can identify at least three generalized models of mobilization in the minds of those Russian statesmen and military planners who came to grips

82. Ibid., 96.
83. For further discussion of these differences, see Robert Jervis, *The Illogic of American Nuclear Strategy* (Ithaca, N.Y.: Cornell University Press, 1984), 126–46.

with the dramatic European events of June and July 1914. One conception was that of Sazonov: mobilization was military ballast in support of coercive bargaining. His intent was to intimidate Austria into going easier on Serbia. Only when this failed did Sazonov begin to understand the nature of the difficulty he had created by insisting upon partial mobilization for deterrence; for partial mobilization was indistinguishable from general mobilization to his enemies, and to most of the Russian military. The objective of his coercive diplomacy was to get Austria to back down from its extreme political demands against Serbia and to deter Austria from military attack against that country. Although he obtained formal approval for partial mobilization as he understood it, Sazonov never convinced the Russian General Staff or the War Ministry of its value, and after the outbreak of war between Austria and Serbia, Sazonov shifted toward the view that mobilization was simply preparation for war.

A second conception of mobilization was that of defensive realism. This concept was held by the head of the mobilization section of the General Staff (Dobrorolsky), by military district commanders, and by the ministers responsible for maritime affairs and transportation.[84] This concept was based on the fear that Russian mobilization would lag too far behind that of Germany, and the fear remained a realistic one, even after the 1912 modifications to the 1910 version of Plan 19. Russian mobilization planners also feared that their alliance commitment to France required a prompt offensive into East Prussia in addition to one against Austria in Galicia, and preparedness for both contingencies would not be possible unless early premobilization measures were taken throughout the country. Finally, the General Staff and its mobilization section feared that a partial mobilization would disrupt later plans for general mobilization, should it be needed.

A third conception of mobilization was that it was tantamount to war, and that measures "preparatory to war" were tantamount to mobilization. However, there was a passive and an active form of this assumption. The active form attributed the conviction that mobilization was tantamount to war to Russia's prospective opponents, especially to Germany. It implied that Russia's forces might be vulnerable to German or Austro-Hungarian preemption unless Russia mobilized without delay at the first sign of a crisis. The passive form placed less emphasis on the potential vulnerability of Russia's slower mobilization system, compared to its probable opponents in the west, and simply noted that for Russia and its military planners, mobilization without war was possible and, perhaps, preferable.

84. Dobrorolsky, "La Mobilisation de l'armée russe en 1914."

As an example of the active form, recall that Sukhomlinov had tried to push Russia into the First Balkan War in November 1912 by getting the tsar to sign off on mobilization against Austria. Only the energetic objections of Sazonov and Count Kokovtsov, chairman of the Council of Ministers at the time, prevented a Russian mobilization that in all likelihood would have led to war. On this occasion Sazonov was quite upset with Sukhomlinov and told him so.[85] Yet, in July 1914, Sazonov expected his plan for partial mobilization to improve Russia's freedom of action vis-à-vis managing the growing crisis. The mobilization of thirteen army corps against Austria was accompanied by messages of reassurance to Germany that Russia's actions were intended solely to deter further Austrian aggression against Serbia and to protect the sovereignty of the latter. Ironically, Sukhomlinov also provides an example, and a somewhat amusing one, of the passive form of the concept that mobilization was tantamount to war. In the 1912 crisis just mentioned, he planned to go abroad for several weeks, *immediately after* having ordered a mobilization, in order to join his wife on the Riviera. The revelation astonished Sazonov and Kokovtsov.

However, Sazonov's message of "flexible response" in July 1914 was a signal that competed with the "noise" of other Russian actions which were interpreted with great suspicion by the Germans, and not without reason. The Russian "period preparatory to war" (called the "premobilization period" in the General Staff gazette) which the tsar authorized on the evening of July 25/26 involved a series of steps that were designed to make general mobilization easier to accomplish at a later time, should the tsar and the appropriate ministers so decide.[86] It made no sense to take the measures preparatory to war unless the leaders expected that general mobilization was imminent. Sazonov's actions from July 24 through 26 sought to use a weak military position to support an assertive diplomatic one. His efforts to extend Russian deterrence further into the crisis by military means, but to avoid having those military means encumber his future choices, was not prejudicial to peace per se. But it did compete with the General Staff's concerns about military preparedness, should deterrence fail, and those concerns resulted in

85. Kokovtsov, *Out of My Past*, 348.
86. Albertini, *The Origins of the War of 1914*, 2:304–6, and Fay, *The Origins of the World War*, 2:303–21. According to Albertini, "however much the General Staff regarded partial mobilization as a mistaken, dangerous and impracticable measure, they were only too ready to carry out the provisions of the 'Regulation concerning the period preparatory to war' which had been approved by the Tsar on 2 March 1913 and partly made up for the slowness of Russian mobilization" (2:305).

the tsar's approval for a second track of military readiness, in the form of "measures preparatory to war," which sent aggressive signals to the Germans once they learned of it. If Sazonov intended to communicate a policy of flexible response to foreign audiences, the premobilization set in motion by the measures preparatory to war suggested something more like massive retaliation.

An example of standard operating procedures for connecting measures preparatory to war with those of general mobilization was the solution to the problem of readiness in the border military districts. The "Regulation Concerning the Period Preparatory to War" went into effect on July 26. It provided, according to procedures reviewed by military and civil authorities and approved by the tsar in 1913, for the fulfillment of two "lists" of activities. These activities included the call-up of territorial and other reserve forces and the complete arming of frontier posts. The border military districts were in fact put on a wartime footing during the period preparatory to war, prior to the tsar's approval of any ukase for general mobilization. Ianushkevich's communication to the commander of the Warsaw Military District on July 26 confirms the qualitative change in the character of readiness that was expected: "His Majesty commands all the fortresses of the District to be placed in a state of war."[87] In addition, measures preparatory to war were ordered not only in the districts relevant to mobilization against Austria, but throughout the entire territory of European Russia.[88]

The views of the "defensive realism" and "tantamount to war" schools were based not only on military-technical considerations but on their proponents' interpretation of recent Russian historical experience. During the Bosnian annexation crisis from October 1908 until March 1909 (Austria-Hungary declared that it would annex the province of Bosnia-Herzegovina, which belonged to Turkey), Serbia and Austria-Hungary mobilized against one another and maintained their forces in a state of readiness for war for months. The crisis ended when Russia, partly in response to German demands, backed away from its support for Serbia's own interest in controlling the disputed provinces.[89] Another crisis broke out in 1912 during the First Balkan War when Serbia, having routed the forces of its Turkish opponent, attempted to incorporate Albania and obtain a port on the Adriatic. Austria-Hungary demanded that Albania be granted independence and mobilized its

87. Fay, *The Origins of the World War*, 2:315.
88. Ibid., 2:315–16, n. 89.
89. Paul K. Huth, *Extended Deterrence and the Prevention of War* (New Haven, Conn.: Yale University Press, 1988), 184.

forces along the Serbian border. As we have seen, in November the Russians almost committed themselves to mobilize against Austria with the attendant risks of a wider conflict, but ultimately backed down. Thus, for the second time in about three years, Russia had appeared to back away from support for its Serbian ally in the face of German and Austro-Hungarian demands.[90] Russia learned mistakenly from this episode and from previous crises in Europe that any lack of decisiveness in providing "extended deterrence" support to its Balkan ally would be interpreted as a sign of Russian weakness by Germany and Austria. For its part, Austria learned that Russian extended deterrence on behalf of Balkan allies was vulnerable to the pressure of Austrian mobilization and the threat of subsequent German mobilization. Both lessons/misperceptions would contribute to an outbreak of war in August 1914.

Comparing Past and Present

The U.S. experience in nuclear-crisis management is not without similar divergence in the views of policymakers as to the significance of mobilization and increased readiness and the interpretations likely to be placed on such moves by potential opponents. During the Cuban missile crisis of 1962, for example, the U.S. Navy implemented its blockade of Cuba according to standard operating procedures. These procedures included the stationing of picket ships outside the range of Cuban aircraft, and they also included the expectation that Soviet submarines entering waters declared off-limits by the U.S. Navy would be forced to the surface or driven off by U.S. antisubmarine warfare units. These expectations on the part of the navy were quite consistent with its standard operating procedures for the conduct of blockades, but they conflicted with some of the nuances of Kennedy and McNamara's political strategy for resolution of the crisis without fighting. On the issue of using force and increased readiness to support coercive diplomacy in Cuba, McNamara and Kennedy preferred to place minimum operational stress on Soviet forces while Khrushchev rethought his political position. The navy worried that a blockade too close to Cuba or antisubmarine operations which were less assertive would create significant military vulnerabilities.

Also during the Cuban missile crisis, readiness for war meant massive U.S. preparations for an invasion of Cuba if coercive diplomacy failed to remove

90. Ibid.

the missiles. These preparations, including the movement of troops and aircraft within the United States to southern locations more advantageous for attack on Cuba, were obviously designed to send a message of U.S. determination to Khrushchev. But they ran the risk of succeeding too well. If Khrushchev decided that an invasion of Cuba was inevitable, he might attempt to accelerate the readiness of Soviet nuclear-capable missiles or preemptively engage in "horizontal escalation" (geographic war widening) elsewhere, say in Europe. Russia's mobilization in 1914 did not deter the Austro-Hungarians, and it provoked the Germans into a wider war that ultimately destroyed three empires in Europe (four, if we count the Ottoman Empire). The distinction between measures preparatory for war, actual mobilization for war, and an outbreak of war might have seemed as obscure to Soviet pessimists in October 1962 as they did to some Russian planners in July 1914.

In July 1914 Sazonov and the Russian military leadership were operating with somewhat different concepts of command and control. Sazonov assumed that political control could be maintained as a process of mobilization was increased in intensity in order to support coercive diplomacy and deterrence. He expected that the carrying out of partial mobilization, together with the credible threat of general mobilization later, would be responsive to the oscillations in relations between Russia and Germany. Even his critics unexpectedly endorse such a theory. For example, Baron Taube criticizes Sazonov for urging on the tsar the declaration of general mobilization on July 30. This was premature, according to Taube, in view of the personal demarches taken by the tsar with regard to the kaiser after the kaiser had volunteered to mediate the conflict between Russia and Austria-Hungary.[91] Sazonov's critics might believe in the possible success of mediation efforts by the German kaiser at this late date, but the Russian foreign minister had resigned himself to the certainty of Russian involvement in war after Austria declared war on Serbia and began its bombardment of Belgrade on July 28.[92]

91. De Taube, La Politique russe d'avant-guerre, 362.
92. Russia received news of this on the 29th. Sazonov, consistent with decisions taken at ministerial councils on the 24th and 25th of July, had authorized partial mobilization against Austria to begin on July 28. At that stage he was still hopeful of containing the crisis. On the 29th, Portales, the German ambassador, informed Sazonov that unless Russia called off its mobilization Germany would be forced to mobilize and this would mean war. This message from Chancellor Bethmann-Hollweg apparently referred to reports received in Germany prior to July 29 about Russian "measures preparatory to war," which were not tantamount to mobilization as such but were necessary preliminaries to general mobilization. The initial German reaction to the news of Russian partial mobilization against Austria was a last-minute effort by

The kaiser had, at a much earlier stage in the crisis, supported Austria-Hungary in the making of its extreme demands against Serbia. His boldness in backing Austria was perhaps motivated by the two setbacks suffered at the hand of Russian "extended deterrence" in the Bosnian annexation and First Balkan War crises.[93] It is equally or even more likely that the kaiser, in providing a general reassurance of German support to Austria-Hungary on July 5, was confident that any demands placed on Serbia by Austria-Hungary would not be excessive as seen by the European powers. He was mistaken in this assumption about the probable moderation of Austrian demands. The kaiser had in earlier crises *not* necessarily sided with Austria against Serbia, and he regarded efforts by Austria to exclude Serbia from access to the Adriatic during the Balkan Wars as "nonsense."[94] Apparently his close friendship with Archduke Franz Ferdinand was one factor limiting the kaiser's ability to appraise with objectivity the crisis that began in Sarajevo on June 28. Another factor making him less cautious about supporting Austria against Serbia in July 1914 was his conviction that the principle of monarchy in Europe was in danger (a source of his annoyance at Russia for backing the antimonarchical Serbs).[95]

In view of Wilhelm II's own misperceptions of Austrian intentions and his miscalculation of the risks of inadvertent escalation, the claim that Sazonov deliberately headed into disaster and circumvented a "Willy–Nicky" rapprochement is very debatable. Sazonov is more accurately held accountable for a failure to understand that his concept of using partial mobilization for compellence was regarded as subversive of war-preparedness by the General

the German chancellor on the evening of July 29/30 to pressure Austria to accept mediation. Thus, the earlier measures set in motion by Russia "preparatory to war" proved to be more alarming to Germany than the later partial mobilization implemented by Sazonov. See Marc Trachtenberg, "The Meaning of Mobilization in 1914," *International Security* (Winter 1990–91): 120–50.

One could also argue that it was only when Bethmann-Hollweg became convinced Britain would not remain neutral in a war between the Entente and Alliance powers that German efforts to restrain Austria began in earnest. See Albertini, *The Origins of the War of 1914,* 2:632–40. Albertini's verdict, that Sazonov bore heavy responsibility for having thought of resorting to partial mobilization, for not turning back when he realized that partial mobilization was impractical, and for advising the tsar to order general mobilization, although this would render war practically inevitable, is unfair to Sazonov if, as some documentary evidence suggests, the immediate impact of Russia's partial mobilization was to temporarily deter rather than provoke Germany.

93. This is Paul Huth's interpretation in *Extended Deterrence,* 183–85.
94. Fay, *The Origins of the World War,* 2:207.
95. Ibid., 2:207–9.

Staff and by the quartermaster general and principal war planner, Danilov.[96] Russia's military moves during the period of July 24–28 also confused the Germans, who did not interpret measures preparatory to war and partial mobilization as bargaining tactics in support of a manipulation-of-risk strategy. Albertini blames Sazonov's failed partial mobilization or manipulation-of-risk strategy for the subsequent "avalanche of mobilizations and war itself."[97] According to Albertini, Sazonov realized too late that partial mobilization would be a "disastrous step," but once having announced that it had been put into effect, Sazonov refused to back down and instead escalated to general mobilization when partial mobilization proved ineffective.[98] However, it is doubtful that the further conclusion drawn by Albertini in this regard can be sustained: namely, that it was "political leaders' ignorance of what mobilization implied and the dangers it involved which led them lightheartedly to take the step of mobilizing and unleashing a European war."[99]

The truth is not so much that leaders approached the problem of mobilization "lightheartedly" in July 1914 but that they approached it with somewhat different perspectives and concepts. Sazonov's manipulation-of-risk strategy might have made more sense to his contemporaries in Russia and elsewhere if they had foreseen with greater clarity the possible consequences of war. One advantage that nuclear-crisis managers have had over their predecessors in 1914 is their ability to foresee clearly what might happen if crisis management should fail and escalation subsequently escapes control. Therefore, Sazonov was not wrong to attempt a risk-oriented approach to deterrence through mobilization, and his approach could have worked if his intentions had been clearer to leaders in other countries and if his own military had developed a plan for partial mobilization in support of coercive diplomacy. Because they had not, their war plans squeezed Sazonov's manipulation-of-risk strategy between the planners in Berlin and those in St. Petersburg who sought to insure their forces against feared early and decisive losses.

---

96. Danilov is quite explicit on this point. A war against the Central Powers had to require of Russia "the maximum of forces and resources" that the country would be capable of furnishing. For this reason, "only a general mobilization of the totality of our forces would suffice for the exigencies of the moment (an outbreak of war), and that in consequence our plan for war on the western frontier only anticipated a general mobilization." Danilov, *La Russie dans la Guerre Mondiale*, 122.

97. Albertini, *The Origins of the War of 1914*, 2:578.

98. Ibid.

99. Ibid., 2:579.

Dynamics of Threat

During the crisis of July 1914, plans for German and Russian mobilization and deployment of forces prior to war contributed to an increased likelihood that war would in fact occur. The Russian war machine could not provide for a partial mobilization against Austria alone which was nonthreatening to Germany, for at least two reasons. First, reserves ticketed for units within the four military districts mobilized against Austria were not drawn exclusively from those districts, as noted above. Only a completely territorial armed force lends itself to the kind of selective mobilization that Sazonov envisioned for the purpose of signaling determination, along with an open door for continued negotiation, to Germany. Second, the critical Warsaw Military District, which was relevant to force generation for a possible war with Germany or Austria, created the same trade-off between readiness and political provocation that, according to John D. Steinbruner, characterizes U.S. nuclear operations at very high levels of alert. Measures preparatory to war taken in that district, any partial mobilization of forces involving that district, could not but alarm Germany.

In turn, Germany would be alarmed because its own mobilization and war plans dictated reliance on preemption, on getting in the first decisive blow in a battle of annihilation. Any improvement in the prospective speed of Russian mobilization was a reminder of Germany's dependence on a military strategy of preemption. Had Germany a defensive instead of an offensive strategy on the eve of World War I, neither Russia's measures preparatory to war nor the subsequent mobilizations would have seemed nearly so provocative to the Germans. Russia is not being excused here: failures in command and control, relative to its leaders' inconsistent understandings of the details and impact of mobilization, have been discussed above. But the Russians' deficiency in command and control, relative to mobilization and deterrence, was different from that of the Germans. Russia was of too many minds about when to begin mobilization and how; Germany, of one military mind (the Schlieffen Plan, modified, which dictated the timetables for mobilization), produced a plan the consequences of which were not apparent until crisis management by the kaiser, the tsar, and others turned into crisis muddlement.

Skeptical historians might say that the issue of inadvertency is irrelevant: the powers were driven into World War I by a number of causes that overpowered in importance any causal relationship between reciprocal fear of preemptive attack and mobilization. It is also true that mobilization was not considered tantamount to war by all the powers; nor were the lines of cleavage always between civilians and military as institutional or professional groupings. The case against World War I as an "accidental war" was under heavy attack by historians long before many political scientists concerned about nuclear strategy revisited the issue.[100] The matter of inadvertency versus deliberateness in reciprocal military mobilization is not so easily laid to rest, however. "Inadvertent" war is not the same as "accidental" war. Inadvertency is the result of a process that takes place between two parties whose expectations are in a field of uncertainty and are subject to distortion in the form of cognitive or motivational bias.[101] An accidental event is a random failure in a system component or in the behavior of a person; no rules established for "normal" cases can prepare one for such a failure.

Inadvertent escalation is likely to be the result of unexpected interactions between two forces for which the rules of engagement have been prescribed without sufficient attention to the problem of escalation control. As an example, consider the interaction between an SDI (Strategic Defense Initiative) space-based defense component, either battle stations or reconnaissance/sensing platforms, and a Russian ASAT (antisatellite) system. The United States could deploy the SDI system with the declared purpose of defending against a hypothetical Russian attack. The Russians have tested and deployed an ASAT system and could conceivably upgrade that system in the future. The U.S. SDI, if deployed, and the Russian ASAT, each designed for "defensive" purposes as understood by its creators (defense against missile attack in the U.S. case; reconnaissance and communications denial to the opponent in a global conventional or nuclear war in the Russian case), might contribute to inadvertent escalation of a crisis. If the successful execution of U.S. war plans were to depend upon the protection provided by SDI, then in a crisis a Russian ASAT system capable of attacking SDI would appear to

100. Geoffrey Blainey, *The Causes of War* (New York: Free Press, 1973), 127–45 et pass. Blainey is especially interesting on this point, since he considers the problem of "causes of war" as intellectually analogous to the determination of the "causes of peace." The idea that war is the norm, and peace the exception that requires logical and historical explanation, provides many insights into the issue of war causation. Ibid., esp. 3–17. For a discussion of general causes of war with reference to the more recent social science literature, see Jack S. Levy, "The Causes of War," in Philip E. Tetlock, J. L. Husbands, Robert Jervis, Paul C. Stern, and Charles Tilly, eds., *Behavior, Society, and Nuclear War*, vol. 1 (New York: Oxford University Press, 1989), 210–333; and for similar up-to-date treatment of literature on World War I, see Levy, "Preferences, Constraints, and Choices in July 1914," 151–56.

101. As this applies to escalation, see Richard Smoke, *War: Controlling Escalation* (Cambridge, Mass.: Harvard University Press, 1977).

U.S. leaders as threatening decisive military loss. If the successful carrying out of Russian war plans depended upon denial to any opponent of its space-based reconnaissance and communications while the Russians preserved their own, then the U.S. SDI could appear as threatening to Moscow as the Russian ASAT system seemed to Washington.[102]

Theories of deterrence applied to international politics have suggested that there are two major components that determine the success or failure of a deterrent threat: the military capabilities of the deterrer to carry out its threat, and the will to do so. This specification cannot be faulted as it stands, but it is so general as to call for more specific refinement. Paul Huth makes a useful distinction between the structural and the behavioral features of a deterrence policy.[103] The structural features of a deterrence policy are found in the balance of forces and other capabilities of two or more antagonists. Behavioral aspects of a crisis deterrence policy include the behavior of the defender in previous international crises, diplomatic strategies used by the defender in a given crisis, and the deployment of military forces during that crisis.[104] This distinction between the structural and behavioral aspects of crisis bargaining could probably be applied to the task of explaining arms races. Crises, like arms races, have structural as well as behavioral aspects; both phenomena have been overanalyzed from the standpoint of structural analysis, to the detriment of behavioral insight.[105]

In the behavioral science literature of international relations, one insight prompted by the paradoxes of nuclear deterrence stability has to do with the trade-off between deterrence and provocation. Nuclear weapons are most successfully employed in threatmaking that leaves some discretion to the party being threatened. The threat that entirely closes off options for negotiation or for retreat by one side is likely to be counterproductive. U.S. and Soviet experience in nuclear-crisis management demonstrated that the last

---

102. This is because space-based ballistic missile defense would, almost by definition, have an ASAT capability against the space-based warning-and-communications satellites of its opponent. For relevant technical issues, see U.S. Congress, Office of Technology Assessment, *Ballistic Missile Defense Technologies* (Washington, D.C.: GPO, 1985).

103. Huth, *Extended Deterrence*, 34.

104. Ibid.

105. Important exceptions are Phil Williams, *Crisis Management* (New York: John Wiley & Sons, 1976); Alexander George and Richard Smoke, *Deterrence in American Foreign Policy: Theory and Practice* (New York: Columbia University Press, 1974); Morgan, *Deterrence: A Conceptual Analysis*; *Psychology and Deterrence*, ed. Robert Jervis, Richard Ned Lebow, and Janice Gross Stein (Baltimore, Md.: Johns Hopkins University Press, 1985); and Lebow, *Between Peace and War*. For an up-to-date assessment of the behavioral science literature on crisis management, see Holsti, "Crisis Decision Making."

clear chance to avoid disaster is almost never obvious to leaders in the midst of a crisis. Only historians very much after the fact have the luxury of ascertaining with clarity who had the last chance to stop the game of "chicken" or to make a cooperative movement toward a solution of the "prisoner's dilemma" game. This is apparent from historical accounts of the July 1914 crisis, which even now differ considerably in the degree of blame they place upon Russia, Germany, and Austria-Hungary for the outbreak of war.

Looking backward at the experience of crisis management preceding World War I and comparing it with today, we are struck by the fact that no true concept of crisis management as we now know it existed then. The assumption made by leaders in July 1914 was that they had surmounted previous crises in the Balkans and would do so again. They counted on deterrence holding against at least one of the major powers in the complicated chess game of alliance diplomacy. Although textbooks argue that the solidifying of alliances prior to World War I was an important factor contributory to war, it is equally true that the fear of alliance partners defecting once war broke out made all the powers more nervous than they otherwise might have been. Thus, the French president and foreign minister sailed into St. Petersburg for meetings with the tsar which took place from July 20 to 23, just as the July crisis was beginning to come to a boil. Having received reassurance from the Russians that the alliance would hold firm in case of war, and providing reciprocal guarantees of French support for Russia, Raymond Poincaré and René Raphaël Viviani were at sea on their return voyage when news broke of the Austrian ultimatum to Serbia.[106] In their absence, important military measures in anticipation of war were taken by the French cabinet and minister of war, including the return of troops to standing quarters and the recall of officers then on leave.[107]

The fluidity of alliance commitments made possible by a multipolar system, in contrast to the lack of flexibility implicit in bipolarity, made resolution of the July crisis more difficult. The amount of decision time and reactive time available to the leaders of Russia and Germany might have sufficed to extricate them from a two-way crisis—say, for example, a dispute over some piece of territory on the border between Russian Poland and East Prussia. Some evidence for this "counterfactual" is provided by the kaiser's reaction on July 28 to the text of the Serbian reply to Austria's ultimatum. Wilhelm II judged the Serbs to have taken a very conciliatory stance and, in

106. Fay, *The Origins of the World War*, 2:277–86.
107. Ibid., 2:482–83.

a note to his foreign minister, proposed that Austria be permitted temporary military occupation of Belgrade as a pledge against any later Serbian change of mind about compliance with the ultimatum. Serbia, the kaiser noted, had been humiliated and forced to retreat: "no more cause for war exists."[108] Wilhelm was now ready to accept England's suggestion to act as mediator between Russia and Austria. Based on this "pledge plan" offered by the kaiser, German Chancellor Bethmann-Hollweg sent a telegram to Vienna outlining Germany's support for a temporary occupation of Belgrade and other Serbian territory to ensure Serbian compliance with Austrian demands. The chancellor's telegram noted that "as soon as the Austrian demands were fulfilled, a withdrawal [of Austrian troops from Serbia] would follow."[109] From the standpoint of the kaiser and Bethmann-Hollweg, Austria could accomplish its strategic aims with minimum and nonprovocative main force operations. The question was whether Austria had as its strategic aim only the intimidation of Serbia or, rather, the permanent incapacitation of Serbia; Germany's initiative stood or fell on the concept of decision time held in Vienna, not that in Potsdam.

The Clock Runs Down

However, this initiative was doomed to fail. The Austrian Foreign Minister, Count Leopold von Berchtold, was determined to impose on Serbia the harshest terms and to bring about permanent capitulation and, perhaps, the dismemberment of Serbian territory. Berchtold had used Germany for Austria's purposes to settle old scores with the Serbs: the role of Germany was to deter the Russians from countermobilization against Austria as Austria imposed its will on Serbia. Chancellor Bethmann-Hollweg, not understanding fully that Berchtold's aim was to win a local crisis and to humiliate Serbia, and that Austria left to Germany the problem of containing expansion of the crisis, failed to persuade Austria to adopt the kaiser's "halt in Belgrade" pledge plan.[110] The kaiser and his chancellor shared the view as of July 28 that Serbia had satisfied all of Austria's essential demands, yet they failed to communicate their desire for further Austrian restraint with sufficient clarity and force. According to historian Sidney Fay, Bethmann-Hollweg was afraid of offending Austria and was also concerned to avoid any appearance that

108. Ibid., 2:421.
109. Ibid., 2:424.
110. Ibid., 2:425.

Germany and Austria had been responsible for starting a European war.[111] If
so, the chancellor failed to appreciate that Germany's stakes in localizing
the conflict were much higher than those of Austria, since Germany had
ample evidence by this time that the Russians had begun to mobilize.

The "Willy–Nicky" telegrams between the kaiser and the tsar, beginning
on July 29, offer some evidence for optimistic historians that the two heads
of state might have worked out arrangements for resolution of the crisis independently of the machinations of Austria and Serbia. There is substantial
evidence that the tsar genuinely sought to avoid war and that he resisted the
pressures of his generals for a declaration of general mobilization, widely
considered tantamount to war, as long as he could. Nicholas's difficulty was
that he and his advisers had to estimate the character of the relation between
deterrence and mobilization in two directions: toward Germany and toward
Austria-Hungary. Germany's priorities were both to forestall Russian mobilization, which might enable St. Petersburg to launch a preemptive attack
against East Prussia and defeat Germany's entire strategy, should war occur,
and to prevent Britain's entry into any war. Austria-Hungary's priorities were
to rapidly crush Serbia and to occupy parts of that country until Serbia's
subject status was reaffirmed by its government and people, and, as a result
of this, to deter future Serbian-sponsored terrorism against the Austro-Hungarian regime. Austria-Hungary planned to win a local war quickly, based
on its assessment of the balance of forces between itself and Serbia.

Following the earlier distinction between the structural and behavioral
aspects of deterrence, the structural aspects of the July crisis included the
expectation by Austria of a rapid and decisive victory over Serbia. According
to John Mearsheimer's analysis of conventional deterrence, prospective attackers have open to them three general strategies: limited aims, blitzkrieg,
and attrition.[112] A limited-aims strategy attempts to seize a piece of territory
or achieve some other objective which is less ambitious than the total defeat
of the opponent's armed forces. Blitzkrieg is an attempt to rapidly defeat the
armed forces of the opponent, and attrition aims at total destruction of the
opposed armed forces and war-supporting resources over a prolonged period.[113]

111. Ibid.
112. John J. Mearsheimer, *Conventional Deterrence* (Ithaca, N.Y.: Cornell University Press,
1984), ch. 2.
113. See also the distinction between a strategy of *sokrusheniye* (destruction) and *izmor*
(attrition) developed by the noted Soviet thinker A. A. Svechin, *Strategiya* (Moscow: Gosvoy-
enizdat, 1926), 250ff.

Austria's ability to effect a blitzkrieg against Serbia was conditional on accomplishing that aim before Serbia's ally Russia could take measures to preempt the Austrian move diplomatically and militarily. Austria prepared the way diplomatically by deceiving all the powers, including its ally Germany, about the timing and content of its demands on Serbia. Austria then declared war on Serbia on July 28, preempting Sazonov's efforts at "direct conversations" between Vienna and St. Petersburg. The Austrian declaration of war on Serbia led to Russia's partial mobilization and to the adoption by Russia of measures preparatory to general war, rendering almost beside the point the "Willy–Nicky" telegram exchanges (which, nonetheless, continued thereafter).[114]

German Chancellor Bethmann-Hollweg sent a blitz of telegrams to his ambassador in Vienna in the early morning hours of July 30, urging that the ambassador impress upon the Austrians that "the refusal of every exchange of views with St. Petersburg would be a serious mistake, for it provokes Russia precisely to armed interference, which Austria is primarily interested in avoiding."[115] Germany had counted on England's remaining neutral in a Balkan war or in any larger European conflict growing out of one, but that optimism was disabused when Bethmann-Hollweg received a telegram the evening of July 29 from Prince Lichnowsky, the German ambassador in London. Arriving at 9:12 P.M., it contained the first warning from Sir Edward Grey, the British foreign secretary, that England might not remain neutral in the event of a general war in Europe. This added urgency to Bethmann-Hollweg's communication to his ambassador in Vienna during the early morning of July 30 (2:55 A.M.) that if "Austria refuses all negotiations, we are face to face with a conflagration in which England will be against us; . . . through England's opposition the main blow will fall on Germany. . . . Under these circumstances we must urgently and emphatically urge upon the consideration of the Vienna cabinet the adoption of mediation in accordance with the above honorable conditions."[116]

One lesson of the July crisis of 1914, then, is that the objectives of crisis management may be in conflict with those of extended deterrence (protection of an ally or protégé offered by another state which acts as guarantor). Russia's extended deterrence commitments to Serbia and Germany's to Austria propelled both powers into a regional and world war that neither the

114. Fay, *The Origins of the World War*, 2:430–31.
115. Bethmann-Hollweg to Tshchirschky, July 30, 1914, ibid., 2:435.
116. Ibid., 2:437.

kaiser nor the tsar had expected to break out in July 1914. Undoubtedly, militarists and annexationists in both Germany and Russia welcomed war and predicted that war was inevitable throughout the decade preceding August 1914, but these cacophonies did not dictate to the cabinets or monarchs of either country that war was necessary or inevitable. Nor was the deterioration of the July crisis into war mainly an accident, despite the inopportune interactions among heads of state and their diplomats during that month.

One of the things that overtook the powers in July 1914 was that they ran out of decision time and reactive time to an extent not previously seen. Austria-Hungary had decided to settle old scores with Serbia, whatever the risk of Russian countermobilization. Germany's reaction to Russia's partial mobilization was certainly going to be one of alarm, and the time for mediation was shortened by the rapid transition from one event to another. Austria's stiff ultimatum to Serbia was followed almost immediately by Russia's "measures preparatory to war" and by the tsar's approval for partial mobilization. Once Russia began to mobilize, Germany could not long defer mobilization. Germany did hold back for a few days while the kaiser, through Bethmann-Hollweg, urged Austrian restraint, but no response to these entreaties by Germany was forthcoming from Vienna. In fact, Austria deliberately expedited its declaration of war against Serbia in order to circumvent expected peace proposals that might rob it of the fruits of a short and decisive victory.

It is not entirely fair to place the blame for short decision and reaction time on the character of Russian, German, and Austrian mobilization plans. Given their political objectives in 1914 and their expectation that wars might be won in an initial period by means of rapid and decisive offensives, the powers' mobilization systems were consistent with their political and grand strategic goals. Where the powers miscalculated was in the expectation that, as in 1908–9 and 1912–13, time would be on the side of one more peace proposal and breathing space which would separate potential combatants and return them to their corners. In July 1914, time for negotiation ran down faster than the time for mobilization speeded up, and the result was to constrain the options of those policymakers who sought to avoid war. It must be said, too, that the leaders of Germany and Russia sought to avoid war in a much more conditional way than did others, such as England. A favorable settlement of affairs in the Balkans was judged by leaders in Austria-Hungary, Germany, and Russia as a more important policy objective than the extension of decision time for the workings of diplomatic efforts toward peace. War became inevitable only after the armed forces, having been marched toward the frontiers by their respective national leaderships, crossed into the valley of death that would destroy four empires and ruin millions of lives.

The July 1914 crisis and the diplomacy of the great powers in Europe during the early twentieth century, together with the war plans of major actors between 1910 and 1914, demonstrate the importance of the trade-off between deterrence and the avoidance of provocation. The great powers of Europe had managed to escape the worst consequences of this trade-off prior to July 1914, but they failed to analyze correctly the delicacy of the situation from July 24 onward. The purchase of additional increments of deterrence could no longer be made cost-effectively, in terms of the marginal costs in additional provocation to potential opponents. War was neither accidental nor inadvertent: it was deliberate, in the sense that the powers in June and July 1914 calculated, but they calculated badly. Mobilization systems failed to contribute to the prevention of war in 1914 because they provided to leaders only a one-way street, supportive of deterrence, without also enabling the transmittal of additional, and equally important, signals of the desire for accommodation and nonprovocation.

The members of the Triple Alliance and Triple Entente failed to recognize that the relationship between deterrence and provocation, in a situation of generalized threat or insecurity, differs from the character of that relationship in an "immediate deterrence" setting, a form of crisis security dilemma. In a condition of generalized perception of threat, the benefits of additional deterrence appear more obvious to leaders than the risks of excessive provocation. The transition from generalized to immediate threat perception reverses this relationship: now there is a higher benefit to be had by emphasizing nonprovocative signals and de-emphasizing more credible deterrence. In addition, a crisis period may include more than one phase of immediately threatening stimuli. Sources on the outbreak of World War I suggest that a relatively more stable situation of immediate deterrence existed prior to the Austrian ultimatum to Serbia, and that afterward a less stable situation made deterrent actions almost indistinguishable from provocative ones. This finding has implications with respect to complacency about deterrence, whether based on force balances in conventional deterrence situations or on survivable basing modes for nuclear retaliatory systems. Force balances and military technology may be more important for stability in a situation of general deterrence, when crisis has not yet broken out, but less important after the beginning of a crisis. Thereafter, military doctrines, operations, and strategies may contribute to the transformation of a crisis security dilemma into a war. In a condition of immediate deterrence, states find it significantly more difficult to signal restraint together with resolution than they do under other conditions. In a time of crisis, then, leaders should assume that all but the most unambiguous signals are subject to misperception of the most dangerous sort.

2

U.S. NUCLEAR STRATEGIC PLANNING FOR WORLD WAR III

Revisiting the Schlieffen Plan?

From the moment that the first nuclear detonation in anger destroyed Hiroshima, U.S. scientists, politicians, and military planners recognized that they had entered another world. The atomic secret of the Manhattan Project had proved itself outside the laboratory, to the discredit of some scientific pessimism that the bomb would never work. Military strategy would obviously have to change in response to this new technology, but how? Theorists during the 1940s and 1950s had large debates over the issue of the impact of nuclear and thermonuclear weapons on military strategy. Politicians and military planners had to make difficult choices about the purchase and operation of forces within budgetary constraints mostly unrelated to strategic priorities or to larger U.S. foreign policy objectives.

U.S. strategic planning was dominated during the first two decades of the Cold War by the prospect of global war with the Soviet Union, whether growing out of war in Europe or from a direct U.S.-Soviet confrontation.

The present chapter argues that the U.S. community of strategymakers had to choose among three admittedly imperfect strategies for the use of nuclear weapons in support of deterrence: retaliatory strategies, intimidation strategies, and bargaining and negotiation strategies. Each of these strategies involved a necessary trade-off in emphasis between deterrence and avoiding provocation during crises (or, in some versions of deterrence theory, during war itself). Although U.S. declaratory policy was stabilized in the mid-1960s around the basic retaliatory strategy of mutual assured destruction, actual war plans included options for fighting a traditional counterforce or counter-military campaign with prompt massive attacks against a comprehensive target set.

THE ROLE OF NUCLEAR WEAPONS

In the years of the U.S. atomic monopoly (i.e., until the Soviet Union detonated its first fission weapon in 1949), Truman administration military planners were uncertain about how nuclear weapons would fit into the process of strategic policy formulation. Their uncertainty was shared by leading atomic scientists and by the most prominent strategic thinkers of the day.[1] The U.S. military services began to develop joint war plans in 1947, and the planning process in 1947 and 1948 represented the first serious effort by the bureaucracy to incorporate nuclear weapons into war plans. The assumption of pandemic availability of large numbers of nuclear weapons and the demonstration of the feasibility of hydrogen weapons still lay ahead. The planning guidance established by U.S. leaders in 1947 and 1948 established broad parameters for subsequent approaches to the construction of war plans that would somehow have to incorporate these most deadly and destructive weapons.

The earliest plans in 1947 and 1948 stipulated as their objectives the slowing down of a Soviet conventional offensive in Europe and the destruction of valued social and economic targets in the East European and Soviet rear.[2]

---

1. See Lawrence Freedman, *The Evolution of Nuclear Strategy* (New York: St. Martin's Press, 1981), chs. 1–5, esp. pp. 47–62, and McGeorge Bundy, *Danger and Survival* (New York: Random House, 1988), chs. 1–5, on the origins of U.S. nuclear weapons policy and the Truman years.
2. Freedman, *The Evolution of Nuclear Strategy*, 54–55.

To these plausible missions for atomic weapons, targeteers under Truman and Eisenhower would add the destruction of Soviet nuclear forces at their bases. At the time, these Soviet forces consisted of air-delivered munitions carried by bombers; significant deployments of missiles awaited the 1960s. Ultimately these missions of counterforce, societal destruction, and retardation of advancing Soviet forces in Europe would be known respectively as the Bravo, Delta, and Romeo target sets for application of nuclear weapons.[3]

During the Truman years the U.S. atomic weapons stockpile was such that war planners could not expect to deliver a knockout blow to a country the size of the Soviet Union by use of nuclear forces alone. In fact, U.S. State Department and Joint Chiefs of Staff planners in 1950–51 doubted that it would be prudent to engage in assertive nuclear diplomacy until U.S. nuclear and other military capability could be built up further. Historian Marc Trachtenberg has argued that one reason for the more serious U.S. consideration of escalating the war in Korea during the later years of the conflict, in contrast to a lack of interest in 1950 and 1951, was U.S. policymakers' growing confidence owing to expansion of the American nuclear arsenal.[4]

Once nuclear weapons were available in numbers that allowed for optional assignment to diverse missions, the Eisenhower administration predicated its strategy for general war on the assumption of an early and massive U.S. nuclear strike against the Soviet homeland and other targets. Some worst-case estimation about bomber gaps and some realistic concerns about second-strike capability during the 1950s pushed analysis toward the deterrence of a surprise "bolt from the blue" launched by Moscow against U.S. forces or overseas bases. But the basic stability of deterrence, in the form of a two-sided capability for infliction of unacceptable retaliatory damage to society, was presumed by the U.S. political leadership—even during the years of "massive retaliation"—as declaratory policy.[5]

Despite growth in U.S. warhead inventories and delivery vehicles during

3. The Strategic Air Command, or SAC, was formally relieved of the Romeo mission in 1956, although some of the components of its target base would have been related to that mission incidentally. See David Alan Rosenberg, "U.S. Nuclear War Planning, 1945–1960," ch. 2 in *Strategic Nuclear Targeting*, ed. Desmond Ball and Jeffrey Richelson (Ithaca, N.Y.: Cornell University Press, 1986), 35–56, esp. 49.

4. Marc Trachtenberg, "A 'Wasting Asset': American Strategy and the Shifting Nuclear Balance, 1949–1954," *International Security* (Winter 1988–89), in *Nuclear Diplomacy and Crisis Management*, ed. Sean M. Lynn-Jones, Steven E. Miller, and Stephen Van Evera (Cambridge, Mass.: MIT Press, 1990), 69–113.

5. Richard K. Betts, *Nuclear Blackmail and Nuclear Balance* (Washington, D.C.: Brookings Institution, 1987), 132–79.

the Eisenhower years, Soviet force enhancements during those same years were sufficient to restrain complacency about the success of counterforce first strikes. U.S. government estimates of U.S. population vulnerability, in any U.S.-Soviet nuclear war from the mid-1950s through the early years of the Kennedy administration, provided little confidence to political leaders that societal damage could be confined to acceptable levels. For example, the Technological Capabilities Panel reported to the Eisenhower administration in 1955 that "neither the U.S. nor the Soviets can mount an air strike against the other that would surely be decisive," and the panel explained the term "decisive" as including prevention of the opponent's ability to strike back after a first strike.[6]

   At least three other reasons for lack of confidence in the U.S. ability to fight and win a nuclear war, despite an apparent superiority in relevant weapons and delivery vehicles during most of the 1950s and in the early 1960s, were significant. Each of these reasons is related to the problem of time and war or of time and crisis management. A major issue that faced planners once nuclear weapons were assigned to the military and were no longer held in custody by the Atomic Energy Commission was the distinction between prompt and delayed missions. Immediate retaliation might be necessary if the Soviet Union attacked the continental United States without warning, although modernized U.S. and Canadian air defenses were supposed to provide improved survivability. Delayed retaliation could be accomplished only if sufficient numbers of U.S. strategic nuclear forces survived not only first but subsequent attacks against their launching or staging areas. A division of labor based on submarine-launched missiles and bomber-delivered weapons for delayed missions (mostly) and land-based missiles for prompt missions (mostly) was eventually worked out, but strategic planning during the 1950s had to be based on mission profiles for bomber forces only.

   The first reason for pessimism instead of optimism in leaders' expectations about war outcomes was that a dearth of timely information might force targeteers to misassign weapons. The United States lacked the ability to conduct a comprehensive preattack reconnaissance of plausible first-strike targets in the Soviet Union until satellites became available for this purpose during the early 1960s. Second, U.S. air defenses, though the beneficiaries of significant expenditures during the 1950s, were never judged as sufficiently competent by U.S. planners to provide high confidence in acceptable dam-

6. Ibid., 169.

age limitation. By the time missiles became the delivery vehicles of choice for prompt missions, defenses would inspire even less confidence.[7] Third, and most strategically significant, the difference between preemption and preventive war was crucial.[8]

PREVENTIVE WAR

A preventive war is one undertaken by a state in anticipation of an enemy intent to attack at some future date or in response to an expected power transition in the international system which the state considers unacceptable and is willing to go to war to prevent.[9] Preemption is a decision to strike first in the belief that an enemy has already decided to attack and is now attempting to implement that decision.[10] Although U.S. political and military lead-

7. For discussion of pertinent issues, see *Strategic Air Defense*, ed. Stephen J. Cimbala (Wilmington, Del.: SR Books, 1989), esp. the chapters by Kenneth Schaffel and Owen E. Jensen.

8. Discussion further to this point is provided by Betts, *Nuclear Blackmail and Nuclear Balance*, 161ff.; Trachtenberg, "Wasting Asset," 96–108; and Rosenberg, "U.S. Nuclear War Planning," 35–56, esp. 44–53.

9. On the preventive motivation for war, see Jack S. Levy, "Declining Power and the Preventive Motivation for War," *World Politics* (October 1987): 82–107. Levy notes that systemic power transitions can occur when a weaker but rising state challenges the status of a dominant power or when a dominant power takes preventive action to forestall the challenge of an aspiring competitor. See also on this subject Robert Gilpin, *War and Change in World Politics* (Cambridge: Cambridge University Press, 1981), and A.F.K. Organski, *World Politics* (New York: Alfred A. Knopf, 1968), ch. 12. Stephen Van Evera, Richard Ned Lebow, and Jack Snyder have applied the concept of preventive war to World War I: see Van Evera, "The Cult of the Offensive and the Origins of World War I," *International Security* (Summer 1984): 58–107; Lebow, *Between Peace and War: The Nature of International Crisis* (Baltimore, Md.: Johns Hopkins University Press, 1981); and Snyder, "Perceptions of the Security Dilemma in 1914," in *Psychology and Deterrence*, ed. Robert Jervis, Richard Ned Lebow, and Janice Gross Stein (Baltimore, Md.: Johns Hopkins University Press, 1985), 153–79. A very important version of the "preventive motivation for war" argument, applied to World War I, is Fritz Fischer, *War of Illusions: German Policies from 1911 to 1914* (New York: W. W. Norton, 1975), 468–70. In this version, offered by some German historians and critiqued by Fischer, Germany went to war in 1914 to forestall an eventual, inevitable attempt by Russia and France to change the balance of power by 1916–17.

10. Preventive and preemptive motives for war both lend themselves to "window of opportunity" arguments. See Richard Ned Lebow, "Windows of Opportunity: Do States Jump Through Them?" *International Security* (Summer 1984): 147–86.

ers flirted with ideas and proposals for preventive war in the 1940s (during the brief period of U.S. atomic monopoly) and again during the 1950s when preventive war options came up in Eisenhower's "Solarium" study, by the autumn of 1954 President Eisenhower and the National Security Council had formally rejected preventive war as a viable policy option.[11]

Preemption was not ruled out, however, and SAC's 1954 war plan called for a massive and simultaneous nuclear strike using more than 700 bombers against a variety of Soviet targets. According to David Alan Rosenberg: "There was no calculated strategy for war winning or termination beyond that of producing as much destruction in multiple Soviet target systems as possible in a single, devastating blow. Increasing emphasis was placed on utilizing high-yield weapons to cause bonus damage and destroy multiple targets simultaneously."[12] Available technology in the form of fusion weapons with large yields that could be delivered by aircraft made possible this kind of planning, but in the judgment of some critics it was a nuclear version of the Schlieffen Plan. It promised to wreak great havoc and destruction on Soviet military capability and society, but it did not provide for a politically acceptable war outcome from the standpoint of American objectives. Just as the Schlieffen Plan raised the probability of destroying France's armies only to bring Britain into the war on France's side, the 1954 SAC war plan promised great damage to the Soviet Union but at the potential cost of losing Western Europe to invading Soviet conventional forces.

As the implications of the details of the Schlieffen Plan were not fully appreciated by Schlieffen's masters (although they were briefed on its contents generally), so too were the details of the SAC 1954 plan for strategic nuclear war obscure to policymakers, and even to higher-level U.S. military commanders. From 1951 to 1955 the basic SAC war plan was not submitted by its commander, General Curtis LeMay, for Joint Chiefs of Staff (JCS) review, and even then LeMay provided only a briefing and summary overview.[13] Dismissing concerns about the vulnerability of SAC to enemy first strikes, LeMay told the deputy chairman of the Gaither Committee, Robert Sprague, that he would launch a preemptive strike against the Soviet Union if U.S. intelligence detected Soviet forces massing for a likely attack.[14] When an incredulous Sprague noted that this was not national policy, LeMay answered: "It's my policy. That's what I'm going to do."[15] It was

11. Rosenberg, "U.S. Nuclear War Planning," 44.
12. Ibid., 45.
13. Ibid.
14. Betts, *Nuclear Blackmail and Nuclear Balance*, 162.
15. Ibid. It is not entirely clear how LeMay expected to accomplish this without presidential

clearly not the expectation of SAC that its main weapon against a Soviet attack on Western Europe would be withheld during the initial period of war, even if Soviet forces had yet to cross the inter-German border or other lines of demarcation between Soviet-controlled territory and that of NATO.

The assumption by LeMay and perhaps others was that there was some significant premium in going first, but even in a narrow military sense the advent of ballistic missiles stimulated rethinking about the advantages and disadvantages of preemption. Compared to preventive war, preemption was more politically acceptable but difficult to bring about in fact. Preemption was defensively motivated by the perception of imminent threat and the decision that war was unavoidable; what remained for leaders was to make certain that the first blow would be struck only "in the last resort." The difficulty was that preemption could be justified only by unimpeachable evidence of the other side's intention to attack. In the age of nuclear missiles, waiting for this evidence robbed the preemptor of the advantage of surprise: the opponent's forces would be launch-ready, too. Thus, preemption was politically feasible only when it was no longer militarily feasible; and it was militarily feasible only when it would not be politically sensible. In reaction to an air force briefing scenario, Eisenhower wrote in his private diary on January 23, 1956: "The only possible way of reducing these losses would be for us to take the initiative some time during the assumed month in which we had the warning of the attack and launch a surprise attack against the Soviets. This would not only be against our traditions but it would appear to be impossible that any such thing would occur."[16]

As ballistic missiles began to enter the inventories of the nuclear superpowers in significant numbers during the 1960s, the feasibility of preemption became so low that it was recognized as a nonviable basis for nuclear strategic target planning. Much earlier, however, the political and military objections to SAC's strategic air offensive, based on the expected authorization for preemption, were voiced within the U.S. government. Army and navy analyses of the SAC war plan for 1957 found that redundant targeting of high-yield weapons would have resulted in unnecessary societal destruction and wasteful allocation of weapons to targets.[17] Debates among the services questioned targeting priorities for strategic nuclear forces if preventive war was precluded by policy and as preemption became more difficult to accomplish against

---

approval, however, so he may have assumed that the president would concur if intelligence was very convincing concerning a Soviet intent to attack.

16. Ibid., 164.
17. Rosenberg, "U.S. Nuclear War Planning," 50.

growing Soviet forces. The U.S. Navy argued in favor of a "finite deterrence" model for target planning, encouraged by the expected deployment of its Polaris ballistic-missile-firing submarines (SSBNs). Backed by the army during debates in Eisenhower's second term, the navy supported nuclear war plans with less ambitious counterforce targeting objectives.[18]

As is usual in the U.S. system, the air force–navy divergence over strategic nuclear targeting was resolved by a political compromise. The Hickey Committee, tasked by the Net Evaluation Subcommittee to review target plans on the basis of instructions designed by the secretary of defense, the chairman of the JCS, and the national security adviser, considered three alternative target systems.[19] These systems were primarily military or counterforce, as preferred by the air force; primarily urban-industrial, as recommended by the army and navy; and an "optimum mix" of the two. It is assumed that the Hickey Committee opted for an optimum-mix target base, including counterforce, command-and-control targets, and many urban centers in the Soviet Union and the People's Republic of China.[20] Thus the Eisenhower administration and the military services compromised between the air force–preferred counterforce strike plan and the original navy version of finite deterrence. This compromise carried over into the preparation of the first integrated operational plan for nuclear war (SIOP-62), approved by the JCS in December 1960 for FY 1962.[21]

SIOP-62 AND THE KENNEDY ADMINISTRATION

The Kennedy administration reaction to SIOP-62, which it had inherited from Eisenhower, was one of great skepticism and disappointment. Policy guidance for SIOP-62 had been provided in two Eisenhower administration documents: *National Strategic Targeting and Attack Policy* (NSTAP) and *Guidance for the Preparation of the Single Integrated Operational Plan for Strategic Attack*. These documents directed the Joint Strategic Target Planning Staff (JSTPS, located at SAC headquarters in Omaha, Nebraska, and headed by the air force general in charge of SAC, or CINCSAC, with a navy flag officer

18. Ibid., 51.
19. Ibid., 52.
20. Ibid., 53.
21. Ibid., 50.

assigned as deputy director) to provide for the "optimum integration" of forces against target categories.[22] Categories of targets (in order of importance) were Soviet strategic nuclear forces, primary military and government control centers, and Soviet urban-industrial targets.[23] SIOP-62 essentially provided for only one option: at the outbreak of war with the Soviet Union, the United States would launch its entire repertoire of strategic nuclear forces in one massive strike against the "optimum mix" target set, which included Soviet, Chinese, and East European cities. Estimated fatalities in the target countries, according to the U.S. Joint Chiefs, were 360 million to 425 million persons.[24]

The Kennedy administration found this plan politically unacceptable and morally dubious. The influence of Rand acolytes who had migrated to Washington produced within the administration a burst of activity on behalf of counterforce strategy and a tectonic shift away from massive retaliation. Robert McNamara's early interest in counterforce was prompted by his desire for a more credible response than a massive "war-gasm" and by his belief that U.S. superiority in numbers of deliverable warheads would make it possible to implement the strategy against an appropriate target set. In Athens in May 1962, McNamara sprang on his European NATO colleagues his important statement of the relationship between a counterforce-oriented SIOP and the "flexible response" strategy he advocated for adoption by NATO. He later restated the same basic concepts in his June 1962 commencement address at Ann Arbor, Michigan: "The US has come to the conclusion that to the extent feasible basic military strategy in a possible general nuclear war should be approached in much the same way that more conventional military operations have been regarded in the past. That is to say, principal military objectives, in the event of a nuclear war stemming from an attack on the Alliance, should be the destruction of the enemy's military forces, not of his civilian population."[25]

McNamara's effort to restore conventional warfighting principles to nuclear strategy rested on the assumption that the ability to fight a controlled nuclear war was more dissuasive to potential opponents than the threat to unleash massive and indiscriminate nuclear destruction. The difficulty with this argument centered on the problem of maintaining control over escala-

22. Desmond Ball, "The Development of the SIOP, 1960–83," ch. 2 in *Strategic Nuclear Targeting*, ed. Ball and Richelson, 61.
23. Ibid.
24. Ibid., 62.
25. McNamara quoted in Freedman, *The Evolution of Nuclear Strategy*, 235.

tion, with respect both to the feasibility and the desirability of doing so. The collocation of counterforce and other target sets in the Soviet Union made it difficult to attack Soviet nuclear forces and military command centers without causing enormous collateral damage in the form of lost lives and destroyed social value. Then, too, Soviet military theory, as it was then known in the West and is arguably so even today, suggested that the view from Moscow was highly skeptical of any U.S. capability for limited nuclear war. Such a capability was regarded by Soviet military and political leaders not as a gesture of restraint, but as a token of a drive for military superiority. The Soviet leadership had not failed to notice the correlation between putative U.S. superiority in strategic nuclear forces during the early 1960s and U.S. government interest in the "no cities" version of counterforce strategy.[26]

Moscow might logically have drawn this conclusion about the direction of U.S. strategy in the early 1960s because the doctrine of flexible response also included an extended deterrence component. The McNamara strategy was not only to allow for the conduct of controlled strategic nuclear warfighting, but also for the limited and constrained use of NATO nuclear weapons in a theater war on the European continent. "Flexible response" became NATO's official strategy in 1967, but only after careful compromises between the U.S.-understood version and the version adhered to by most European members of the alliance. The U.S. version held that controlled strategic nuclear warfighting was designed to coexist with controlled escalation below the level of strategic nuclear conflict. The brink would be approached in increments, from the first engagements of conventional war at the inter-German border through the final step over the threshold of nuclear exchanges between the U.S. and the Soviet homelands. The European members of NATO hoped, to the contrary and for the most part, that the Soviets would largely disbelieve this notion of incremental nuclear escalation by NATO. Feeling less of an immediate sense of Soviet military threat compared to the Americans, European members of NATO preferred not to worry overmuch about the refinements of targeting for extended deterrence. Blowing up a great many things on the Soviet side of the line would probably dissuade all but the lunatic fringe in the Kremlin, many sophisticated European strategic planners and thinkers believed. It was all right if the United States sought to calibrate its nuclear responses according to some step-by-step progression of

26. The development of Soviet views on nuclear war during this period is covered in David Holloway, *The Soviet Union and the Arms Race* (New Haven, Conn.: Yale University Press, 1983, 2d ed. 1984), ch. 3.

escalation, but this was mainly for the amusement of the Americans and should in no way be considered a likely outcome in any actual nuclear war. McNamara eventually came round to this "European" view, at least with respect to the controllability of general nuclear war, although the U.S. secretary of defense never gave up pressing for increases in allied NATO conventional forces. Gradually McNamara moved away from the "no cities" version of counterforce strategy in declaratory policy, although the growing U.S. arsenal allowed for a majority of weapons to be assigned to military and war-supporting targets. By 1966 McNamara had endorsed without reservation the "assured destruction" metric as the basis for U.S. force sizing, though not for targeting doctrine. However, this was not obvious to the U.S. public or to Congress, which simply concluded that more weapons favored counterforce, and fewer weapons favored assured destruction. The qualitative implications of targeting plans were harder to explain and were highly classified in any event.

ESCAPING FROM NUCLEAR RIGIDITY

The McNamara effort to escape from the 1950s version of a nuclear "Schlieffen Plan" was only partly successful. McNamara acknowledged defeat on the effort to make either feasible or politically acceptable the notion of controlled nuclear war. On the other hand, he was in favor of additional options for the SIOP, including "withholds" of attacks against highly valued targets for bargaining and intrawar deterrence. McNamara's unresolved dilemma was that finding a politically acceptable way to fight a nuclear war might make nuclear war more probable. He and his successors in the nuclear age have been unable to reconcile the Clausewitzian view of military force, as subservient to policy under any conditions, and the technological uniqueness of nuclear force, which argues against the traditional view of controlled and rational warfighting. Ian Clark points to one of the ironic outcomes of this discrepancy between policy desiderata and technological autonomy: "While, historically, various belligerents have had interests in various forms of limitation, and these interests have not always been mutual and equal, it is probably true that, at no previous time, would one country's adoption of a limited strategy have constituted an act of aggression, or been seen as being more provocative than a threat of total war. Whatever other arguments might be levelled against limited-war strategies, they have seldom been charged with being more hostile than their total war counterparts."[27]

The technology of nuclear weapons and intercontinental delivery vehicles threatened to overturn Clausewitz's model of the force–policy relationship not only because of the destruction they could cause but also, and most important for present discussion, on account of the short *time* in which they could cause it. The short flight times of ballistic missiles meant that the normal decisionmaking processes by which states opted for war or for peace were in many scenarios irrelevant. Institutions would have to be substituted for deliberation. Standard operating procedures and other institutionalized, bureaucratic decision rules would now limit, if not dictate, the actual choices political leaders had in responding to a nuclear attack, or even to a warning of attack. Preplanned strike packages offering little in the way of flexibility for unexpected contingencies would provide the entire menu of choice for presidents faced with plausible but uncertain warning of nuclear attack. Deterrence by organizational prearrangement argued for an inflexibility that spoke loudly to the priority of deterrence over nonprovocation in nuclear strategic planning.

Leaders, perceiving this risk, sought to avoid being drawn by organizational decisionmaking into a nuclear Schlieffen Plan, which would leave them dependent on crisis management timetables and military options inappropriate for the circumstances. Depending on how the ballistic missile was based, it could widen instead of narrow the windows of time. During the 1960s, silo-based ICBMs were not threatened with prompt destruction by their counterparts in the hands of potential opponents. The improved accuracies of delivery systems and the MIRVing of warheads were not yet at hand. It was assumed by U.S. military planners during the Kennedy and Johnson administrations that enough ICBMs could ride out any Soviet first strike and then retaliate, guaranteeing along with other surviving forces the accomplishment of the assured destruction mission. In later decades, after MIRVing and improved accuracies changed the force ratio of attacker to defender in favor of the attacker, the ICBM became the weapon of fixation for those who argued in favor of "windows of vulnerability."

The submarine-launched ballistic missile (SLBM) added further still to the decision time of policymakers and commanders. Unlike its ICBM coun-

27. Ian Clark, *Limited Nuclear War: Political Theory and War Conventions* (Princeton, N.J.: Princeton University Press, 1982), 145.

terpart, its prelaunch survivability against plausible first strikes would not be eroded by technology during the 1970s and 1980s. To the contrary, SLBMs today seem more survivable than ever before. Submarines are growing quieter and will be even harder to detect in the future than they are now. Evidence of this is the U.S. willingness under a START agreement to limit U.S. as well as Soviet ballistic missile forces to 6,000 accountable warheads. Observance of this agreement would probably limit U.S. ballistic missile submarine (SSBN) deployments to eighteen. Some two-thirds would be out of port, meaning either on patrol or in transit to and from patrol locations, at any given time.[28] Thus, the United States would be dependent upon the survivability of twelve ballistic missile submarines in the event of a surprise attack without warning.[29]

This seems like a small number of ballistic missile submarines, but their survivability depends on the competency of Soviet strategic antisubmarine warfare (ASW) and on U.S. countermeasures. The countermeasures, in which U.S. military planners have high confidence, include quieter and faster submarines and U.S. strategic ASW, including prompt attacks on an opponent's ballistic missile and attack submarines. Some critics of the U.S. SSBN modernization program have called for the deployment of more and smaller submarines, with fewer missiles and warheads per boat, in the interest of improved survivability. But the U.S. lead in strategic ASW and in ASW countermeasures seems assured for the near future, especially with regard to software development for acoustical science. Continuing high confidence in the prelaunch survivability of SSBNs makes the problem of survivability for other legs of the U.S. strategic "Triad" less acute.[30] The vulnerability of ICBMs brought about by improved accuracies and MIRVing in the 1970s and 1980s was mitigated by the lesser vulnerability of ballistic missile submarines to preemptive attack.

By the end of the 1980s, however, the submarine-launched ballistic missile had turned another page. The accuracy of the Trident II (D-5) SLBM,

---

28. Presumably the entire U.S. SSBN fleet would be Tridents.

29. U.S. planners assume that submarines in port would be destroyed in a surprise attack, and that those on station or in transit would suffer attrition rates of about 10 percent. See Ted Corbin, Arsen Hajian, and Kosta Tsipis, *Nuclear Arsenals for the 21st Century*, Report no. 23, Program in Science and Technology for International Security (Cambridge: Massachusetts Institute of Technology, January 1991), 16.

30. As officially acknowledged by the Scowcroft Commission in closing the putative "window of vulnerability" for the U.S. strategic nuclear deterrent. See President's Commission on Strategic Forces, *Report* (Washington, D.C.: April 1983).

planned as the replacement for Trident I with Trident II deployments beginning in 1989, was comparable to that of the MX/Peacekeeper ICBM, the
most accurate land-based missile in the U.S. strategic nuclear arsenal.[31] Owing to its improved accuracy and larger payload compared to its SLBM predecessors, Trident II would be able to attack hardened targets in the Soviet
Union that were not previously vulnerable to sea-launched ballistic missiles.
Although U.S. planners might assume that these strikes against hardened
targets in the Soviet Union would be retaliatory attacks, a Soviet net assessment of U.S. first-strike capabilities would have to include the improved sea-
based missiles.

It is also possible that sea-based first-strike capabilities were considered
more of a threat to crisis stability by Soviet leaders than by their U.S. counterparts. In the United States, submarine-launched ballistic missiles became
associated at birth with the navy's justification for those systems as contributory to finite deterrence and assured destruction. Advocates of finite deterrence regard second-strike counterforce capabilities as superfluous; advocates
of assured destruction consider them potentially dangerous.[32] The reasons for
skepticism are sound: flexible nuclear response strategies can appear to the
other side as first-strike–aspiring strategies. Even securely based and highly
survivable second-strike weapons can be employed as part of a first-strike
package if they are sufficiently accurate and prompt. ICBMs had this two-
hatted potential during the 1960s, and SLBMs may have it now. According
to a study by the U.S. Congressional Budget Office of the Trident II system:
"From the Soviet perspective, hard-target warheads are more threatening if
based on SLBMs than on ICBMs; U.S. submarines can be deployed nearer
to the Soviet Union, reducing the time between detection and arrival of an
attack. Furthermore, if the United States has enough prompt hard-target
capability to attack and destroy a high percentage of the Soviet strategic

31. Estimated circular error probable (CEP) for the Trident II (D-5) is given as .07 nm,
compared to the estimated CEP of .05 nm for the MX. See U.S. Congressional Budget Office,
Modernizing U.S. Strategic Offensive Forces (Washington, D.C.: U.S. Congressional Budget
Office, November 1987), 86–87; Corbin, Hajian, and Tsipis, *Nuclear Arsenals for the 21st
Century*, 11.
32. Much depends on whether second-strike counterforce capabilities are thought necessary
for the deterrence of general war or for the control of escalation during limited war. Advocates
of second-strike counterforce have argued both positions. For pertinent arguments, see Scott
D. Sagan, *Moving Targets: Nuclear Strategy and National Security* (Princeton, N.J.: Princeton
University Press, 1989), ch. 2, and Robert Jervis, *The Meaning of the Nuclear Revolution: Statecraft and the Prospect of Armageddon* (Ithaca, N.Y.: Cornell University Press, 1989), ch. 3.

facilities, the Soviet Union would have to assume that the United States might consider employing that capability in a first strike."[33]

One does not have to agree with this judgment to draw out one of its implications: different components of the U.S. strategic nuclear force structure have the potential to send different signals to external audiences, including foreign governments in a crisis. The U.S. strategic bomber force is an example of different meanings within the same force package. Although the United States has more experience with bomber forces than with missiles, the complexity of balancing the requirement for survivability against the equally desirable objective of nonprovocative crisis management is not fully appreciated by lay or expert audiences. Approximately 30 percent of the bomber force remained on runway alert until 1991. Even the survivability of much of this force could be in doubt if submarine-launched ballistic missiles and undetected cruise missiles from sea-based or airborne platforms reached coastal targets within six minutes. Therefore, at a certain alert status the commander-in-chief of SAC (CINCSAC) (now Strategic Command) can order the bombers dispersed among a larger number of airfields for increased survivability.[34] And if the danger seems sufficiently acute and time is short, a portion of the bomber force can be placed on airborne alert. Popular literature assumes that, once aloft, alerted bombers would automatically proceed to "fail safe" points from which they would turn back unless they receive further and specific authorization from the National Command Authority (the president, the secretary of defense, and/or their successors). Nothing prevents a president, however, from ordering portions of the bomber force to be placed on airborne alert without having all planes fly directly to "fail safe" destinations (presumably over northern Canada in most cases). During the 1950s and 1960s, SAC regularly maintained a portion of the bomber force on peacetime airborne alert; the practice was later discontinued as a result of several nuclear accidents. Bomber operations are complex not only because of the command-and-control options available to leaders, but also because bombers carry the most diverse arsenal of nuclear weapon loadings: gravity bombs; air-launched cruise missiles (ALCMs); and air-to-

33. U.S. Congressional Budget Office, *Trident II Missiles: Capability, Costs, and Alternatives* (Washington, D.C.: GPO, July 1986), 21–22.

34. Sagan notes that the distinction between dispersal of the U.S. bomber force to alternate bases during a crisis and the actual launching of the bomber force might not be obvious to Soviet intelligence. See Sagan, *Moving Targets*, 170.

ground short-range attack missiles (SRAMs). Each type of weapon is specialized for use against certain classes of targets as opposed to others. Of necessity, the various force components of the U.S. strategic nuclear deterrent, even leaving aside NATO theater nuclear forces, must operate according to somewhat different conceptions of the relationship between mobilization and deterrence. Formally, a simple series of graduated defense conditions (DEFCONs) from 5 to 1, in order of systemic preparedness for war, covers all arms of service. In practice, there is great variation in what individual force components, such as aircraft carrier battle groups, army divisions, and marine amphibious brigades may be doing at the same level. Mobilization does not mean the same thing for ground forces as it does for naval forces, and its meaning can be as various as that between naval surface forces and submarines. One acknowledged example of this variation in U.S. force component mobilization is that SAC was kept at DEFCON 4 in normal peacetime conditions during the cold war, although other elements remained at the lowest level of readiness, DEFCON 5. Thus, although laypersons and even some experts have the impression that mobilization is menu-driven and of a piece, in actual fact the alerting of U.S. nuclear and other forces involves diverse activities based on differing assumptions about the organizational mission. The process is much more "subsystem dominant" than can be appreciated from a schematic view of the DEFCON system.[35]

One might infer from U.S. force structure that the various force components are based on diverse concepts of mobilization. This point is distinct from the equally valid concern about each service's ideology and ethos resulting in a uniquely "army," "navy," or "air force" perspective on war and military organization.[36] Interservice rivalry marked the early years of the nuclear missile and space age, with spirited debates over which service, for example, would control land-based missiles: the army, because they were launched from the ground; or the air force, because missiles fly through the

35. I gratefully acknowledge helpful conversations with Bruce Blair on this subject, but he bears no responsibility for the arguments made here. See Blair, "Alerting in Crisis and Conventional War," ch. 3 in Managing Nuclear Operations, ed. Ashton B. Carter, John D. Steinbruner, and Charles A. Zraket (Washington, D.C.: Brookings Institution, 1987), 75–120.

36. See the discussion of "servicism" in Samuel P. Huntington, "Organization and Strategy," ch. 11 in Reorganizing America's Defense: Leadership in War and Peace, ed. Robert J. Art, Vincent Davis, and Samuel P. Huntington (New York: Pergamon/Brassey's, 1985), 230–54. This book was among the intellectual stimuli contributing to the Goldwater-Nichols military reform legislation of 1987, which among other objectives strengthened the roles of the JCS chairman, the JCS staff, and the commanders-in-chief (CINCs) of unified and specified commands.

air. At least with regard to strategic nuclear force structure, these issues settled into an accepted pattern of navy control over Polaris-Poseidon submarines, air force ownership of ICBMs and bombers, and army concern with ballistic missile defense. But these disagreements on force structure masked something equally critical: implicit notions about force "generation" or mobilization from peacetime into wartime readiness.

Each force component in the U.S. strategic nuclear arsenal was predicated on a somewhat different time schedule for operational readiness. ICBMs were "warm" in their fixed silos (mobiles present somewhat different sets of problems, although they can be made launch-ready almost as fast) and were counted on for immediate launch even from peacetime status once presidential authorization was given and the appropriate emergency action message (EAM) disseminated. Ballistic missile submarines were designed to disperse across a vast oceanic template and to vanish from detection to the extent possible. They were mainly, though not exclusively, tasked as a last-ditch, countervalue retaliatory force after the initial stages of a nuclear war had been fought. Bomber operations were more complicated than those for either of the other two types of strategic nuclear weapons. Some portion of the bomber force, about 30 percent, remains in constant readiness for short-warning takeoff. The remaining bombers are vulnerable to surprise attack against their bases without warning; they require "strategic" as well as "tactical" warning to escape in time before warheads detonate and destroy them on the ground or during takeoff.

In a way, we can describe the ICBM mobilization/readiness model as one designed on the premise that "mobilization is tantamount to war." Always ready for prompt launch, land-based strategic missiles were once highly survivable against the kinds of attacks that either the Soviet Union or the United States could make against them. Accuracy improvements and MIRVing reduced the prelaunch survivability of silo-based ICBMs if the head of state was not willing to "launch on warning"; thus, there was a destabilizing situation in the event of a crisis in which two sides deployed such forces. In contrast, the SLBM deployment/readiness model is one based on the premise of "defensive realism." A certain portion of the force is on patrol and launch-ready but, because of its high degree of survivability, not on a hair trigger. Bombers are not as "laid back" as submarines and not as "forward-leaning" as ICBMs. The complexity of bomber operations is an asset for crisis time policymakers, for the U.S. strategic bomber force can be used to send signals to potential adversaries in a way that land- and sea-based missiles cannot. Bombers can be surged and recalled, dispersed to alternate airfields, or even sent overseas during a crisis. Therefore, they lend themselves to a mobilization/readiness model of "support for coercive bargaining." We will see in the next section that these models have approximate equivalents in history: namely, in the concepts of the relationship between mobilization and deterrence held by Russian civilian and military leaders immediately prior to World War I.

Components of the U.S. strategic nuclear force structure also suggest different models of deterrence in a larger than mobilization and readiness sense. Capabilities for hard-target, prompt-response strikes in retaliation can appear to potential opponents as first-strike capabilities, compounding the difficulty of resolving a crisis on mutually acceptable terms. U.S. net assessments of the Soviet "threat" during the Cold War years frequently focused on the potential of Soviet ICBMs to destroy significant portions of the U.S. land-based missile force, although little evidence was available to suggest that the Soviet intentions ever led in this direction. U.S. misperceptions of Soviet intent were reciprocated by Soviet misperceptions of U.S. intent, likewise inferred from an analysis of capabilities. Soviet leaders perceived U.S. strategic nuclear counterforce capabilities as first strike–oriented or as designed to support policies of extended "compellence" against Soviet efforts to maintain the political and military status quo.[37] U.S. assessments of Soviet intent questioned why the Soviet Union needed prompt, hard-target counterforce for destroying silos and command centers if, according to the U.S. view of deterrence, the capacity for assured retaliation was sufficient for mutual deterrence.[38] Soviet leaders questioned why, if the United States held to an "assured retaliation" view of deterrence, the United States needed extra insurance in the form of counterforce nuclear warfighting capabilities.[39]

---

37. For further development of this point, see Raymond L. Garthoff, *Deterrence and the Revolution in Soviet Military Doctrine* (Washington, D.C.: Brookings Institution, 1990), 24–28.

38. One answer provided by U.S. pessimists was that the Soviet Union sought a counterforce capability sufficient to destroy portions of the U.S. retaliatory force in a first strike (primarily ICBMs and the nonalert portion of the bomber force). Remaining Soviet forces could then hold hostage U.S. cities, coercing a U.S. president into capitulation. Or, in a softer version of the same scenario, U.S. leaders might be coerced to yield in a crisis by Soviet superiority in prompt, hard-target capabilities. See Paul Nitze, "Assuring Strategic Stability in an Era of Detente," *Foreign Affairs* 54 (1976): 207–33. For counterarguments, see Benjamin S. Lambeth, "Uncertainties for the Soviet War Planner," *International Security* (Winter 1982–83), in *Soviet Military Policy*, ed. Sean M. Lynn-Jones, Steven E. Miller, and Stephen Van Evera (Cambridge, Mass.: MIT Press, 1989), 347–74.

39. Marshal N. V. Ogarkov, then chief of the Soviet General Staff, characterized the Reagan administration's strategy as one of "direct confrontation" with the USSR on a global and regional scale, and he distinguished it from the U.S. strategy in the 1970s of "realistic deter-

Both sides' force structures were obviously driven by internal imperatives, too, but the present point is that both probably deployed more counterforce capabilities than they need have in order to achieve deterrence, and in the process each sent signals to the other that led to erroneous inferences about intentions.

PREFERRED STRATEGIES

In the U.S. case, different constituencies in the government and diverse schools of strategic analysis have supported various notions of what it would take to guarantee the stability of deterrence. These constituencies, broadly speaking, have grouped around strategies of retaliation, strategies of intimidation, and strategies of bargaining and negotiation.[40] Each category of strategy calls for different kinds of military capabilities.

Retaliation strategies are based on posing to a potential attacker the credible threat of unacceptable social destruction in response to an attack of any significance on the U.S. homeland, and perhaps in the aftermath of a failure of "extended deterrence" in Europe. In retaliation strategies, the capability of U.S. forces to survive and to inflict unacceptable societal damage was a necessary and sufficient condition for the success of basic deterrence (against homeland attack), but it was not necessarily a sufficient condition for the deterrence of conventional or nuclear attacks on allies (extended deterrence).

Intimidation strategies call for superior U.S. counterforce offensive and active defensive capabilities in order to preclude Soviet crisis coercion and to provide for favorable war outcomes should deterrence fail.[41] Intimidation

---

rence." See Ogarkov's *Vsegda v gotovnosti k zashchite Otechestva* (Moscow: Voyenizdat, 1982), 15, and *Istoriya uchit bditel'nosti* (Moscow: Voyenizdat, 1985), 67–69.

40. For a different but useful distinction—among strategists favoring damage limitation, punitive retaliation, and military denial—see Charles L. Glaser, *Analyzing Strategic Nuclear Policy* (Princeton, N.J.: Princeton University Press, 1990), 50–54. The distinctions between the damage limitation and punitive retaliation schools are very clearly drawn, but the distinction made by Glaser between the damage limitation and military denial schools would not be noticed by many in the punitive retaliation camp. Nevertheless, Glaser has correctly noted the distinction between those who support limited options (including limited counterforce options) for bargaining purposes and those who support limited nuclear options as part of a damage denial strategy. Glaser's arguments are usefully compared with those of Sagan, *Moving Targets*, ch. 2, and Jervis, *The Meaning of the Nuclear Revolution*, ch. 3. See also Glaser's discussion of counterforce in his *Analyzing Strategic Nuclear Policy*, ch. 7.

41. Colin S. Gray, "Nuclear Strategy: The Case for a Theory of Victory," *International*

strategies did not necessarily require a U.S. nuclear first-strike capability (although they did not disparage it), but they did require that no asymmetry favorable to the Soviet Union in active defenses or in counterforce first-strike capabilities could lead to wartime exchange ratios favorable to the Soviet Union.[42]

Bargaining and negotiation strategies, like intimidation strategies, assume that assured destruction capabilities are necessary but insufficient for credible deterrence. The purpose of counterforce weapons in bargaining and negotiation strategies was different in kind and in degree from the purpose of such weapons in intimidation strategies. In bargaining and negotiation strategies, the purpose of counterforce capabilities and limited nuclear options was to de-escalate a war and to terminate it, while obtaining as many of one's preferred political objectives as one could.[43] The assumption of nuclear bargain-

---

Security (Summer 1979), in *Strategy and Nuclear Deterrence*, ed. Steven E. Miller (Princeton, N.J.: Princeton University Press, 1984), 23–56. I prefer the term "intimidation" for this strategy, rather than "damage denial," because the major purpose of the improved counterforce and active defense capabilities is not to actually fight a nuclear war, but to improve the quality of U.S. deterrence.

42. The shift from the "Schlesinger Doctrine" of 1974 to the countervailing strategy of the Carter administration was, according to my analysis, a transition from a strategy of nuclear bargaining and negotiation to a strategy of intimidation. This judgment would be disputed by some proponents of countervailing strategy. See the Hon. Harold Brown, Secretary of Defense, "Remarks Prepared for Delivery at Convocation Ceremonies for the 97th Naval War College Class, Newport, Rhode Island, October 20, 1980," for the authoritative public exposition of U.S. countervailing strategy by a U.S. government official. For context, see Desmond Ball, "Counterforce Targeting: How New? How Viable?" *Arms Control Today* (February 1981), reprinted with revisions in *American Defense Policy*, ed. F. Reichart and Steven R. Sturm (Baltimore, Md.: Johns Hopkins University Press, 1982), 227–34. Countervailing strategy is critiqued extensively in Robert Jervis, *The Illogic of American Nuclear Strategy* (Ithaca, N.Y.: Cornell University Press, 1984), passim. Carter administration nuclear strategic planners and other officials characterized countervailing strategy as evolutionary from the Schlesinger Doctrine and its emphasis on limited nuclear options, and from that perspective Reagan's "prevailing" strategy is held to be fundamentally different from "countervailing" strategy. I disagree with that assessment, holding that the shift from an emphasis on bargaining to an emphasis on favorable war outcomes occurred under Carter. For counterarguments, see Walter Slocombe, "The Countervailing Strategy," *International Security* (Spring 1981), in *Strategy and Nuclear Deterrence*, ed. Miller, 245–54, and Leon Sloss, "The Strategist's Perspective," ch. 2 in *Ballistic Missile Defense*, ed. Ashton B. Carter and David N. Schwartz (Washington, D.C.: Brookings Institution, 1984), 24–48.

43. Academic studies on conflict resolution and bargaining were influential in the development of this perspective, inside and outside government, especially the work of Thomas C. Schelling. See Schelling's *The Strategy of Conflict* (Cambridge, Mass.: Harvard University Press, 1960) and *Arms and Influence* (New Haven, Conn.: Yale University Press, 1966). On the problem of limited war between nuclear-armed states, see Morton Halperin, *Limited War in the Nuclear Age* (New York: John Wiley, 1963), and Ian Clark, *Limited Nuclear War* (Princeton, N.J.: Princeton University Press, 1982). Also influential have been studies of coercive diplo-

ing and negotiating strategies was that brinkmanship tactics could be extended from crisis management into the conduct of war itself. A gradually increasing and shared risk of escalation would lead nuclear combatants to pull back from Armageddon even after they had embarked on a war of uncertain dimensions. The Schlesinger Doctrine, promulgated by the U.S. secretary of defense in 1974, was mostly based on this logic, which emphasized improvements in command and control, wartime communications between opponents, and the withholding of attacks against certain categories of targets that were considered especially useful as hostages for bargaining purposes.[44]

Unlike the cases of retaliation strategies and intimidation strategies, bargaining and negotiation strategies were based on a construction that was more *process-oriented* than *outcome-oriented*. Bargaining strategies emphasized the possibility that nuclear exchanges could be conducted for the purpose of de-escalation. This smacked of casuistry to adherents of retaliation strategies and as pussyfooting to those who preferred intimidation strategies. Advocates of bargaining strategies in the government did not have an easy time of it, for they were less interested in force building than they were in improvements to strategic command, control, communications, and intelligence (C3I) for prewar alert management and wartime communication with adversaries. Whereas those who preferred intimidation strategies wanted enough forces to maintain an advantage even after repeated nuclear strikes had been carried out, advocates of bargaining and negotiation strategies thought that highly competent counterforce capabilities were useful only if they were far less than adequate for a first strike. Bargaining strategists preferred second-strike counterforce in order to reduce vulnerability to the opponent's coercion in crisis and wartime.

---

macy and the psychology of deterrence, which yielded some conclusions relevant to the control of escalation in nuclear war, although the contributors to these genres were not sympathetic to the idea of limited nuclear war. See Robert Jervis, *Perception and Misperception in International Politics* (Princeton, N.J.: Princeton University Press, 1976); Alexander L. George and Richard Smoke, *Deterrence in American Foreign Policy: Theory and Practice* (New York: Columbia University Press, 1974); Alexander L. George, David K. Hall, and William E. Simons, *The Limits of Coercive Diplomacy: Laos, Cuba, Vietnam* (Boston: Little, Brown, 1971); and relevant sections in Gordon A. Craig and Alexander L. George, *Force and Statecraft: Diplomatic Problems of Our Time* (New York: Oxford University Press, 1983), chs. 14 and 15.

44. See Secretary of Defense James R. Schlesinger, press conference on January 10, 1974, excerpts in *Survival* (March–April 1974): 86–90. See also Ball, "The Development of the SIOP, 1960–1983," 57–83, and Desmond Ball, *The Evolution of United States Strategic Policy Since 1945: Doctrine, Military Technical Innovation, and Force Structure*, Reference Paper no. 164 (Canberra: Strategic and Defense Studies Centre, Research School of Pacific Studies, Australian National University, January 1989).

An important distinction between the intimidation and bargaining schools lay in the rationale provided by each for improvements in command and control. An intimidation strategy required improved command and control in order to be able to fight a nuclear war, including a massive or protracted nuclear war, under any conditions. A bargaining and negotiation strategy would use nuclear weapons not as instruments of destruction but as signaling devices, albeit of a morally ambiguous and highly destructive sort. The different rationales offered for command-and-control improvements in the two kinds of strategies tell us something basic about a difference in purpose. The purpose of limited nuclear war in an intimidation strategy is to destroy the opponent's capabilities and, by that means, to influence the opponent's judgments about escalation. In a bargaining strategy, on the other hand, the purpose of limited nuclear war is to shock the opponent to come to his senses and to agree to stop fighting before a process of escalation runs out of control. A strategy of intimidation depends on the capability to destroy; a strategy of bargaining, on the capability to coerce, which is fundamentally a capability for persuasion.[45]

U.S. advocates of nuclear bargaining strategies found themselves in a position very similar to that of Russian Foreign Minister Sazonov during the crisis of July 1914. They sought to use military instruments for diplomatic persuasion, and they encountered skepticism from professional military planners, who despise half-measures in time of war, and from dovish critics, who are doubtful of any distinction between barking dogs of war and biting dogs. The experience of the July crisis suggests that the demonstrative uses of mobilization are as fraught with uncertainty and peril as the demonstrative uses of nuclear weapons would have been. The argument here goes beyond the much-quoted assertion that World War I was a war by timetable. "Timetable war" may be an accurate characterization of the *inflexibility* of mobilization plans as they were put into action, but this valid point about World War I

45. Robert Powell makes a distinction of this sort, distinguishing between manipulation-of-risk strategies and limited-retaliation strategies. The logic of a manipulation-of-risk strategy "works through an array of risk and ultimately appeals to the sanction of an unlimited nuclear attack or, more generally, to a sanction that no state would ever deliberately be the first to impose. The strategy of limited retaliation, however, never appeals to the possibility of an unlimited attack. The array of punishment is used to impose limited sanctions in order to make the threat of future destruction sufficiently credible that an adversary will be coerced into coming to terms" (Powell, *Nuclear Deterrence Theory: The Search for Credibility* [Cambridge: Cambridge University Press, 1990], 25). I would add to this the caution that one cannot exclude the threat of ultimate sanction from limited nuclear use, although strategies can differ in the degree of explicitness by which the threat is conveyed.

mobilization omits the equally important dimension of the *bargaining context* within which such plans are carried out.[46]

One can imagine that under the right circumstances an inflexible war plan might be advantageous. Indeed, some have argued that the inflexibility of Schlieffen's original plan for the invasion of France was its strength, and that Moltke's hasty decision to withdraw two corps from the right wing while the offensive was in progress, in order to strengthen the German defenses in East Prussia, was a fatal mistake.[47] This judgment is probably unfair to Moltke, and it certainly ignores the numerous transportation, supply, and command-and-control problems that plagued the German offensive in the west in the autumn of 1914. Inflexibility in planning and execution is less costly against a slower-reacting opponent. But the great cost of inflexibility in mobilization and deployment of forces *prior* to war, as in nuclear-crisis alerting procedures which might be too rigidly prescribed, is the lack of clarity that either rigid mobilization or timetable alerts can introduce into political leaders' intended signals. The timetable aspect of the Schlieffen Plan was important before war began as well as afterward. It had not only operational-tactical consequences, but political ones.

Because of what Germany and its potential opponents *believed* about the Schlieffen Plan and about mobilization in general, they favored strategies of preemption or "prompt launch" of forces into enemy territory instead of

46. On the importance of inflexibility as an aspect of military decisionmaking, see Martin Van Creveld, *The Transformation of War* (New York: Free Press, 1991), 104.

47. Command-and-control failures and logistical problems had more to do with the failure of the Schlieffen Plan in the west. The Germans planned for a rate of advance that required motorization and mechanization not yet available to their forces. Inadequate transportation caused supplies to lag behind the requirements of advancing troops. General Staff headquarters was too far behind the front, with the result that dependable communications between Moltke and his army commanders were not available (e.g., no exchange of information occurred between Moltke and his army leaders from September 5 to 9, 1914). See Holger Herwig, "The Dynamics of Necessity: German Military Policy During the First World War," ch. 3 in *Military Effectiveness. Vol. I: The First World War*, ed. Allan R. Millett and Williamson Murray (Boston: Unwin Hyman, 1988), 93–94, and Martin Van Creveld, *Supplying War: Logistics from Wallenstein to Patton* (Cambridge, Mass.: Harvard University Press, 1977), 113–41. The first careful study of transportation and supply problems attendant to the Schlieffen Plan was ordered up by Moltke one month after assuming his post as chief of the General Staff in 1906. The head of the railway section of the General Staff, Lt. Col. Groner, was in charge of the study, which concluded that the plan as it stood had little chance of success. In addition, Van Creveld argues that Moltke's reduction in size of the large right wing of his invading armies must be viewed in the context of his decision to avoid violation of neutral Dutch territory. By this decision, Moltke avoided having to commit perhaps two corps to deal with the armed forces of the Netherlands in the earliest phase of the war. See Van Creveld, *Supplying War*, 119–21; also see references cited in Chapter 1, above.

delay-oriented strategies based on slower-reacting and more defensively postured forces. As the German General Staff viewed the Russians, and as the Russians viewed the Germans during the July 1914 crisis, neither could afford the luxury of risking a type II error (wait and see) as opposed to a type I error (attack when in doubt). Neither, as analyzed by its prospective adversary, could substitute a bargaining and negotiation strategy for a strategy of intimidation. Partial mobilizations were distrusted by General Staff planners as misbegotten measures that would complicate later efforts to wage total war. The message-sending aspects of mobilization were judged to be less important than the logistical and tactical ones.

Although official U.S. policy during the Cold War was that we would never launch a nuclear first strike, this declaration was embedded in policy-planning guidance for the operation of nuclear forces, and in the expectations of force operators themselves, that seriously qualified any reassurance about no first strike. Nuclear "first use" of tactical weapons deployed in Europe under NATO command, in response to a Soviet conventional attack against Germany, was never precluded. Once the first tactical nuclear weapons had been exploded, U.S. strategic nuclear forces would be raised to their highest alert levels and poised for "prompt launch" in response to clear indications of enemy attack. Reassurances from defense planners and political leaders that these alerts could be managed safely and without undue provocation of a destabilizing Soviet response amounted to assertions short of credible proof. For example, careful analyses of the vulnerability of the U.S. nuclear command, control, and communications (C3) system suggested that surprise strikes against vital nodes might "decapitate" key elements of the U.S. political leadership or destroy command-and-control facilities needed to reconstitute forces.[48] The result of command vulnerability to nuclear attack was that U.S. force operations would be short war–oriented. Leaders could not count on the survival of their command centers and communications for very long after massive attacks had struck the U.S. homeland, and even limited but carefully timed attacks might immobilize much of the command structure relevant to mindful prosecution of a war.

Complacency about this issue of U.S. nuclear command-and-control vulnerability was motivated by an expectation on the part of some planners and nuclear strategists that nuclear war could never be fought in a coherent manner anyway. The only object of retaliatory forces and command systems was

---

48. Bruce G. Blair, *Strategic Command and Control: Redefining the Nuclear Threat* (Washington, D.C.: Brookings Institution, 1985).

to deter attack; if deterrence failed, there was no meaningful distinction among degrees of loss. This position—that degrees of loss would not matter after deterrence failed—posited only massive and suicidal attacks by Americans against Soviets or vice versa. The same position also assumed that only deliberate attacks were possible; degrees of loss and the ability to terminate a war short of holocaust would matter a great deal if a war had begun inadvertently and leaders sought to terminate it. As the prominent nuclear strategist and international relations scholar Robert Jervis noted, in his work *The Meaning of the Nuclear Revolution*, assured destruction never assumed that a president would have *no* ability to wage limited war by means of flexible options.[49]

What prevented the U.S. and Soviet military-political leaderships from developing confidence in their ability to employ limited options along with negotiations, in order to end a war begun inadvertently, was not a lack of hardware or military options. The preventive force was the existence of certain "operational codes" or mind-sets on the part of military planners as well as many persons who provided those planners with relevant policy guidance for the use of nuclear forces. These operational codes served as convenient sets of assumptions about how any war would be fought, or must be fought, in order to ensure that U.S. foreign policy objectives were attained. Military definitions of these operational codes emphasized massive and prompt retaliatory strikes, and even preemptive attacks if feasible or necessary. Military training habituated commanders and planners to the assumption that planning must be based on worst-case estimates of enemy intentions and capabilities. Any response suitable for the worst case would also suffice for lesser conditions.

Along with this went the professional armed forces' traditional aversion to restraints imposed on military operations, including the management of alerts and the conduct of field forces, by politicians. U.S. military fears of amateurish meddling in war plans were exacerbated after Vietnam by their fears that civilians addicted to graduated deterrence and flexible options would deny the means for victory to harried commanders. The same fears

---

49. See Jervis, *The Meaning of the Nuclear Revolution*, 74–106. As Jervis explains in his discussion of MAD-4, a correctly understood version of mutual assured destruction: "The argument that MAD is flawed because it can threaten only an unlimited response to any Soviet aggression is incorrect. MAD-4 foresees that limited wars, even limited nuclear wars, might be possible. But more options would not reduce American vulnerability, and it is the knowledge that it would be destroyed in an all-out war rather than the lack of carefully crafted options that inhibits the United States" (p. 99).

applied to nuclear-crisis management and the expected conduct of nuclear war as applied to conventional war. If war was unavoidable, then U.S. military tradition suggested that the most massive and decisive blows needed to be struck promptly against the sources of aggression. Applied to nuclear force operations, this meant that ambiguous indications of enemy preparation for attack might justify provocative alert measures or preemptive strikes if the president were convinced that war was inevitable.

During the Cold War, the pressure on a U.S. president to use nuclear forces before the command system for employing those forces coherently was destroyed was comparable to the pressures facing the German General Staff in July and August 1914. Faced with a Russian decision to enact "measures preparatory to war," German leaders still held back from ordering mobilization or the officially declared warning period prior to mobilization (*Kriegsgefahrzustand*).[50] Later evidence of Russian partial mobilization in the military districts facing Austria-Hungary led Chief of the German General Staff Helmuth von Moltke and War Minister General Erich von Falkenhayn to call for this *Kriegsgefahrzustand* ("threatening danger of war"), but political leaders still resisted a German mobilization. Evidence of Russian general mobilization reached Berlin on August 30 and prompted Germany's decision for general mobilization. Historian Marc Trachtenberg uses this evidence to argue against any assessment that political leaders in Germany lost control of their armed forces or that they capitulated to urgent military demands for action when the chancellor and the kaiser could have exercised restraint.[51]

Trachtenberg's argument might be reassessed in terms of the operational codes by which German planners had developed their military strategy. Although political leadership had approved the Schlieffen Plan in its various forms, they had not fully appreciated the implications of the Schlieffen Plan for crisis management, as opposed to warfighting. If war were truly inevitable (as in the case of a Russian or French preemptive attack into German territory based on mistaken notions that Germany was already attacking), then the Schlieffen Plan offered the most economical and militarily efficient road to victory, *given Germany's problem of a two-front war*. If the opportunity for stopping a crisis short of war still existed, on the other hand, then the Schlieffen Plan placed political leaders in a situation where the risks of delay were much greater than the risks of mistaken preemption (type II errors were much riskier than type I errors, in terms of statistical decision theory).

50. Marc Trachtenberg, *History and Strategy* (Princeton, N.J.: Princeton University Press, 1991), 88.
51. Ibid., 90.

The Schlieffen Plan had this character, as noted in the preceding chapter, because of its two most important attributes: it called for *total* victory, and it called for a *rapid* decision.[52] In similar fashion, despite decades-long U.S. declaratory policy in favor of flexible nuclear response and limited options, the operational codes of Cold War U.S. nuclear strategic planners emphasized the avoidance of vulnerability to nuclear "Pearl Harbors" and the capability of responding rapidly and massively to any surprise attack.[53] The result of the emphases in the Schlieffen Plan and its nuclear-age successors was not the usurpation of political auspices for decision by the military, as Trachtenberg correctly surmised. But the Schlieffen Plan and U.S. Cold War nuclear war plans *did shift leaders' expectations about the character of risk* from a marginal emphasis on the avoidance of war to a marginal emphasis on the successful conduct of a first decisive military strike in war.[54]

NUCLEAR WEAPONS AND STABILITY AFTER COLD WAR

During the Cold War years from 1945 to 1989, theorists assumed that nuclear weapons contributed to international stability, provided certain conditions could be met. These conditions were quite exceptional. First, strategic nuclear bipolarity conferred an exceptionality on U.S. and Soviet foreign policy and on the relationship between the two nuclear superpowers.[55] Bipolarity defined the character of their political and military compe-

52. For an interesting argument that the German "tradition" from Frederick the Great was one of total war for limited objectives, aiming at prompt and decisive battlefield victories followed by a negotiated peace, see Dennis Showalter, "Total War for Limited Objectives: An Interpretation of German Grand Strategy," in *Grand Strategies in War and Peace*, ed. Paul Kennedy (New Haven, Conn.: Yale University Press, 1991), 105–24.

53. Blair, *Strategic Command and Control*, passim. See also Paul Bracken, *The Command and Control of Nuclear Forces* (New Haven, Conn.: Yale University Press, 1983).

54. Trachtenberg concedes the point made here by describing what happened in Berlin on July 30, 1914, when news arrived of Russia's decision for general mobilization. When the news about Russian mobilization reached Berlin, says Trachtenberg, "the issue had been overtaken by events" (*History and Strategy*, 88). What can such a statement mean? It can mean only that Germany's war plan required the launching of a prompt *offensive* against France and through Belgium whether or not Russian mobilization included a prompt offensive against East Prussia. Russia's alliance with France required Russia to undertake an early offensive against East Prussia, but the requirement for early Russian assistance to France was based on correct appreciations by Russia and France of the Schlieffen Plan and its implications.

55. John Lewis Gaddis, "The Long Peace: Elements of Stability in the Postwar International System," *International Security* (Spring 1986): 1–44.

tition. On one hand, in a bipolar world the reach of U.S. and Soviet interests was worldwide; any balancing behavior in response to assertiveness by
one side had to come from the other. On the other hand, both sides had a
large stake in preserving the status quo. Even without nuclear weapons, it is
hard to see how Washington and Moscow could have justified going to war,
given the enormous sacrifices made by the two sides in World War II and the
lingering memories of those costs in the minds of the first generation of Cold
War leaders (especially Soviet leaders).[56]

The argument that bipolarity was at least as important as nuclear weapons, if not more so, in stabilizing the postwar world is fundamental to accurate historical assessment and to successful prediction of the conditions related to international and regional European stability. Because the
Americans and Soviets dominated the international military chessboard during the Cold War years, a tradition grew with regard to the management of
nuclear force operations in peacetime and in crisis. That tradition was the
result of nuclear learning that took place, in Washington and in Moscow, as
a result of their confrontations and arms control negotiations during the
Cold War years. A "dialogue" conducted openly at arms control sessions,
such as those which continued under the Strategic Arms Limitation Talks
(SALT) umbrella for several decades, was one path by which nuclear learning occurred. The two sides evaluated one another's force deployments,
aided by the revolution in surveillance and reconnaissance technology. Sat-
ellite-based photographic and electronic surveillance made transparent any
attempt to hide from discovery the numbers and kinds of new weapons sufficient in quality or quantity to overturn the strategic nuclear balance.

The dialogue between the U.S. and Soviet leaderships during arms control
negotiations accomplished more than the agreement to limit numbers of
arms or destabilizing arms modernization. It also gave the professional military leadership on each side important insights into the norms and procedures by which the other side operated its nuclear forces. The political leaders of both countries sought to guarantee against accidental or inadvertent
nuclear war. This was more of a problem than guaranteeing against military
usurpation of political power. It also required that the operating norms of
military organizations be reconciled with the crisis management objectives
of policymakers. This could not be done by textbook, but only by U.S. and

---

56. For related arguments, see John Mueller, "The Essential Irrelevance of Nuclear Weapons: Stability in the Postwar World," *International Security* (Fall 1988), in *Nuclear Diplomacy
and Crisis Management*, ed. Lynn-Jones, Miller, and Van Evera, 3–27.

Soviet experience in nuclear-crisis management. Leaderships of both sides discovered, in the course of managing nuclear force operations in peacetime and during crises, that the transmission of policymakers' values into the operations of military (or other) bureaucratic organizations could not be taken for granted.

One result was the establishment of special-purpose organizations for the operation of strategic nuclear forces and for the acquisition and dissemination of warning-and-intelligence information about the possibility of nuclear attack to force commanders and policymakers. In the U.S. case, for example, the Strategic Air Command was created during the 1940s as a unique organizational entity with the major mission of delivering strategic nuclear weapons against designated targets in the Soviet Union. Its ethos and norms grew up around the expectation that SAC would be the lead operating arm in carrying out this mission. On the other hand, for SAC to carry out its mission it had to avoid vulnerability to surprise attack. Given the speed with which nuclear weapons could be delivered against targets in the continental United States by Soviet ballistic missiles, continuous streams of warning information available in "real time" and a capability for rapid assessment of that information became necessary conditions for strategic stability. At the same time, the tight coupling of warning-and-intelligence information with the responsive forces that would carry out orders to retaliate made the problem of crisis stability two-sided.

Instantaneous warning-and-intelligence information could provoke norm-driven military organizations to raise their levels of alertness. This increase in alert levels would then be noticed by the warning-and-intelligence systems of the other side. A ratcheting effect might then be set in motion by the two sides' monitoring and reacting to one another's crisis moves. At an extreme, state leaderships in Washington and Moscow, in an ironic action–reaction process, might squeeze the hair triggers that connected their nuclear warning-and-intelligence systems to one another.[57] This "spiral effect," or reciprocal growth in the wariness of both sides, could lead to an expectation by one side that the other was about to strike. Even more complicated was the problem that the expectation of one side that the other was about to launch a first strike did not depend on a decision by side A that side B had made a rational, deliberate decision to attack. Side A could conclude erroneously that side B had lost control of its own decisionmaking and nuclear-crisis management.

57. For an expansion of this point, see Bracken, *The Command and Control of Nuclear Forces*.

"Loss of control" in the preceding sense is something more subtle, and more dangerous for crisis management, than the loss of control implied by popular U.S. films such as *Dr. Strangelove*. In this popular movie, directed by Stanley Kubrick in the 1960s, a deranged U.S. SAC general is able to order an attack on the Soviet Union despite the desire of the U.S. and Soviet leaderships to avoid war. Another loss-of-control scenario which had more basis in fact than mad colonels and generals was the possibility of a technical malfunction causing inadvertent crisis tension or war. Radars spoofed by flocks of geese or other natural phenomena which might be mistaken for incoming Soviet bombers were among the incidents reportedly taking place during the development of U.S. warning-and-assessment systems in the 1950s. More recently, several incidents reported during the Carter administration included a failed computer chip, which caused a simulated Soviet submarine attack on the U.S. East and West coasts, and a misplayed training tape at North American Aerospace Defense Command (NORAD) that momentarily impressed observers as the real thing.

U.S. leaders worked during the 1950s and 1960s to develop procedures that were proof against usurping officers and technical malfunctions leading to actual U.S.-Soviet preparations for attack or even to inadvertent war. Electromechanical locks (permissive-action links, or PALs) were placed on most U.S. nuclear weapons in order to preclude unauthorized tampering or firing. Authentication and enabling codes would have to be provided from the highest levels of the political and military leadership before weapons could be mated to delivery vehicles or launched. In addition, other procedural controls ensured that a temporarily confused situation of political authority would not lead to military usurpation of political authority. We are not certain how the Soviets arranged this during the Cold War years, although some evidence has appeared in the writings of expert U.S. analysts. In the U.S. case, though, important safeguards against military usurpation included the precise specification of a National Command Authority (the president, the secretary of defense, and/or their duly authorized successors) atop the military chain of command, including the chain of command for releasing and firing nuclear weapons.

The specification of nuclear command authority was necessary to ensure that, during a crisis over presidential succession or incapacity, the nuclear forces of the United States would not remain paralyzed during a credible warning of surprise attack. The problem of avoiding nuclear surprise attack required not only that the U.S. president lawfully grant nuclear release to subordinate commanders, but also that the delegation of nuclear command authority for exceptional wartime conditions be preserved alongside the constitutionally specified devolution of civil executive power. The Presidential Succession Act and the Twenty-fifth Amendment to the U.S. Constitution establish clearly the order of succession to the office of the presidency. However, this line of succession establishes the order of political legitimacy, not the effective capacity for nuclear warfighting or war termination.

The problem of loss of control may be viewed within a broader context. According to Richard Ned Lebow, loss of control is one of three major sources of crisis instability; the others are miscalculated escalation and preemption.[58] Preemption is self-explanatory: the decision to launch a first strike in the mistaken belief that the opponent has already decided to attack. Loss of control and miscalculated escalation are more complicated and, in some instances, are related. Joseph F. Bouchard further develops Lebow's ideas on the sources of crisis instability in his explanation of the concept of "crisis security dilemma."[59] A crisis security dilemma is a version of the concept of "security dilemma." As explained by Robert Jervis, a security dilemma is the result when efforts by one state to increase its security are perceived to threaten the security of one or more other states.[60] A crisis security dilemma, according to Bouchard, occurs when actions taken by states to increase their security, to deter escalation, or to improve their bargaining positions decrease the security of an adversary.[61]

From Bouchard's definition of the crisis security dilemma and his application of Lebow's and others' discussions of the loss-of-control problem, it follows that certain kinds of crisis management behavior are repeated offenders. Three dangerous behavior patterns are 1) those which suggest to the adversary an intent to launch a preemptive strike; 2) those which convince the opponent that the crisis can no longer be resolved peacefully (i.e., war is inevitable); and 3) those which result in a use of force not fully controlled by state political leaders.[62] The use of force not fully controlled by state leaders does not have to include explicit or deliberate violation of orders. Rules of engagement and standard operating procedures often allow consid-

58. Robert Ned Lebow, *Nuclear Crisis Management: A Dangerous Illusion* (Ithaca, N.Y.: Cornell University Press, 1987).

59. Bouchard, *Command in Crisis: Four Case Studies* (New York: Columbia University Press, 1991), 1–36, esp. 17–23.

60. Robert Jervis, "Cooperation Under the Security Dilemma," *World Politics* (January 1978), in *International Politics: Anarchy, Force, Political Economy, and Decision Making*, ed. Robert J. Art and Robert Jervis (New York: Harper Collins, 1985), 86–100 and 185–207.

61. Bouchard, *Command in Crisis*, 34.

62. Ibid., 20.

erable latitude to lower echelons for reacting to fairly predictable and standardized events. And operational and tactical commanders, whose first consideration in crisis management and in war must always be the avoidance of
surprise strikes causing decisive losses to their forces, also have considerable
latitude to react to unexpected events.

To many civilians, military organizations appear to epitomize the hierar-
chical concentration of authority in a single action channel which flows from
the top down. As many close students of military history have noted, however, this image is far from the decisionmaking reality pertinent to strategic,
operational, and tactical military operations within a large state. Even authoritarian systems allow for considerable discretion by field commanders
faced with anticipated or unanticipated situations of crisis management or
wartime duress. The nuclear age has created a specialized field of military
crisis management among academics and their fellow travelers, but it has not
introduced anything new into the difficulty of controlling far-flung operational and tactical forces, whether equipped with nuclear weapons or not.
The conventional weapons of today are capable of enormous destruction in
a short time, as the government of Iraq, on the receiving end of U.S. and
allied coalition weapons, learned in January and February 1991.

Students of bureaucratic politics and organizational process have noted
two kinds of factors that inhibit rational decisionmaking, both in crisis and
under normal day-to-day conditions. Bureaucratic politics emphasizes the
degree to which policy decisions are the outcome of bargaining and negotiation among the leaders of important government agencies. In this perspective, policy is the result of bargaining games among bureaucrats, and the
positions of the players are fairly predictable on the basis of agency self-
interest: "where you stand depends upon where you sit."[63] Organizational
process models explain policy decisions as the result of standard operating

---

63. For an explanation and critique of this perspective, see Robert J. Art, "Bureaucratic
Politics and American Foreign Policy: A Critique," *Policy Sciences* 4 (1973): 467–90. Bureaucratic politics models are discussed in Graham T. Allison, *Essence of Decision: Explaining the
Cuban Missile Crisis* (Boston: Little, Brown, 1971), chs. 5–6; in Morton H. Halperin, *Bureaucratic Politics and Foreign Policy* (Washington, D.C.: Brookings Institution, 1974); and in *Read-
ings in American Foreign Policy*, ed. Morton H. Halperin and Arnold Kanter (Boston: Little,
Brown, 1973), 1–42. Art contends that "second wave" theorists of bureaucratic politics admit
that organizational position does not determine policy stance for *senior* policymakers. However,
conceptual flexibility on this point is purchased at the cost of irrelevancy. If organizational
position determines the policy stance of followers but not of leaders, then the bureaucratic
politics model is merely a special case of the organizational process model, absent leaders.
Moreover, it fails to account for the very behaviors within an organization that may be most
important: the goal setting and other major decisions taken by its top echelons.

procedures and preprogrammed routines, activated by stimuli which are anticipated by the organization on the basis of experience. According to the organizational process model, the best prediction of what an organization will do next is what it is doing now. Organizations will "naturally" carry out standard repertoires of behavior in response to expected stimuli, and the same repertoires will be used to respond to sources of threat that are unexpected, even if those decision routines are inappropriate under the circumstances.[64]

Bureaucratic politics and organizational process factors explain how the day-to-day activities of an organization may be decoupled from the long-range policy objectives of its leadership, but they do so for very different political panoramas. Bureaucratic politics has more to do with the interagency maneuvers for position and power; organizational process, with the accumulated impact of institutional microdecisions based on precedent and stimulus–response interactions of the past. The problem, for any particular case of crisis management, is in deciding whether bureaucratic politics and organizational process factors can be inhibitors of innovation or necessary correctives against false confidence in improvised solutions. For example, during the Cuban missile crisis, it was important for President Kennedy to appreciate that even the most "surgical" air strike could not guarantee that all the Soviet MRBM and IRBM installations would be destroyed. Therefore, were any of those sites operational at the time of attack, one or more missiles might be launched in retaliation against the continental United States.

Robert Art has emphasized in his revisionist critiques of bureaucratic politics that actors can have goals which embody their views of the national interest, notwithstanding their institutional commitments and bureaucratic proclivities.[65] The point is incontestable, although it is difficult to separate the motivational construct of the secretary of defense who values additional resources for his department from the conviction on the part of the same individual that U.S. national security exists in a state of imminent peril. Whether actors take institutional or "national interest" positions during crisis management depends on many factors, including the structure of the

<hr/>

64. On the crisis management implications of the organizational process model, see Allison, *Essence of Decision*, passim. Organizational process explanations often rely heavily upon cybernetic analogies and concepts. The finite information-processing capabilities of organizations and the cognitive limits on individual rationality combine to force most decisions into a preset pattern of stimulus and response. See John Steinbruner, *The Cybernetic Theory of Decision: New Dimensions of Political Analysis* (Princeton, N.J.: Princeton University Press, 1974).
65. Art, "Bureaucratic Politics and American Foreign Policy."

decisionmaking process and the relationships among those persons included in the process. For example, President Kennedy went outside the normal chain of civilian political and military institutional command to create an ad hoc group of advisers during the Cuban missile crisis. The relationships among members of this "ExComm" (Executive Committee, National Security Council) were deliberately structured by Kennedy to be nonhierarchical, and participants were encouraged to air dissenting views, even those views which differed from the president's own. The result was an unusual mix of candor and indeterminacy in the deliberations, which forced to the surface alternatives and disagreements that would in all likelihood have been overlooked in a more structured and institutionally focused decisionmaking process.

Bureaucratic politics and organizational process models can mistakenly convey the impression that delegated authority and discretion is the same as unintended leakage of authority from top to bottom. All bureaucratic organizations must delegate discretion. The question is how to do so. U.S. military organizations face special problems in delegating responsibility because they are organized as separate service branches in peacetime but must fight and prepare for war during crises as combined arms commands.[66] Defense legislation of the 1950s, modified by the Goldwater-Nichols reforms of defense decisionmaking passed by Congress in 1986, enhance the importance of the CINCs: the commanders-in-chief of the various unified and specified commands who will oversee the actual conduct of war or of maneuvers in crises involving the possibility of war. For example, General Norman Schwarzkopf, in charge of U.S. Central Command (CENTCOM) during the Gulf crisis and war of 1990–91, had under his jurisdiction forces from the U.S. Army, Navy, and Air Force assigned to his theater of operations. Schwarzkopf reported through the Joint Chiefs of Staff (through its chairman) to the secretary of defense. He did not report to the secretary of the army, whose responsibilities are administrative and not operational. Under a president with the operating philosophy of George Bush, favoring maximum delegation of military responsibility to the theater commander on the scene, Schwarzkopf operated with considerable autonomy and little of the "micromanagement" about which line officers customarily complain.[67]

66. Important issues in the evolution of U.S. military service and Department of Defense command and control are reviewed in C. Kenneth Allard, *Command, Control, and the Common Defense* (New Haven, Conn.: Yale University Press, 1990), esp. 123–47.
67. Although newspaper reports after the conclusion of the Gulf War carried accounts of Schwarzkopf's chafing at Pentagon reporting requirements, the incidents were few and trivial

The problem of loss of control in military command organizations is one that policymakers have sometimes alleged to exist only after the fact of a failed operation. Political leaders reaching for post hoc explanations for military failure are tempted to place the blame on bad military advice or execution instead of on ill-conceived war aims. U.S. policy in Vietnam offers a very compelling illustration of the decoupling of military instruments from effective policy guidance, because those responsible for policy were unable to reach consensus on their own objectives. The U.S. military moved gradually from a posture designed for counterinsurgency support to the government of South Vietnam to the assumption by the U.S. armed forces of responsibility for driving North Vietnamese and Viet Cong armed forces from the field. Meanwhile, the coercive air war against North Vietnam continued as a separately conducted campaign by which political leaders sought to influence the leadership in Hanoi in favor of a negotiated peace settlement. In addition, the disintegration of South Vietnamese civil society under the stress of warfare caused a U.S.-directed pacification effort to be mounted under the guidance of officials whose agenda and expertise were in internal security and rural development. The internal security, conventional ground, and air wars ran through separate chains of political or military command, sought different hierarchies of objectives, and defied combination into a coherent statement of war aims that could be made to trickle down bureaucratic channels.

U.S. nuclear command-and-control systems for most of the Cold War rested on the setting of a "snooze alarm" and were activated only during serious crises as defined by the political leadership. In theory, the DEFCONs allow policymakers to surge forces and command-and-control systems in a smooth progression. In practice, even modest increases in nuclear command-and-control system readiness during the Cold War carried more ominous overtones. Soviet warning and intelligence would be alerted almost instantly to U.S. alerting decisions, especially for those which involved U.S. or allied NATO nuclear weapons capable of reaching Soviet territory. During the autumn of 1983, for example, NATO's exercise Able Archer so concerned Soviet observers that high officials in Moscow ordered the KGB and other intelligence organs to watch U.S., British, and other Western capitals for telling movements of presidents, prime ministers, and other principals. During the Paris summit of 1960, infamous for Soviet Premier Khrushchev's

---

compared to alleged episodes of Pentagon or White House micromanagement in prior administrations.

decision to disrupt the proceedings after Soviet air defense shot down a U.S. U-2 reconnaissance plane, U.S. Secretary of Defense Thomas Gates decided to test the readiness of the U.S. military command-and-control system. For this purpose, he ordered a worldwide military alert for U.S. conventional and nuclear forces from a command post at a Paris residence, with the apparent approval of President Eisenhower and Secretary of State Christian Herter. The resulting Joint Chiefs declaration of a DEFCON 3 alert left U.S. military personnel and the Pentagon press office in a state of confusion. As the prominent Washington journalist Walter Lippmann noted, "The timing of the exercise was just a shade worse than sending off the U-2 on its perilous mission two weeks before the Summit."[68]

The nature of the work that military organizations do influences the assignment of tasks to organizational subunits and the degree of delegation of authority and discretion acceptable to top decisionmakers. For example, U.S. Army and Navy command-and-control expectations reflect differences in their operational environments. U.S. Navy ship captains are used to more autonomy and independence from higher authority than are commanders of ground force divisions. Within the navy, aviators, surface ship, and submarine crews each have a distinct organizational ethos and different normative expectations for appropriate behavior. U.S. Air Force pilots, like those in the armed forces of other countries, are surrounded with a special aura of derring-do and invincibility, as the legends of the Red Baron of World War I and the role model of "ace" in air combat attest. U.S. Marine Corps advertisements project a very discrete image of that organization and its officer corps. U.S. Army special operations units, including airborne or airmobile troops and Green Berets, attempt to stimulate a perception of special identity within a larger and more corporate army organizational framework.

Nuclear command-and-control organizations are highly specialized collections of civil and military personnel. Many parts of these organizations are coordinated through the sharing of information and expertise across normal bureaucratic channels. For example, organizations that are keyed for attentiveness to certain warning and threat indicators are coupled through infor-

---

68. Michael R. Beschloss, *Mayday: Eisenhower, Khrushchev, and the U-2 Affair* (New York: Harper & Row, 1986), 281. See also Scott D. Sagan, "Nuclear Alerts and Crisis Management," *International Security* (Spring 1985), in *Nuclear Diplomacy and Crisis Management*, ed. Lynn-Jones, Miller, and Van Evera, 159–99, esp. 162–65. According to Sagan, the military-readiness measures resulting from this decision and implemented on May 16, 1960, were not dangerous in themselves, but the visibility of the alert outside military channels, especially to the public and to the Soviets, was unexpected by the policymaker who approved it.

mation chains to other organizations tasked with the collection and prompt assessment of continuous intelligence streams. The surging of Soviet ballistic missile submarines from their home ports at Severomorsk or Petropavlovsk-Kamchatka during Cold War crises of the 1970s or 1980s would have reverberated immediately throughout the entire U.S. military command-and-control system worldwide. Other ambivalent indicators might or might not have provoked a heightened U.S. alert status. One unanswered question from years of U.S.-Soviet Cold War interaction is how sensitive each side's warning-and-intelligence indicators were to military movements, including heightened levels of alert for nuclear forces. The issue is difficult to resolve without further access to Soviet Cold War archives. For example, Khrushchev reports that during the Cuban missile crisis he raised the alert levels of all Soviet military forces, but U.S. analysts doubt this actually took place.[69]

According to David Holloway and Condoleezza Rice, Khrushchev may have decided against alerting his nuclear forces during the Cuban missile crisis for military-technical or political reasons. He may have doubted that Soviet forces could be maintained on high alert for more than a short period of time. Or Khrushchev may have feared that moving launch vehicles or mating them with warheads might have caused U.S. leaders to authorize a preemptive attack, based on an erroneous but justifiable expectation that the Kremlin was preparing to strike.[70] There was reason for Khrushchev's concern about one side's misperceptions of the other's intent. During the denouement of the crisis, Khrushchev received a telegram from his ambassador

69. Khrushchev contended after the Cuban missile crisis that the Soviet government had ordered the entire Soviet armed forces establishment, "above all the Soviet intercontinental and strategic rocket forces, the anti-air missile defense and fighter aviation of the PVO (Air Defense Forces), strategic aviation and the Navy" into a condition of full combat readiness. Khrushchev added that during the October 1962 crisis the Soviet submarine fleet, including "the atomic fleet," occupied "its appointed positions" (presumably assigned patrol or port stations from which firing would be authorized). Khrushchev, Pravda, December 13, 1962, and October 24, 1962, cited in Kurt Gottfried and Bruce G. Blair, Crisis Stability and Nuclear War (New York: Oxford University Press, 1988), 152, n. 19. Blair contends that the Soviets actually alerted at least some parts of their nuclear forces and command system in 1960, 1962, 1968, and 1973 concurrently with U.S. alerts. See Blair, The Logic of Accidental Nuclear War (Washington, D.C.: Brookings Institution, 1993).

70. Holloway and Rice, cited ibid., 129. See also Sagan, "Nuclear Alerts and Crisis Management," 189. Sagan reports that the Soviet Union announced on October 24, 1962, that its nuclear forces were being placed at a high state of readiness, and the claim was repeated by Khrushchev on December 13; CIA intelligence summaries for October 25 noted that "we still see no signs of any crash procedures in measures to increase the readiness of Soviet armed forces."

to Cuba, Aleksandr Alexeev, indicating that Alexeev had just conferred with Cuban Premier Fidel Castro. Castro allegedly had reliable information that the United States was going to invade Cuba within hours. The contention of Castro via Alexeev was supported by other Soviet intelligence sources, according to Khrushchev. Castro's response to this intelligence stunned the Soviet leader: the Cuban premier suggested that Khrushchev order an immediate preemptive strike against the United States.[71]

The problem of loss of control is more than one-dimensional, as incidents during the Cuban missile crisis and in other historical confrontations between opposed states make clear. There are at least three different kinds of loss of control that policymakers and academic analysts are discussing in their scholarly debates and personal memoirs. The first kind is the unpredictable character of interactions between interdependent choices. As Thomas C. Schelling has pointed out, the term "game" in the theory of games has a special connotation; it denotes something beyond the common sense of "game" as amusement. As Schelling explains, games are sequences of *interdependent* decisions taken by players whose interests are partly or totally opposed.[72] Not all applications of game theory require that the parties communicate directly with one another, but many interesting applications to international relations, including applications to deterrence and crisis management, do. Players in international bargaining games may also communicate by means of the moves they make and the decisions they take, as interpreted by the opponent. Regardless of the form of communication, important assumptions in international or other bargaining games are 1) that the "rationality" or logical consistency of choices by one side are at least partly dependent on what the other side does, and 2) that both sides *maintain a minimum interest in preserving the basic structure of the game* as opposed to making an "illegal" move which makes continuation of the game irrelevant. This second basic assumption of game theory is not spelled out as carefully or as often as the first by game theorists. For example, the bargaining of two teenage drivers playing the game of "chicken" assumes that neither really

71. Khrushchev, *Khrushchev Remembers: The Glasnost Tapes*, trans. and ed. Jerrold L. Schecter and Vyacheslav V. Luchkov (Boston: Little, Brown, 1990), 176–77.

72. Schelling, "What Is Game Theory?" in *Contemporary Political Analysis*, ed. James C. Charlesworth (New York: Free Press, 1967), 218–38; reprinted in *Approaches to the Study of Politics*, ed. Bernard Susser (New York: Macmillan, 1992), 318–46. See also Schelling, *The Strategy of Conflict*. A discussion of the Cuban missile crisis as a game of "chicken" is presented in Steven J. Brams, *Game Theory and Politics* (New York: Free Press, 1975), 39–47; the introduction to Brams's work offers a very concise explanation of what rationality means in the context of game theory.

prefers martyrdom, although each may be willing to run some unpredictable degree of risk such that "martyrdom" may result inadvertently from their interdependent driving decisions. In the film *Dr. Strangelove*, the decision by the Russians to create a Doomsday Machine without announcing its existence is tantamount to an "illegal" move which goes outside the existing game structure.

This first kind of loss of control is the probability that interactions between forces in a crisis situation will lead to a sudden and dramatic shift in expectations which was not intended by the governments responsible for controlling those forces. The problem in this instance is not illegal or unauthorized military action, but unexpected consequences from authorized actions. U.S. Navy antisubmarine warfare in the Caribbean during the Cuban missile crisis was authorized by President Kennedy. The rules of engagement by which U.S. ASW cruisers and other ships trailed suspected Soviet submarines had been approved by the president and the secretary of defense. The implications of applying ASW hunter-killer submarine search in this context were not entirely foreseeable, however. Soviet submarine captains and the Soviet political leadership had to make choices in responding to U.S. search procedures. Fortunately, no incident at sea resulting from U.S. ASW led to any acknowledged exchange of fire between U.S. and Soviet naval forces.

A second kind of loss of control results from changes in crisis management expectations such that at least one side is convinced that war is inevitable. The issue is no longer to maximize gains or to minimize losses within a stable bargaining context, but to prepare for war and, perhaps, to launch preemptive attack at the earliest possible moment. There are two variations of this change in expectations. The first occurs when one side becomes convinced that its opponent has already decided to attack; the only remaining choices for the second side are capitulation or preemption. The second variant of the "war is inevitable" scenario is the judgment by policymakers that war now is better than war later, and that the probability of war later is a near or absolute certainty. A judgment of this sort was made by Germany's leaders in the months preceding the outbreak of World War I. The German General Staff, concerned about the problem of a possible two-front war against France and Russia, feared that improved Russian mobilization capabilities subsequent to 1912 would make the tsar's empire harder to defeat in 1916 or 1917 than in 1914. This assessment of Russian competency led to the judgment by some civilian and military leaders in Germany that war sooner, with a higher probability of victory, would be better than war later with a lesser likelihood of prevailing. That such judgments lend themselves to self-fulfilling prophecies destructive of the peace is as apparent as the judgmental character of the decision that war is inevitable. War is actually inevitable only if at least one side has so decided and takes action on that assumption which provokes the other side into an irrevocable commitment.

A third kind of loss of control results from the inability of policymakers to control force operations during crises. This happens because modern military forces are complex organizations, the details of which cannot be known to high-level officials. This problem is related to but distinct from the problem of unexpected interactions between the forces of two or more states. In the present instance, the issue is the correctness of the understanding held by policymakers of the capabilities of their military organizations, of their operational norms and institutional ethos, and of the kinds of fault trees to which military and crisis decisionmaking in these organizations may be subject. The present concern is the intrastate coherence of policy and operations, although there is an obvious relationship with interstate communication of intentions.

An example is provided by the U-2 incident in 1960 which wrecked the Paris summit conference in May of that year. President Eisenhower had personally authorized U-2 flights since 1956 and approved their individual routes. He had approved the ill-fated Francis Gary Powers flight that left Adana, Turkey, on May 1, 1960, and was shot down near Sverdlovsk in the Soviet Union. But Eisenhower gave his approval for the Powers flight on the basis of two assumptions, relying on briefings from CIA managers of the U-2 program. First, Eisenhower believed that no pilot could survive the downing of a U-2 aircraft by a Soviet surface-to-air missile (SAM). Second, the president was told that the U.S. reconnaissance plane was equipped with a self-destruct device so that it could never be captured intact. In fact, both assumptions were erroneous, as the embarrassed president discovered in the aftermath of Powers's capture. Not only had Powers survived the crash, but much of his plane had been captured intact along with its roll of film. The "self-destruct device" turned out to be one that the pilot was required to activate, and it was a charge insufficient in power to destroy the entire plane. The CIA had simply assumed that any SAM hit on a U-2 would demolish completely such a lightweight aircraft; U-2 managers failed to consider the outcome of a *near miss* from a SAM.[73]

73. Stephen E. Ambrose with Richard H. Immerman, *Ike's Spies: Eisenhower and the Espionage Establishment* (Garden City, N.Y.: Doubleday, 1981), 279–92.

On October 27, 1962, a U.S. U-2 strayed into Soviet airspace over the Chukhotsk peninsula, located across the Bering Sea from Alaska. Sensitive to foreign aircraft penetration even under normal peacetime conditions, Soviet air-defense commanders scrambled fighter interceptors based on Wrangel Island to meet the "intruder." The U.S. pilot, who had accidentally lost his way on an air-sampling mission over the North Pole, requested assistance from U.S. air-defense fighters based in Alaska. The U.S. Air Force operations deputy to the Joint Chiefs of Staff during the Cuban missile crisis has reported the reaction of Secretary of Defense McNamara to the news of the U-2 "stray" as nearly hysterical: "The word came into the 'tank' where McNamara and the Chiefs were meeting. . . . He turned absolutely white, and yelled hysterically, 'This means war with the Soviet Union.' "[74] However, McNamara's reaction, if accurately reported, was not necessarily hysterical. Khrushchev complained about the U-2 stray in his letter of the following day, in which he agreed to remove Soviet missiles from Cuba. "One of your planes violates our frontier during this anxious time we are both experiencing, when everything has been put into combat readiness," wrote Khrushchev, adding that "an intruding American plane could easily be taken for a nuclear bomber, which might push us to a fateful step."[75]

U.S. military experts might scoff at the possibility that a U-2 reconnaissance plane could be confused with a B-52 bomber, but the stresses attendant to crisis management can influence the perceptions of leaders about the present in a way that renders their expectations about future states of affairs more pessimistic. For example, the Soviet shootdown of the Korean Air Lines 007 passenger jet on September 1, 1983, seemed incomprehensible to Western observers, who wondered how air-defense commanders could fail to distinguish the civilian aircraft from a military reconnaissance intruder. Therefore, the U.S. government initially charged the Soviet government with deliberately and cold-bloodedly destroying the airliner, regardless of the cost in innocent lives. However, information available to U.S. Air Force intelligence suggested that Soviet interceptors may have confused the large Boeing 747 with the smaller RC-135 U.S. military reconnaissance aircraft. The flight path of an RC-135 that evening did take it near the actual, although not reported, flight path of KAL 007 before the RC-135 returned to its base in Alaska. Soviet air defenses following the flight of the "intruder"

74. Lt. Gen. David A. Burchinal, "Oral History" (Carlisle Barracks, Pa.: U.S. Army Historical Institute), 114–15, cited in Sagan, "Nuclear Alerts and Crisis Management," 178.
75. Ibid., 179.

may have *expected* to see, as a result of this coincidence, a military reconnaissance aircraft for which standing rules of engagement called for a shootdown.[76]

Political relations between the Americans and the Soviets were very sour
at this time. The Reagan administration was pressing for modernization of
theater nuclear forces, including Pershing II ballistic missiles deployed in
West Germany which the Soviet leadership regarded as prompt threats to
command-and-control systems in the western military districts of the Soviet
Union. Reagan defense guidance for 1984–88 had called for capabilities to
fight a protracted nuclear war, and a U.S. "full-court press" against the Soviet Union on all diplomatic and military fronts was being advocated by
White House officials.[77] This atmosphere may account for some of the immediate reactions by American military officers in the Pacific, after having
been provided with summaries of National Security Agency cable traffic.
Some senior army and navy officers became "emotional," according to one
officer's report to the journalist Seymour Hersh. Several officers reportedly
began to consider provocative actions against the Soviet Union. According
to Hersh: "At least one reckless decision was made in the first twenty-four
hours [following the shootdown]. Six [U.S.] F-15 interceptors and an
AWACS electronics surveillance aircraft were temporarily assigned to Misawa
Air Base and ordered to orbit adjacent to Soviet territory near Sakhalin.
The unstated goal was to provoke an incident: the F-15 pilots were instructed
'to take advantage of the situation,' one officer recalled, in the event they
were challenged by Soviet SU-15 or MiG-23 interceptors. No one in Washington had cleared such instructions in advance, or knew of them."[78]

As Scott Sagan noted, the specific cause for the U-2 stray incident during
the height of the Cuban missile crisis has never been established with convincing certainty.[79] Although the official explanation of navigational error
has not been disproved, it is arguably insufficient as an explanation of the

76. Background on this incident is provided in Seymour M. Hersh, *"The Target Is De-
stroyed": What Really Happened to Flight 007 and What America Knew About It* (New York:
Random House, 1986), and Alexander Dallin, *Black Box: KAL 007 and the Superpowers*
(Berkeley: University of California Press, 1985).

77. For discussion of the political climate and its implications for KAL 007, see Oliver
Clubb, *KAL Flight 007: The Hidden Story* (Sag Harbor, N.Y.: Permanent Press, 1985). Although this work contains hostile prejudgments of Reagan administration motives, it provides
an interesting critique of the most widely believed explanation for the KAL 007 disaster: that
the Korean crew mistakenly programmed an erroneous flight path into their navigational com-
puters and followed it unknowingly to their doom.

78. Hersh, *"The Target Is Destroyed,"* 74.

79. Sagan, "Nuclear Alerts and Crisis Management," 180.

awkward *timing* of the U-2 flight. Policymakers obviously did not intend for any U-2 even to fly close to Soviet airspace during the intense negotiations to resolve the crisis. Sagan suggests the possibility that a local U.S. commander might have felt a last-minute need for up-to-date reconnaissance in case of an actual outbreak of war, although Sagan acknowledges that this is an "unlikely" explanation for this specific case.[80] The U-2 would not have been the aircraft of choice for the most plausible last-minute reconnaissance assignments, such as establishing the locations and frequencies of Soviet air-defense radars.[81] Regardless of the cause for the U-2 stray into Soviet airspace, it is important to note that Soviet air defenses acted on standing authority to intercept the intruding plane, and the U-2's call for assistance was responded to by U.S. fighter interceptors also following standard rules of engagement. A very dangerous incident could have followed from an accident compounded by *authorized* patterns of military response, well within the guidance laid down by higher-level U.S. and Soviet political-military leaders who did not anticipate a situation in which the limitation of prompt response would be as important as its guarantee.

Individual incidents of operations not in keeping with policy intent might be explained by the inevitable complexity of bureaucratic organizations, especially those dealing in advanced technology. The sociologist Charles Perrow has suggested that certain types of complex organizations involved with high-risk technology, such as nuclear power plants and space transportation systems, are logically and organizationally prone to "normal accidents."[82] Perrow's cases provide an interesting counterpoint to the often simplistic analyses that blame "human error" or technical component failure for systemic catastrophes; his argument is that there are decisionmaking pathologies built into the complexity of human–machine interactions in certain kinds of organizations. At the extreme, it may appear that the organization has lost control of itself.

Two examples of Cold War crisis management may provide illustrations of the appearance, if not the reality, that accountable government officials might have lost control over events. In the first instance, during the Cuban missile crisis Soviet Premier Khrushchev apparently concluded that a U.S. invasion of Cuba was imminent because President Kennedy had lost control over the U.S. military. Khrushchev, according to his memoirs, drew this

80. Ibid.
81. Ibid.
82. Perrow, *Normal Accidents: Living with High-Risk Technologies* (New York: Basic Books, 1984).

inference from his Cuban ambassador's reports to Moscow about Cuban intelligence findings that a U.S. invasion would take place within hours. At about the same time, Khrushchev received from his U.S. ambassador, Anatoly Dobrynin, a summary of Dobrynin's October 27 meeting with Robert Kennedy. Dobrynin, according to Khrushchev, was asked by Robert Kennedy to pass the message that President Kennedy wanted to resolve the crisis peacefully. However, the president feared that events were rapidly moving out of control; war might break out inadvertently owing to the logic of escalation and despite his best efforts to prevent it. Robert Kennedy explained to Dobrynin in this context that some of President Kennedy's military advisers were advocating stronger measures than the quarantine already imposed, and that advocates of escalation would soon carry the day in policy-making circles unless Khrushchev relented. The Soviet leader, seeing the U.S. system through his own dark fears, understood this not as a comment on the probable outcome of ExComm policy debates, but as a forecast by Robert Kennedy of military usurpation against his brother in favor of war.[83] Khrushchev's comment in his memoirs is quite explicit with regard to his recall of the gist of Dobrynin's report: "If the situation continues much longer, the President is not sure that the military will not overthrow him and seize power. The American army could get out of control."[84] There may be some selective recall in Khrushchev's recollections on this point, but even the possibility that during the most important crisis of the nuclear age a Soviet leader might have drawn the conclusion that the president had lost control to the military offers relevant speculative food for policy-relevant thought.

Another illustration of the potential for loss of control, in the form of "Who's in charge?" was the widely reported U.S. global military alert during the October War of 1973. A cease-fire sponsored by the United States and the Soviets broke down on October 24 along the Suez Canal, and the Third Army Corps of Egypt was faced with potential destruction. Egyptian President Anwar as-Sadat asked for U.S. and Soviet troops to enforce the cease-fire, and Soviet President Leonid Brezhnev sent a priority message to the Americans calling for the United States and the Soviet Union to "urgently dispatch" military forces from both states to Egypt. Brezhnev added in his message of October 24 that if the United States found it impossible to join with the Soviet Union in such an undertaking, the Soviet Union would be

83. Khrushchev, *Khrushchev Remembers*, trans. and ed. Strobe Talbott (Boston: Little, Brown, 1970), 498.
84. Ibid.

faced with the "necessity urgently to consider the question of taking appropriate steps unilaterally."[85] Members of the Washington Special Action Group (WSAG) were convened by Secretary of State Henry Kissinger to consider responses to Brezhnev's message, which U.S. leaders interpreted as an ultimatum.

Having received reports that Soviet airborne forces might begin to arrive in Egypt the next morning, WSAG members debated whether an alert of conventional forces only or a global military alert, including U.S. strategic nuclear forces, would be necessary to impress on Soviet leaders the U.S. determination not to permit Soviet military intervention in the Middle East.[86] The WSAG decided in favor of a global military alert including U.S. nuclear forces, and U.S. military commands worldwide were ordered to DEF-CON 3. U.S. officials transmitted to Soviet President Brezhnev the next morning a message which stated that any unilateral Soviet intervention in the crisis would have "incalculable consequences," a not very veiled reference to the risk of direct U.S.-Soviet fighting and possible escalation to nuclear war.[87] The U.S. DEFCON 3 alert and other measures were clearly intended as signals that the U.S. was willing to run an unknown risk of military confrontation with the Soviet Union, with the potential of any such confrontation for escalation into nuclear war.

Until we know exactly what Soviet leaders expected to gain from their threats of unilateral involvement to impose a cease-fire and rescue the Egyptian Third Army Corps it remains unclear whether the U.S. nuclear alert "worked." An airlift of thousands of Soviet troops to Egypt would almost certainly have involved the Soviets and the Israelis in a shooting war even if the Americans initially remained uncommitted to direct military action. The Soviets, then, would have faced the prospect of heavy losses by their airborne forces prior to any direct fighting with American reinforcements for Israel. Intervention would not necessarily have been an advantageous move for the Soviet leadership even if it had taken place in time to rescue the Third Army Corps. Soviet military intervention in the Middle East, even without provoking an immediate U.S.-Soviet military confrontation, would

85. Sagan, "Nuclear Alerts and Crisis Management," 183. See also Barry M. Blechman and Douglas M. Hart, "The Political Utility of Nuclear Weapons: The 1973 Middle East Crisis," *International Security* (Summer 1982): 132–56.

86. Sagan, "Nuclear Alerts and Crisis Management," 184.

87. Blechman and Hart, in "The Political Utility of Nuclear Weapons," suggest that the language of "incalculable consequences" was intended by Kissinger quite deliberately to suggest the possibility of inadvertent nuclear war, though not of any deliberate U.S. intention to initiate nuclear operations. See also Sagan, "Nuclear Alerts and Crisis Management," 186.

have wrecked détente and President Nixon's triangular diplomacy, whereby the United States sought to balance suitors for its favor in Moscow against those in Beijing. Nevertheless, the possibility cannot be excluded, given Brezhnev's apparent impression of Israeli noncompliance with the cease-fire and his obvious feeling that the United States supported Israel in this position, that Soviet and U.S. misperceptions could have resulted in a dangerous escalation of the war into a superpower crisis.

Thus, it remains an unfortunate historical note that President Nixon was not consulted by the WSAG prior to its decision to call a global DEFCON 3 alert, including the alert of strategic nuclear forces, as a means of signaling resolve to Moscow. Nixon was regarded as unavailable for consultation by the members of the WSAG, who believed that immediate action was necessary and who chose in the president's absence to include a nuclear alert in that action.[88] One can argue that they had to do something in response to Brezhnev's ultimatum, although it is far from obvious that the only responses open to them were military. Indeed, the WSAG also dispatched that evening a message to Sadat which caused him to drop his request for U.S. and Soviet intervention in favor of United Nations troops on October 25.[89] U.S. Soviet expert Raymond Garthoff cautions against attributing too much significance to the U.S. alert as a coercive measure that purportedly resolved the crisis. The United States and the Soviet Union, Garthoff argues, "shared fundamentally the same objectives" during the crisis of October 24–25: to obtain Israeli compliance with the cease-fire, previously sponsored by the United States *and* the Soviet Union, and to bring the fighting to a conclusion short of decisive defeat for *either* Israel or Egypt.[90]

In a technical and very legalistic sense, the actions of the Washington Special Action Group (actually a modified form of the National Security Council as it operated on October 24, 1973) did not amount to any loss of control by the U.S. government over military operations. Nor can it be convincingly argued that an unknown but very high risk of escalation was being run in a reckless manner. U.S. officials had information suggesting

88. White House Chief of Staff Alexander M. Haig judged the president "too distraught to participate in a preliminary discussion" of the Brezhnev message or the U.S. reaction. See Raymond L. Garthoff, *Detente and Confrontation: American-Soviet Relations from Nixon to Reagan* (Washington, D.C.: Brookings Institution, 1985), 378.
    89. Sagan, "Nuclear Alerts and Crisis Management," 187.
    90. Garthoff, *Detente and Confrontation*, 382. Of course, Kissinger's own diplomatic objective of excluding Soviet *political* influence from the postwar peace settlement was divergent from Soviet political objectives, but the U.S. desire to prevent Soviet *military* intervention was compatible with Soviet political aims in the crisis.

that Soviet nuclear forces were not being alerted, although alert levels for Soviet airborne divisions were raised and other indications of possible military intervention in Egypt were noted by U.S. intelligence. Despite the apparent lack of a two-sided nuclear alert and the evident congruity of goals between the political leaderships, the October 24–25 alert raises several questions about decision probity and government policy. First, President Nixon knew nothing about the decision and was not involved in it. He was not informed of Brezhnev's ultimatum until the next day. Second, the potential for escalation subsequent to the U.S. nuclear alert was serious, had U.S. efforts to make Israel comply with the U.N. cease-fire not worked. Third, Soviet and U.S. fleets in the Mediterranean during the crisis shadowed and targeted one another very dangerously. The possibility of an imminent outbreak of war as a result of an incident at sea was not trivial even without any immediate Soviet response to the U.S. DEFCON 3 alert.[91] The "good news" offsetting these concerns is that the U.S. nuclear alert system, like the system for nuclear retaliatory response, cannot be paralyzed by the unavailability or incoherence of the chief executive.

U.S. nuclear strategic planners after 1945 faced difficulties similar to those which Germany's strategic thinkers at the turn of the century had to confront. The prospect of a nuclear war, for American political leaders and strategic planners of the Cold War years, offered no acceptable linkage between the use of force and U.S. grand strategic objectives. Like Germany's Schlieffen Plan, U.S. nuclear war plans were exercises in making the best of a bad situation. Germany's strategic predicament on two fronts, by the paradoxical logic of military strategy, required Germany to prepare for aggressive operational-tactical moves in the earliest stages of a war. Despite the rhetoric of global power–oriented German theorists and the inflated reputation of the German General Staff, the strategic predicament of Germany in continental Europe was considerable in the event of any actual outbreak of war. In the same fashion, U.S. and Soviet strategic nuclear forces did not confer on them grand strategic (i.e., world policy) influence of the kind implied in the term "superpower." Strategic nuclear weapons conferred on the Soviet Union and the United States important advantages at the bargaining table during international crises, but the same weapons also brought them closer together in shared nuclear danger.

The Schlieffen Plan imposed a "usability paradox" on the Germans prior

91. Bouchard, *Command in Crisis*, 160–87.

to World War I. They could not threaten to wage partial war in defense of limited objectives in Central Europe. Germany's guarantee to Austria-Hungary against Serbia in 1914, in the expectation that subsequent action by Austria-Hungary against Belgrade could be localized, did not dampen the European crisis but helped to escalate it. U.S. nuclear war plans and the destructive power of nuclear weapons imposed a similar usability paradox on American policymakers during the years of Cold War. The history of U.S. nuclear strategic planning from the 1960s through the 1980s is a history of attempted escapes from the all-or-nothing character of war plans that were based on the expectation of a massive Soviet surprise attack and the requirement to deter such a contingency above all else. War plans oriented to the worst-case scenarios proved to be inflexible instruments for those U.S. presidents and Soviet leaders who sought usable options short of mutual assured destruction. Although theorists consoled themselves with the thought that war plans of such destructiveness were too terrible ever to be used, the result was that U.S. nuclear-crisis management proceeded on the basis of military improvisation tailored to fit the situation at hand. During the Cuban missile crisis the United States and the Soviet Union fortunately escaped the consequences of failed nuclear-crisis management, but both sides acknowledged a dangerous near miss. Subsequent Cold War arms control measures owed no small debt to the sobering confrontation of October 1962 and to the postcrisis recognition by U.S. and Soviet leaders that any plan for nuclear war owed more to Schlieffen than to Liddell Hart.

3

THE OPENING PHASE OF WAR

Balancing Readiness and Steadiness

The opening phases of a war can be the preliminaries to further and prolonged fighting, or those phases can provide a well-prepared surprise attacker with the opportunity for a rapid and decisive victory. Surprise attack is a gambler's strategy; despite the apparent high risks for high gains, surprise attacks frequently succeed. However, this success is contingent. Whereas surprise on a tactical or theater scale is quite common in the experience of modern armies, truly strategic surprise which denudes the opponent of all capacity for resistance is very rare. Since surprise attacks often turn into military and political stalemates, the aftermath of surprise often requires that diplomacy and war support one another in order for attacker and defender to make eventual arrangements for an acceptable peace settlement. However, fighting armies and wartime policymakers are often indifferent to the benefits of constrained fighting and military bargaining, trading in the bargaining chips of eternal hope for those of diplomatic and military subtlety.

This chapter considers the signals sent by war preparations for the initial period of military conflict as well as the messages sent, intentionally or not, by a state's warfighting strategy during that period. Preparedness for the opening phase of a war requires that leaders make painful choices among grand strategic options. A mobilization plan designed for deterrence by threat of prompt offensives may defeat itself by provoking other states to attack. Forward-leaning mobilization thus exacerbates the crisis security dilemma discussed in earlier chapters. On the other hand, counting on losing in the initial phase of a war, regrouping forces, and restoring disputed fronts can be costly, too, as the Soviet military-political leadership on whom this strategy was forced in June 1941 soon discovered. The Soviet reading of its military-historical experience will be compared in this chapter with other states' decisions in favor of "forwardist" or "rearwardist" grand strategies. Reference will also be made to some of the carry-forward dilemmas passed from Soviet military thinking and perceived geopolitical predicaments to the Russian General Staff.

THE INITIAL PERIOD OF WAR

According to Soviet military historians, the initial period of a war was the period of time from the commencement of hostilities until friendly forces were within grasp of their initial operational and strategic military objectives.[1] The authoritative study of S. P. Ivanov on this subject, published in

1. S. P. Ivanov, *Nachal'nyi period voiny: Po opytu pervykh kampanii i operatsii vtoroi mirovoi voiny* [The Initial Period of War: On the Experience of the First Campaigns of the Second World War] (Moscow: Voyenizdat, 1974), is an important reference and is available in the U.S. Air Force Soviet Military Thought series (Washington: GPO, n.d.). I am most grateful to John Yurechko, Defense Intelligence Agency, for the opportunity to read his draft manuscript on this topic, and to Jacob Kipp, Foreign Military Studies Office, U.S. Army Command and General Staff College, Ft. Leavenworth, Kansas, for helpful insights. The Soviet *Voenno-istoricheskii zhurnal* [Military-Historical Journal] covered this topic extensively. See, for example, Lt. Gen. A. I. Yevseev, "O nekotorykh tendentsiyakh izmenii soderzhaniya i kharaktera nachal'nogo perioda voiny" [On Certain Tendencies in the Changing Content and Character of the Initial Period of War], *Voenno-istoricheskii zhurnal*, no. 11 (November 1985): 10–20. See also A. A. Grechko et al., *Istoriya vtoroi morovoi voiny, 1939–1945* [History of the Second World War] (Moscow: Voyenizdat, 1974), 2:174–82 et pass., for a discussion of Soviet military doctrine from 1936 to 1939. For an appraisal of Soviet threat assessment between the two world wars, see John Erickson, "Threat Identification and Strategic Appraisal by the Soviet Union, 1930–1941," ch. 13 in *Knowing One's Enemies: Intelligence Assessment Before the Two World Wars*, ed. Ernest R. May (Princeton, N.J.: Princeton University Press, 1984), 375–424.

1974, was part of a broader Soviet military interest in the problem of threat assessment and the avoidance of surprise attack.[2] The initial period of war is a time during which a defender may suffer strategic losses that, if not blunted by a stout defense and routed by a counteroffensive, may leave its armies with no future options other than delaying actions. Traditional military theory posits that the initial period of war is a window of opportunity for well-prepared attackers and a window of vulnerability for unprepared defenders. Modern military technology, even apart from nuclear weapons, makes possible a reversal of this dogma: the "defender" may surprise the "attacker" during the initial period of war, especially if the defender is provoked by hostile declarations and suspicious military buildups on the part of the other side.

According to Lieutenant General M. M. Kir'yan, the initial period of war is "the time during which the belligerents [fight] with previously deployed groupings of armed forces to achieve the immediate tactical goals or to create advantageous conditions for committing the main forces to battle and for conducting subsequent operations."[3] Major General M. Cherednichenko noted in a 1961 article that prior to World War II, the initial period of war was defined in Soviet military theory according to World War I experience. This meant, according to Cherednichenko, the period from the official declaration of war and the start of social mobilization to the beginning of main battle force engagements.[4] Soviet planners, following this model, assumed that covering forces deployed in the border military districts were to fight the first phases of the defensive battle. Their mission was to cause attrition to enemy forces and to delay the enemy advance until the Soviet second-echelon forces counterattacked. During the interwar years, however, the widespread introduction into the armed forces of tanks, aviation, and other means of armed conflict "revealed a strong possibility of surprise offensives and the achievement of decisive aims at the beginning of war."[5]

2. For overviews of this issue, see Richard H. Phillips, *Soviet Military Debate on the Initial Period of War: Characteristics and Implications* (Cambridge, Mass.: Center for International Studies, Massachusetts Institute of Technology, November 1989), and Jacob W. Kipp, *Barbarossa, Soviet Covering Forces and the Initial Period of War: Military History and AirLand Battle* (Ft. Leavenworth, Kans.: Soviet Army Studies Office, n.d.).

3. Lt. Gen. M. M. Kir'yan, "Nachal'nyi period Velikoi Otechestvennoi voiny" [The Initial Period of the Great Patriotic War], *Voenno-istoricheskii zhurnal*, no. 6 (June 1988): 11–17.

4. Maj. Gen. M. Cherednichenko, "O nachal'nom periode Velikoi Otechestvennoi voiny" [On the Initial Period of the Great Patriotic War], *Voenno-istoricheskii zhurnal*, no. 4 (1961): 28–35.

5. Ibid., 29.

Kir'yan's article in the June 1988 *Voenno-istoricheskii zhurnal* [Military-Historical Journal] contends that Soviet military theory during the 1930s taught that a surprise attack with premobilized forces could "give the expected results only against a small state" and that, for an offensive against the Soviet Union, a definite time of mobilization, concentration, and deployment of the German main forces would be required.[6] Soviet military analysts have charged the political and armed forces leadership on the eve of war with errors in addition to the theoretical ones. Failures in the assessment of warning intelligence and the reluctance of the political leadership even to take sensible preparatory measures in the western border districts of the USSR allowed the Soviet defense to fall below adequate standards for readiness. This indictment of the Soviet armed forces high command and of Stalin personally was offered by A. M. Nekrich in his classic *1941 22 Iyunya* [June 22, 1941].[7]

Studies by Western specialists on the Soviet armed forces have supported much of Nekrich's verdict, if not all of his analysis in detail. John Erickson has noted the effects on the proficiency of Soviet command, in the early stages of World War II, of Stalin's purges of the armed forces' leadership from 1937 to 1939.[8] Much of the prewar theory of deep operations and mechanized-motorized warfare which had been pioneered in Soviet professional military writing of the 1920s and 1930s was forgotten in the aftermath of the military purges and had to be relearned in the hasty reorganization of Soviet defenses after June 22, 1941. Misinterpretation of the experience of the Spanish Civil War by the Soviet postpurge armed forces leadership created a hiatus with regard to the development of theory and force structure for large-scale offensive and defensive operations. Only after bitter disappointments in their war against Finland, and after having observed the successes of the Germans against Poland and France, did the Soviet high command turn to the practical reequipping and retraining of the armed forces for large-scale, mobile offensive and defensive operations. Unfortunately for the Soviets, they were caught in the midst of reorganization and reequipment, and their concept of the strategic defensive had not been carefully thought out.[9]

6. Kir'yan, "Nachal'nyi period Velikoi Otechestvennoi voiny," 13.
7. A. M. Nekrich, *1941 22 Iyunya* [June 22, 1941] (Moscow: "Nauka," 1965), in *June 22, 1941: Soviet Historians and the German Invasion*, ed. Vladimir Petrov (Columbia: University of South Carolina Press, 1968), 24–245. This source also contains excerpts from debates among Soviet military historians about the responsibility for Barbarossa.
8. John Erickson, *The Soviet High Command: A Military-Political History, 1918–1941* (New York: St. Martin's Press, 1962), 447–509.
9. Col. David M. Glantz, *Soviet Operational Art and Tactics in the 1930s* (Ft. Leavenworth, Kans.: Soviet Army Studies Office, 1990).

Former Soviet Premier Nikita S. Khrushchev, who was a member of the military council in the Kiev Military District, in the southwestern front, and at Stalingrad during the Second World War, places the blame for Soviet unpreparedness directly on the highest political and military leaders of the Soviet state: Stalin and the high command. According to Khrushchev's memoirs, the argument that the Soviet Union did not expect a German attack is without any logical or historical support: "no one with an ounce of political sense should buy the idea that we were fooled, that we were caught flat-footed by a treacherous surprise assault."[10] Khrushchev argues that Stalin knew exactly what fate Hitler intended eventually for the Soviet Union and its armed forces. Stalin hoped, according to Khrushchev, to buy time with the Molotov-Ribbentrop Pact (which temporarily aligned the Soviets and Germans from August 1939 until June 1941) in order to rebuild Soviet defense capabilities, including the military cadres decimated in Stalin's earlier purges.[11]

Failures of estimation with regard to the actual timing of Operation Barbarossa acted like compound interest, added to the incorrect anticipation of German operational methods. According to Major General V. Matsulenko, despite the availability of reliable information on German preattack troop concentrations, Soviet forces in the western military districts were not brought to a condition of proper combat-readiness.[12] Matsulenko notes several specific shortcomings. First, most of the first-echelon divisions of Soviet covering-force armies at the outbreak of war were located in training camps 8 to 20 kilometers from planned deployment lines. Second, comparatively few units were positioned directly adjacent to the frontier. Third, artillery and engineer units and signals subunits in certain armies were undergoing combat training in centers away from their parent formations. Fourth, the covering forces' second echelons, usually mechanized corps, were 50 to 100 kilometers from the border, and the district second-echelon and reserve forces were as far away as 400 kilometers.[13] Not all of this can be blamed on

10. Khrushchev, *Khrushchev Remembers: The Glasnost Tapes*, trans. and ed. Jerrold L. Schecter and Vyacheslav V. Luchkov; foreword by Strobe Talbott (Boston: Little, Brown, 1990), 49.
11. Ibid., 50–52.
12. Maj. Gen. V. Matsulenko, "Nekotorye vyvody iz opyta nachal'nogo perioda Velikoi Otechestvennoi voiny" [Certain Conclusions from the Experience of the Initial Period of the Great Patriotic War], *Voenno-istoricheskii zhurnal*, no. 3 (1984): 35–43. On Soviet failures to respond to warning, see Nekrich, *1941 22 Iyunya*, and Barton Whaley, *Codeword Barbarossa* (Cambridge, Mass.: MIT Press, 1973), chs. 3–5.
13. Matsulenko, "Nekotorye vyvody iz opyta nachal'nogo perioda Velikoi Otechestvennoi voiny."

Stalin's willful neglect of political and strategic warnings of Hitler's hostile intentions, warnings received from numerous foreign and some domestic sources.[14] Some of the lack of preparedness in the border districts resulted from the changed borders that occurred following the conclusion of the German-Soviet pact of 1939. Pushing the borders westward extended Soviet defensive lines over a broader front and required greater echelonment in depth for defense against a blitzkrieg. It also implied improvements in rear logistical support, aircraft survivability, and command and control (of which, more below), areas in which the Soviet forces were inadequately trained and equipped by June 1941.

Lack of combat-readiness in the western-border military districts forced the Soviet leadership into operations to restore the disrupted strategic defensive front during the first weeks of war. The dilemmas presented to Russian commanders were not unlike those which might recur in a modern version of Barbarossa in the 1990s.[15] Restoration of a disrupted strategic front required that the Soviet leadership rethink political and military command-and-control arrangements. For strategic leadership of the war on June 23, 1941, the Main Command Headquarters (Stavka Glavnogo Komandovaniya) was created, consisting of S. K. Timoshenko (chairman), K. Ye Voroshilov, V. M. Molotov, I. V. Stalin, G. K. Zhukov, S. M. Budenyi, and N. G. Kuznetsov. The Main Command Headquarters was subsequently transformed, on July 10, into the Supreme Command Headquarters (Stavka Verkhovnogo Komandovaniya), headed by Stalin and B. N. Shaposhnikov. On August 8 Stalin was named supreme commander-in-chief, and the headquarters was renamed Headquarters, Supreme High Command (Stavka, Verkhnogo Glavnokomandovaniya; or Stavka–VGK).[16] To ensure unity of political and military command, Stavka–VGK carried out activities under the direction of the Party (VKP–b; for All-Union Communist Party, Bolshevik) Central Committee and Politburo, and according to guidance laid down by the State Committee for Defense (GKO, also headed by Stalin).

The most important measures to repel the German aggression and to restore the broken strategic defensive front were discussed at joint sessions of members of the Politburo, GKO, and Stavka–VGK.[17] In order to improve

14. On this see John Erickson, "Threat Identification," in *Knowing One's Enemies*, ed. May, and Whaley, *Codeword Barbarossa*, passim.
15. For contemporary aspects of the initial period of war, see my "Intelligence, C3, and the Initial Period of War," *Journal of Soviet Military Studies* 3 (September 1991): 397–448.
16. See Maj. Gen. P. T. Kunitsky, "Vosstanovlenie prorvannogo stratigecheskogo fronta oborony v 1941 gody" [Restoration of the Disrupted Strategic Front in 1941], *Voenno-istoricheskii zhurnal*, no. 7 (1988): 53.
17. Ibid.

the effectiveness of command and control and to facilitate leadership of military actions of the wartime fronts by the Supreme High Command, the State Defense Committee approved the creation of three intermediate command-and-control organs on July 10. These intermediate organs were termed "main commands of troop directions (axes)," or *glavnyye komandovaniya voysk napravleniya*, and were established as northwestern, western, and southwestern axes headed respectively by Marshal of the Soviet Union (MSU) K. Voroshilov, MSU S. K. Timoshenko (from July 19, MSU Shaposhnikov; from July 30, Lt. Gen. V. D. Sokolovskiy), and MSU S. M. Budenyi (from September 1941, Timoshenko).[18]

These timely adjustments in command and control helped the Soviet armed forces to stabilize and to reestablish the strategic defensive across several fronts during the summer and autumn of 1941. The creation of large defensive groupings of forces that had not existed prior to war was accomplished by regrouping forces within fronts, by transferring units from one front to another, and by moving up strategic reserves from the interior of the USSR.[19] Of course, this was hard going during the initial weeks of war, when German command of the air disrupted lines of communication and support and forced Soviet units into battle under maldeployed and otherwise unfavorable conditions.

Even later, Soviet forces were not always prepared for a rapid shift from offensive to defensive operations. For example, when the German Army Group Center aimed at the Smolensk-Moscow axis shifted to the offensive for its final lunge at Moscow in late September 1941, it caught many of the defenders unprepared. A headquarters directive to Soviet forces on September 27 to halt their offensives in that sector and shift to defensive operations caught most commanders unprepared and with insufficient time to prepare terrain, to complete engineering work, and to reorganize formations for defensive battle.[20] Therefore, the Germans broke through the strategic defensive front and created a critical situation for the defense of Moscow. The Supreme High Command was forced to transfer units quickly from the northwestern and southwestern axes and to commit new strategic reserves against the thrusts of Army Group Center.[21] Within approximately one week the Soviets had organized what amounted to a new defensive configuration on the Moscow axis, contributing to the stalled German offensive of October.

18. Ibid., 54.
19. Ibid., 56.
20. Ibid., 57.
21. Ibid.

This success in slowing the advancing Germans along the Moscow axis also bought time for the establishment of a more favorable strategic defense of the Moscow axis by early November, including the forces of several fronts and of the Moscow Defense Zone which halted the German offensive at the gates of Moscow.[22]

A command-and-control challenge of equal seriousness confronted the Supreme High Command as early as June 1941, when the Soviets faced the need to conduct a general withdrawal of their decimated forces on the western strategic axis. It was clear to the Soviet leadership by June 25 that the main thrust of the German offensive was not against the southwestern axis (Kiev), as prewar planners under the influence of Stalin had assumed, but on the western axis long the line of Minsk-Smolensk-Moscow. Once this situation was clear, Stavka–VGK began to move forces of seven armies to restore the disrupted front and to reinforce the forces defending the Moscow axis. Between June 27 and July 10 the Soviets transferred five combined-arms armies (some 36 divisions) to the western front. An additional thirteen combined-arms armies (104 divisions and 33 brigades) were eventually sent there in order to reinforce the defense of the Moscow axis against the onslaught of Army Group Center.[23] The building of defensive structures and obstacles at rapid rates, together with the reinforcement of reserves from Supreme High Command and the transfer of forces from other fronts, allowed the Soviet defenders to effect a stubborn resistance against enemy attackers and to cause delay and attrition sufficient to force the German Army Group Center onto the defensive by the end of July.[24]

If the Soviet command system provided for some necessary adaptations to the strategic defensive, it has nevertheless been held by Soviet military historians for numerous shortcomings in the command and control of troops. For example, in 1988 Lieutenant General P. V. Maltsev authored an article in *Voenno-istoricheskii zhurnal* entitled "Who Is to Blame?"[25] Maltsev was commander of a machine-gun platoon in the 111th Rifle Division on the

22. Ibid.

23. Ibid., 57–58. See also Albert Seaton, *The Battle for Moscow, 1941–1942* (New York: Stein & Day, 1971).

24. Kunitsky, "Vosstanovlenie prorvannogo strategicheskogo fronta oborony v 1941 gody," passim.

25. Lt. Gen. P. Malt'sev, "Kto vinovat? . . . Nekotoryye voprosy organizatsii i osushchestvleniya upravleniya voyskami zapadnogo fronta nakanune i v nachal'nom periode voiny" [Who Is to Blame? Certain Questions on the Organization and Implementation of Troop Command on the Western Front on the Eve and in the Initial Period of War], *Voenno-istoricheskii zhurnal*, no. 10 (1988): 21–28.

northwestern front in June 1941. His article points to a number of shortcomings in the command-and-control arrangements for the defense of the Western Special Military District (later the western front).

Staffs were, according to Maltsev's account, deficient in numbers of personnel and in communications equipment. Even the district signals troops lacked regulation communications equipment. Communications with troops were based on permanent telephone and telegraph lines of the USSR People's Commissariat of Communications. This state wire network was organized according to a radial plan in which communications centers and lines were concentrated in large industrial and administrative centers. Thus, overhead communications lines along major rail and road arteries and communications centers in heavily populated areas were vulnerable to air interdiction and other kinds of attack.[26] Radio communications were inadequate for combat tasks; the training of radio operators in the district forces was inadequate. Military councils of the district and its armies had no concept of the speed with which a surprise attack could inflict devastating losses; they lacked skill in organizing and maintaining cooperation between various branches of troops, and they were restricted by a lack of initiative. Front command was prohibited by order of the people's commissar of defense from undertaking "provocative" actions, the term "provocative" being defined to include what most other armies fighting on the defensive would consider to be reasonable measures for self-defense.

Disruption of communications by enemy sabotage groups added to the confusion created by the complexity of code tables. Commanders often issued orders in the clear which were intercepted by the enemy, and many communications arrived too late for most formations to take up their required defensive positions on time.[27] The front commander issued combat orders, one after another, which failed to take into account the actual situation; the staff of the front did not know whether orders were actually reaching the troops.[28] According to Maltsev, loss of control over the troops and ignorance of the true state of affairs on the part of district commanders (who in turn were cut off from Supreme High Command for a considerable period) led to decisions that were "unrealistic and infeasible" as well as to an "absence of control over the execution of issued orders."[29]

Writing in the Military-Historical Journal in 1988, Major General Kunitsky

26. Ibid., 23.
27. Ibid., passim.
28. Ibid., 26.
29. Ibid.

asks how it could happen that the Soviet armed forces carried out a successful winter offensive in 1941–42 that pushed the enemy back from Moscow.[30] Yet, by mid-July 1942, the strategic initiative was again in enemy hands: German troops had achieved another breakthrough of Soviet strategic defenses and had placed the armed forces of the USSR in extreme jeopardy in the southwest, in the direction of Stalingrad and the northern Caucasus. (Three breakthroughs had occurred during offensives of the previous year's campaigns.) The standard explanation for the ability of the Germans to regain the initiative in 1942, writes Kunitsky, had been German superiority in forces. He rejects that explanation and presents statistics to support his case: to the effect that, in crucial levels of manpower and equipment, Soviet forces were not patently inferior to the German forces.[31] The main reason for the ability of the Wehrmacht to breach the Soviet defensive front once again, he argues, was miscalculation on the part of Stavka–VGK in the planning of the summer 1942 campaigns. The Supreme High Command overestimated the capabilities of the Soviet armed forces relative to the German forces on the basis of the successful offensives conducted by the Red Army during the previous winter. The Soviet General Staff had offered more pessimistic assessments of Soviet capabilities relative to those of the Wehrmacht, but they were not listened to.[32]

According to Kunitsky, Stavka–VGK also erred in its prediction of the direction of the main thrust of German forces at this time. Soviet military intelligence reported to the General Staff on March 18, 1942, that German troop movements indicated preparations for a spring offensive with its center of gravity on the southern sector toward Stalingrad and the northern Caucasus. Stavka–VGK judged instead that the Germans would probably launch their main thrust on the flank of Soviet Army Central Grouping, with the objectives being Moscow and the central industrial region of the USSR.[33] This mistaken prediction was not corrected until the pressure created by the German offensives forced rethinking at the end of June, when the Soviet

30. Maj. Gen. Kunitsky, "Esli oborona prorvana . . . k vosstanovleniyu prorvannogo strategicheskogo fronta oborony na yugo-zapadnom napravlenii" [If Defense Is Disrupted: On Restoration of the Disrupted Strategic Defensive Front on the Southwestern Direction], Voenno-istoricheskii zhurnal, no. 12 (1988): 3–10.

31. Ibid., 4.

32. Ibid. During the spring of 1942, Soviet forces had not yet developed the level of mastery with regard to strategic, operational, and tactical deception (maskirovka) that they would later acquire. See David M. Glantz, Soviet Military Deception in the Second World War (London: Frank Cass, 1989), 24.

33. Kunitsky, "Esli oborona prorvana," 2.

high command began the process of reorganizing the defensive fronts in the region. On July 12 the new Stalingrad front was established, including three reserve armies from Stavka–VGK.[34] In the northern Caucasus sector, the southern and northern Caucasus fronts were combined into a single northern Caucasus front on July 28. To ensure effective command and control in the Stalingrad sector, Stavka–VGK decided on August 5 to split the Stalingrad front into two independent fronts: the Stalingrad front (commanded by Lt. Gen. V. N. Gordov) and the southeastern front (commanded by Gen. A. I. Yeremenko). For operational purposes, the Stalingrad front was ordered to cover the city from the west and northwest and to defeat the enemy which had broken through the inner defensive perimeter at the boundary of the Twenty-first and Sixty-second armies. The southeastern front was to stop the German advance toward the southern face of the outer defense perimeter and to prevent the Wehrmacht in that sector from reaching the Volga, to the south of Stalingrad.[35]

Another aspect of military preparedness for the Second World War was how well the general staffs of the various armed forces understood the operational doctrines of potential opponents.[36] Intelligence must not only convey adequate "order of battle" data and indications of hostile intent, it must also establish how the opponent is going to fight if it comes to that. As Richard K. Betts and other experts on intelligence have pointed out, there is a great difference between adequacy of *warning* and effectiveness of *response*.[37] Between warning and response is the psychologically based but intelligence-driven "threat perception," which is highly subjective. Part of this threat perception is the military-operational doctrine according to which war plans will be carried out. For example, it makes a great deal of difference to potential defenders whether the opponent's strategy is one of blitzkrieg or of slow attrition.[38] Or, in nuclear strategy, it may matter whether selective and lim-

34. Ibid., 6.
35. Ibid.
36. The importance of this factor is stressed in Erickson, "Threat Identification."
37. Richard K. Betts, *Surprise Attack: Lessons for Defense Planning* (Washington, D.C.: Brookings Institution, 1982). See also Ariel Levite, *Intelligence and Strategic Surprises* (New York: Columbia University Press, 1987); Richard K. Betts, "Surprise, Scholasticism, and Strategy: A Review of Ariel Levite's *Intelligence and Strategic Surprises*," *International Studies Quarterly* 33 (1989): 329–43; and Levite's response to Betts in the same issue (pp. 345–49). Also see Michael I. Handel's *Perception, Deception, and Surprise* (Jerusalem: Leonard Davis Institute, Hebrew University of Jerusalem, 1976) and *War, Strategy, and Intelligence* (London: Frank Cass, 1989), esp. 229–81.
38. The point is explained in John J. Mearsheimer, *Conventional Deterrence* (Ithaca, N.Y.: Cornell University Press, 1983), ch. 2. I develop this point more fully in the last section of the present chapter.

ited attacks are planned in the initial phases of a conflict, regardless of whether the actual outcome of such a war was judged to be "winnable" by either side. Deterrence of nuclear attack might be affected by the expectations held by leaders about the willingness of either state to respond to limited attacks by selective rather than general retaliation.[39]

As Michael Handel has noted, a critical issue for students of surprise attack is the time lag between adequate attacker preparations for surprise assault and adequate defender preparations to meet the attack. The difference between attacker and defender preparedness for war is more complicated than the comparatively simpler issue of warning time. Warning may be given, but response (in the form of timely mobilization by the defender) may be delayed or postponed entirely.[40] Since surprise is rarely complete and total, defenders have usually begun *some* process of mobilization and response. The more precise question then becomes: How much mobilization, and how timely? Handel refers to the gap between the victim's preparations for war and the attacker's preparations as the "readiness gap." The ratio between the readiness gap and the defender's actual mobilization is therefore posited by Handel as a valid conceptual indicator of the effectiveness of a surprise attack.[41] Two exceptions to this rule deserve special note. First, a defender, having obtained irrefutable information of a forthcoming attack, decides to preempt even though his forces have not yet been fully mobilized. A second exception, which may occur during an extended crisis, happens when one side has won the race to mobilize fully but delays its attack, allowing the opponent time and opportunity to improve its own preparations. An example of the first kind of exception might be the Israeli attack on Egypt in 1967; for the second exception, one may find several examples during the July crisis of 1914.[42]

39. The case for limited nuclear options is argued by Albert Wohlstetter and Richard Brody, "Continuing Control as a Requirement for Deterring," ch. 5 in *Managing Nuclear Operations*, ed. Ashton B. Carter, John D. Steinbruner, and Charles A. Zraket (Washington, D.C.: Brookings Institution, 1987), 142–96. For counterarguments, see Robert Jervis, *The Meaning of the Nuclear Revolution: Statecraft and the Prospect of Armageddon* (Ithaca, N.Y.: Cornell University Press, 1989), chs. 2–3.

40. Handel, *War, Strategy, and Intelligence*, 238. For other cases and theory, see *Strategic Military Surprise*, ed. Klaus Knorr and Patrick M. Morgan (New Brunswick, N.J.: Transaction Books, 1983).

41. Handel, *War, Strategy and Intelligence*, 238.

42. Ibid., 239. See Richard Ned Lebow, *Between Peace and War: The Nature of Brinkmanship Crises* (Baltimore, Md.: Johns Hopkins University Press, 1981), on the nature of brinkmanship crises. Lebow finds a significant number of historical cases in which a state's commitment was challenged by another on the assumption that the first state would yield, an assumption that flew in the face of a great deal of information to the contrary.

Colonel General M. A. Gareev, then deputy chief of the Soviet General Staff, wrote in 1985 that Soviet military theory and operational plans on the eve of World War II gave insufficient attention to the proper conduct of the operational and strategic defensive. He noted that the "idea of the continuous shifting of war at its very outset to enemy territory (and the idea was unsound both scientifically and backed up neither by an analysis of the actual situation or by operational calculations) had so beguiled certain leading military workers that the possibility of conducting military operations on our own territory was virtually excluded."[43] This same assessment was offered by Andrei Kokoshin and Valentin Larionov in this discussion of the battle of Kursk as a model for the implementation of the doctrine of defensive sufficiency.[44] The authors do not dwell on the fact that Kursk was an example of very active defense, nor that it was based on the acquisition of very precise intelligence about the opponent's intentions. Kursk was also a case of an operational counteroffensive planned and conducted after war had been declared and fought for several years. Thus it provided little in the way of guidance for harried Russian or All-Union commanders who might be tasked to defend expansive borders on the basis of a force posture and military doctrine that excluded preemption or even active defense as an option.

DEFENSIVE MILITARY DOCTRINE: FROM SOVIET EXPERIENCE TO RUSSIAN UNKNOWNS

The withdrawal since 1990 of most Russian forces formerly deployed elsewhere to locations within the territory of the Russian Federation establishes a westward defensive perimeter that demands a mobile, active, and flexible defense. The same possibility of imminent vulnerability to border aggression will face the Russian republic whether it stands alone or serves as the nucleus for a Commonwealth of Independent States (CIS) as adhered to in December 1991 by eleven of the twelve republics remaining on the territory of the former Soviet Union. Denuclearization of Russia and the other republics,

43. M. A. Gareev, M. V. Frunze—Voyennyi teoretik [M. V. Frunze: Military Theorist] (New York: Pergamon/Brassey's, 1988), 208 (in English).
44. Andrei Kokoshin and Valentin Larionov, "Kurskaia bitva v svete sovremennoe oboronitel'noe doctriny" [The Battle of Kursk in View of Contemporary Defensive Doctrine], Mirovaya ekonomika i mezhdunarodnye otnosheniya, no. 8 (1987): 32–40.

should it come about, would only increase the emphasis on routine and active nonnuclear defenses. Such a defensive posture places extreme stress on
command-and-control systems and on the commanders who must operate
them. In addition, the further backward from Central Europe the western
Soviet defense perimeter is pushed, the more important it is to anticipate
correctly the intentions of the opponent and to limit the consequences of
any surprise attack. Territory between the state's own borders and a potential
attacker's borders performs a function in the deterrence of conventional warfare comparable to that performed by redundancy of weapon systems in strategic nuclear deterrence. Contiguous nonthreatening territorial zones, like
redundant basing systems for nuclear weapons, create additional time and
opportunity for defenders to rally their forces. Therefore, such territories
reduce the pressure on the defender to preempt if attack is feared.

Additional nuclear weapons, especially if they are survivable, also serve to
reduce the defender's sense of vulnerability to surprise and, therefore, contribute to stability. A complication with nuclear weapons, of course, is that
a state can overdo it, deploying so many weapons of such diversity that the
other side fears not only the loss of its first strike but also the loss of its
retaliatory strike. If this analogy has any validity, then Soviet defenders
pushed back into the territorial USSR will, in the event that a crisis develops
in which war seems possible, be more inclined to preempt than not. NATO
during the Cold War always felt that, from its perspective, the idea of a
NATO attack on the Soviet Union was inherently absurd. The difficulty is
that one can find in Soviet writing equally vehement insistence upon the
purely defensive character of their policies during the same period. Thus,
war would most likely have begun not with premeditated attack prepared
over many months, but during an intensifying crisis over a few weeks or days.

Control and combat stability are separate but related considerations for
Russian military planners and commanders in their assessment of what can
be accomplished under modern conditions, fighting from offensive or defensive strategic deployments. The operational configuration of tailored ground
and air units must be carefully thought out, and the coordination (*vzaimodeistvie*) among the various headquarters and force components thoroughly
rehearsed.[45] Control, according to authoritative Soviet military discussions,
had to be stable, continuous, efficient, and covert.[46] Stable (*ustoychivyi*)

45. On the concept of *vzaimodeistvie*, see *The Voroshilov Lectures: Materials from the Soviet
General Staff Academy*, Ghulam Dastagir Wardak, comp., and Graham Hall Turbiville, Jr., gen.
ed. (Washington, D.C.: National Defense University Press, 1989), glossary, 1:365, 380 (for
operational and strategic coordination, respectively).
46. V. G. Reznichenko et al., *Taktika* [Tactics] (Moscow: Voyenizdat, 1987), 94. The Soviet

command and control means that command and control must be conducted successfully regardless of enemy pressure, and continuous (*nepreryvnyi*) command and control signifies that control must be maintained without interruption. Efficiency (*operativnost'*) of command and control meant the "swift implementation of all troop command and control measures during preparation and in the course of battle in such a way as to forestall the enemy in operations."[47] Covertness was the requirement to disguise plans and to implement measures as diverse as limiting the number of persons privy to plans, maintaining secure communications, and establishing camouflage and deception measures.[48]

The "covertness" dimension of control implied active as well as passive deception measures. From the death of Stalin through the mid-1980s, Soviet military doctrine placed surprise among the most important principles of military art. An important component of surprise was deception, or *maskirovka*, an inclusive concept in Soviet military thought. According to Colonel David M. Glantz, who studied extensively the Soviet use of deception in World War II, Soviet military theorists contended that surprise could be achieved by one or more of the following methods:

- misleading the enemy with regard to one's intentions;
- maintaining the secrecy of one's plans;
- concealing combat preparations;
- using new weapons, techniques, and forms of combat;

---

frame of reference with regard to the theory of military art and strategy, relative to command and control, is entirely different from the American or Western. See A. S. Milodov and V. G. Kozlov, *Filosofskoe nasledie V. I. Lenin i problemy sovremennoy voiny* [Philosophical Heritage of V. I. Lenin and Problems of Contemporary War] (Moscow: Voyenizdat, 1972), trans. in U.S. Air Force, Soviet Military Thought series (Washington, D.C.: GPO), 45–47, 106–7, 110–16, 126–27; *Osnovy teorii upravleniya voyskami* [Fundamentals of the Theory of Troop Control], ed. P. K. Altukhov (Moscow: Voyenizdat, 1984); D. A. Ivanov, V. P. Savel'yev, and P. V. Shemanskiy, *Osnovy upravleniya voyskami v boyu* [Fundamentals of Troop Control in Battle] (Moscow: Voyenizdat, 1977); Stephen M. Meyer, "Soviet Nuclear Operations," ch. 17 in *Managing Nuclear Operations*, ed. Carter, Steinbruner, and Zraket, 470–531; and John G. Hines and Phillip A. Petersen, "The Changing Soviet System of Control for Theater War," *International Defense Review* 3 (March 1986), revised in *Soviet C3*, ed. Stephen J. Cimbala (Washington, D.C.: AFCEA International Press, 1987), 191–219. An updated and revised version of the Hines-Petersen study appears in *The Soviet Challenge in the 1990s*, ed. Cimbala (New York: Praeger, 1989), 65–120. Much of the Soviet literature is well traced in *Soviet Defense Notes*, a publication of the Soviet Security Studies Working Group, headed by Stephen M. Meyer at MIT.

47. Reznichenko et al., *Taktika*, 96; see also 94–95.
48. Ibid., 97–98.

- choosing correctly the direction of the main blow and correctly timing its delivery;
- the surprise use of all types of forces, especially air, artillery, and armored forces;
- maneuvering rapidly and acting decisively to forestall enemy responses;
- using fraudulent structures, communications, or other means for deception (e.g., dummy weapons, false communications);
- using effectively the terrain, weather, and seasonal factors.[49]

According to Glantz, *maskirovka* applied directly to five of these nine conditions and affected all of them indirectly. One implication for Cold War Soviet planners was that the command and control of friendly forces, including the initial organization of forces, must be concealed to the extent possible. Demonstrations, simulations, and diversionary attacks could confuse enemy intelligence about the choice of a primary attack sector. Disinformation (*dezinformatsiia*) exploits enemy perceptions of one's own capabilities and intentions.[50] Disinformation, in this context, might allow the Russian or All-Union leadership to exploit divisions within an opposing coalition whose members lacked consensus on goals or methods.[51]

The Soviet General Staff analysis of the successful counteroffensive at Stalingrad, beginning November 19, 1942, and resulting in encirclement of the German Sixth Army, attributed high significance to surprise and deception as components of a successful operational plan. The enemy, according to General Staff assessments, underestimated the strength of the Red Army and overestimated its own strength; it was demoralized by the great scope of the Soviet counteroffensive, especially by the deep penetration of Soviet mobile forces into the strategic rear of the German forces. The Stalingrad counteroffensive proved to Soviet planners that surprise could be achieved, and secrecy maintained, even during a period of long penetration and for an operation conducted over several fronts. Among the most important factors identified by Soviet analysts in the aftermath of their success at Stalingrad were these: informing only a small number of persons about the planning for

49. Glantz, *Soviet Military Deception in the Second World War*, 583. Glantz draws extensively on M. M. Kir'yan, *Vnezapnost' v Nastupatel'nykh Operatsiyakh Velikoy Otechestvennoy Voyny* [Surprise in Offensive Operations of the Great Patriotic War] (Moscow: "Nauka," 1968). For a typology of deception, see Handel, *War, Strategy, and Intelligence*, 315; Handel's entire chapter on this topic is very useful.
50. Glantz, *Soviet Military Deception in the Second World War*, 584.
51. Ibid.

the operation; concealing troop concentrations and means of reinforcement, including the limitation of many movements to nighttime; maintaining radio silence in attacking units; preserving scrupulous headquarters security; advance probing of the entire front by shock detachments in order to establish potential areas of vulnerability; and assigning missions orally wherever possible.[52]

Of particular importance in any future war, according to Soviet assessments of their experience in the Great Patriotic War, would have been Soviet efforts to deceive potential opponents with respect to their preferred method for initiating hostilities. For example, an enemy might be led to believe that mobilization of the Soviet military machine and economic base for war required considerable time. Instead, measures would be implemented to prepare forces for war without depending upon massive and highly visible general mobilization. New technical means might be used to rapidly and secretly reinforce selected forward-deployed forces. Another approach to mobilization without detection could have exploited Soviet and Russian experience in generating new units from existing "cadre"—skeletal units which are kept in standby status with only portions of their necessary wartime equipment and personnel available in peacetime.[53] Wartime force strength and operational configurations might not have been apparent from the Soviets' peacetime deployment and organization of their ground and tactical-air forces during the Cold War years, according to expert Western analysts. Peacetime force structure might have performed administrative and *maskirovka* functions. Forces could have been rearranged on a geographic or functional ("operational configuration," or *operativnoe postroenie*) basis during the period immediately prior to war or in the initial period itself. An example given by Glantz is that prior to the dissolution of the Warsaw Pact, the nineteen-division Group of Soviet Forces, Germany (GSFG) was expected by Western intelligence to produce a single wartime front (roughly comparable to a NATO army group). In fact, with minimum reinforcement and with resubordination of units on a more logical geographic or functional basis, the GSFG during the early and middle 1980s could actually have formed two fronts, each having at least three armies.[54]

52. Ibid., 130–31. See also B. V. Panov, V. N. Kiselev, I. I. Kartavtsev et al., *Istoriya voyennogo iskusstva* [The History of Military Art] (Moscow: Voyenizdat, 1984), ch. 7, pt. 2, on the Stalingrad counteroffensive.

53. Glantz, *Soviet Military Deception in the Second World War*, 584–85. See also Christopher N. Donnelly, *Red Banner: The Soviet Military System in Peace and War* (Alexandria, Va.; Jane's Publishing Co., 1988), ch. 8, 135–70.

54. Glantz, *Soviet Military Deception in the Second World War*, 586.

Military deceptions can be active or passive and can be directed at misleading the opponent with regard to a state's capabilities or intentions.[55] Many actions that Western analysts have classified as deception fell into very distinct programs in Soviet Cold War intelligence policy and were therefore the responsibility of different security organizations. These Soviet activities included *maskirovka*, counterintelligence, and active measures.[56] *Maskirovka* was the kind of deception most directly applicable to Soviet military planning; it included camouflage, cover and denial of information to the opponent, as well as active and passive efforts to deceive him.[57] *Maskirovka* was applied at the strategic, the operational, and the tactical level of Soviet military planning; at all levels it supported the objectives of 1) protecting the secrecy of Soviet planning and operations and 2) disorienting the enemy with regard to Soviet intentions and capabilities.[58] As Michael Handel has noted, the success of deception operations, especially complicated ones, depends upon the slow and persistent creation of misleading images and expectations in the mind of the opponent. Therefore, successful deception requires that sufficient time be permitted for the various threads to be brought together by the enemy's own intelligence services. In addition, deception operations cannot be designed with excessively redundant, and thus self-defeating, complexity. The image that deceivers want to implant must arise

55. Types of deception are discussed in Handel, *War, Strategy, and Intelligence*, ch. 7. See also *Knowing One's Enemies: Intelligence Assessment Before the Two World Wars*, ed. Ernest R. May (Princeton, N.J.: Princeton University Press, 1986), 503–42, for May's summary of intelligence failures in estimating capabilities and "proclivities."

56. Richards J. Heuer, Jr., "Soviet Organization and Doctrine for Strategic Deception," ch. 2 in *Soviet Strategic Deception*, ed. Brian D. Dailey and Patrick J. Parker (Lexington, Mass.: Lexington Books, 1987), 21–54. See also, in the same volume, John J. Dziak, "Soviet Deception: The Organizational and Operational Tradition," 3–20; Richard H. Shultz and Roy Godson, *Dezinformatsia: Active Measures in Soviet Strategy* (New York: Pergamon/Brassey's, 1984). According to Ladislav Bittman, Soviet intelligence agencies distinguish three types of "special operations," which U.S. analysts would call "active measures": disinformation, propaganda, and influence operations. See Bittman, *The Deception Game* (New York: Ballantine Books, 1972), 19 et pass. Also see the essays in *Strategic Military Deception*, ed. Donald C. Daniel and Katherine L. Herbig (New York: Pergamon Press, 1982), esp. the chapter by Earl F. Ziemke.

57. Heuer, "Organization and Doctrine for Deception," 42.

58. Ibid., 43; Glantz, *Soviet Military Deception in the Second World War*, notes that the Soviet experience in World War II demonstrated to Soviet planners the essential unity of all types of deception at the tactical, operational, and strategic levels (p. 559ff.). Strategic deception may be a special case on account of the high stakes and involvement of senior-level policymakers; see Handel, *War, Strategy, and Intelligence*, ch. 8, on strategic and operational deception, esp. his discussion of the strategic and operational deception plans by Gen. Edmund Allenby in Palestine in 1917 and the similarity of the latter to successful World War II deceptions (pp. 366–67).

"naturally" in the course of the victim's intelligence collection and estimation.[59]

The importance of strategic and operational deception in wartime operations was demonstrated, according to Soviet military historians, by the successful carrying out of the 1945 strategic operation in the Far East against Japan's Kwantung Army. This operation was a triumph over significant obstacles to the timely regroupment of forces, to the logistical support of forward, fast-moving tactical elements in battle, and to the command and control of a multifront operation .that was partly dependent for its success on deceiving the Japanese as to the exact timing and method of attack.[60] In order to accomplish their objective of defeating the Kwantung Army and preventing any of its elements from withdrawal outside of Manchuria, the Soviets were required to use the combined forces of three fronts on widely separated axes over a frontage of more than four thousand miles. The main thrust was launched by forces of the Transbaikal front, which was required to move four all-arms armies and a tank army across the Great Khingan mountains. Planning for the Manchurian offensive began in March 1945, and a major regroupment of forces from Europe to Asia took place from May through July of that year.[61]

59. Handel, *War, Strategy, and Intelligence*, also notes: "During the shorter wars of the future, deceivers may not have the time to implement intricate deception operations; instead, cover plans will have to be prepared *before the outbreak of war in order to be used in its initial stages and may be much more difficult to apply at later stages*" (p. 387).

60. My discussion of the Manchurian operation is derived from David M. Glantz, *August Storm: The Soviet 1945 Strategic Offensive in Manchuria* (Ft. Leavenworth, Kans.: Combat Studies Institute, February 1983); Lilita I. Dzirkals, *"Lightning War" in Manchuria: Soviet Military Analysis of the 1945 Far East Campaign* (Santa Monica, Calif.: Rand Corp., 1976); Glantz, *August Storm: Soviet Tactical and Operational Combat in Manchuria, 1945* (Ft. Leavenworth, Kans.: Combat Studies Institute, June 1983); and Peter H. Vigor, *Soviet Blitzkrieg Theory* (New York: St. Martin's Press, 1983), 102–21. Important Soviet sources include Ivanov, *Nachal'nyi period voiny* [The Initial Period of War], ch. 12, and Panov, Kiselev, Kartavtsev et al., *Istoriya voyennogo iskusstva*, ch. 9.

61. Glantz, *August Storm: The Soviet 1945 Strategic Offensive in Manchuria*, ch. 1. According to S. P. Ivanov, editor of the highly regarded *Initial Period of War* and chief of staff of the Soviet Far East Command in August 1945, the Transbaikal front had four combined-arms armies, a tank army, a group of Soviet-Mongolian troops, an air army, and an air-defense army in addition to reinforcement formations and other support. Its total complement included 654,000 men, 7,000 guns and mortars, 2,416 tanks and self-propelled guns, 1,360 antitank guns, 601 antiaircraft guns, 583 rocket launchers, and 1,334 aircraft. See Ivanov, *The Initial Period of War*, U.S. Air Force Soviet Military Thought series (Washington, D.C.: GPO, 1986), 250. The Far East Command structure and order of battle are given by Glantz, *August Storm* (February 1983), 199–213. In addition to the forces of three fronts, the Soviets also employed maritime forces from the Amur Flotilla and the Pacific Fleet. Operational statistics, including

The massive regroupment of Soviet forces prior to launching the Manchurian operation also required a major change in previous wartime command-and-control practices. Both the regroupment and the command-and-control arrangements had to be concealed from Japanese intelligence until the moment of truth. Already by 1944, Soviet experience in World War II had demonstrated an ability to conduct operations over several fronts and multiple axes of advance, under the coordination of Stavka representatives dispatched by Stalin to the various theaters of operation. Planning for the offensive against the Japanese in Manchuria soon revealed, however, that an innovative arrangement in the command system would be required for the Far Eastern theater.

Thus, a Far Eastern theater headquarters was established under Marshal A. M. Vasilevskii, who was responsible for all land, air, and sea operations in the Far East and Transbaikal regions.[62] The Far East high command carried out a plan to defeat the Kwantung Army by a strategic "Cannae," or envelopment using three fronts, each assigned a strategic axis of advance: the Transbaikal front, on the Transbaikal-Manchurian axis; the Second Far Eastern front, on the Amur-Manchurian axis; and the First Far Eastern front, on the Maritime-Manchurian axis. The forces of the Transbaikal front were to advance rapidly against major Japanese defensive bastions, including Mukden, and eventually to link up with the forces of the First Far Eastern front to complete the encirclement.

From the point of view of Soviet strategic and policy objectives, it was important not only to defeat the remnants of the Kwantung Army in Manchuria, but to do so quickly and decisively. Accordingly, deception planning

the width of attack frontage, depth of advance, and tempo of advance for the three main fronts of the Soviet attack in Manchuria, are enumerated in Glantz, *August Storm*, 215–16 and 44–47. Chief of Staff of the Transbaikal front, Gen. M. V. Zakharov, has written extensively about the Manchurian campaign; see *Final: istoriko-memuarny ocherk o razgrome imperialisticheskoi iapony v 1945 gody* [Finale: A Historical Memoir Record of the Rout of Imperialist Japan in 1945], ed. Zakharov (Moscow: "Nauka," 1969).

62. Glantz, *August Storm* (February 1983), 39, and Dzirkals, "*Lightning War*," 38–39 and app. A. Dzirkals notes that the position of Far East commander-in-chief was not officially created until July 30, 1945, "after Vasilevskii's first weeks on location had proven that his authority as Stavka representative was insufficient" (p. 39). As we have seen, in the earliest stages of the war against Germany (June–July 1941) Soviet forces in the west were organized into three large fronts, which were de facto theater commands. These commands were subsequently broken into smaller commands, which became directly subordinated to the Stavka, Supreme High Command, and the Soviets did not return to the early system until the closing stages of the war. See Dzirkals, "*Lightning War*," 38, and Gen. of the Army S. Shtemenko, "Triumph of Soviet Military Strategy," *New Times*, no. 18 (May 1975): 5, cited by Dzirkals.

had to allow for the unprecedented regrouping and concentration of forces ("the largest regrouping of forces in history," according to S. P. Ivanov, who as chief of staff of the Soviet Far East Command in August 1945 is understandably enthusiastic).[63] In any case, it cannot be denied that the movement of equipment and supplies from the European to the Far Eastern theater of operations covered a distance of 9,000 to 12,000 miles, over rail and road networks that were far from optimal for the purpose. This redeployment doubled the strength of Soviet forces in the Far East within a few months, from a previous forty divisions to more than eighty. According to David M. Glantz:

> The movement of men and material eastward involved constant use of screening, cover, and secrecy. The Soviets relied heavily on night movement to deceive the Japanese as to the grand scale of redeployment. Use of assembly areas remote from the border masked attack intentions, but ultimately required units to move to the attack in August over a considerable distance. Many high ranking commanders moved into the theater under assumed names and wearing the rank of junior officers. While the sheer size of Soviet movements made them impossible to mask, deceptive measures obscured the scale of Soviet redeployments and caused the Japanese to underestimate the Soviet ability to attack.[64]

The importance of the Manchurian campaign for the present-day student of deterrence and defense policy lies in several areas. First of all, it illustrated the importance of the use of surprise, decisively exploited and followed up, as a component of a successful strategic offensive operation. S. P. Ivanov, noted Soviet military theorist and chief of staff of the Far East Command, underscored this in his research. The Far Eastern campaign against Japan, he noted, was "truly one of blitzkrieg warfare" which had a "decisive influence" on the Japanese decision to end their participation in World War II (more decisive, according to Ivanov, than the dropping of the atomic bombs by the U.S. at Hiroshima and Nagasaki).[65] In addition, the study of the Far East campaign contributed a great deal to the development of the modern Soviet art of war from the end of World War II to the latter 1980s.

One lesson, according to Ivanov, was that surprise "was a decisive factor

63. Ivanov, *Initial Period of War*, 253.
64. Glantz, *August Storm* (February 1983), 4.
65. Ivanov, *Initial Period of War*, 261.

in achieving rapid success in the campaign," as was the ability of the Soviet high command to keep secret the plans for the offensive, the time of launching the attack on Japanese forces, the main strategic directions of attack, and the composition of the attacking Soviet forces.[66] A second lesson from the Manchurian campaign, perhaps more profound, was that an essentially rearward-looking mobilization posture in a major theater of military action can be turned rapidly into a forward-leaning capability for rapid and decisive first strike. As studies by Handel and other experts on military surprise have shown, surprise does not need to be total to strategic (i.e., politically or militarily decisive) in its effects.[67] Historical cases of surprise also show that the weaker side can exploit the vulnerability of the stronger to overconfidence. Finally, the defender can surprise the attacker, by moving more rapidly than thought possible from an essentially defensive posture to a potentially offensive one. Strategic nuclear weapons make this transition from defensive/nonthreatening to offensive/threatening postures possible within minutes, as is widely acknowledged. Less widely acknowledged is the possibility of doing the same, over a longer period, with conventional forces, especially if one side has the historical experience and military art as incentives to try.

Given the vastness of Russian and allied CIS territory, the most active defense using a variety of means for stopping attackers from more than a single direction will have self-evident appeal for some military planners. According to Major General A. S. Kulikov and Major General A. D. Nefedov, writing in the March 1990 issue of *Voennaia mysl'* [Military Thought], the experience of the Second World War proved that a major enemy offensive could be halted only by a defensive operation using both positional and maneuver elements and with the involvement of several fronts.[68] The same authors ask how positional and maneuver operations would be correlated in a

66. Ibid.

67. Handel, *War, Strategy, and Intelligence*, 234, notes that modern technology has offsetting effects both on the surpriser and the intended victim. Familiarity with blitzkrieg tactics together with photographic and electronic reconnaissance aid defenders and reduce the probability of surprise, especially surprise "out of the blue." On the other hand, nuclear weapons and high-technology conventional weapons make it theoretically possible for one side to win a decisive victory within minutes. The balance is not entirely equal, however: despite technology favoring the defense, the basic problems of surprise are not technological, but psychological and perceptual. See also Handel's chapter on "Technological Surprise in War," 131–83 in the same volume, and his comments in the introduction to *Clausewitz and Modern Strategy*, ed. Handel (London: Frank Cass, 1986).

68. Maj. Gen. A. S. Kulikov and Maj. Gen. A. D. Nefedov, "Position and Maneuver Actions: Role and Place in Defensive Operations," *Voennaia mysl'*, no. 3 (1990): 23–31.

modern defensive operation, assuming "that the attacking side conducts military actions according to the concept of air-land operation (*vozdushno-nazemnaia operatsiya*) or engagement (*srazhenie*)."[69] This means that Russian or allied CIS defenders could expect to face deep conventional firepower, the results of which the attacker would attempt to exploit rapidly by airmobile and airborne operations and by armored force groupings. The attacker's objective would be to split the defender's combat formation and disrupt the integrity of the defense, in order to defeat the defender's first echelon and advancing reserves by preventing the successful coordination of their efforts.

Positional aspects of a defense under these conditions, according to Kulikov and Nefedov, can hardly be separated from the maneuver aspects. The defender must at all costs prevent the attacker from penetrating the tactical defensive zone and linking up the efforts of those forces operating from the front with those at the rear of the defender.[70] The positional stability (*ustoichivost'*) of the defense presumes active maneuver, the importance of which for improving the positional stability of defenses is increasing.

Maneuver is also the basis for the defender's preparation and conduct of counterattacks and counterthrusts, according to Kulikov and Nefedov. However, they caution that training exercises in the Soviet armed forces had excessively stylized counterthrusts and counterattacks. Counterattacks are not always advisable. They should not be undertaken when there is a significant risk of their resulting in unjustified losses and disruption of the defense. Such an unfavorable outcome for the defender is likely if the attacker has been able to premobilize a large superiority (say five- or sixfold) over the defender on the selected axes of attack prior to the outbreak of war. It may be more expedient under some conditions for the defender to forgo counterattacks, hold stubbornly to defensive positions, and inflict damage by using reserve and second-echelon forces from preplanned lines of firing positions.[71]

Several principles concerning the relationship between position and maneuver aspects of defensive operations, current and future, are deduced by Kulikov and Nefedov. These principles may influence the kinds of defensive operations that Russian or CIS forces can expect to have to conduct in the early stages of any conflict in which they are forced to fight on the defensive, at least initially. First, maneuver is the basis for the successful conduct of counterstrikes and counterattacks. Second, the activeness of contemporary

69. Ibid., 27.
70. Ibid., 28.
71. Ibid., 29.

defense is mainly determined by the maneuverability of the delivery of conventional firepower. This changes the nature of counterattacks: combined-arms forces must now take maximum advantage of a curtain of mobile firepower in order to accomplish their missions. Third, securely holding the tactical zone of defense is of decisive importance "especially in the initial period of war," and for this to be accomplished "troops must optimally combine position and maneuver warfare, and the fundamental aim of maneuver actions is seen as ensuring the stability of the defense."[72]

The discussions by Kulikov and Nefedov contribute some insight to the problem of using position and maneuver under modern conditions on the defensive, and they further explicate some of the conditions under which Kokoshin and Larionov's most offensively constrained options might be viable. However, substantial uncertainty remains about whether the political aspects of any defensive military doctrine, emphasizing nonprovocation of potential adversaries over the robustness and promptness of any prepared retaliatory strike, can be fully reconciled with the inclination of professional officers to engage in decisive counterattacks and counteroffensives immediately after blunting the attacker's first thrusts.

POLITICS, ARMS, AND RESTRUCTURING THE ARMED FORCES

In an article in the December 1989 issue of the theoretical Party journal *Kommunist*, then Soviet defense minister and subsequent coup plotter Dmitri Yazov set down his view of a change in the relationship between the political (or sociopolitical) and military-technical levels of Soviet military doctrine.[73] Yazov acknowledged that a contradiction has marked the past development of Soviet military doctrine: a contradiction between its political and its military-technical aspects. If in its political aspects military doctrine was always defensive, stipulating the rejection of military attack on anyone at all, on the military-technical plane reliance was placed on "decisive offensive actions" in the event a war was unleashed against the Soviet Union and its

72. Ibid.
73. D. T. Yazov, "Novaya model' bezopasnosti i vooruzhennye sily" [A New Model of Security and the Armed Forces], *Kommunist* 18 (December 1989): 61–72.

allies. It was also assumed that, the higher the capability of the Soviet armed forces for such actions, the more solid the defense and the less likely an attack by the enemy. Eventually this resulted in a contradiction that had to be acknowledged and resolved; the defensive thrust of the political aspect of military doctrine was in contradiction, according to Yazov, with its military-technical emphasis on offensive action. Therefore, "in the contemporary contents of our doctrine, brought into action in 1987, this contradiction is completely eliminated."[74] The contradiction was resolved, according to Yazov and in conformity with authoritative Party guidance at the time, by movement toward a posture of reasonable sufficiency for defense which would be apparent in changes to Soviet defense budgets and force structure.

A pertinent question for future Russian or CIS planners is the impact of force reductions or restructurings on the prospects for deterring attack, or for victory denial in the initial period of war, while forestalling nuclear escalation. Future Russian or CIS planning could be based on a smaller, more modernized force which is trained and equipped for rapid, fast-moving offensive operations, a sort of mini-blitz force. Such a force would offer hedges against surprise, which defensively oriented armed forces have historically regarded as necessary. Second, if modernization lags, commanders may prefer to retain a larger-than-efficient force structure in order to compensate for the technological advantages of such potential opponents as, say, Germany. This force would, however, be smaller than the present force, especially in the western military districts of Russia, Belarus, and Ukraine.

A third option is to restructure the CIS armed forces by redefining the relationship between regular forces and reserve or militia forces. This was a matter of some contention within the Soviet leadership during the 1920s. Debates between Mikhail Frunze and Leon Trotsky involved, among other issues, the appropriate relationship between professional cadre armies and territorial militia forces.[75] The discussion of manpower policy again became a contentious issue in Soviet military and other journals during the Gorbachev years, and members of the USSR military leadership entered into the controversy in public media.

For the most part, the Soviet military leadership remained skeptical of any program that would rely on militia forces mainly to provide the balance of

74. Ibid., 66.
75. See Condoleezza Rice, "The Making of Soviet Strategy," ch. 22 in *Makers of Modern Strategy; From Machiavelli to the Nuclear Age*, ed. Peter Paret (Princeton, N.J.: Princeton University Press, 1986), 648–76. The importance of Mikhail Frunze in resolving these issues is discussed in Gareev, M. V. *Frunze*, 225–36.

fighting power in the early stages of a war. Modern war would seem to demand of units great cohesion under pressure of unprecedented destruction and confusion. This could hardly be expected of forces that had not trained together repeatedly and were not kept at high peacetime levels of readiness. Trotsky had originally advocated a complete shift from reliance upon a professional standing army to a territorial militia posture, but Frunze and others prevailed in favor of a mixed system. However, the concept held by Frunze while in charge of the People's Commissariat for Defense was that the territorial militia *would* be kept at high peacetime levels of readiness and training. According to Gareev: "As a whole, rather high demands were placed on the territorial formations and units. M. V. Frunze considered them to be first-line troops which should be ready to enter battle simultaneously and on equal footing with the regular troops. He saw that the best trained commanders and political workers were sent to these formations. He also demanded the creation of the best conditions for them in terms of supply and service."[76]

Frunze's optimism in this regard was not fully justified. But the concept of combining a professional cadre with a large military-mobilization base did take hold. During the Cold War, the Soviet military district system was designed to provide for the operational commanders a steady stream of mobilized manpower once war had begun. According to Christopher Donnelly, divisions in the Soviet armed forces during that time were maintained at four levels of combat-readiness.[77] Fully deployed formations were maintained at or near wartime levels of personnel and equipment and could be activated within hours. Semideployed formations could complete mobilization within one to three days, having available all of their combat equipment though relying on the civilian sector for some logistics, and could have 50 to 75 percent of wartime personnel. Cadre formations might have been able to mobilize within several days, but actually required several weeks to attain combat-readiness. They were typically manned at 15 to 30 percent of wartime tables of organization and may have held older types of equipment. Finally, second-generation formations could have been created when a parent formation left behind deputy commanders down to battalion commanders, who then formed a potential command cadre for any new division.[78]

The estimation of a country's military-mobilization potential is not unre-

---

76. Gareev, M. V. Frunze, 238.
77. Donnelly, Red Banner, 156–57.
78. Ibid., 157.

lated to the estimation of its potential for a short-warning surprise attack. There are, nevertheless, significant differences of emphasis in the types of intelligence material collected and in the ways such materials are related to other indicators. In his review of British successes and failures in intelligence between World Wars I and II, Donald Cameron Watt cites several examples of how intellectual preconceptions and domestic politics can influence intelligence estimates.[79] British strategic planning proceeded on the general assumption that Germany would go for a short and decisive military campaign against its adversaries to the west. British planners based this estimate on an assumption that Germany did not have the resources to sustain a protracted war in the face of British economic pressure.[80] Air staff estimates of Luftwaffe force development in 1934 assumed that stereotypically methodical and efficient Germans would introduce new air divisions with large time intervals between each, allowing for maximum amounts of testing and quality control, instead of engaging in a rapid and sustained buildup. In 1935 the cabinet forced expansion of the Royal Air Force at a faster rate than the air staff thought appropriate, and in 1936 air staff estimates still held that the Luftwaffe would not exceed parity with the French air force. Air staff underestimates of Luftwaffe production were ironically combined with excessive pessimism about the capability of the German air force for long-range, strategic bombardment, although German planning concentrated on aircraft that could provide close air support and interdiction on the battlefield.[81]

One of the most difficult kinds of estimation, as the preceding examples bear witness, is the assessment of a state's military doctrine and its influence on military operations. Assumptions by American, Italian, and British advocates of strategic air bombardment assured doubters that the bomber would prove to be a decisive arm of service in the next war, and without the necessity for exhausting ground and naval engagements or prolonged societal wars of attrition. John Erickson has noted that one of the most significant failures of Stalin's intelligence apparatus was its lack of appreciation for the significance of German operational and tactical doctrine for the combined-arms employment of infantry, tanks, and aircraft in blitzkrieg operations.[82] The failure was all the more surprising in view of the exposure given German

79. Donald Cameron Watt, "British Intelligence and the Coming of the Second World War in Europe," ch. 9 in Knowing One's Enemies, ed. May, 237–70.
80. Ibid., 252.
81. Ibid., 259.
82. Erickson, "Threat Identification," 418.

tactics during their war against Poland and France, and in view of Soviet weaknesses plainly demonstrated in the war between the USSR and Finland. This "doctrinal surprise" is something for which intelligence assessors in Britain and France (less so the Soviet Union) can be forgiven, to a point. Hitler himself did not resolve the issue of the desirability of blitzkrieg operations, given the skepticism on the part of his General Staff, until the spring of 1940 on the very eve of the invasion of France and the Low Countries.[83] Less defensible is the degree of German reliance on grossly inadequate information about Soviet industrial production, military-mobilization potential, and reserve forces prior to the actual decision in favor of Operation Barbarossa.[84] The German military-intelligence staff organization under the army high command was divided into Foreign Armies West and Foreign Armies East. The Soviet Union was not a priority target for Foreign Armies East until the very eve of war. Other sources, including German agents and foreign government sources, supplied some order-of-battle information about the Red Army to German intelligence, but this dealt exclusively with Russian deployments in the border military districts.[85] The German high command did not know the numbers of tanks or aircraft in the Soviet Union, nor did it have reliable information on the numbers of Soviet peacetime (or potential wartime) divisions. An official, secret handbook published by Foreign Armies East in January 1941 concluded that the Red Army "was not fit for modern war and could not match a boldly led and modern enemy."[86] Hitler's strategy for Plan Barbarossa envisioned a short war that would defeat the Red Army over an expanse extending from Archangel to Astrakhan, roughly a thousand miles into Soviet territory from its western border. The question of what to do if when this point was reached the Soviet state continued to function was pushed aside; the assumption was that the Soviet Union was a weak multinational empire waiting to topple, if helped along by a judicious push from the outside.[87]

Estimation of the wartime environment from the peacetime environment was difficult enough prior to the age of automation and "electronization." In the future, additional complexity will be added to efforts to extrapolate from peacetime to wartime: by the higher degree of uncertainty about wartime command and control and by the higher degree of interdependency among

---

83. Mearsheimer, Conventional Deterrence, 105–12, esp. 111.
84. Albert Seaton, The Russo-German War, 1941–45 (New York: Praeger, 1970), 43–49.
85. Ibid., 44–45.
86. Ibid., 46.
87. Ibid., 53.

command, communications-control, and intelligence functions. Three immediate implications for Russian or All-Union military planners suggest themselves. First, the battle for control over the electromagnetic spectrum will become more intense in the future: electronic countermeasures and counter-countermeasures (ECM and ECCM, respectively) will figure more prominently in procurement and exercises for all modern armies, navies, and air forces. Second, the pressure to get additional combat power from a reduced or restructured force, albeit one postured defensively, means that command must be pushed downward as far as possible. Tactical flexibility will be a necessary condition for the accomplishment of battlefield objectives that otherwise would remain at risk. Soviet operations in the Great Patriotic War were designed for a command-and-control system that maximized the flexibility of operational and strategic commanders at the expense of very restrictive guidelines for tactical commanders (in the Soviet ground forces, division or lower).[88] During the 1980s and until the dissolution of the former Soviet Union in the aftermath of the failed coup of August 1991, the Soviet high command had adjusted computer and chips to the requirements and traditions of centralized command: speeding up calculations and computations so that the flow of information upward could be matched to the speed of events in battle.

Defensive military doctrine and electronization of the battlefield will create stronger pressures for the decentralization of decisionmaking authority in all modern militaries, along with more widely distributed information technology needed by commanders to perform traditional tasks faster. Although armed forces are frequently studied from the perspectives of their military doctrine or combat tactics, they are less frequently analyzed as holistic institutions subject to periods of institutional steadiness or stress. Institutions are norm-driven organizations which will attempt to adapt to the unfamiliar by retracing their steps through familiar repertoires of memory, information, and procedure.[89] Beyond a certain point, incremental adaptation to a radically different environment is no longer possible: the organization must change its institutional ethos or cease to function with the same set of role

---

88. Richard H. Phillips, "Problems in Soviet Tactical Training," *Soviet Defense Notes*, no. 4 (July 1990): 5–8, indicates a carryover from Soviet practices in the Second World War to a "rote-ness" in the conduct of exercises even today. Critiques of Soviet exercises for their lack of imagination and rigid adherence to formula have marked the Soviet military press for many years.

89. Paul Bracken brings out this point nicely with regard to military organizations. See his chapter in *Controlling and Ending Conflict: Issues Before and After the Cold War*, ed. Cimbala and Sidney R. Waldman (Westport, Conn.: Greenwood Press, 1992), 183–96.

perceptions; it can continue as an organization but not as the same institution it once was. Russian or All-Union military-traditional patterns of command and control will have to adapt to the democratization of politics and of military discipline brought about by new social forces. As Morris Janowitz noted many years ago with regard to Western armed forces, future armed forces may be drawn away from excessive reliance upon authoritarian patterns of command and toward more adaptive and follower-oriented modes of leadership.[90]

Adoption of defensive military doctrine does not necessarily change the Russian perception of its own security dilemma. In an age in which information (timely delivered and properly analyzed) and electronic warfare are as important as firepower, the relationship between offense and defense is a precarious one. So, too, is the relationship between a surpriser and his intended victim. Military deception in the form of gross force deployments, suddenly moved by stealth to the decisive point of concentration, may be a thing of the past, at least for major powers in confrontation with one another. Nonetheless, mobilization and preparedness for war involve many activities not normally detected by photographic or electronic surveillance, or perhaps not detected in time to provide for an effective response.[91] Many analysts now consider war in Europe, or war between major powers outside Europe, impossible. This optimism may ignore the potential application of "Handel's law" to the problem of strategic and operational military surprise: the more improbable a given attack seems, the more surprising it is; the more surprising, the more tempting to prospective attackers; and the more tempting it is, the more gains it promises if unaware defenders can be caught in a vulnerable position.[92]

90. Janowitz, using studies of U.S., British, and German officers, has documented a "shift from authoritarian domination to greater reliance upon manipulation, persuasion, and group consensus," such that "the central concern of commanders is no longer the enforcement of rigid discipline, but rather the maintenance of high levels of initiative and morale." See Janowitz, *The Professional Soldier: A Social and Political Portrait* (New York: Free Press, 1960), 8–9.

91. In Soviet military theory, this subject matter falls into the category of "strategic deployment" of the armed forces. See *The Voroshilov Lectures*, 1:205–32. I gratefully acknowledge Graham H. Turbiville, Jr., for contributing to my understanding of this topic.

92. See Handel, *War, Strategy, and Intelligence*, passim. Also see Handel, "Strategic Surprise: The Politics of Intelligence and the Management of Uncertainty," ch. 15 in *Intelligence: Policy and Process*, ed. Alfred C. Maurer, Marion D. Tunstall, and James M. Keagle (Boulder, Colo.: Westview Press, 1985), 239–69. See also the essays in *Strategic Military Deception*, ed. Donald C. Daniel and Katherine L. Herbig (New York: Pergamon Press, 1982).

POLITICAL DISINTEGRATION AND THE NATIONALIZATION OF ARMS

The Soviet Union faced the problem of armed national formations during its civil war, and subsequent efforts to incorporate national formations into the Soviet armed forces were frequently commented upon in the Soviet military press. During the Gorbachev years the debate between military traditionalists, who argued for the suppression of nationally based formations or nationality sentiments in the armed forces, and reformists of various camps, more or less sympathetic to ethnically and nationally based formations, was especially intense. Nor was the Soviet Union the only crumbling empire to feel the sharp edge of social and political revolution on the bayonets of disaffected soldiers. Leaders of the Soviet armed forces recalled the experience of the tsar and of Kerensky's Provisional Government in 1917; both were undermined by the collapse of soldier loyalties for tsar and country, in favor of a variety of causes, including social-revolutionary ones.

In a remarkably short time, the apparently intimidating Soviet armed forces became a hollow shell by 1990, consumed by rifts within the armed forces leadership and between the more senior commanders and their lower-ranking and more politicized junior officers. Several jolts hit the proud Soviet armed forces and its military tradition of ethnic and national inclusiveness between 1985 and 1990. First, the mission of the armed forces was called into question by the willing surrender of Soviet political control over its formerly contiguous empire in Eastern Europe. The fruits of World War II had seemingly been abandoned without firing a shot; NATO had "won" the Cold War. Second, the Soviet economy was openly acknowledged by Gorbachev and his advisers to have failed utterly. Gorbachev, initially optimistic about economic reform of the communist system, was pushed by events as the 1980s drew to a close to acknowledge that the Soviet socialist economic model was a catastrophe for the peoples of the USSR. Third, and related to the second, the Soviet socialist economy had been created by a unique sort of political system, directed by one dominant party which had assumed responsibility for the destiny of the state and its economy. It followed by the inexorable logic of Marxism-Leninism that the "superstructure" of the state was rotten to the core if the "substructure" of its economic performance had failed to fulfill its promises.

The demise of the myth of "Sovietism" opened the door to the counter-myth of political salvation by nationalism. The inclusive polity based on an authoritarian political system would be displaced by a plural political system founded on allied nationalities, each with its own accountable political system. For practical purposes, the nationalities in the Soviet Union were too numerous to expect that each would have its own state, however rapidly the Soviet empire disintegrated. It soon became clear that the new nationalism which would displace Soviet imperialism would be a nationalism organized around the various republics of the USSR. Their governments and leaders would accept political devolution resulting from the breakup of the former Soviet empire and the demise of the Communist Party on its territory. In December 1991 eleven republics of the former Soviet Union, led by the Russian Federation, formed a loose association called the Commonwealth of Independent States. On Christmas Day 1991 President Bush recognized Russia and five other republics as sovereign states.

Problems of military command and control presented themselves in the immediate aftermath of the official political pluralization of the former Soviet Union: nuclear weapons, military loyalties, and uncertain borders. Nuclear weapons received the most attention in the Western news media. There are four republics (Russia, Belarus, Ukraine, and Kazakhstan) which held all of the former Soviet Union's strategic nuclear weapons, capable of being mated with delivery vehicles of intercontinental range. The Russian Federation held the greater part of these 15,100 strategic nuclear weapons as of July 1991. In addition, some 12,300 "tactical" nuclear weapons (actually anything other than strategic) were distributed mostly among those same four republics. The immediate problem for Boris Yeltsin and the other leaders of the Commonwealth in December 1991 was to ensure reliable command and control over these nuclear charges.

Expert Western analysts supposed that the strategic nuclear weapons, mostly in Russia, remained under single command and control even in the aftermath of the failed coup of August 1991. Reports in Western news media and elsewhere indicated that there were three "fingers" on the nuclear button during the coup and immediately thereafter. One belonged to Gorbachev, then president of the floundering but still legally alive Soviet Union. Another belonged to the Soviet minister of defense. Prior to the coup, that had been Dmitri Yazov, who turned up among the leading coup plotters; after the coup failed, Yazov was replaced by Yevgeny Shaposhnikov, former chief of staff of the air force, who had played a key supportive role during the critical days of August 19–21.[93] A third finger on the button had been

93. According to press rumors, Shaposhnikov refused to carry out Defense Ministry orders

that of the Chief of the Soviet Armed Forces General Staff, General Mikhail Moiseev. His allegiance during the coup had been uncertain; he was replaced afterward.

Between the failed coup and the meetings that formed the Commonwealth of Independent States in December 1991, nuclear command and control resided in the hands of Russian Federation President Yeltsin and Defense Minister Shaposhnikov. Each guaranteed that stable command and control over all nuclear weapons would be maintained. Each called for the repatriation of all nuclear weapons to the Russian republic. I say "repatriation" here because it soon became clear that Yeltsin's political agenda called for Russia to assume the legal and political place of the Soviet Union in important international forums, including the U.N. Security Council. Other republics, however, were not as ready to resolve outstanding issues of military command and control as they were to throw off the former Soviet yoke. Leaders of the Ukrainian parliament and Ukrainian President Leonid Kravchuk indicated a long-term desire to become "nuclear-free" but an interim shrewdness about using nuclear weapons as bargaining chips. Strategic nuclear weapons located in Ukraine would not necessarily be relocated in Russia, at least not right away. Ukrainian leaders and other republics outside Russia wanted reassurance that they would have some say in the political control over any use of nuclear weapons.

Yeltsin was forced to accommodate Ukrainian demands and those of the very assertive and capable leadership of Kazakhstan provided by Nursultan Nazarbayev with respect to shared control of nuclear weapons. Under agreements reached in December 1991 by leaders of the eleven republics that formed the Commonwealth of Independent States, political control over nuclear weapons on the territory of the former Soviet Union would rest with Yeltsin, but an affirmative decision by him for nuclear release or use required concurrence by the other republics holding nuclear weapons. Military control over nuclear forces resided in the office of Commonwealth Defense Minister Shaposhnikov.

Supposing that nuclear weapons could be kept under wraps, the second problem for the post-Soviet military was the political allegiance of the armed forces. The political disintegration of the Soviet Union occurred at more than one level. First, central authority of the Soviet Union as a single territorial state had been delegitimated by the disestablishment of the Commu-

---

for air attacks on the Russian parliament building where Boris Yeltsin was holed up during the coup.

nist Party from a monopoly of political power, by the poor performance of the economy under centralized state guidance, and by the turncoat behavior of state officials during the failed coup. Second, the authority of the individual republics was in some instances up for grabs—owing to internal power struggles, as in Georgia; or owing to the presence of minority national enclaves within the borders of a republic dominated by other national and ethnic groups, as with conflicts between Armenians and Azerbaijanis in Nagorno-Karabakh. Third, the authority of "Soviet" armed forces commanders was rendered somewhat ambiguous by the decision of leaders of several Commonwealth republics, including Russia and Ukraine, to nationalize armed forces stationed on their territories. Presumably this referred to the ground forces of the former Soviet Union deployed in those locations. It was less clear what would become of air force, navy, and national air-defense units, which might be harder to disaggregate or to divide among the various republics according to an acceptable measuring rod. By early January 1992, for example, Russia and Ukraine were in dispute over "ownership" of the Black Sea Fleet. Russia argued that it was nuclear-capable and should therefore be assigned to Russia for reasons of nuclear command and control. Ukraine contended that the fleet presently carried no nuclear weapons and was therefore properly included in those forces nationalized under its political sovereignty. The two republics eventually agreed later that same year to divide the fleet.

A divided political sovereignty on the territory of the former Soviet Union was easier to declare into existence than was the fine print of subdividing and reallocating Soviet military assets, including ready and reserve forces of the former USSR. Not only internal but external pressures on Commonwealth leaders made it difficult to postpone this issue. The matter of secure borders for the Commonwealth and for its constituent republics was bound up with the division of post-Soviet military assets. One reason why Ukraine, for example, might have wanted to hold onto its nuclear weapons, at least temporarily, was that they offered a grisly kind of insurance against potential Russian or other hostile republican irredentism. Kazakhstan also indicated to Yeltsin that the matter of assigning all nuclear weapons not destroyed by the new regimes to the Russian republic would require protracted negotiation and consultation. The same point might be made about the major conventional components of the formerly Soviet armed forces. The better-armed and -equipped divisions and armies—if they were successfully nationalized and their troops were turned into loyalists for Ukraine, Belarus, Russia, or other individual republican states—would represent a potent symbol of actual and political military might. Nationalized forces based on territorial militias could be "checkmate forces," sufficiently strong to withstand invasion but insufficient to commit aggression against other republics.

This vision of eleven or (counting Georgia, not a founding member of the Commonwealth) twelve republics loosely associated for the purpose of international defense was based on the not very egalitarian reality of preponderant Russian power, both nuclear and conventional. Any aggression against the territory of the former Soviet Union would have to be deterred and fought primarily by Russian forces, assuming the enemy posed a significant threat of invasion with major forces of division size or larger. It was difficult to imagine who might pose such a threat in 1991, but a more completely disillusioned and disintegrated Commonwealth military establishment in the middle to latter 1990s might be tasked to resist border attacks from China, Iran, Turkey, or (very selectively) Japan.

A political map of uncertain dimensions returns Russian planners to the fundamentals, such as those grappled with by Tsar Peter the Great in his effort to create a modern Russian army. Peter found it necessary to redo the relationship between government and citizen, between people and polity, in the process. The "modernization" of the Russian armed forces required that several other things be accomplished during the eighteenth and nineteenth centuries. A reliable system of administration for the armed forces, and indeed for the government as a whole, had to be set up. Ministers who could be relied upon to follow through on reforms had to placed in key positions and given the tsar's backing. A political system that Russians found it worthwhile to defend had to supersede the ethnonational particularisms of an empire that was growing faster geographically than could be assimilated politically and socially. The relationship between people and polity, and therefore between army and regime, sustained a nearly fatal blow as a result of Russia's defeat by Japan in 1905. The First World War toppled the entire edifice.

A return to military fundamentals requires rethinking the Russian experience in offensive and defensive military strategy.[94] It has become a cliché among post–World War II Soviet military historians that Hitler's near success in Operation Barbarossa resulted from inadequate prewar attention in Soviet military theory to the importance of the strategic defensive. Actually, Soviet military theory passed through several stages between the wars, oscillating between periods of offensive- and defensive-mindedness. The noted

94. Draft military doctrine for the post-Soviet Russian armed forces appeared in a special May 1992 edition of *Voennaia mysl'*.

Soviet military theorist A. A. Svechin argued in the 1920s that the two
dominant strategic paradigms of contemporary warfare ("forms of conducting
military operations") were annihilation or destruction (*sokrushenie*) and attrition (*izmor*).[95] Svechin drew this contrast from the earlier work of the
German military historian Hans Delbruck, who postulated two ideal types of
war: *Ermattungsstrategie* (attrition or exhaustion) and *Niederwerfungsstrategie*
(destruction or annihilation).[96] In Svechin's usage, "attrition" was a collective designation for anything other than a strategy of "annihilation," but the
polarity of the two ideal types is an important part of his analysis. The political goals of the war should, according to Svechin, dictate the preferred form
of military operations. A strategy of destruction calls upon the armed forces
to destroy rapidly and completely the fighting power of the enemy field
forces. Forces ready for combat in the initial period of war are all-important,
for reserve forces mobilized later may be omitted from the decisive battles.
Attrition strategies, according to Svechin, admit of more variety in the form
of operations, but they have in common an absence of dependency on a rapid
and decisive military victory over the opponent's field forces. The "weary"
path of a strategy of attrition which "leads to the expenditure of much
greater resources than a short destructive strike aimed at the heart of the
enemy" is, for the most part, chosen only "when a war cannot be ended by
a single blow."[97]

One important distinction between attrition and destruction strategies,
according to Svechin, is that attrition strategies call upon political leaders
to make difficult decisions during war about the emphasis to be placed on
various theaters of operation or fronts. His analysis of French decisionmaking
during the First World War helps to illustrate Svechin's point. After the
Schlieffen Plan for a six-week victory against France had been thwarted, the
leaders of France continued to act as if the French front were the most important strategic theater of operations. In a strategy of destruction Germany
was indeed the most important enemy for French planners to take into account. But, according to Svechin, once the war had been turned into a war
of attrition, the defeat of Austria-Hungary was probably more important
than that of Germany. Austria-Hungary represented the "strategic line of

95. Aleksandr A. Svechin, *Strategiia* [Strategy] (Moscow: Voennyi vestnik, 1927), trans.
and ed. Kent D. Lee (Minneapolis, Minn.: East View Publications, 1992), esp. 239–50.
96. Other German writers used the term *Vernichtungstrategie* for the strategy of annihilation.
See Gordon A. Craig, "Delbruck: The Military Historian," ch. 11 in *Makers of Modern Strategy*, ed. Edward Mead Earle (Princeton, N.J.: Princeton University Press, 1943), 260–87.
97. Svechin, *Strategy*, 247.

least resistance" in the Triple Alliance from the standpoint of a war of attrition. Therefore, as Germany's emphasis shifted in 1915 to its attacks on the Russian front, Britain and France should have deployed a 500,000-man combined army on the Danube. According to Svechin, such a deployment would have relieved German pressure on the Russian front, which then could have held onto Russian Poland, accelerated the collapse of Austria-Hungary, and shortened the war by two years.[98]

One does not have to buy into Svechin's analysis of the priority of weakening Austria after the Schlieffen Plan had broken at the Marne to apply his thinking about strategic paradigms to other cases. Churchill's plan for forcing the Dardanelles was a brilliantly conceived strategic stroke attempting to circumvent the stalemate on the western front in Europe. The Gallipoli campaign ended in disaster, but the attempt to shift the war of attrition toward a dominant strategy of destruction was not necessarily ill-conceived. For this attempted shift of concept was missing one thing: an adequately trained and provisioned expeditionary force. Admittedly the forcing of the Dardanelles and the seizure of the Bosporus might not have created all the havoc that Churchill hoped to create: opening a rapid strategic highway to the support of beleaguered Russia and, meanwhile, offering a thrust line through southeastern Europe into the heartland of the Austro-Hungarian Empire. Churchill via the sea and Svechin via troop movements on the Danube both recommended courses of action which they saw as accepting the reality that the war had become a war of attrition, and both tried to turn that corner favorably for the Entente and to the disadvantage of the Alliance.

Another issue in choosing a strategy of attrition in preference to a campaign of annihilation is that mobilization in an attrition strategy can take place *during* war as well as prior to it. A threatening premobilization is not necessary to support political objectives that can be obtained by one or more kinds of attrition strategy. From the time of the great reforms under War Minister Dmitri Miliutin in the late 1870s until the revision of war plans in 1912, Russian grand strategy and military strategy for war in Europe were essentially defensive. Even as late as 1910, plans envisioned conceding a significant portion of Russian Poland to the invading Germans on account of Russia's assumed slower rate of mobilization compared to that of Germany. Russian Poland was an exposed salient that was potentially vulnerable to a

98. Ibid. Svechin assumed that the deployment of an Anglo-French army of half a million strong on the Danube would have forced Bulgaria to remain neutral, would have cut off German communications with Turkey, and would have had other side-effects combining to reduce pressure on the Russians and increase the constraints on Austria-Hungary.

two-pronged attack, by Germany from East Prussia and by Austria-Hungary through Galicia. Russian war plans between the 1905 defeat by Japan and 1910 were strategically defensive for another reason: some of Russia's leading military strategists feared another conflict in the Far East, suggesting a more cautious and less offensively oriented strategy in the West.[99]

By 1912, some of Russia's confidence in its armed forces had been restored, and more was promised by the Great Program of that year which was designed to build toward a substantially improved mobilization capability by 1916. Then, too, a new and more aggressive French leadership assumed office in 1912, and the French General Stuff urged upon Russia a more offensively oriented strategy that would guarantee prompt Russian attacks into East Prussia by the fifteenth day of mobilization. Fears of war in the Far East had receded, but war planners such as Quartermaster General Iurii Danilov remained pessimistic about Russia's chances for simultaneous offensives against Germany and Austria. The 1912 version of War Plan 19 was laid down in two variants: one assumed that the bulk of Germany's armies would attack westward against France in the first period of the war; the other was intended for the less likely contingency that Germany would direct its stronger offensive eastward against Russia. The first variant, plan A for Austria, therefore supposed that the larger proportion of Russian armies would be deployed against Austria; the second variant, plan G, supposed heavier deployment against Germany. According to General Danilov, the main variant was plan A, based on intelligence and a sensible reading by the Russians and French of German military doctrine.[100]

99. For background on Russian war planning in the latter nineteenth and early twentieth centuries and assessments of Russian planning competency pertinent to World War I, see Jack Snyder, *The Ideology of the Offensive: Military Decision Making and the Disasters of 1914* (Ithaca, N.Y.: Cornell University Press, 1984), chs. 6 and 7; I. I. Rostunov, *Istoriya pervoi mirovoi voiny* [History of the First World War] (Moscow: "Nauka," 1975); I. I. Rostunov, *Russkii front pervoi mirovoi voiny* [The Russian Front in the First World War] (Moscow: "Nauka," 1926); Iurii Danilov, *La Russie dans la Guerre Mondiale, 1914–1917* (Paris: Payot, 1927); William C. Fuller, Jr., *Civil-Military Conflict in Imperial Russia, 1881–1914* (Princeton, N.J.: Princeton University Press, 1985), 219–58; and Forrestt A. Miller, *Dmitri Miliutin and the Reform Era in Russia* (Nashville, Tenn.: Vanderbilt University Press, 1968), esp. 182–230. Implications of the Russian mobilization system for the performance of the armed forces are discussed in N. N. Golovin, *The Russian Army in the World War* (London: Humphrey Milford/Oxford University Press, 1931), republished by Yale University Press and by Archon Books (1969), esp. 15–74.

100. Rostunov, *Istoriya pervoi mirovoi voiny*, 251–54; Danilov, *La Russie dans la Guerre Mondiale*, 134–36; Rostunov, *Russkii front pervoi mirovoi voiny*, 92–94 and 110. A unit-by-unit roster and timetable for Russian troop concentrations on the western border, according to the 1912 changes in the 1910 mobilization plan, appears in A. M. Zaionchkovskii, *Podgotovka Rossii k imperialisticheskoi voine: Ocherki voennoi podgotovki i pervonachalnykh planov* [Preparation of Russia for Imperialist War: Record of Military Preparations and Initial Plans] (Moscow: State

The issue of whether plan A or plan G would be adopted was pertinent to the "short war" scenario that all countries had more or less counted on. The doctrine of a battle of annihilation grew out of positive and negative calculations made by leaders in the years immediately preceding the outbreak of World War I. The positive calculations were the optimistic expectations that any war would be brought to a rapid conclusion, regardless of the winning side; the negative estimates were the pessimistic economic analyses, offered by soldiers and economists alike, which warned that the economies of the European powers could not withstand a prolonged war. The war turned out to be a contest of societal endurance, not of military strategy. One might facetiously argue that this was a war in which military strategy had very little to do with the outcome, and there would be some truth to that.

The danger for a state in relying on a strategy of destruction is that it implies a quick-reacting or preemptive military cast to war planning. Strategies of attrition are not so dependent on rapid and total victory, so forces need not be poised on a hair trigger. But there are risks in a strategy of attrition, too. A state cannot necessarily depend on its larger territory, manpower reserves, or economic potential to obviate the consequences of a fallible military strategy. Although Svechin noted that leaders must be prepared to adopt an attritional or destructive strategy as conditions dictated, he basically felt that for the Soviet Union, given its state of economic development in the 1920s, a strategy of attrition made more sense.

It may be the case that, in general, a strategy of attrition deliberately risks conceding important gains in the initial period of war to the opponent, emphasizing as it does the society's preparedness for a longer struggle. But there is no necessary correlation between attrition and limited political or military aims, nor between a strategy of destruction and total objectives.[101] In the American Civil War, for example, a strategy of attrition was used by the North against the South for the pursuit of political objectives that were as total as one might imagine: the destruction of the Confederacy and its way of life.[102] On the other hand, British foreign policy objectives in the First World War included restoration of the balance of power in continental Eu-

---

Military Publishing House, 1926), 373–400. Important first-person assessment is provided by the Russian head of the mobilization section of the General Staff; see S. Dobrorolsky, "La Mobilisation de l'armée russe en 1914," *Revue d'Histoire de la Guerre Mondiale*, no. 1 (1923): 144–65.

101. Michael Howard, "British Grand Strategy in World War I," ch. 3 in *Grand Strategies in War and Peace*, ed. Paul Kennedy (New Haven, Conn.: Yale University Press, 1991), 31–42.

102. Ibid., 32.

rope and the erasure of any subsequent German "will to power" for European hegemony. They did not include the kinds of objectives for which World War II was fought by Britain and its allies, including the complete overthrow of the enemy regime and the remaking of its political and social order.[103] World War I was the anomaly of a conflict nearly total in its destructiveness and in its consequences for the sociopolitical order of Europe and the Near and Middle East but, at the same time, a conflict that was fought for "restorationist" rather than "revisionist" goals by most members of the victorious coalition.

Like a strategy of attrition, an annihilation strategy can be combined with total or limited political objectives. One assessment of Prussian and German strategy in the eighteenth and nineteenth centuries argues persuasively that the Prussian-German model of the relationship between force and policy was one of total war for limited objectives.[104] Growing out of the experience of Frederick the Great and the victories of Austria in 1866 and France in 1870, German grand strategy from the 1880s until the First World War emphasized the use of armed forces to inflict rapid and decisive defeats on the opponent's forces, in order to compel him to sue immediately for peace. As Dennis Showalter has argued, German planning immediately prior to World War I was not directed to mobilization of the entire economy for war, but to the improvement of armed forces mobilization in order to expedite victory in a short campaign.[105] German leaders, like heads of state and military chieftains in the other capitals of Europe, doubted their economic and societal staying power for a long war. It followed that, for Germany, victory meant "less the destruction of the Entente than its neutralization," following a series of battles of annihilation that would not destroy the Entente's capacity for war but would erode its will to continue fighting.[106]

Unfortunately for the German and British grand strategies in the First World War, they ran aground on the problem of grand tactics. No one could win a decisive engagement on the western front, and no one could figure a way to induce the opposed coalition to discontinue fighting without exhausting its war potential. The powers therefore blundered into a war of attrition for which expanded political objectives were later tacked on. For want of means to win quickly for limited aims, the coalitions staggered into a test of

103. Ibid., 34.
104. Dennis E. Showalter, "Total War for Limited Objectives: An Interpretation of German Grand Strategy," in *Grand Strategies in War and Peace*, ed. Kennedy, 105–24.
105. Ibid., 113–14.
106. Ibid., 114.

economic capacity, social cohesion, and military endurance which left Europe in ruins and destroyed the German, Russian, Austro-Hungarian, and Ottoman empires. There is no small irony in the fact that although the war plans of the powers were marked by an emphasis on the rapid destruction of opposed forces in order to secure an early military victory, the technology and tactics dictated preparedness for a longer war. So did the coalition character of the combatants: membership in the Entente and the Alliance, once war had begun, made it more difficult for any of the individual powers, like Austria, to withdraw, despite strong national sentiment to do so well before the war was actually concluded. Coalition memberships and preemption-prone strategies of destruction both contributed to an offensive-mindedness that provoked rather than deterred an outbreak of war for which, in the event, states, societies, and armed forces were ill-prepared.

The drift of military doctrine in post-Soviet Russia is not entirely clear at this writing. To judge from the draft doctrine for the Russian armed forces published in the journal *Military Thought* in May 1992, there are significant continuities between this and the previously published Soviet military doctrine of November 1990. The later, Russian doctrine includes both politico-military and military-technical aspects, as did its recent Soviet predecessor. "War prevention" and "readiness to repel an aggressor" are included in the politico-military components of the draft Russian doctrine of May 1992; the military-technical components include defensive sufficiency, personnel acquisition policy, and "defense on all azimuths."[107] The draft doctrine identifies five principal sources of "military danger," defined as a condition in international relations such that the possibility of war is inherent, though not imminent. These five sources of military danger are 1) the persistent aim of some states or coalitions to dominate the world or selected regions; 2) the continued existence of "powerful military groupings" in some states and coalitions and the continued basing of their military might near the Russian border; 3) unstable politico-military situations combined with some states' military force building, proliferation of nuclear and other weapons of mass destruction, and international terrorism; 4) the potential use of military blackmail or political and economic pressure against Russia; and 5) violation of the rights of Russian citizens or persons in former Soviet republics who identify themselves ethnically or culturally with Russia.[108]

107. Lt. Col. James F. Holcomb, *Russian Military Doctrine: Structuring for the Worst Case*, Central and East European Defense Studies (The Hague: SHAPE, August 4, 1992).

108. C. J. Dick, *Initial Thoughts on Russia's Draft Military Doctrine*, SSRC Occasional Brief no. 12 (Sandhurst: Soviet Studies Research Centre, Royal Military Academy, July 12, 1992). I gratefully acknowledge Prof. Dick for sharing this important and insightful study.

The draft Russian doctrine is the product of the General Staff and reflects very traditional concerns about Russian vulnerability to pressures against its borders or to nationalist risings in nearby states with the possibility of territorial spillover into Russia. The General Staff's phrase "coalitions of states" was an apparent reference to NATO, and the reference to states operating from a position of strength or employing blackmail seems directed at the United States.[109] A Russian deputy minister of defense appointed in 1992 expressed the opinion in July of that year that the West might use the issue of international control over nuclear weapons as a pretext for intervention in the former USSR.[110] According to the May 1992 draft doctrine, Russia will seek to maintain parity with the United States in strategic nuclear weapons, although the adherence of the Russian political leadership to this tenet is in some doubt. The draft doctrine does carry over into the post-Soviet Russian era the stance in favor of an *eventual* complete elimination of nuclear weapons (with military-strategic parity in the interim). Although the draft renounces military force as a means for attaining political objectives, it is acknowledged that a potentially serious source of conflict lies in the violation of the rights of Russian citizens and persons in former Soviet republics who identify themselves *ethnically* or *culturally* with Russia (the fifth possible source of "military danger," above).[111] This last provision can be an open door for intervention in the affairs of other former Soviet republics.

An interesting aspect of Russia's May 1992 draft military doctrine is the impression made on the authors by the U.S. and allied victory in the Gulf War of 1991. The effects of conventional, high-precision weapons in the Gulf War obviously impressed Russian General Staff planners with the potential of high-technology conventional weapons for the accomplishment of strategic victory in the initial period of war. Since conventional high technology is the strong suit of the United States and its allies, and given the geostrategic shrinkage imposed on the Russian military by the collapse of the Warsaw Pact and the Soviet Union, Russia's nuclear deterrent may now become its first line of defense from the perspective of its General Staff.[112] Russian Minister of Defense and Army General Pavel Grachev, in a June 23, 1992, interview in *Krasnaya zvezda* [Red Star], noted that strategic nuclear offensive weapons are "the main means of safeguarding Russia's national se-

109. Holcomb, *Russian Military Doctrine*, 3.
110. Ibid., 3–4.
111. Dick, *Initial Thoughts on Russia's Draft Military Doctrine*, 3.
112. Holcomb, *Russian Military Doctrine*, 5.

curity and are a guarantee of deterrence against *nuclear or conventional war.*"[113] It is also asserted in the draft military doctrine that if, in the course of a war, an aggressor attempts actions "involving the purposeful disruption of strategic nuclear forces and the destruction of nuclear power and other potentially dangerous installations, even by conventional means, this will be taken as a transition to the use of weapons of mass destruction."[114]

The General Staff's perception of May 1992 that strategic defeat can be inflicted by the conventional weapons of potential opponents in the initial period of war gives that time period decisive importance in future warfare. We have already noted the verdict of Soviet historians about its importance in past wars, including wars of the twentieth century. We have also introduced comparisons between Soviet-Russian experiences and those of other countries in modern times. What these experiences seem to show is that the expected outcomes of wars have a great deal to do with leaders' expectations about what can be accomplished during the initial period. Leaders are tempted by the expectation that victory can be accomplished in a short time, and especially by the possibility of a strategically decisive victory which entirely routs the forces of the defender. On the other hand, this temptation toward victory in a short war is one of the major causes for wars, including wars that turn out unexpectedly for the aggressors. In addition, the short war–victory temptation pushes planners toward rapid-deployment and mobilization schemes which may undermine crisis management and contribute to inadvertent escalation. A nation seeking to deter its potential opponents from any expectation of victory in the initial period of war should approach the problem from the opponent's perspective, making certain that the effort to deny the opponent quick victory at acceptable cost is not accomplished by dysfunctional means which provoke the very attack one seeks to avoid. Deterrence without nonprovocative constraints seals the scorpions inside the bottle.

This chapter has considered the circumstances surrounding the initial period of war when states fight with previously mobilized and deployed forces toward initial operational or strategic objectives. Although historically some states have accomplished strategic aims in this time period, for modern major powers pitted against other powers the track record for blitzkrieg strategies is quite mixed. A blitzkrieg strategy that is entirely dependent on smashing the opponent's capability for resistance may be less fault-tolerant than one that

---

113. Ibid., 6; emphasis added.
114. Dick, *Initial Thoughts on Russia's Draft Military Doctrine*, 4.

allows for the interplay of force and diplomacy in the pursuit of limited aims. Hitler's plan for invasion of the Soviet Union was a plan for operational success that left open the issue of what to do in the event of a strategic stalemate owing to Soviet persistence. Japan's foray at Pearl Harbor was undertaken despite Japan's own prewar estimates that the United States could not be defeated in a protracted war. However, neither Imperial Japan in 1941 nor Hitler in the same year offered inducements for their victims to do anything other than respond with massive and overwhelming reprisals. Although the Soviet campaign in Manchuria in 1945 is represented by some of their historians as exemplary of success through strategic surprise, the Manchurian fighting was a campaign *within a war*, not a war unto itself. It makes the case for strategic surprise in a multifront theater of operations quite apparent, but it does not lift the burden of political thinking from invaders or defenders about what terms short of annihilation might be acceptable in order to resolve disputed political issues.

The relationship between deterrence and nonprovocation is illuminated further by revisiting World War I from the perspective of the grand strategies available to members of the great power coalitions which fought in that conflict. Forces and military planning were oriented to a strategy of destruction, implying rapid defeat of the opposed forces in battle in order to force an expeditious peace settlement on the opposed governments. Unexpectedly, superior technology for the tactical defensive stalled campaigns of annihilation, and the powers were driven into strategies of attrition for which their governments and societies were not prepared. Ironically, had the powers been operating with attrition-oriented grand strategies and had they based prewar plans on those strategies, the July 1914 crisis might not have been so dangerous and preemption-prone. Because strategies of destruction emphasized rapid victory in the initial period of war, planners and political leaders worried about the first weeks of battle only. Assuming that forces vulnerable to early surprise would necessarily suffer total defeat, the powers competed to devise workable strategies of destruction and led their ill-prepared forces into a labyrinth of attrition. Ironically, too, the strategic planners who so feared the consequences of a long war were not therefore led to speculate more consistently about how force and diplomacy could support one another, either before or after war had actually broken out.

4

COERCION IN WAR AND DIPLOMACY

Deterrence and Compellence in the Persian Gulf

The Gulf crisis and war of 1990–91 might seem inappropriate venues for demonstrating the subtlety of the problem of successful threatmaking. Saddam Hussein seemed to present the kind of leader who could only be bludgeoned into submission; otherwise, he would hold onto Kuwait, and possibly advance further, at any apparent risk. Saddam might represent the prototype of the undeterrable leader. While there is undoubtedly much to be discovered about the Iraqi leader's personality, the complexity of deterrent and compellent threatmaking, not its simplicity, is supported by the Gulf experience. In order to achieve their political objectives at acceptable cost, the United States and its Gulf War allies had to manipulate the credible risk of

I am grateful to Prof. David W. Tarr, University of Wisconsin, for permission to read his draft manuscript on the Gulf crisis and for calling my attention to other works of his on this topic.

military escalation in synchronization with the credible promise of deescalation and war termination once Iraq's occupation of Kuwait had ceased.

During the months immediately preceding the outbreak of war in the Persian Gulf in January 1991, both the U.S.-led coalition and Iraq engaged in
massive preparation for war. Each side expected the other to back down in
the face of its deterrent measures. U.S. political objectives were more ambitious than those of Iraq once Iraq had conquered Kuwait: compellence of
Iraqi withdrawal was harder than deterrence of an attack that had not yet
taken place. Even after war began, the first phase of battle was a coercive air
war designed to bring about prompt Iraqi surrender and withdrawal from
Kuwait on the terms offered in U.N. resolutions, thereby avoiding a potentially costly ground war. Iraqi prewar resistance to U.S. and allied pressure,
despite the overwhelming military superiority of Iraq's opponents and in the
face of diplomatic isolation, cautions against the expectation that force superiority alone can allow one side to prevail in crisis management. The inferior side retained important bargaining assets throughout the various stages
of crisis and warfighting, and it used those assets to obtain for itself the
survival of important parts of its armed forces and its political leadership.

PHASES OF COERCION

Opening Moves

Iraqi armed forces invaded Kuwait in the early morning of August 2 without
provocation and rapidly subdued resisting Kuwaiti defenders within several
hours. Within a week Iraq had moved forward into Kuwait some hundred
thousand troops, armed with modern equipment including surface-to-surface
missiles. Iraqi President Saddam Hussein announced that the government of
Kuwait had been deposed and that a new regime would be installed more
consistent with Saddam's definition of Islamic polity. The emir of Kuwait
and his retinue had fled ahead of Saddam's tanks.

With regard to the invasion of Kuwait in 1990, the United States was in
a position somewhat similar to that faced by President Harry S. Truman and
his advisers in June 1950, when North Korean forces crossed the 38th parallel and crashed into South Korea. Prior to the North Korean attack, various persons, including leading military experts and political figures at the

time, were uncertain whether South Korea lay within the U.S. "defense perimeter."[1] Once the attack was actually under way, President Truman and his advisers quickly recognized its strategic importance: the loss of all of Korea to the North Korean regime would be a catastrophic setback for U.S. policy and an immediate strategic threat to America's principal ally in the Far East, Japan.

To say that the North Koreans and the Soviets were disappointed by the reaction of Harry Truman to the North Korean attack would be a considerable understatement. They, the North Korean and Soviet regimes, had miscalculated badly. They had forgotten that great powers do not necessarily define all the interests for which they will fight ahead of time in peacetime. War, or the imminent prospect of it, changes calculations.[2] The North Koreans and the Soviets were disappointed in a way that most students of U.S. foreign policy find quite reassuring. Not all disappointments are of this sort. In 1956, after Egyptian President Gamal Abdel Nasser had nationalized the Suez Canal and the British, French, and Israelis mounted an invasion to depose him, the United States chose to define its strategic interest quite unexpectedly: with Nasser, and against its NATO and Israeli allies. The attack had to be called off, Nasser emerged from the crisis as a hero, and the advertisement of the limitations to French and British global reach, compared to the American, was to have long-run effects still being felt in the region.

Saddam Hussein calculated, as Kim Il Sung had in 1950, that he could bring about a fait accompli, in the form of a complete and total military conquest of Kuwait and the replacement of its regime with an Iraqi puppet. The essential political and military objectives would be accomplished while the United States, its NATO allies, and the other states in the Persian Gulf/ Southwest Asia cauldron dithered about what to do. It was a reasonable supposition on the part of the impetuous Iraqi ruler. The United States had not completely shed the "Vietnam syndrome" with regard to intervention in foreign countries outside Europe. The NATO allies of the United States were preoccupied with winding down the Cold War in Europe and with the changes going on in the Soviet Union. The Soviet Union, which had for

1. U.S. Secretary of State Dean Acheson is said to have raised doubts about the importance of Korea in a speech given in January 1950, in which he defined a number of U.S. vital interests in Asia, not mentioning Korea specifically. This was not, however, a formulation that excluded the possibility of a U.S. response to North Korean aggression, as North Korean Premier Kim Il Sung and Soviet General Secretary Joseph Stalin soon learned.

2. Geoffrey Blainey, *The Causes of War*, 3d ed. (New York: Free Press, 1988), 146–56.

many years built up the Iraqi armed forces through military aid, equipment, and training, would at worst, according to Saddam's reckoning, turn a deaf ear to the entreaties of the Americans or the United Nations. Even the United States had, within recent memory, shown more official and unofficial sympathy toward Iraq than Iran during the war those two states fought for most of the 1980s. Undoubtedly, Saddam believed that the Arab states of the Gulf, Southwest Asia, and North Africa would live up to their well-deserved reputations for finding excuses not to oppose his version of Arab imperialism.

All these calculations might have been reasonable, but they were very far from being accurate in the event. Most astonishing to the Iraqis was the unequivocal U.S. reaction. President Bush laid down the general thrust of U.S. policy in his address to the nation of August 8, 1990. The U.S. president outlined four policy objectives that had to be met in order to resolve the crisis on terms judged satisfactory to American interests. First, the United States insisted upon the "immediate, unconditional and complete withdrawal" of all Iraqi forces from Kuwait.[3] Second, the legitimate government of Kuwait had to be restored. Third, the stability and security of the Persian Gulf were defined explicitly by the president, as by more than one of his predecessors, as vital U.S. interests. And fourth, President Bush indicated that he would be concerned about the lives of American citizens living abroad, including those in Kuwait and Iraq.[4]

Bush ordered an immediate embargo of all trade with Iraq and, with allied cooperation, froze all Iraqi and Kuwaiti financial assets in the United States and elsewhere. U.S. diplomacy sought to isolate Iraq as an aggressor state and to mobilize international opinion against it. Toward that end, U.S. leaders succeeded in getting the U.N. Security Council on August 6 to approve for the first time in twenty-three years mandatory sanctions under Chapter 7 of the U.N. Charter. This gave international blessing to the U.S. effort to ostracize Iraq from military, economic, and political support. Further to the discomfiture of Iraq, the Soviet Union under Gorbachev did not even make sympathetic noises in the direction of Baghdad. Instead, Gorbachev sided with Bush and with the United Nations in declaring the Iraqi aggression illegal, and in calling for a restoration of the status quo ante. This was the first post–Cold War crisis in which the superpowers acted in diplomatic con-

3. White House, Office of the Press Secretary, *Address by the President to the Nation,* August 8, 1990.
4. Ibid.

cert, and it gave to the Americans a virtual carte blanche for a military response of the most unambiguous sort.

The response was not long in coming. Bush immediately authorized the deployment of elements of the Eighty-second Airborne Division to Saudi Arabia; much more would follow. By the middle of September 1990, the United States had some hundred and fifty thousand troops in the region, including air force and naval personnel. This expectation was realized, along with the commitment of forces and support from a total of twenty-six countries, including forces from Egypt, Morocco, and Syria. Many more U.S. forces were to follow in October and November, with increasing controversy over the political objectives motivating the deployments.

Coercive Deterrence

The United States had at first poured this sizable contingency force into the Gulf and its environs as an exercise in deterrence. The particular form of deterrence chosen was what Alexander George has termed "coercive diplomacy": the combined use of arms and diplomacy in order to induce an opponent to behave in a preferred way, but stopping short of actual war.[5] The objective was not to get into a large, face-to-face shooting war between the United States and Iraq, but to discourage further Iraqi aggression, notably an attack on Saudi Arabia. Because it partakes of coercion rather than war, coercive diplomacy is intellectually demanding on the resources of military planners and policymakers alike.

Coercive diplomacy is an influence strategy designed to get the target of the influence to calculate that it is in its own interest to comply with the demands being made by the threatener. As Thomas C. Schelling noted in his book *Arms and Influence*, coercion differs from the forcible denial of an objective to an opponent.[6] Coercion requires two elements: 1) a credible threat to inflict undesired costs if the threat is not complied with and 2) a promise to withhold the punitive action if the threatened party complies. Coercive diplomacy uses the threat of force in order to make a political point. Under certain conditions, according to Alexander George and others,

5. George, "The Development of Doctrine and Strategy," ch. 1 in Alexander L. George, David K. Hall, and William E. Simons, *The Limits of Coercive Diplomacy* (Boston: Little, Brown, 1971), 1–35.

6. Schelling, *Arms and Influence* (New Haven, Conn.: Yale University Press, 1966), passim.

it may be necessary to use a little force in order to deter the outbreak of a wider conflict. Thus, the United States during the Cuban missile crisis of 1962 employed a "quarantine" around Cuba which was a naval blockade in fact, if not in declaratory policy. This was a warlike act, but far less so compared with other options that President Kennedy could have chosen, including attacks against the sites of the Soviet missiles deployed in Cuba or even an invasion of Cuba by U.S. forces. The president chose the quarantine in order to coerce the Soviets into withdrawal of their offensive nuclear-capable missiles from Cuba. For understandable and obvious reasons, he preferred coercion to direct superpower fighting.

Like Bush in the Gulf crisis of 1990, Kennedy in 1962 had a two-part problem: deterrence and compellence. Although the U.S. blockade would interdict any further shipments of Soviet missiles to Cuba, those missiles already deployed there would not be removed by the blockade alone. The United States either had to squeeze the Soviets out by a combination of military and political pressures, or it had to remove the missiles forcibly. In other words, pure deterrence did not suffice to accomplish President Kennedy's primary objective: the removal of the Soviet missiles from Cuba. Compellence of the Soviet Union, or the inducement of Soviet leaders to reverse a course of action that was already in motion, was also required.[7] In the final analysis, the United States was able to obtain this necessary degree of compellence by combining the credible threat of crisis escalation into war with promises not to invade Cuba and tacit agreements about the future of U.S. Jupiter missiles deployed in Turkey.[8]

One can overstate the difference between deterrence and compellence, implying that deterrence is always passive, compellence always active. This is far from the case. It is sometimes impossible to make a deterrent threat credible by words or military preparedness without an actual demonstration in battle. At this point, defense and deterrence may be commingled. One can respond to an attack with forcible defense per se, which is designed simply to defeat the attack, destroy the attacking forces, and eliminate their combat power. Or one can use defense as a way of making a statement relative to intrawar deterrence: defense, once in progress, makes more apparent

7. An explanation of the distinction between "deterrence" and "compellence" appears in Schelling, *Arms and Influence*, 69–91.
8. For recent documentation on Cuban missile crisis decisionmaking, see James G. Blight and David A. Welch, *On the Brink: Americans and Soviets Reexamine the Cuban Missile Crisis* (New York: Hill & Wang, 1989), and Raymond L. Garthoff, *Reflections on the Cuban Missile Crisis*, 2d ed. (Washington, D.C.: Brookings Institution, 1989).

the willingness of the defender to pay actual costs in lives lost and resources expended in battle. What was previously a hypothetical possibility—viz., that the defender would resist—is now a certainty.[9]

The idea of intrawar deterrence is not so self-contradictory as it might sound. The purpose of fighting can be twofold: 1) to force the attacker to use up combat power and 2) to send a message that the continuation of combat presents a potentially higher risk for the attacker than for the defender. The United Nations sought to send both messages during the Korean War. The North Koreans were put on notice that the conventional defenses of the United States, the South Koreans, and other allies would deny to North Korea an inexpensive victory or, once the fighting had stabilized in 1951, any victory at all. North Korea was also led to believe, as was China, that continued fighting might expand in ways that were not simple extensions of the ground and tactical air warfare previously fought to a standstill. Through intermediaries, the Eisenhower administration warned the Chinese and the North Koreans that the United States would not necessarily confine future fighting to the Korean peninsula unless more progress was made toward the conclusion of an armistice in 1953. The deterrent threat against further North Korean or Chinese escalation was posed in part by the availability of American and other forces that were prepared to continue fighting, and in part by the possible expansion of the war into other theaters of operation and by the U.S. potential use of tactical nuclear weapons.[10]

President Bush and his advisers assumed that the ability to exclude Iraq from meaningful allied support was a necessary condition for the establishment of escalation dominance in the crisis. The United States moved rapidly and successfully on the diplomatic front to obtain military and other support from NATO allies, and troop commitments were obtained from Egypt, Syria, and Morocco for deployments in support of U.S. forces in Saudi Arabia. The Soviet Union was also engaged in support of the U.S. aim to reverse the results of the attack on Kuwait. The U.N. Security Council supported the embargo of trade with Iraq in goods other than foodstuffs and medicine. As the diplomatic noose closed on Saddam as a result of effective U.S. international politicking and a globally shared dependency on oil, Iraq's options became more limited. Divested of support for its war effort on the part of its former Soviet ally, Iraq in desperation turned to its former enemy, Iran.

9. Schelling, *Arms and Influence*, 78.
10. Richard K. Betts, *Nuclear Blackmail and Nuclear Balance* (Washington, D.C.: Brookings Institution, 1987), 31–47.

During September 1990, Saddam Hussein offered attractive terms to Iran for terminating their conflict, including the repatriation of Iranian prisoners of war. Further diplomatic isolation of Iraq was brought about by its own incompetence: the sacking of the French embassy in Kuwait resulted in a French decision in September to dispatch an additional four thousand troops to the region.[11] France had previously declined to join in the active naval quarantine against Iraq, on the grounds that doing so would make it a cobelligerent.

The diplomatic aspects of crisis management were supported by an extensive military buildup, which would rise to some four hundred thirty thousand U.S. troops in the Persian Gulf region by the end of January 1991. Having inserted the trip-wire force to establish U.S. commitment, the Bush administration then built it into a formidable air-, ground-, and sea-based force, supported by allied deployments that were more than ceremonial. The commitment of other Arab forces to the defense of Saudi Arabia testified to the isolation that Saddam's diplomacy had imposed on him. The difference between the U.S. ability to mobilize international support for its position and Iraq's inability to do so created military alternatives for the Americans and limited the military options available to Iraq. As the U.S. and allied military buildup proceeded, the window of opportunity for a blitzkrieg against Saudi Arabia, of the kind Saddam had imposed on Kuwait, rapidly closed.

Therefore, the United States had succeeded by mid-September 1990 in employing a variant of coercive diplomacy which prevented Iraq from accomplishing further aggressive aims in the region. This variant is termed by Alexander George the "try and see" approach.[12] This is the more passive of the two basic forms of coercive diplomacy; the other form is an ultimatum with a time limit for compliance attached to it. The difference between the two variants can be illustrated by reference to the Cuban missile crisis of 1962. The try-and-see approach was represented by the blockade imposed against further shipments of missiles into Cuba; the blockade could preclude additional shipments of medium- or intermediate-range ballistic missiles, but it could not by itself cause the Soviet Union to remove missiles. Only the additional pressure of an ultimatum that the missiles had to be removed within twenty-four hours, with the warning that if the Soviets could not do so the United States would, finally forced Khrushchev's hand on October 28.[13]

11. *Time*, September 24, 1990. This raised the total of French forces committed to the immediate theater of operations to 7,800.
12. George, "The Development of Doctrine and Strategy," passim.
13. It has become a somewhat contentious point, among historians of the Cuban missile

Having deployed a blocking and deterring force in Saudi Arabia and the Gulf region, the United States was in a position analogous to that of President Kennedy after he imposed the quarantine against Soviet missile deliveries to Cuba in October 1962. The United States had established a line that Saddam could not cross without raising the risk of escalation, just as Khrushchev could not have repeatedly violated the quarantine without risking at least conventional war between the superpowers. The analogy is to one's approach to decisionmaking, and to the character of the relationship between force and policy. Obviously the United States was in a superior military position relative to that of its antagonist, in 1962 as in 1990. The United States could have won a conventional war in the Caribbean in 1962; the Soviet Union would have been left with the option of nuclear escalation or conventional war in Europe with a very high probability of nuclear escalation. In similar fashion, the U.S. position of force superiority relative to Iraq was obviously a very important factor in calculations being made in Baghdad and in Washington. An all-out war in the Gulf would be costly, but the eventual expulsion of Iraq from Kuwait and the destruction of Saddam's regime seemed to be highly probable, if not inevitable, outcomes.

From Deterrence to Compellence

The deterrent objectives of the U.S. deployments seemed easier to accomplish than the compellent ones, however. It did not suffice, according to U.S. policy, merely to deter Saddam from an attack on Saudi Arabia. U.S. political objectives, as noted, included the withdrawal of Iraqi forces from Kuwait and the restoration of the emirate government in power prior to the invasion. This compellent mission was more complicated than the deterrent one, both politically and militarily. Politically, the allied and U.N. support that the United States had signed onto the deterrent mission now complicated the planning for any use of military force for the purpose of compellence. The Soviet Union was not eager to go beyond its commitment to the slow squeeze on Iraq by blockade and embargo. Tightening the blockade by

---

crisis, as to whether Robert Kennedy did or did not issue an ultimatum through Soviet Ambassador Anatoly Dobrynin on October 27. In his report to the Supreme Soviet on the Cuban crisis, Premier Nikita Khrushchev noted that "we received information from Cuban comrades and from other sources on the morning of October 27th *directly stating* that this attack (a U.S. air strike and/or invasion of Cuba) would be carried out in the next two or three days. We interpreted these cables as an *extremely alarming warning signal.*" Quoted in Graham T. Allison, *Essence of Decision: Explaining the Cuban Missile Crisis* (Boston: Little, Brown, 1971), 64–65.

the interdiction of air traffic to and from Iraq was proposed by nine European states for consideration by the U.N. Security Council on September 18. This further refinement of the "try and see" variant of coercive diplomacy would be complicated to administer, and it posed the risk of inadvertently strafing or forcing down a civilian jetliner.

Compellence required the Iraqi leadership to reverse a course of action previously undertaken, as opposed to the simpler task of deterring any further aggression perhaps being contemplated. An unprovoked attack on Iraq launched by U.S. forces without U.N. approval would not have broad international, allied NATO, or Gulf Cooperation Council support. The United States needed a compellent option that supported the diplomacy of "slow squeeze" and ate away at the Iraqi military position. Instead, during September Iraq moved further toward the termination of its war with Iran, transferring its forces from that front into Kuwait. U.S. planners, who in August had anticipated an Iraqi force in Kuwait of some two hundred fifty thousand troops, faced the prospect that by the end of December 1990 there might be as many as six hundred thousand Iraqi troops deployed in forward defensive positions or in operational reserves of high readiness stationed behind the covering forces. However inferior in professional competency to the crack U.S. divisions being deployed in Saudi Arabia when fighting on the *offensive*, the Iraqi forces in Kuwait presented a significant defensive capability against any ground invasion.

On November 8, 1990, Bush announced a virtual doubling of the U.S. military deployments to the Gulf. This was taken by many in Congress and in the news media as a shift from a defensive to an offensive strategy. Congressional leaders, although Congress had gone into recess following the election two days earlier, indicated their concern and demanded to know whether the Bush administration had abandoned the blockade for a course of action leading to war. From the perspective of the Bush administration, the addition of some two hundred thousand combat troops to the estimated two hundred thirty thousand U.S. troops already deployed in Persian Gulf area did not constitute a transition to an offensive military strategy. Instead, it amounted to a tightening of the screw, an increase in compellent pressure by a show of force that might, or might not, be used. As explained by a U.S. "senior official" in early November 1990, "What we are trying to do is tell Saddam Hussein, 'Look, we are serious.' "[14] The administration was not yet

---

14. Dan Balz and R. Jeffrey Smith, "Bush Ordered Escalation to Show Resolve, Aide Says," *Philadelphia Inquirer*, November 11, 1990.

prepared to issue an ultimatum demanding Saddam's withdrawal, although the ground was being prepared for that next step as the compellent pressure on Iraq was being tightened. U.S. Secretary of State James Baker sought and received the approval of the Soviet leadership for a conditional use of force if other options were to no avail. And U.S. officials worked with other U.N. delegations throughout November on candidate resolutions authorizing the use of force against Iraq; American diplomats were working against the clock, for the U.S. chairmanship of the U.N. Security Council was to expire on December 1.

The same "senior official" cited above also noted, in contrast to some other Bush administration policymakers, that the new U.S. military deployments were not related to any assumed failure of economic sanctions. The official told reporters that it was too soon (early November) to draw any conclusion about how well sanctions might ultimately work.[15] The new deployments were designed to support the sanctions by conveying to Saddam a sense that his time for compliance was not unlimited: they thus represented an ultimatum of a sort, albeit with no specific time line for compliance.[16] This relatively passive form of compellence failed to move Iraq; in response, Saddam Hussein mobilized another two hundred thousand troops for deployment to or near Kuwait, raising his expected total to more than six hundred thousand by January 1991. It therefore became clear to U.S. officials that a stricter form of coercive diplomacy would be necessary, one of the more active forms of compellence.

In the last week of November 1990, the United States worked at a hectic pace to establish a consensus among the permanent members of the U.N. Security Council in favor of dropping the other shoe. On November 29, the Security Council voted twelve to two (one abstention) to authorize the use of force against Iraq if Iraq did not withdraw from Kuwait by January 15. During the forty-seven-day period following passage of the authorization to use "all necessary means" to enforce the U.N. resolutions on Kuwait, announced the Security Council, there would be "pause of good will" and a concentration on diplomatic approaches to resolve the crisis.[17] This made little immediate impression on Iraq, which vowed defiance immediately prior to the expected Security Council resolution authorizing force if necessary.

U.S. officials indicated that they sought the time limit not as a guarantee

15. By Christmas, however, Vice-President Dan Quayle was stating in public that sanctions had failed to dislodge Saddam from Kuwait.
16. Balz and Smith, "Bush Ordered Escalation."
17. *New York Times*, November 30, 1990.

that American and allied forces *would* take the offensive after that date, but as an open door through which subsequent attacks could be launched at any time. Although this seemed to give the United States the upper hand, the "ultimatum" variant of the coercive strategy was not without risk. An ultimatum gave Iraqi planners an outside date to use as a guideline for military preparedness. Possible first-strike moves by Iraq in the interim between the authorization of force and the arrival of the deadline were not precluded. Iraq also had the option of selective "reprisal" attacks in response to the U.N.-imposed deadline, attacks short of all-out war but putting stress on the coalition supporting U.S. and U.N. objectives.

One obvious unknown, at the time of the passage of the U.N. resolution authorizing force against Iraq, was how the U.S. Congress would figure into the equation of U.S. compellence. A Congress strongly in support of the president would add to the credibility of compellent threats, but forcing Congress to stand up and be counted on this issue risked defeat for the administration, which lacked a congressional majority. Both houses of Congress eventually voted to authorize U.S. use of force against Iraq in January and, armed with these resolutions together with that of the United Nations, Bush was legally and politically protected against charges of "presidential war." In the weeks ahead, this would prove to be a considerable asset for him, with regard to the support of the international community, Congress, and the U.S. public.

By virtually doubling the size of the force deployed in the Persian Gulf immediately after the fall elections, Bush had circumvented a congressional and public debate over the shift from deterrence to compellence as the mission of U.S. forces. A force of roughly two hundred thousand could be maintained in Saudi Arabia almost indefinitely without a significant strain on U.S. resources and patience, but a force of four hundred thousand or more was too large for such an extended, constabulary mission. Pressures would surely build within the armed forces and within the administration for a resolution of the crisis, either by war or by Iraq's voluntary withdrawal from Kuwait. While Bush administration officials publicly scorned the idea of "saving face" for Saddam and viewed his aggression against Kuwait as criminal and inadmissible, they understood that the avoidance of war would require some kind of bargaining over minor aspects of the crisis, if not the major stakes. The other option was to fight, and the Bush coercive strategy could threaten to fight with more credibility following the U.N. resolution of late November.

However, once the guns speak military persuasion is not silent, to paraphrase a famous saying. The United States would still be fighting for political objectives, holding together a diverse multinational coalition, including Arab states of heterogeneous ideological persuasion and regime character. The "economy of violence" recommended by Machiavelli would call for a rapid and decisive campaign against Iraqi forces in Kuwait, but it was less clear how much further the United States and its allies ought to go. Military forces find targets of opportunity hard to resist, and plenty of hints emitted from high places in Washington to suggest to Saddam Hussein that his regime's days, and perhaps his own, were numbered should war begin.

TARGETING FOR COERCION

The uppermost question in the minds of U.S. and allied planners, with regard to planning for the outbreak of war should compellence fail, was the decision about whether Saddam Hussein should be permitted to survive in power. Wartime operations might give the coalition the opportunity to depose him, but not necessarily at an acceptable cost in battlefield casualties and allied disunity. Saddam's strategy for the conduct of war could be assumed to include a postwar world in which he maintained effective control over Iraq's armed forces and security services, allowing for his later return to the Middle East and Persian Gulf stage of prime-time players.

U.S. planners probably included "decapitation" attacks against the Iraqi regime in their target folders for wartime operations. The U.S. Joint Chiefs of Staff had concluded that only massive uses of airpower against a wide variety of targets could force Iraq out of Kuwait and bring the war to an acceptable conclusion.[18] Air force planners interviewed academics, journalists, "ex-military types," and Iraqi defectors to determine "what is unique about Iraqi culture that they put a very high value on? What is it that psychologically would make an impact on the population and regime of Iraq?"[19] Israeli sources advised that the best way to hurt Saddam Hussein was to target his family, his personal guard, and his mistress.[20]

A U.S. Air Force chief of staff who discussed these and other targeting

18. Rick Atkinson, "Hussein, Baghdad Would Be Air Force's Top Targets," *Philadelphia Inquirer*, September 17, 1990.
19. Ibid.
20. Ibid.

considerations with reporters was summarily dismissed by Secretary of Defense Dick Cheney. Chief of Staff, General Michael J. Dugan had offended political sensibilities, but he contributed inadvertently to a broader discussion of just what it is that targeting is supposed to accomplish. Planners frequently approach the problem of targeting as a question of the destruction of so many physical things: bridges, air defenses, depots, and so forth. This is a legitimate concern but, from the perspective of the relationship between force and policy, not the most important issue.

Targeting can also be treated as an effort to disrupt or destroy the coherence of an enemy organization. The command system of an opponent is its "brain," without which the body is susceptible to paralysis or disintegration. Targeting the command-and-control system of an opponent, including the opponent's leadership, is thought by some analysts to be an economical approach to victory, compared to a prolonged war of attrition. The counter-command approach commends itself especially when political power and enemy leadership are concentrated in one or a few hands. Undoubtedly this was one reason why the headquarters of the dictator Muammar Qaddafi were specifically targeted during the U.S. raids against Libya in 1986.

However, targeting for coercion, as opposed to targeting for destruction, is more complicated than the killing of one individual or the elimination of a few persons in a leadership group. Targeting for coercion is an influence process directed at a reactive military organization.[21] Military organizations react and adapt to changed conditions according to procedural repertoires and professional expectations. The U.S. and Allied bombing offensives against Germany in World War II proved to be less effective than the most optimistic proponents of strategic airpower had assumed, precisely because of the ability of the German civil and military organization to adjust previously established routines and priorities. Similarly, the air-delivered knockout blows against the British Isles expected by many military strategists prior to World War II, on the basis of worst-case extrapolations from World War I experience, proved less damaging to British society and morale than Germans hoped, or Britons feared.[22]

The idea of rapidly and decisively eliminating the command structure of the opponent is in part, and ironically, the result of conceptual seepage from nuclear strategic thought into conventional war planning. It provides one

21. Paul Bracken, *The Command and Control of Nuclear Forces* (New Haven, Conn.: Yale University Press, 1983), 92–93.

22. See George H. Quester, *Deterrence Before Hiroshima: The Airpower Background to Modern Strategy* (New York: John Wiley & Sons, 1966).

indicator of the nuclearization of conventional strategy referred to earlier, although one could even find prenuclear roots for the concept in Western strategic thought. The development of bomber aviation prior to World War II suggested to some theorists the possibility of decisive blows not only against an opponent's society but also against his command-and-control system. Even if the head of state or the principal military command could not be knocked out entirely, the enemy's strategy could be so discredited that it would be forced to sue for peace for want of viable options.

Consider, in this context, the German effort in 1940 to obtain mastery over the skies of southern England in order to pave the way for a cross-Channel invasion. Although depicted by some as a contest between British air defenses and German bomber aviation in a campaign of attrition, it was in fact a competition between command-and-control systems. Technical factors—e.g., the decisive contribution made by radar to the British defenses—played their part, but the more interesting competition, from the present perspective, was not technical but command-strategic. The Luftwaffe expectation with regard to the "Battle of Britain" was that the effectiveness of British air defenses would be defeated by a strategy of superior command and control. British air-defense controllers would use up their available fighter interceptors faster than those interceptors could exact unacceptable attrition against German bombers. Were it not for the perspicacity of Air Marshal Hugh Dowding, who correctly inferred the German strategy and husbanded his fighters in order to thwart that strategy, the Germans might have prevailed, with unforeseeable consequences. As it was, Dowding solved a highly complicated "optimization" problem by getting the maximum number of bomber kills from the most efficient allocation of a minimum number of interceptors. Today he would be praised as a brilliant game theorist; his reward at the time was to be sacked when other officers complained about his refusal to mass larger numbers of interceptors against the endless waves of bombers in attack formation.

As a counterexample, which the Germans got right and their opponents did not, consider the development of the German blitzkrieg tactics in 1939 and 1940 and the inability of the Allies to respond defensively. As in the preceding case, this was not a question of the side that ultimately prevailed in battle having the greater numbers and outlasting its opponent by simple attrition. Instead, the Germans literally stumbled upon a daring strategy which combined close air support and armored-mechanized spearheads in a way that the French and Allied defenders had not expected. Since the high commands of the German armed forces (OKW) and German army (OKH) had resisted the development of armored blitzkrieg tactics, it was partly serendipity that led Hitler and the high commands to opt for them in the spring of 1940. Until then, Hitler and his principal military advisers planned for a "limited aims" campaign in the west, regarding the possibility of a larger and more decisive victory as beyond their capabilities.[23] The serendipitous nature of the German "discovery" of blitzkrieg tactics made it harder for Allied intelligence organizations to anticipate them, although some aspects were apparent in the earlier campaign against Poland in 1939.

What is most interesting about the German version of blitzkrieg, as seen in the May 1940 offensive westward, was its impact upon the command and control (including the operational cohesiveness) of the defending French forces. The Germans selected an unexpected attack sector (the Russians would say strategic "direction," or *napravleniye*) through the Ardennes, thought by the defenders to be virtually impassable by armored forces. They also accompanied their fast-moving armored spearheads with tactical air cover of the most assertive kind, relying on dive-bombers which were effective as much for the shock value of their tactics as for the actual tonnage of bombs dropped or the target values destroyed.[24] In addition to the shock value of armored spearheads and the Stukas, the Germans also made innovative use of command-and-control technology in their 1940 campaigns. By fitting radio receivers and transmitters into tanks they enabled commanders to regroup and reroute forces in what today is called "real time." Most important, the Germans thwarted the basic strategic concept on which the French command-and-control system rested: an "impregnable" forward defense backed up with small numbers of mobile reserves.

The point of our discussion here is not to revisit familiar history, but to draw from the larger historical record observations that lead to a deeper understanding of "targeting" than is customarily available in military or academic accounts. Nuclear-oriented targeting concepts emphasize the destruction of "aim points" or physical things because the entire idea of a nuclear "strategy" seems inappropriate, if not macabre, in the context of a total U.S.-Soviet conflict. Even in the case of strategic nuclear war, horrible as that might be, it would be important for planners and political leaders to

23. John J. Mearsheimer, *Conventional Deterrence* (Ithaca, N.Y.: Cornell University Press, 1983), 99–133.
24. A point made by the noted British historian of Soviet military affairs Peter H. Vigor, Royal Military Academy, Sandhurst, who experienced the German tactics firsthand during the Second World War. See Vigor, *Soviet Blitzkrieg Theory* (New York: St. Martin's Press, 1983), on the lack of German unified doctrine with regard to blitzkrieg operations (pp. 96–97).

have some notion of priority and sequence in targeting. Not everything need be destroyed at once, and some things not at all. Moreover, the objective of destroying the opponent's command system in a nuclear war conflicts with the objective of preserving enough parts of that system intact to make possible some war termination short of total societal destruction.[25]

Despite the evident need for policy control over choices of targets in nuclear as well as conventional warfare, the latter is more interesting because it is more imaginable and more amenable to being compared with historical precedent. What we learn from the history of command-and-control systems is that there is no one "right" way to organize a defense establishment or a fighting force. It follows that there is no all-purpose magician's trick that will destroy the opponent's cohesion.[26] It follows that coercive diplomacy in war or crisis cannot be based on the assumption of toppling the opponent's command system. In some cases the "system" will consist of one dominant leader and his or her immediate coterie of retainers. Destruction of this group of persons might change short-term war aims, but there is little historical evidence that the change would be for the better. Hawks are as likely as doves to emerge from the rubble when the top leadership group is eliminated by internal coup or external attack.[27] As Fred Charles Iklé noted in his definitive study of conflict termination, it is arguable whether those who favor continuation of fighting or those who are prepared to surrender an unfavorable position are truly "patriots" or "traitors." It frequently happens that a "peace of betrayal" can be brought about only by a military hero from an earlier era.[28]

The matter of targeting options is related to the chronology of U.S. approaches to resolution of the Gulf crisis from August to December 1990 in the following manner. In the days and weeks immediately following Saddam's attack against Kuwait, the United States might have initiated punitive air attacks against targets highly valued by the leadership of Iraq. Priority targets in a U.S. and allied air campaign during August 1990 might have

25. For further discussion, see George H. Quester, "War Termination and Nuclear Targeting Strategy," ch. 14 in *Strategic Nuclear Targeting*, ed. Desmond Ball and Jeffrey Richelson (Ithaca, N.Y.: Cornell University Press, 1986), and the Hon. Harold Brown, Secretary of Defense, "Remarks Prepared for Delivery at Convocation Ceremonies for the 97th Naval War College Class, Newport, Rhode Island, October 20, 1980."

26. A generalization aptly documented in Martin Van Creveld, *Command in War* (Cambridge, Mass.: Harvard University Press, 1985).

27. Fred Charles Iklé, *Every War Must End* (New York: Columbia University Press, 1971), 59–83.

28. Ibid., 66.

included both counterforce and countercommand targets, including the headquarters of the military and political leadership. The purpose of such attacks would not have been to defeat the Iraqi armed forces in battle, but to coerce Saddam Hussein into terminating his occupation of Kuwait. Some observers felt that the United States could have conducted selective, punitive air raids against Iraq almost indefinitely once air superiority had been established in an initial campaign of several days.

The vulnerability of various Iraqi targets to air interdiction was obvious— but not necessarily connected to the determination of Iraq's leadership to hold onto Kuwait. Saddam had the option to attack the structure of collective security by adapting his own targeting strategy to the political cohesion of the allied coalition that opposed him. For example, he might have attacked Israel in response to any U.S. or allied attack against Iraq prior to January 1991. Saddam made this threat explicit in December 1990, undoubtedly as a deterrent; but the threat could not be dismissed as fanciful, since the Iraqi leader had the capability to strike at Tel Aviv and other cities in Israel with surface-to-surface missiles carrying chemical or biological weapons. In the event, he carried out this threat repeatedly once actual warfighting had begun. Thus, even in a losing military campaign, Iraq could threaten either unacceptable or at least highly undesirable consequences for one or more of the members of the coalition that opposed it. Israeli self-restraint in the face of repeated attacks by Iraqi Scud missiles was induced by U.S. promises to make the Scuds a high-priority target for the air campaign. U.S. and allied planners also kept Israeli planes from the wartime skies by denying to their aviators the necessary "identification, friend or foe" (IFF) codes which would identify them as friendly craft, immune from attack.

The larger politico-military aspects of removing the Iraqi regime suggested a necessary connection between international system stability and the tolerance of any particular international system for "deviant" (i.e., destabilizing) behavior. International systems need core values which promote stability along with flexible programs of adjustment for those states whose aims cannot be satisfied within the context of system stability. If too many powerful states develop antisystemic objectives and strategies, the system will fall. As the United States attempted to shift from a Cold War system to a post–Cold War collective security model, it needed to recognize that the connection between system strategies and "dissatisfied actor" options was one that required further attention by diplomats and soldiers.

SYSTEM STABILITY AND MODELS OF WAR

Robert Osgood's definitive study defines limited war as one in which the belligerents restrain their political objectives and military exertions deliberately.[29] Osgood, in this seminal work, advanced important propositions about the relationship between the structure of the international system and its polarity, on one hand, and the propensity of states to seek moderate or ambitious foreign policy goals, on the other. As he explains it: "The limited objectives of eighteenth-century warfare sprang directly from the prevailing international political system, the balance of power. In accordance with this system a dozen or so major states of roughly equal power continually combined, separated, and combined again in ever-shifting alliances and alignments in order to prevent any single power or coalition from gaining preponderance and thereby threatening the common interest of all powers in maintaining a stable international order."[30] Preservation of the balance of power was not a mechanistic, scientific, or self-equilibrating exercise, however. Leaders of states had to be willing to act with a "system interest" (my phrase, not Osgood's) which was not an altruistic one. It was in the interest of the greater number of major powers that certain rules of the game be established concerning the avoidance of system disruption, especially with respect to the elimination of major state actors.

A second important observation made by Osgood about war limitation is that the balance of power is not the automatic result of a multipolar distribution of potential power. One cannot assume that a distribution of major military assets across many countries instead of one or two automatically preserves the equilibrium of the system. The structure of the system is a necessary condition for the preservation of the balance of power, but not a sufficient one. It was also necessary to fight small wars and to engage in limited military interventions in order to prevent larger, and possibly system-destroying, conflicts. As Osgood acknowledges:

> The balance-of-power system did not prevent war. It would have been miraculous if three hundred or more sovereign states, large and small, had been able to adjust their interests within a delicate equilibrium by peaceful means alone. However, it did moderate the nature of the

29. Robert Endicott Osgood, *Limited War: The Challenge to American Security* (Chicago: University of Chicago Press, 1957), esp. 13–27.
30. Ibid., 77.

issues which led to war and hence the objectives for which wars were fought. For in the eighteenth century, war was truly a continuation of political intercourse. *The objectives for which states fought were substantially the same as the ones for which they resorted to war in the first place,* and diplomacy kept the political aspects of the struggle foremost throughout hostilities.[31]

It might seem self-evident that the objectives for which states "fight" are the same as the ones for which they "resort to war." Osgood's point is that this will be true only if there is a "system interest" perceived and shared by the major actors in keeping wars limited. Otherwise, the momentum of military operations and ideological, religious, or nationalist hatreds will carry war beyond the original aims for which the leaders embarked upon it.

This is an extremely important observation, implicit in Osgood's work, about the causes of limitations of escalation. Escalation can be limited only if major actors recognize that they share a systemic interest in doing so and then adapt their foreign policies and military instruments for that purpose. Recognition of a systemic interest in war limitation is not unknown in international history; efforts in the field of international law, including efforts to outlaw the resort to war altogether, have marked European deliberations about world politics for centuries. The point here is more specific. It involves a level-of-analysis issue: the systemic level of analysis directs attention to factors other than the objectives of states and the means available to them for making war. The systemic level of analysis emphasizes the *interaction* among the major actors' goals and capabilities and the shared interest that some actors have in preserving a systemic equilibrium, though admitting of wars and revolutions which allow the system to continue within its essential parameters.

For example, the wars between Prussia and Denmark, and between Prussia and Austria, during the 1860s did not threaten the basic structure of the international system which existed at that time. Prussia was still building up a head of steam that would culminate in its successful war against France in 1870. Prussia's victory in the Franco-Prussian War *did* constitute a threat to the existing system, though, unlike its victory over Austria four years earlier. This was so for two reasons. First, lasting grievances between the French and the German Empire (resulting from the outcome of the Franco-Prussian War) prevented future flexibility of alignment on which the balance-of-

31. Ibid., 78; emphasis added.

power system depended for its dynamic stability. Second, the unification of Germany in the center of Europe changed the potential balance of military and economic power on that continent. Both factors pushed the system toward instability and disequilibrium which erupted in full measure in August 1914.

The point is, the frequency of wars of limited aim or partial victory may be related not only to limited objectives of states but also to the "systemic" structure from which states' objectives are partly deduced. Some leaders acknowledge no interest in preserving the existing system, as Napoleon did not. The Soviet government, despite ideologically antisystemic declaratory policy, did recognize an interest in system preservation after World War II when it emerged as one of two "superpowers" with the capacity for global application of military power.[32] The question raised by Osgood is not so easily answered about the Cold War, even if we grant the supposition that the Soviet Union sought both to preserve its superpower status as long as possible and to avoid nuclear war.

States may moderate their foreign policy goals and their military ambitions for reasons having little or nothing to do with a system interest. They may lack the resources to engage in war, or they may have no significant grievances against the existing international order. Liechtenstein is an example of the first category; Switzerland, of the second. This autolimitation of military means or political objectives does not necessarily guarantee a stable international *system*. The major actors in the system must prefer the existing distribution of power to any drastic alternative, and they must be prepared to commit their national military power, if necessary, toward this end. The U.N. Security Council, like the Concert of Europe after the conclusion of the Napoleonic Wars in 1815, is an attempt to formalize a system interest in preserving international stability against the disruption of peace and security.

If the concept of partial victory or limited aim in war implies a systemic interest on the part of major international actors, as Osgood suggests, then the absence of a systemic interest pushes states toward wars that expand beyond the expectations of the statesmen who start them. World War I provides an excellent illustration of this tendency for military operations that turn out unexpectedly to lead to expanded political aims and, ultimately, to antisystemic ones. Restoration of the balance-of-power system after World

32. See John Lewis Gaddis, *The Long Peace: Inquiries into the History of the Cold War* (New York: Oxford University Press, 1987), esp. ch. 8.

War I proved to be impossible owing to the growing power of antisystemic actors compared to those which favored the status quo.

Critics of the balance-of-power concept have attacked it on many grounds, some of them quite valid.[33] Overly mechanistic concepts of international balancing make nations sound like children on either end of a seesaw, like billiard balls on a table. The mechanistic versions of balance-of-power theory are not the interesting ones, however, just as mechanistic explanations of arms races tell us very little about the causes of arms races. The more interesting aspects of balance-of-power theory are those which call our attention to the dynamics, not the statics, of the relationship between war and politics. Clausewitz, for example, operated without any systemic concept of why wars might be fought with military restraint and for limited aims, although he says some interesting things about the reasons why individual states might prefer, or be forced, to fight a less than total war. His perspective is thus actor-oriented and richly informative therein.

International relations theorists seeking to explain why some historical periods are more warlike than others, and why some distributions of power are more enduring than others, have sought to identify some explanatory variables in the validity and obviousness of the distinction between offensive and defensive military strategies and technologies. Robert Jervis approaches this issue from the standpoint of the security dilemma: the probability that, under conditions of international political anarchy, gains in one state's security may reduce the perceived or actual security of others.[34] Jervis emphasizes the interaction between two conditions that may exacerbate or reduce the force of the security dilemma: 1) whether offensive strategies and technologies can be distinguished from defensive ones and 2) whether the offense or the defense is presumed by leaders to have relative advantage in war. When the offense has the advantage and there is no clear distinction between offense and defense, even status quo states are pushed toward preemption; the result is a great deal of systemic instability.

Robert Gilpin argues that important system transformations are the results of hegemonic wars.[35] According to Gilpin, disturbed international systems

---

33. Hans J. Morgenthau's widely used textbook provides an exemplary statement of balance-of-power theory. See Morgenthau and Kenneth W. Thompson, *Politics Among Nations: The Struggle for Power and Peace*, 6th ed. (New York: Alfred A. Knopf, 1985).

34. Robert Jervis, "Cooperation Under the Security Dilemma," *World Politics* (January 1978): 167–214, in *International Politics: Anarchy, Force, Political Economy, and Decision Making*, ed. Robert J. Art and Robert Jervis (New York: Harper Collins, 1985), 86–100 and 185–207.

35. Robert Gilpin, *War and Change in World Politics* (Cambridge: Cambridge University Press, 1981).

are characterized by an imbalance, or disequilibrium, between the older and newer distributions of political, military, and economic power. The old order resists the new; the aging top dogs resent the upstarts who challenge them for positions on the international ladder of prestige. A hegemonic war redistributes power in an obvious and visible way: the enhanced status of the victors and the reduced status of the losers undergo a visible audit.[36] Hegemonic wars are usually characterized by their unlimited means, by a wide geographic scope, and by the tendency for such wars to involve all or almost all of the major powers in the system. One condition that often precedes the outbreak of hegemonic war is the perception on the part of the current leading states that their international preeminence is imminently threatened by aggressive challengers. The conclusion is sometimes drawn by the status quo leading powers that resistance to this challenge in the form of war is inevitable, and the sooner the better. Notably, states that embark on hegemonic wars, such as World War I, often fail to forecast correctly either the political or the military outcome of the fighting.[37]

Unfortunately, according to Gilpin, hegemonic wars have served as ordering mechanisms in international relations. They have resolved ambiguities about the balance of power and about the governance of the international system. Removal of ambiguities concerning prestige and power increases system stability until the existing status quo is threatened by new challengers, posing the threat of a new distribution of international power and prestige. Two problems with this explanation for system change are apparent. First, though devoid of short-run determinism, in declining to predict any specific outbreak of hegemonic war within particular years or decades, there is an assumption of long-run determinism. Sooner or later the existing order must be challenged by rising hegemons, and the likelihood is that the old order will forcibly resist the new. Second, in the nuclear age, hegemonic war could result in mutually assured destruction of all major combatant forces and their societies. The cost of going to war in order to certify a new distribution of international power may be prohibitive for challenger and challenged alike. Proliferation to many states not previously holding nuclear weapons of mass destruction may be the functional equivalent of hegemonic war. Unconstrained nuclear proliferation would create a "unit veto" international system in which even small powers could deter much larger ones by threatening to impose socially unacceptable costs in the form of heavily damaged or destroyed capital cities.

36. Ibid., 198; see 197–209 for additional discussion by Gilpin of this concept.
37. Ibid., 201.

Nuclear weapons have in some ways made clearer the systemic interests of states, and in other ways have helped to obscure them. The fact that two states, and not three or more, developed large, redundant, and survivable strategic nuclear arsenals was an important cause of postwar international stability. One can see this in the work of U.S. deterrence theorists throughout the nuclear age and, within the past few years, in the work of Soviet theorists also. A system interest in avoiding nuclear war has been proclaimed as official Soviet policy since at least 1977; as early as 1956, Khrushchev's declaration that war between capitalism and socialism was not "fatalistically inevitable" was an acknowledgment that nuclear weapons had established a new international system.[38]

On the other hand, the implications of nuclear multipolarity for international order have been controversial.[39] As the preceding footnote attests,

38. David Holloway, *The Soviet Union and the Arms Race*, 2d ed. (New Haven, Conn.: Yale University Press, 1983), esp. 32. For Soviet military doctrine on the prevention of war as viewed by the armed forces leadership during the Gorbachev era, see MSU Sergey Akhromeyev, "Doktrina predotvrashcheniya voyny zashchity mira i sotsializma" [Doctrine for the Prevention of War, the Defense of Peace and Socialism], *Problemy mira i sotsializma*, no. 12 (December 1987): 23–28, and Minister of Defense D. Yazov, "Novaya model' bezopasnosti i vooruzhennyye sily" [A New Model of Security and the Armed Forces], *Kommunist*, no. 18 (December 1989): 61–72. Yazov's article included important comments on the previous disjunction between the politico-military level of Soviet military doctrine, explicitly defensive in its orientation for decades, and the military-technical level of doctrine, formerly offensive in its emphasis. According to Yazov, "If in its political respect military doctrine was always defensive, stipulating the rejection of military attack on anyone at all, and the rejection of the first use of nuclear weapons, on the military-technical plane reliance was placed on decisive offensive actions in case of the unleashing of war against the Soviet Union and its allies" (p. 65). This contradiction, according to Yazov, had now been eliminated. See also Raymond L. Garthoff, *Deterrence and the Revolution in Soviet Military Doctrine* (Washington, D.C.: Brookings Institution, 1990), 160 and chs. 4–5. For the role of war prevention in current Russian military doctrine, see the May 1992 special issue of *Voennaya mysl'*. Interpretations of the significance of the draft Russian military doctrine of 1992 appear in C. J. Dick, *Initial Thoughts on Russia's Draft Military Doctrine*, SSRC Occasional Brief no. 12 (Sandhurst: Soviet Studies Research Centre, Royal Military Academy, July 14, 1992), and Lt. Col. James F. Holcomb, *Russian Military Doctrine: Structuring for the Worst Case*, Central and East European Defence Studies (Brussels: SHAPE, August 4, 1992). I am indebted to Prof. Charles Dick, SSRC, for calling these sources to my attention.

39. A very useful discussion of this issue is John Lewis Gaddis, *Nuclear Weapons and International Systemic Stability*, International Security Studies Program, Occasional Paper no. 2 (Cambridge, Mass.: American Academy of Arts and Sciences, January 1990). See also Kenneth N. Waltz, *The Spread of Nuclear Weapons: More May Be Better*, Adelphi Paper no. 171 (London: International Institute of Strategic Studies, 1981). Important conceptual insights on this issue are provided in Michael Mandelbaum, *The Nuclear Revolution: International Politics Before and After Hiroshima* (Cambridge: Cambridge University Press, 1981), and Robert Jervis, *The Meaning of the Nuclear Revolution: Statecraft and the Prospect of Armageddon* (Ithaca, N.Y.: Cornell University Press, 1989).

some theorists have argued that the dispersion of nuclear weapons will in-crease international stability, other theorists have contended that nuclear proliferation is highly destabilizing, and still others have taken an agnostic position. There are many facets to the issue of nuclear proliferation and international stability that cannot be developed here. Our present interest is in the effects of nuclear weapons on the propensity for the development of a system interest which is recognized by major actors as a genuine interest apart from their own specific goals. If historical precedent is any guide, the impact of nuclear weapons will not be to lower the risk of deliberate aggres-sion, but to raise the risk of inadvertent war and escalation. Outside of Eu-rope, the spread of nuclear weapons might embolden nuclear-armed states to engage in "nuclear blackmail" against those not possessing nuclear weap-ons, or to launch conventional wars on the assumption that their nuclear weapons will act to establish superiority in intrawar deterrence if need be. Given the level of U.S. and Soviet anxiety about the spread of nuclear weap-ons to Third World states, an aspiring regional hegemon might be better served by using its nuclear weapons as a backdrop for conventional aggression and as a last-ditch escape from a conventional military defeat. A nuclear first strike against another regional actor, say by Israel against Iraq or India against Pakistan, would risk the alienation of both the United States and the Soviet Union, widespread political condemnation inside and outside the world of developing states, and eventual retribution by the victim or its allies as soon as capabilities permitted.

The emphasis on nuclear proliferation in much Western writing has ob-scured the more immediate risk to regional balances of power inherent in the spread of ballistic missiles of long, medium, and short range.[40] If the development of nuclear weapons technology was fortuitously concentrated in a handful of states after World War II, the potential for the dispersion of long-range missiles capable of firing chemical, nuclear, or other rounds was a disturbing introduction to the 1990s. The path to destabilization of the international system might be an accretion of tensions in regions far from Europe and over which the superpowers might have little direct control. Long-range ballistic missiles are sought by aspiring regional hegemons such as Libya, Iraq, and Syria as much for their symbolic and status value as for their military capabilities, but the latter are significant in their own right. According to expert analysts Janne Nolan and Albert Wheelon, ballistic

40. See Janne E. Nolan and Albert D. Wheelon, "Third World Ballistic Missiles," *Scientific American* (August 1990): 34–40.

missiles in the hands of Third World states could be very destructive. A Scud B (Soviet surface-to-surface missile; range, 180 mi.) releasing 1,200 pounds of VX (a chemical nerve agent) 4,000 feet above an airfield would kill about half of the people in a corridor three-tenths of a mile wide and two and a half miles long in the direction of prevailing winds.[41] Accuracy, as important as yield in determining the lethality of munitions, is steadily improving as a result of better guidance technology. Third World states already have access to ballistic missile guidance technologies that would allow them to achieve a circular error probable of 200 feet at a range of 500 miles, or 120 feet at 200 miles. Such accuracies, according to Nolan and Wheelon, would permit the destruction of most point targets by means of high-explosive warheads and the elimination of troop concentrations and cities by means of cluster bombs or poison gas.[42]

Nuclear weapons increased the U.S. and Soviet span of control. The spread of ballistic missiles and chemical weapons outside Europe tends to work in the other direction, toward a reduction of that span of control. One might argue, against this, that decentralized "system maintenance" will occur instead of U.S.-Soviet bipolarity. A multipolar system of heavily armed regional hegemons will find its own stability regardless of what the Americans and Soviets do. This alternative is not foreclosed, but it will require some self-conscious effort on the part of regional hegemons to limit their aspirations to intraregional goals and to restrain other regional giants whose ambitions threaten to become global. If, for example, India or Japan chooses to exercise its right to a much more assertive, internationalist foreign and defense policy in the 1990s and beyond, who is to moderate such aspirations in favor of "systemic" constraints? The U.S. and Soviet span of controls over regional actors will be limited, based on diplomatic suasion instead of military deterrence. Beijing might balance the ambitions of India and Japan in Asia, but the unlocking of China's capability for regional checkmate might extrapolate into a stronger Chinese interest in global reach.

This relationship between regional or global multipolarity and nuclear or high-technology proliferation is certainly still at issue. John Mearsheimer's prognostication for the 1990s, of an inevitable nuclear proliferation in Europe which will be either well or poorly managed, indicates how wide the spectrum of contingent prediction may be.[43] Prediction of specific events is

41. Ibid.
42. Ibid., 39.
43. John J. Mearsheimer, "Back to the Future: Instability in Europe After the Cold War," *International Security* (Summer 1990): 5–56.

less the issue than is the ability to foresee pertinent general trends.[44] My argument here is that it will be insufficient for the United States to have a military strategy or a foreign policy strategy for the 1990s unless it also has a "systems strategy": a sense of the predominant trends in international politics and a notion of the extent to which the United States or other states can add impetus to favorable trends and slow down unfavorable ones. Iraq's sudden attack on Kuwait on August 2, 1990, forced U.S. and allied leaders to work backward from the outbreak of a specific crisis to the improvisation of an expedient systems strategy for the international containment of an aspiring regional hegemon.

FROM COERCIVE DIPLOMACY
TO COERCIVE WAR

The United States and its allies launched on January 16, 1991, a massive air campaign against Iraq. The objective of the campaign was to induce Iraqi compliance with the demands of President Bush and the United Nations for a prompt withdrawal of Iraqi forces from Kuwait. The U.S. and allied air campaign was unprecedented in its scope. More than two thousand U.S. and other coalition aircraft flew as many as three thousand sorties per day. The setting for the application of air power was ideal. Bombing targets were not obscured by jungle, woods, or other natural interference and camouflage. Iraq's air force was no match for the combined air power of the allies. As former U.S. Air Force Chief of Staff, General Michael Dugan noted, "If there was a scenario where air power could be effective, this was it."[45]

From an operational standpoint, the U.S. air campaign against Iraq had four overlapping phases. The first phase involved attacks against Iraqi command-and-control targets; against nuclear, chemical, and biological warfare manufacturing facilities; and against other components of the Iraqi military infrastructure. In the second phase, the suppression of Iraqi air defenses was emphasized in order to clear the skyways for the operation of coalition aircraft throughout Iraqi battle space. In the third phase, an interdiction cam-

---

44. Yu. V. Chuyev and Yu. B. Mikhaylov, *Prognozirovanie v voennom dele* [Forecasting in Military Affairs] (Moscow: Voyenizdat, 1975), provide an interesting Soviet discussion of forecasting methodology and its relevance to military affairs.

45. Gen. Michael Dugan, "The Air War," *U.S. News and World Report*, February 11, 1991.

paign was designed to isolate Saddam Hussein's crack Republican Guard and other forces from reinforcement and resupply. In the fourth and final phase, air support would be provided to the ground forces of the coalition as they moved against Iraqi forces remaining in Kuwait.[46] Notably missing from this list, as described by General Dugan, is the "air superiority" mission traditionally considered as a first-priority mission by U.S. and other air commanders: prevailing in air-to-air combat against the forces of the opponent.

The reason for this omission was that the Iraqi air force, including its air defenses, was caught by surprise on January 16. This might seem monumentally absurd, since President Bush had long before received U.N. authorization to use force against Iraq. The expectation that the United States would attack eventually did not transfer into an accurate prediction by Iraqi intelligence about the specific timing of the attack. In a classic case of "signals-to-noise" confusion, the flurry of last-minute diplomatic exchanges and proposals in search of a peaceful resolution to the Gulf crisis by various world leaders probably obscured from Iraq the resolution and immediate preparation for war of the U.S. and allied air forces. The initial attacks on January 16 were devastating, hitting Iraqi air defenses and command-and-control targets with such effectiveness that the Iraqi air force was essentially out of the picture of air-superiority combat.

These initial successes in the strategic air war left the missions of interdiction and close air support for the ground phase of the war still to be accomplished. The interdiction campaign against a "target-rich environment" included Iraq's entire military infrastructure, not omitting its stationary defensive forces in Kuwait and its mobile-armored and mechanized forces in Kuwait and Iraq. The objectives of the interdiction campaign were 1) to weaken further the command and control of the Iraqi armed forces, so that they would be forced to fight in disaggregated globules; 2) to reduce the combat power of Saddam's crack Republican Guard so that they could not intervene decisively to rescue other Iraqi forces later cut off and destroyed in Kuwait; and 3) to continue the destruction of other military and defense-related targets in order to increase the price Iraq would have to pay to keep fighting.

The third point is most pertinent to our discussion here. The U.S. and allied air campaign was designed not only to destroy a complex of targets in

---

46. Ibid. Gen. Dugan's description of the phased air campaign notes that the phases are overlapping, as noted above. Otherwise, one might assume that air defenses were attacked only after all missions had been fulfilled in phase one, which is very unlikely.

Iraq for the purpose of *denying* those capabilities to Saddam Hussein, but also to *punish* the Iraqi leadership by influencing their expectation of further damage to come. The air campaign was as much a war of coercion as it was a war of destruction. The hope in some compartments of the U.S. and allied governments was that the bombing campaign by itself might induce the Iraqis to withdraw from Kuwait, without the need for a major ground offensive.

It will be recalled that General Dugan had been dismissed by Secretary Cheney from his post as U.S. Air Force chief of staff in the autumn of 1990 for suggesting that air power alone might accomplish all strategic missions in any war against Iraq. This offended the U.S. defense "tradition" of recent decades, and sensitivities on the subject were even keener since the passage of the Goldwater-Nichols legislation in 1986. Translated from the bureaucratic environment into the combat environment, "jointness" means that each service must have a piece of the action. Whether from a tactical standpoint air power could have accomplished U.S. and allied objectives in the 1991 Gulf War, it was not a politically admissible option to exclude other arms of service once war had begun.[47]

A distinction must be made between the operational-tactical and the strategic level of warfare, relative to the political objectives of President Bush and the U.S. allies, in order to assess the limits of coercive air war in the Gulf.[48] Even under the most optimistic assumptions about the effectiveness of air power, ground operations would be necessary in order to mop up those Iraqi forces remaining in Kuwait, unless Iraq chose to withdraw them voluntarily. Air power can neither hold ground nor forcibly disarm soldiers in their defensive redoubts. These limitations of air power are acknowledged but are incidental to the argument over whether air power alone could accomplish the strategic objectives of the United States in Iraq. The theory that it could rested on assumptions about the coercive effectiveness of air power in both punishment and denial roles.

Western strategists generally accept that the punishment capabilities of nuclear weapons are more meaningful for deterrence than their denial capabilities. Most U.S. strategists also generally assume that, for conventional forces, the reverse is true: conventional denial capabilities are more important than conventional deterrence based on the threat of retaliatory punishment. Thus, it would be argued by many strategists that a coercive air cam-

47. For more on this, see Eliot Cohen, "The Unsheltering Sky," *The New Republic*, February 11, 1991.
48. For comparison, see the analysis of U.S. air power in Robert A. Pape, Jr., "Coercive Air Power in the Vietnam War," *International Security* (Fall 1990): 103–46.

paign with conventional forces should be counterforce rather than countervalue. Its objective would be to destroy the opponent's instruments of military power, in order to induce the opponent to see the futility of further fighting.[49] In addition to avoiding gratuitous attacks on civilians, a counterforce-oriented campaign reduces the competency of the enemy force, thereby influencing the decision calculus of the enemy leadership against continued fighting.

Although these arguments are widely held in the U.S. defense community, they must be qualified in several ways. First of all, in conventional war, the decision calculus of an opponent may not be amenable to influence based on subjective estimates of future losses, until the point at which the back of the opponent's entire war machine is broken. Instead of gradually shifting his will to fight from the "yes" into the "no" column, air and other attacks may meet with stiff resistance until a "catastrophic fold" appears in his ability to fight back. Sudden collapse of an opponent's fighting power may shift his decision calculus overnight from extreme optimism to extreme pessimism. Hitler insisted that wonder weapons, including newer versions of V-2 rockets, would come to his rescue even as his leading generals saw their forces collapse on the eastern and western fronts. During the last months and weeks of the war, Hitler issued orders affecting imaginary or mostly destroyed forces. Only the virtual collapse of the city of Berlin on the führer's head finally persuaded him that all was lost.

A second qualification is that air power, especially in the massive doses administered by the allied coalition against Iraq in January and February 1991, is not a surgical instrument. The precision of bombing has improved dramatically since World War II, and even since Vietnam; nonetheless, the collocation of civil and military installations and the inevitable bombing errors ensure that massive numbers of sorties against "military" targets will also bring significant amounts of "collateral damage." There is no such thing as a counterforce air war, except on a very small and therefore insignificant scale. This argument, if correct, implies that not only the denial aspects of counterforce campaigns, but also the inadvertent punishment that inevitably accompanies them, are important in inducing the opponent to "cooperate" by negotiating for war termination.

Third, coercion of an enemy government that is losing a military campaign is more likely to be successful if that government is divided into various factions. The "outs" can exploit the losses already sustained by the armed

---

49. For an argument to this effect, see Pape, "Coercive Air Power," passim.

forces and by the civilian population to bring policy judgments to bear against the prior decisions of the "ins." If, on the other hand, the enemy leadership is united in its pursuit of war aims, or if the dissenters lack powerful and influential voices compared to those in favor of continued war, the potential for coercive influence is diminished.[50] One of the factors that limited the effectiveness of U.S. air power in Vietnam was the lack of any "peace party" within the political leadership of North Vietnam. Although they emphasized tactical flexibility in their use of diplomacy and fighting tempo, North Vietnam's strategic compass never deviated from the objective of taking over South Vietnam. In similar fashion, Saddam brooked no opposition to his decisions, thus reducing the opportunity for any dissident faction to organize in favor of early war termination. In cases such as these, the coercive influence of air power may be as dependent upon the expectations of an undivided enemy leadership about future punishment, including their own survival, as it is dependent upon the diminished future competency of their armed forces. Conventional deterrence, unlike nuclear deterrence, depends upon punishment and denial capabilities that are based in the same military forces.

The U.S. air war against Iraq is but one case among many which demonstrate that the coercive and attritional aspects of the use of force cannot easily be separated in many cases. Policymakers may adopt a "try and see" variant of coercive punishment just as they have adopted "try and see" variations of crisis diplomacy.[51] The Bush administration in 1991 clearly would have *preferred* to induce Saddam Hussein to withdraw his forces from Kuwait voluntarily, just as President Kennedy would have preferred to induce Khrushchev to withdraw his missiles from Cuba voluntarily. Kennedy avoided actual war and Bush did not, although the military balance in both cases favored the United States one-sidedly. Nevertheless, the initial phase of the U.S. war against Iraq was not just a campaign designed to bring about the destruction of Iraqi military capabilities. President Bush indicated repeatedly that the destruction would stop if Saddam withdrew from Kuwait, and that the destruction would continue if Iraq did not withdraw. Given the U.S. declaratory objective of compelling Iraqi withdrawal from Kuwait and nothing more, the Bush model of coercive air power fit the paradigm of "coercive bargaining in war."

One argument for the goodness of fit between the U.S. and allied air war against Iraq and a coercive bargaining model was that the choice of contin-

---

50. Iklé, *Every War Must End*, 60–83.
51. George, "The Development of Doctrine and Strategy," 1–35.

ued suffering was left up to Saddam Hussein. Bush would have been under great pressure from the U.S. Congress and from members of the allied coalition, especially Arab members, if Saddam Hussein had taken up the challenge of conciliation and had begun to remove his troops from Kuwait in January or early February 1991, even at a slow pace. Saddam would not play this diplomatic card until later, after coalition air attacks had caused significant, if not decisive, losses to his ground forces deployed in Kuwait and Iraq. Only the imminent expectation of total military defeat for his forces in Kuwait would change Saddam's decision calculus for or against continued war. This defeat might also be accompanied by the destruction of the remainder of his offensive military power, as he surely realized by the middle of February, and perhaps by his own political disestablishment.[52]

Saddam Hussein's "strategic" objectives, once crisis management faded into combat, were apparently threefold. First, he sought to create a war of attrition, including an extended phase of ground fighting, which would make the war unpopular with the U.S. public, Congress, and news media. Extended ground fighting with high casualties would also alienate allied members from the U.S. coalition. Saddam's second objective was to expand the war geographically (horizontal escalation) by bringing in Israel. This would also, in his view, separate some Arab members of the coalition from the United States. A third Iraqi objective became clear only in February, as Saddam entertained visits from Soviet officials offering to mediate the conflict. This third objective was to hold the United States to its declaratory objective—the removal of Iraqi forces from Kuwait—and to deter or otherwise prevent the expansion of U.S. and allied war aims to the destruction of all of Iraq's military power and the removal of Saddam as a player in the postwar world.

The problem for Iraq was that each of these objectives required that elements of a coercive strategy, of bargaining while fighting, had to be amalgamated with elements of traditional warfighting in order to succeed. But Iraq was unable to impose any unacceptable costs on the United States and its coalition partners. As the coalition proceeded to destroy Saddam's air and ground forces, his bargaining leverage for the postwar world diminished pro-

52. U.S. Secretary of State James A. Baker III outlined postwar U.S. objectives for the Gulf and Middle East regions in testimony before the U.S. Congress, House Foreign Affairs Committee, on February 6, 1991. His statement hinted at a continued U.S. military presence in the region and included among five major goals the economic reconstruction of Iraq. Baker was noncommittal about insisting that Saddam Hussein resign as a precondition for U.S. postwar aid. *New York Times*, February 7, 1991.

gressively. When the effectiveness of his armed forces reached the point of "catastrophic" failure, Saddam's future influence rested solely on his potential to prolong an already lost military campaign. Having missed the opportunity to negotiate for war termination while a coercive strategy was still open to Iraq, Saddam Hussein ensured that the final terms of armistice would be that much more unfavorable for his country.

The coalition war against Iraq in 1991 and the crisis management phase that preceded it offer important lessons for students of threatmaking and force application. There is a significant probability that these lessons will be mislearned. Professional military and other observers of the Gulf War concluded that the path to future victory was to use overwhelming force from the outset. Theater commanders were to be unrestricted in their selection of military operational plans, targeting priorities, and objectives. In short, the U.S. and allied strategy in the Gulf War was successful because it inverted the reasons for U.S. failure in Vietnam: the Gulf War was an anti–Vietnam War, the negation of a negation. This Hegelian view of what the United States did correctly in the Gulf in contrast to Vietnam missed much of the essence of the Gulf crisis and of wartime coercive bargaining. Prior to and during the war, the United States and its allies continually advertised to Iraq their willingness to settle for partial victory in return for Iraqi compliance with U.N. demands. In the event, the ground war was rapidly terminated as soon as the immediate political objective, that of expelling Iraq from Kuwait, was attained.

The air war against Iraq was both an exercise in coercive bargaining and a campaign of attrition to reduce Iraq's wartime and postwar military capabilities. The coercive aspects were most apparent in the early destruction of Iraq's air defenses, command and control, and facilities for making weapons of mass destruction. A calculating adversary might have quit right there, but Saddam Hussein was not using the decision calculus of Western deterrence theory. The Iraqi leader assumed that he could prolong the war to his political advantage, despite military and civil losses. Saddam misestimated the point at which a coercive air war would be expanded, by virtue of his unwillingness to bargain, into a campaign of widespread destruction of his armed forces and military-supporting infrastructure. Nevertheless, he exploited the weak links in the coalition political consensus in order to obtain war termination under conditions allowing for his own political survival as well as that of his regime.

5

FIGHTING AND ENDING WARS ON TERMS

Deterrence and Conciliation in War

Interstate conflicts are resolved by some combination of coercion and persuasion, but not all international conflicts lead to war. Once a war has begun, states must reach some "agreement" in order to end it; most wars are ended when a potential losing side sees no benefit in continuing to fight, and this point is usually well short of total military or political defeat. Bringing the fighting to a conclusion presupposes that leaders can threaten credibly to impose further costs on their opponents by continued fighting, and can offer prompt relief from suffering if acceptable terms can be worked out.

The preceding chapter showed that the avoidance of excessive demands by

I gratefully acknowledge contributions to my thinking on this subject and pertinent references from Jack S. Levy and Sidney R. Waldman. This chapter grows out of research done for a conference, "Conflict Termination After Cold War," held at Haverford College in April 1990. I am especially grateful to Prof. Sidney R. Waldman for his encouragement and suggestions pertinent to this topic.

ultimate victors and the willingness to trade off values between apparent victors and losers was characteristic even of the most one-sided coalition war of the Cold War years. The capacity to make threats plausible was partly dependent on making clear the benefits of compliance with the terms of the threats as well as making obvious the punishment that would follow if threats were ignored. The preceding chapter also showed that the process of threatmaking was a dynamic one in which the credibility of threats was context-dependent on the capabilities of the sides for continued punishment or denial via warfare. The chapter noted, and the present chapter will expand upon this point, that the success of crisis-ending or war-terminating threats backed up by military power is related to the two-sided character of military persuasion. To threaten a regime with unacceptable hurt may be counterproductive of the aim to induce its cooperation, even if the unacceptable hurt is contingent upon the regime's cooperative behavior. To threaten acceptable hurt with the possibility of greater, possibly unacceptable destruction may be more persuasive, because the negatives of possible future destruction are offset by the positives of preferable and acceptable present suffering.

In the discussion that follows, three of the essential components of the concept of war termination are considered: an agreed battle, escalation control, and coercive diplomacy. An "agreed battle" defines the boundaries of a fight, although those boundaries may be indistinct at the outset of battle. "Escalation control" is the capacity to fight and to negotiate within limitations preferred by policymakers, despite pressure to expand the fighting in counterproductive ways. "Coercive diplomacy" is a framework for the exercise of crisis or wartime influence in which forceful suasion is mixed with nonmilitary instruments in order to attain preferred policy objectives. The present chapter discusses how these aspects of crisis or war termination involved hard choices between deterrence and nonprovocation during the Cold War years, and those observations shed light on the significance of nonprovocative conflict termination in the post–Cold War world. The U.S. experience in the Cuban missile crisis shows with particular force the importance of nonprovocative deterrence in crisis management.

AN AGREED BATTLE

The first component of any concept of war termination is the idea of an agreed battle.[1] An agreed battle is a conflict fought for less-than-total objec-

1. See Paul Bracken, "War Termination," ch. 6 in *Managing Nuclear Operations*, ed. Ash-

tives by mutual agreement. Because it is fought for less-than-total objectives, it is conducted within "rules" that may be apparent only as the fighting unfolds. An illustration is provided by the conduct of the Korean War on the part of the United States and the People's Republic of China (PRC). Each government was determined to achieve certain policy objectives, but not at the cost of allowing the war to expand into a total war. The Chinese limited their acknowledged involvement to "volunteers." The United States intervened in Korea and later, under the aegis of the United Nations, fought the Chinese who intervened. There were also important restraints on how both sides conducted the fighting. The United States did not authorize bombing attacks on targets in the Chinese mainland, and the Chinese did not contest U.S. Pacific sanctuaries from which reinforcements and war-supporting matériel were provided. The war was thus "frozen" into a more-or-less tightly bounded geopolitical context, much to General Douglas MacArthur's displeasure and to the confusion of many American citizens.[2]

In some sense, the United States "discovered" the idea of limited war in the course of fighting the Korean War.[3] The United States did not plan to include South Korea within its strategic defense perimeter in the Far East. During the spring of 1949, General MacArthur, as supreme commander for the allied powers in the Far East, gave a newspaper interview in which he outlined a U.S. "line of defense" in the Far East that excluded the Korean peninsula. And in a speech before the National Press Club on January 12, 1950, Secretary of State Dean Acheson outlined a U.S. "defense perimeter" that also left out Korea. Thus, President Truman's reaction to the North Korean invasion surprised not only the North Koreans and the Soviets, but also many advisers in his own administration. At first the United States reacted by providing air support to the beleaguered South Koreans, but it soon became apparent that this support would be insufficient to stem the tide. Accordingly, Truman authorized intervention of American ground forces, which at that moment were in a state of preparedness far below that required for sustained combat in the Korean peninsula. As the North Koreans pushed U.S. and Republic of Korea (ROK) forces into the Pusan perimeter in 1950, it soon became clear to Americans that they were in for a sustained commitment with apparently high costs.

ton B. Carter, John D. Steinbruner, and Charles A. Zraket (Washington, D.C.: Brookings Institution, 1987), 202.

2. For a discussion of limitations in Korea, see Robert Endicott Osgood, *Limited War: The Challenge to American Security* (Chicago: University of Chicago Press, 1957), 163–94.

3. Thomas C. Schelling, *Arms and Influence* (New Haven, Conn.: Yale University Press, 1966), 130, conveys some of this.

But Truman was determined that those costs not be so high as to preclude the United States from assisting Europe in a defense against Soviet attack there, should one materialize. Nor was the United States so plentifully supplied with nuclear weapons that it could afford to use them in Korea without jeopardizing the stockpile which might be required for war in Europe. Moreover, nuclear weapons seemed disproportionate to the accomplishment of U.S. objectives in Korea: the North Koreans had attacked an American ally with conventional weapons, and the Soviet Union had issued no nuclear threat to back up the North Koreans. After the Chinese intervened, the United States was also determined not to expand the conflict into a war against the PRC mainland. Truman's military advisers noted that the United States lacked the wherewithal to fight the Soviet Union and the PRC simultaneously, and it was not clear that the United States, even with nuclear weapons, could accomplish any meaningful political objective in a war against China.

MacArthur was not alone among U.S. military commanders who failed to understand the evolving concept of limited war within the context of the larger "Cold War" now developing on several fronts.[4] Public confusion was also evident. Initially high levels of public support for U.S. intervention began to vitiate as the war became more protracted, costs mounted, and a clear and decisive outcome seemed nowhere in sight. This pattern was to be repeated in Vietnam, although other causes contributed as well. But one factor which made Korea different from Vietnam was that American policymakers approached the latter war after having lived through the first. The idea of self-imposed limitation in war with Soviet surrogates or allies was no longer in principle a contradiction, although in practice military planners of the Vietnam era resented the "gradualism" imposed by civilian policymakers.

Military resentment notwithstanding, constraints were placed on U.S. air and ground operations during the Vietnam War, as well as on declaratory political objectives. The United States did not officially declare war on North Vietnam, nor did it invade that country. The United States did not go to war against the Soviet Union or China, even though both provided essential aid for the North Vietnamese military campaign against American forces. And, most important, by 1968 the U.S. policymaking process had

---

4. See Robert E. Osgood, "The Post-War Strategy of Limited War: Before, During, and After Vietnam," ch. 4 in *Strategic Thought in the Nuclear Age*, ed. Laurence Martin (Baltimore, Md.: Johns Hopkins University Press, 1979), 93–130.

made further increases in American military commitment impossible. Johnson's refusal to run for reelection and his de facto reversal of policy, toward military and political deescalation, established a context for future Vietnam decisionmaking very different from that which prevailed prior to the Tet offensive of January 1968. Subsequent to the Tet offensive, and especially after Johnson's policy reversal and "resignation" from politics, U.S. objectives emphasized the conditions for war termination. The purpose of U.S. military activity after Johnson's turnaround in policy, reaffirmed by Richard Nixon after assuming office in 1969, was to avoid losing a military stalemate and thereby to preserve bargaining leverage for a pacific settlement of the conflict.

This assessment conflicts with military-traditionalist notions of how a war ought to be fought, notions undoubtedly reinforced by the outcome of the U.S. and allied coalition air war against Iraq in January 1991. The air attacks unleashed by the United States against Iraqi counterforce and command-system targets on January 16, 1991, and thereafter will be used as proof by future advocates of air power that force used in massive doses rather than gradually is the proper recipe for military victory. The U.S. air "blitzkrieg" against Iraq offered to many observers convincing proof that the hobbling of our air power in Vietnam until late in 1972 was largely responsible for the protracted and stalemated character of that war.

However, the parallel between the accomplishments of air power in Iraq in 1991 and the potential accomplishments of withheld air power in North Vietnam decades earlier is imprecise.[5] The political setting of the war against Iraq, which enjoyed no support from the Soviet Union or other potential allies as a result of Saddam's own inept diplomacy, was conducive to an unrestrained use of force. The United States had been authorized by the United Nations to use force to expel Iraq from Kuwait, and the U.S. Congress had also signed on to the use of force in January 1991. Apart from the possibility of horizontal escalation of the conflict by involving Israel, the risks of escalation attendant to a strategy of annihilation against Iraq's military forces ranged from minimal to nonexistent. This was not the case in Vietnam, nor in Korea. The end of the Cold War in Europe and the support of the Soviet leadership under Mikhail Gorbachev for U.S. and U.N. objectives cleared the way for the application of U.S. military power against Iraq almost without constraint.

5. On U.S. coercive bombing in Vietnam, see Robert A. Pape, Jr., "Coercive Air Power in the Vietnam War," *International Security* (Fall 1990): 103–46.

Almost, but not quite; for external as well as self-imposed constraints on U.S. military options existed. President Bush had declared in his television announcement of Operation Desert Storm on January 16 that the U.S. objective was neither to destroy nor to occupy Iraq. Implicit in Bush's announcement was also the "carrot" that the driving of Saddam's forces from Iraq would not necessarily result in the demise of his regime. But it was clear as early as the first day of war that it would be difficult to draw clear lines between three possible objectives of U.S. and allied military action against Iraq: first, eviction of Iraq's occupational army from Kuwait; second, destruction of the remainder of Iraq's offensive military power; and third, removal of Saddam Hussein from effective political and military control of the state, its armed forces, and its internal security apparatus. The limitation of U.S. political objectives, as explained by President Bush, had more to do with keeping in line a precarious coalition of twenty-nine countries, including key Arab states such as Egypt and Syria, than it did with a conceptual framework for the application of U.S. military power. Given Iraq's military weakness relative to the coalition mobilized against it, the "agreed battle" terms would be imposed, not negotiated, once war had started.

Strategic theorists could still argue over whether the actual war had begun with the strategic air assault launched against Iraq on January 16 or with the onset of ground fighting between coalition and Iraqi forces. This is not a facetious question. Bush had obtained congressional and U.N. authorization to use force, and the amount of destruction inflicted on Iraq by the air campaign was impressive by any standard. From most philosophical standpoints, judged by its intent or consequences, this was war.

There was another level at which the air campaign of January and February 1991 could be understood by strategists, however. It could also be interpreted as something short of "war proper," as a campaign of coercive violence, brutal and ugly, designed to induce the "cooperation" of the Iraqi leadership by inflicting some punishment while withholding other, potentially more decisive, attacks. The context of the air war against Iraq was not a test of strength between the Iraqi and the U.S./allied air forces; the outcome of any such test of strength was not in doubt. It was an attempt to use coercion in war in order to avoid a more destructive and more expansive war. As Schelling has characterized it: "War appears to be, or threatens to be, not so much a contest of strength as one of endurance, nerve, obstinacy, and pain. It appears to be, and threatens to be, not so much a contest of military strength as a bargaining process—dirty, extortionate, and often quite reluctant bargaining on one side or both—nevertheless a bargaining process."[6]

Between warfighting and ultimate surrender, nonetheless, Iraq retained assets that could extract enormous costs from U.S. and allied forces, including some six hundred thousand troops deployed on the ground in southern Iraq and Kuwait. Those who did not desert or give up in futility, provided their units maintained organizational cohesion, would have to be rooted out by ground and air assault. The allied coalition obviously preferred to avoid a protracted ground war involving heavy casualties, and President Bush was very much aware that extended and costly fighting could turn U.S. public and congressional opinion against the war.

U.S. Secretary of State James Baker outlined five political objectives for the postwar Middle East in early February 1991, anticipating a military outcome favorable to the coalition. The first of these was a new security arrangement among states of the Persian Gulf, in order to stabilize the balance of power there. Second, he mentioned an arms control agreement among supplier states which would restrict Iraq's postwar rebuilding of its nuclear, chemical, and biological weapons. The third objective listed in Baker's February 6 statement was a program of economic reconstruction in the Arab world, and a fourth plank called for new initiatives to settle Arab–Israeli and Israeli–Palestinian conflicts. Baker's fifth objective called for the United States to devise a comprehensive strategy to reduce its dependency on imported oil.[7]

The difference between "termination of war" and "conflict termination" might be addressed in this context. Wars involve the use of organized military forces on behalf of state policy. Not all conflicts, therefore, are wars.[8] I believe this is sufficiently obvious not to require discussion. In the special case of coalition wars, the distinction between war termination and conflict termination is more meaningful and less a matter of words per se. In a coalition war, members of the coalition buy into the objectives of the coalition

6. Schelling, Arms and Influence, 7.
7. New York Times, February 7, 1991.
8. For pertinent concepts and documentation, see Quincy Wright, A Study of War (Chicago: University of Chicago Press, 1942); Lewis F. Richardson, Statistics of Deadly Quarrels (Pittsburgh: Boxwood Press, 1960); J. David Singer and Melvin Small, The Wages of War, 1816–1965: A Statistical Handbook (New York: John Wiley & Sons, 1972); and especially the classification in Measuring the Correlates of War, ed. J. David Singer and Paul F. Diehl (Ann Arbor: University of Michigan Press, 1990) among interstate disputes, militarized interstate disputes, militarized interstate crises, and interstate war.

to varying degrees. The United States was much more committed to destroying Iraq's offensive military power, for example, than were some of its alliance partners, especially the Arab partners. Because members of an international coalition have different preference orderings with regard to
objectives, they also value differently consequences and outcomes associated
with attaining those objectives. For example, some Arab members of the
coalition were willing to fight defensively in Saudi Arabia or offensively in
Kuwait, but not in Iraq. U.S. officials also feared that Iraq might drag Israel
into the war, changing the alignment of coalition versus Iraq into something
much more confused. Disaggregation of the U.S.-led anti-Iraqi coalition
would complicate the problem of war termination considerably.

Beyond the immediate termination of war between the U.N. coalition and
the Iraqi government, the larger issue of conflict termination between Israel
and its Palestinian and other Arab neighbors loomed importantly. Saddam's
attempt to link two issues—Kuwait's status and a Middle East peace conference—prior to war were deflected successfully by U.S. diplomacy. But in the
aftermath of a destructive Gulf war, pressure from Arab states and other
coalition members for a broad-gauged peace conference on Middle East po-
litical-conflict termination seemed inevitable. In turn, U.S. willingness to
agree to this broader forum for *conflict* termination might expedite termination of the *war* against Iraq. In turn, success in this or in other multinational
forums that resolved differences between Israelis and Palestinians could prevent the outbreak of future wars in the Middle East. Much the same argument, in favor of a broad-based forum for conflict termination in order to
reduce the likelihood of war, was made in Europe for the CSCE process,
including as it did the former Warsaw Pact states, those of NATO, and neu-
tral/nonaligned nations under a common negotiatory framework.

Agreed Crisis?

The notion of an agreed battle might be extended into that of an "agreed
crisis" under any of the following conditions. When more than one of these
conditions is present, the continuation of crisis management as an alternative to war receives multiple reinforcement. Nonetheless, the presence of
one or more of these conditions is no guarantee that war will *not* break out.
At this stage of social science research, the conditions related to war's outbreak or prevention cannot be subjected to causal modeling with statistical
precision. The reasons have to do with more than technique; the subject

matter is inherently complicated, and the "human factor" introduces a great deal of indeterminacy.[9]

First, neither side seeks military victory because the costs of fighting successfully are judged to be disproportionate to the objectives being sought. Second, technology and leaders' perceptions of its effects make victory impossible for either side. Third, the relationship between the probable success of offensive or defensive strategies is one that favors the defense or at least deters preemption. Fourth, leaders are able to communicate with each other with sufficient fidelity to make known their preferences for crisis resolution as opposed to actual fighting. Fifth, the structure of the international distribution of power and other systemic attributes favor the status quo over challenges to it. Sixth, there is at least one "system" actor whose leadership places a higher value on the avoidance of war, or on stability based on the political status quo, compared to system change brought about by war.[10]

Although U.S. and Soviet forces fought no "agreed battles" against one another, they did conduct "agreed crises" with certain ground rules.[11] During

9. For an assessment of social science and crisis management, see Ole R. Holsti, "Crisis Decision Making," ch. 1 in *Behavior, Society, and Nuclear War*, ed. Philip E. Tetlock, Jo L. Husbands, Robert Jervis, Paul C. Stern, and Charles Tilly (New York: Oxford University Press, 1989), 1:8–84. On methodology of the social sciences, especially behavioral psychology, sociology, and decisionmaking studies as applied to war prevention and crisis management, see Philip E. Tetlock, "Methodological Themes and Variations," ch. 5 in *Behavior, Society, and Nuclear War*, ed. Tetlock et al., 1:334–86.

10. A large literature supports these observations. See in particular Lawrence Freedman, *The Evolution of Nuclear Strategy* (New York: St. Martin's Press, 1981); Kurt Gottfried and Bruce G. Blair, *Crisis Stability and Nuclear War* (New York: Oxford University Press, 1988); Robert Jervis, Richard Ned Lebow, and Janice Gross Stein, *Psychology and Deterrence* (Baltimore, Md.: Johns Hopkins University Press, 1985); Klaus Knorr and Patrick M. Morgan, *Strategic Military Surprise* (New Brunswick, N.J.: Transaction Books, 1983); Richard Ned Lebow, *Between Peace and War: The Nature of International Crisis* (Baltimore, Md.: Johns Hopkins University Press, 1981); Richard Smoke, *War: Controlling Escalation* (Cambridge, Mass.: Harvard University Press, 1977); Jack Snyder, *The Ideology of the Offensive: Military Decision Making and the Disasters of 1914* (Ithaca, N.Y.: Cornell University Press, 1984); Jack S. Levy, "The Causes of War: A Review of Theories and Evidence," in *Behavior, Society, and Nuclear War*, ed. Tetlock et al., 1:209–33; and Jack S. Levy, "Preferences, Constraints, and Choices in July 1914," *International Security* (Winter 1990–91): 151–86. Levy's "Preferences" piece is especially valuable on the issue of whether World War I occurred as a result of accident, misperception, or miscalculation, about which a large debate among historians and political scientists has existed for many years.

11. See Alexander L. George, "The Search for Agreed Norms," ch. 2 in *Windows of Opportunity: From Cold War to Peaceful Competition in U.S.-Soviet Relations*, ed. Graham T. Allison and William L. Ury with Bruce J. Allyn (Cambridge, Mass.: Ballinger Publishing Co., 1989), 45–66. George has contributed a large literature to the topic of crisis management and escalation, including his *Managing U.S.-Soviet Rivalry* (Boulder, Colo.: Westview Press, 1983)

the Cuban missile crisis, for example, U.S. and Soviet leaders alike refrained from actions that would certainly have provoked war, including a possible nuclear war. The United States sought to compel Khrushchev to withdraw the missiles by imposing a "quarantine" around Cuba. The quarantine was chosen because it was intended to send a message to the Soviets about U.S. resolve, while allowing Khrushchev an opportunity to withdraw without humiliation.[12] Some of President Kennedy's advisers preferred an immediate invasion of Cuba or a U.S. air strike against Soviet missile installations in Cuba. Although his "ExComm" group of specially selected advisers appeared to be leaning in favor of the air strike during some of the tensest moments of the crisis, Kennedy held back from that option to give Khrushchev more time to reconsider.

The Soviets, for their part, did not turn over to the Cubans the missiles or the decision to fire them once assembled. Thus, when Khrushchev finally acquiesced in Kennedy's demand for removal of the missiles, Castro was reportedly frustrated at the obvious appearance of his superfluous status in Soviet crisis decisionmaking. The Kremlin could not turn over to Cuba, for obvious reasons, a decision that might have resulted in U.S.-Soviet conflict. The motives for Khrushchev's willingness to risk placing the medium- and intermediate-range missiles in Cuba were quite complicated, and they remain less than fully clear even now.[13] More can be said about this under the topic of coercive diplomacy, below. What is immediately apparent is that the Soviet motives for missile deployment in Cuba might not have been perceived correctly by the Americans. An agreed crisis might easily have turned into a war.

In similar fashion, U.S. actions during the crisis might have been misper-

---

and U.S.-Soviet Security Cooperation: Achievements, Failures, Lessons, ed. Alexander L. George, Philip J. Farley, and Alexander L. Dallin (New York: Oxford University Press, 1988).

12. There is a large literature on the Cuban missile crisis. An early classic is Graham T. Allison, Essence of Decision: Explaining the Cuban Missile Crisis (Boston: Little, Brown, 1971). More recent documentation appears in James G. Blight and David A. Welch, On the Brink: Americans and Soviets Reexamine the Cuban Missile Crisis (New York: Hill & Wang, 1989). See also Welch and Blight, "The Eleventh Hour of the Cuban Missile Crisis: An Introduction to the ExComm Transcripts," International Security (Winter 1987–88): 5–29, and comments in Blight and Welch, On the Brink, 333–34, n. 5. Other important studies include Herbert S. Dinerstein, The Making of a Missile Crisis: October 1962 (Baltimore, Md.: Johns Hopkins University Press, 1976); Raymond L. Garthoff, Reflections on the Cuban Missile Crisis (Washington, D.C.: Brookings Institution, 1987, 1989); Roberta Wohlstetter, "Cuba and Pearl Harbor: Hindsight and Foresight," Foreign Affairs (July 1965): 691–707; as well as memoirs by U.S. and Soviet participants in the crisis.

13. Khrushchev's reminiscences about Cuba appear in Khrushchev Remembers, ed. and trans. Strobe Talbott (Boston: Little, Brown, 1970), 488–505.

ceived by the Soviets. The United States apparently forced a number of Soviet submarines in the Caribbean and Atlantic to surface during the crisis; some were undoubtedly nuclear-armed.[14] A U.S. U-2 reconnaissance aircraft took a mistaken reading from a star and overflew Soviet territory on October 27, during one of the most tense periods of the crisis. Soviet interceptors scrambled to meet the inadvertent intruder, and Khrushchev commented after the crisis with some asperity that Soviet leaders might easily have interpreted this as a prestrike reconnaissance.[15] In order to avoid Soviet misunderstanding of U.S. intentions, President Kennedy ordered the original blockade line brought closer to Cuba. The president intended to provide to the Soviet leadership as much time as possible to reverse their course of action short of an outbreak of hostilities at sea. That the crisis was conducted as an agreed battle is more evident from the U.S. side, since we have more testimony from American participants than we have for Soviet ones. We do have evidence of Khrushchev's recognition that the boundaries of crisis management could not be pushed too far beyond a minimal risk of inadvertent war. Once the missiles had been discovered and Kennedy revealed this fact to the world, Khrushchev recognized that brinkmanship had gone too far. Had he been able to emplace the missile complexes before their locations were verified by U.S. photographic intelligence, he might then have presented Kennedy with a fait accompli and offered to trade the missiles for a much higher stake than he (Khrushchev) eventually received. However, Khrushchev was not prepared to gamble on provoking an American invasion of Cuba or an air strike against Soviet installations on the island of Cuba. The first of these two U.S. options, an invasion of Cuba, would have disestablished the Cuban government or forced Khrushchev into countermeasures to save face (or both, such as abandoning the Castro government to its military fate and engaging in escalation elsewhere). U.S. officials who advised against the immediate need for military escalation warned of the options open to the Soviet Union for creating diversionary or major attacks in thea-

14. Allison, *Essence of Decision*, 138.
15. Ibid., 141. The U-2 pilot issued an open radio signal for help, and American fighters in Alaska were surged to escort the plane home safely. An encounter between U.S. defensive escorts and Soviet planes in the Arctic was not inconceivable, and the U.S. interceptors were almost certainly armed with nuclear weapons. Kennedy expressed regret for the incident in his next exchange of messages with Khrushchev and said that he would make certain that "every precaution is taken to prevent recurrence"; the next day Kennedy ordered a stand-down of all U-2 flights around the Soviet Union. An aspect of the crisis never satisfactorily explained is why the stand-down of potentially provocative intelligence flights into or near Soviet airspace was not ordered immediately at the outset of the crisis, or shortly thereafter. For additional discussion of this incident, see Scott D. Sagan, *Moving Targets: Nuclear Strategy and National Security* (Princeton, N.J.: Princeton University Press, 1989), 147–48.

ters of operation other than the Caribbean, say, in Europe. The air-strike option would have killed Soviet soldiers guarding missile sites and at other locations; less than totally successful air strikes (leaving surviving IRBMs and MRBMs) could prompt a Soviet nuclear first strike or preemption (for fear of being attacked) against targets in the continental United States.

In the Cuban missile crisis, the "agreed crisis" or nuclear analogue to an agreed battle was conducted with some important tacit understandings by the participants. First, starting a U.S.-Soviet war, especially a nuclear war, was not worth the stakes in Cuba, whatever they were perceived to be. Second, each side must have some face-saving story with which to confront political opponents and skeptics at home. For Kennedy, photographic confirmation of the missile deployments was a great personal and political embarrassment, given his previously stated public warnings and assurances. For Khrushchev, the discovery of the missiles before they were fully operational meant that he had to retreat in humiliation or get some public and face-saving promise about future U.S. intervention in Cuba.[16]

Third, both sides avoided to the extent possible side-of-the-board moves which would have suggested to the other side that they were preparing to launch a nuclear first strike. The United States clearly threatened nuclear war against the Soviet Union in response to a Soviet *nuclear* strike anywhere in the Western Hemisphere. The implication was that any less drastic Soviet behavior would have met with a nonnuclear response, at least in the Caribbean theater of operations. The Soviet Union did not, as it might have, pose a threat to Berlin immediately after the missiles were discovered, followed by a refusal to bow to the U.S. ultimatum about removal of the missiles. The U.S. ultimatum, in turn, was not stated in terms that foreclosed Soviet options about how to carry it out; Kennedy did not set a time limit after which the United States would necessarily initiate any of its escalatory options.

Agreed Battle and Nuclear War

Crises might be discussed as surrogate battles, with appropriate recognition of the danger attached to crises. A more difficult question is whether a nu-

---

16. Many U.S. observers are inclined to dismiss the importance of this "concession," which is certainly less important than other aspects of the crisis resolution. However, the concession is not a trivial one, given the campaign the United States ran prior to the missile crisis and subsequently to dislodge Castro by covert and overt means. Khrushchev's acceptance of these terms for withdrawal provided a thin cover for his retreat, not a thick one.

clear war, especially one involving the Americans or Soviets, could be so limited. We may consider whether such a battle could be limited by the ends for which the opponents fought, by the means employed, or by the conditions imposed by technology or other outside forces. Nor is such an exercise one of "Cold War nostalgia" with no relevance to current and future policy. The end of the Cold War does not mean the end of nuclear weapons, nor of nuclear danger, and the Americans and Soviets even after START I would deploy some seven or eight thousand strategic nuclear vehicles on each side. In addition, the proliferation of nuclear weapons and of medium- or long-range missiles to countries outside of Europe and North America looms as a potentially destabilizing factor in international relations for the 1990s and beyond.

Rather obviously, nuclear use would not be contemplated by the United States, the Russian republic, or any other current nuclear power unless important, indeed vital, objectives were thought to be at risk. What objectives could be that important? A deliberate attack by one side against the homeland-based forces or society of the other would undoubtedly provoke retaliation. The objectives of such retaliation would be to reduce the arsenal of the opponent that remained after its first strike, in order to limit further damage and to strike at other highly valued targets in order to impose unacceptable costs. The expectation of unacceptable costs and less-than-expected damage to the defender's forces should, according to the logic of deterrence theory, deter any first strike by a putative attacker. The expectation of unacceptable costs alone should suffice to deter attack by the standards of any actual political leaders who contemplate seriously what nuclear weapons can do. Nevertheless, the momentum and madness of a crisis atmosphere might lead one side to move toward a capability for preemption, alarming the other into a "defensive" first strike. In addition, military leaders are professionally conservative planners who desire the sort of overinsurance that, in peacetime, might generally reinforce deterrence but, during a crisis, might contribute to an opponent's fear of attack.[17]

The reasons why attackers might be motivated to strike despite the expec-

17. These issues are discussed extensively in Robert Powell, Nuclear Deterrence Theory: The Search for Credibility (Cambridge: Cambridge University Press, 1990), ch. 5; Thomas C. Schelling, The Strategy of Conflict (Cambridge, Mass.: Harvard University Press, 1960), 205–54; Robert Jervis, The Meaning of the Nuclear Revolution (Ithaca, N.Y.: Cornell University Press, 1989), ch. 5; Richard Ned Lebow, Nuclear Crisis Management: A Dangerous Illusion (Ithaca, N.Y.: Cornell University Press, 1987), passim; and Freedman, The Evolution of Nuclear Strategy, passim.

tation of almost certain and unacceptable losses do not lend themselves to standardized descriptions. During the Cold War years, military experts agreed that a "bolt from the blue" by U.S. or Soviet forces, in which one side attacked the other despite the absence of any apparent crisis or confrontation, was impossible or highly improbable.[18] A more probable path to war between the United States and the Soviet Union, prior to 1985, was the expansion of a war between NATO and the Warsaw Pact from a regional, conventional war into a global, nuclear one.[19] War might also have grown out of crisis misperceptions based upon prewar mobilization plans that were perceived to limit the choices of policymakers: between striking within a short window while forces were at maximum readiness or relinquishing the objective being contested by the opponent. Leaders during the July 1914 crisis in Europe leading to the outbreak of World War I may have felt this sense of options being closed off, between windows of vulnerability and windows of opportunity.[20]

By whatever path the United States and the Soviet Union might have gotten into a nuclear war, their political leaders would have been strongly motivated to try to stop it as soon as possible. Unless the war had begun by a massive surprise attack against one side's forces and urban industrial targets, policymakers would have had significant incentives, though not necessarily compelling ones, to stop the fighting before very many minutes or hours had elapsed. Consider, for example, the possible outbreak of conventional war in Europe, prior to 1985, escalating to exchanges of tactical nuclear weapons in Western or Eastern Europe. Assuming that these exchanges had been limited to targets within Europe outside the Soviet Union, the USSR would have had some strong incentives to stop the war before its

18. On the possibility of nuclear surprise attack, see Richard K. Betts, "Surprise Attack and Preemption," ch. 3 in Hawks, Doves, and Owls: An Agenda for Avoiding Nuclear War, ed. Graham T. Allison, Albert Carnesale, and Joseph S. Nye, Jr. (New York: W. W. Norton, 1985), 54–79, and William R. Van Cleave, "Surprise Nuclear Attack," ch. 21 in Soviet Strategic Deception, ed. Brian D. Dailey and Patrick J. Parker (Lexington, Mass.: D. C. Heath, 1987), 449–66.

19. For discussion of possible European escalation scenarios for the early 1980s, see Fred Osler Hampsen, "Escalation in Europe," ch. 4 in Hawks, Doves, and Owls, ed. Allison, Carnesale, and Nye, 80–114.

20. For contrasting perspectives, see D.C.B. Lieven, Russia and the Origins of the First World War (New York: St. Martin's Press, 1983), esp. 148–49 on the questions of Russian mobilization, and L.C.F. Turner, Origins of the First World War (New York: W. W. Norton, 1970), esp. 104–8. Arguments on the issue of whether the outbreak of World War I was inadvertent are analyzed in Marc Trachtenberg, "The Meaning of Mobilization in 1914," International Security (Winter 1990–91): 120–50. See also the references in notes 24 and 25, below, for counterarguments to Trachtenberg.

homeland came under attack. So, too, would the Americans. The possibility that the two superpowers, at any time from the latter 1960s (when the Soviet Union achieved effective strategic parity with the United States) through the middle 1980s, might have agreed to fight a "limited" nuclear war in Europe was a source of constant tension and anxiety among the European members of NATO. The concern was not illogical. Europeans sensed that, whatever might be said about alliance unity in peacetime for purposes of deterrence, in time of war the separate interests of states in survival and conflict termination short of mutual annihilation would be powerful, centrifugal tendencies.

Whether the Soviet Union would have considered getting into any conflict that was to be fought according to the rules of limited nuclear war was not known with certainty. Doctrinal pronouncements in the Soviet military literature and by Party leaders expressed skepticism about the possibility of limiting any nuclear war. Nevertheless, the possibility of fighting for limited aims, or of restricting the kinds of targets taken under attack, was not foreclosed by Soviet planners. Soviet military doctrine from the 1960s through the 1980s deliberately left ambiguous the conditions under which it would be propitious, or inadvisable, to use nuclear weapons in a restrained manner. Much would depend upon the circumstances surrounding the start of war. Major variants considered by Soviet planners included 1) a large U.S. nuclear surprise attack on the Soviet homeland; 2) a first use by NATO in Europe, followed by escalation to large-scale theater nuclear war on that continent and perhaps thereafter to intercontinental exchanges of strategic nuclear weapons; 3) preemption by Soviet strategic nuclear forces after leaders in the Kremlin concluded that the USSR was about to be struck by a U.S. surprise attack; and 4), though not discussed in literature made available to Western readers, the option of a Soviet first strike in order to prevent an anticipated U.S. escalation to strategic nuclear war, on the basis of strategic rather than tactical warning of enemy intent.[21]

21. See Stephen M. Meyer, "Soviet Perspectives on the Paths to Nuclear War," ch. 7 in *Hawks, Doves, and Owls*, ed. Allison, Carnesale, and Nye, 167–205; Raymond L. Garthoff, *Deterrence and the Revolution in Soviet Military Doctrine* (Washington, D.C.: Brookings Institution, 1990), esp. 157–85; Harriet Fast Scott and William F. Scott, *Soviet Military Doctrine: Continuity, Formulation, and Dissemination* (Boulder, Colo.: Westview Press, 1988), esp. 147–49; *The Voroshilov Lectures: Materials from the Soviet General Staff Academy*, Ghulam Dastagir Wardak, comp., and Graham Hall Turbiville, Jr., gen. ed. (Washington, D.C.: National Defense University Press, 1989), vol. 1; William T. Lee, "Soviet Nuclear Targeting," ch. 4 in *Strategic Nuclear Targeting*, ed. Desmond Ball and Jeffrey Richelson (Ithaca, N.Y.: Cornell University Press, 1986), 84–108; Edward L. Warner III, *Soviet Concepts and Capabilities for Limited Nuclear War: What We Know and How We Know It* (Santa Monica, Calif.: Rand Corp., February

If the concept of agreed battle was to be extended into nuclear war, some notion of thresholds or saliences was implied. Thresholds or saliences are those boundaries between one kind of political-military action and another.[22] A first threshold or salience, the crossing of which could change the entire character of a crisis or war, was the actual shooting of Soviet forces by U.S. forces, or vice versa: the outbreak of war itself. A second threshold was the first nuclear detonation, with all its symbolism and suggestion. A third was the exchange of "tactical" nuclear weapons, either inside or outside Europe, including possible nuclear warfighting at sea. A fourth potential threshold remaining after the first three have been exceeded was the exchange of nuclear weapons massively against Soviet and U.S. (or allied) forces, but not against the homeland-based forces of either Washington or Moscow. A fifth significant threshold was the unrestrained nuclear bombardment of U.S. and Soviet society.

To articulate these potential thresholds of nuclear use is to reinforce the notion that any nuclear first use would have been the threshold of most importance. It would have violated a taboo that had held firm since the U.S. bombing of Nagasaki. It would have signaled to the opponent the most expansive of war aims and the unwillingness to exercise self-restraint. The possibility that an agreed battle could still be conducted after nuclear first use is something that NATO was required to plan for, in order to maintain peacetime alliance cohesion. Options between blowing up the world and capitulating to Soviet wartime demands were demanded by successive U.S.

1989); Notra Trulock III, "Soviet Perspectives on Limited Nuclear War," ch. 3 in *Swords and Shields: NATO, the USSR, and New Choices for Long-Range Offense and Defense*, ed. Fred S. Hoffman, Albert Wohlstetter, and David S. Yost (Lexington, Mass.: Lexington Books, 1987), 53–86; Marshal N. V. Ogarkov, *Vsegda v gotovnosti k zashchite Otechestva* [Always in Readiness to Defend the Fatherland] (Moscow: Voyenizdat, 1982), 16; N. V. Ogarkov, *Istoriya uchit bditel'nosti* [History Teaches Vigilance] (Moscow: Voyenizdat, 1985), 89–90; Col. Gen. M. A. Gareyev, *M. V. Frunze: Voyennyi teoretik* [M. V. Frunze: Military Theorist], translated into English and published by Pergamon/Brassey's (New York, 1988), 213–14. The most recent evidence of Soviet views on controlling and possibly terminating a major war, while withholding significant military assets for bargaining, is noted in Garthoff, *Deterrence and the Revolution in Soviet Military Doctrine*, ch. 5.

22. The issue of terminology is explored in Smoke, *War: Controlling Escalation*, who prefers the term "saliency" becauce it implies changes in the field of future expectations concerning the behavior of the opponent. Thresholds also define points at which the expansion of military operations creates a qualitative change in the nature of fighting though not necessarily a change in the future expectations of the actors. The two notions are not so far apart, however; it is a matter of relative emphasis on battlefield outcomes and near-term options, in the case of thresholds, and on longer-term future expectations, in the case of saliences. On thresholds, see Herman Kahn, *On Escalation: Metaphors and Scenarios* (New York: Praeger, 1965).

presidents and NATO secretaries-general from the 1950s through the 1980s. However, the need for political compromise took primacy over the requirement for coherent military strategy. In truth, NATO's "flexible response" doctrine allowed U.S. and NATO European planners to leave ambiguous the conditions under which first use might occur and the provocations which in their judgment would require additional uses. In actual fact, NATO's real military strategy, once the Soviet Union acquired enough strategic nuclear weapons to destroy North America, was a strategy of temporary resistance of any aggression by conventional forces, followed by a demonstrative first use which, it was hoped, would persuade the Soviet leadership to call off the attack.

Speaking broadly and somewhat unfairly, we may say that NATO Europeans shared a common frame of reference with regard to an agreed battle in Europe: they opposed the idea as a weakening of deterrence. Flexible response, in the judgment of many European politicians and planners during the 1960s and 1970s, meant surrender of Europe to save North America. U.S. leaders saw flexible response as providing for a delay of nuclear first use *and*, subsequently, for a graduated set of responses that would postpone as long as possible the awful moment of decision for or against strategic nuclear war. Soviet leaders, to judge from their declaratory doctrine and force posture from the mid-1960s to the mid-1980s, would have fought an agreed battle with conventional forces, provided those forces were accomplishing wartime missions without nuclear escalation. However, Soviet leaders acknowledged that NATO's doctrine of nuclear first use made it unlikely that such an agreed battle without nuclear escalation (and also sparing the Soviet homeland from direct attack) could be fought in Europe.

ESCALATION CONTROL

The second dimension of war termination as a concept is escalation control. The idea of escalation control suggests several things about war termination. First, wars have political objectives, and it is sometimes contributory to the accomplishment of those aims to limit war instead of expanding it. Presumably this also applies to limitation of nuclear war. Second, there are voluntaristic as well as deterministic elements in limiting escalation. The process is partially controllable by the participants and partially beyond their control. Third, escalation is not always sequential or linear; it does not always proceed in small increments or in a direct line from one step to another. Escalation can take place in sudden and dramatic changes from the status quo to a new condition entirely unexpected by one or more of the combatants.[23] Because escalation is both deliberate and accidental, somewhat under the control of the participants but not totally, the concept of "escalation control" allows for variable approaches to the limitation of war aims or military means.

It might seem self-evident that political objectives are important in determining the outcomes of wars. But those engaged in war or planning for war have not always understood this as clearly as they ought, or as clearly as readers with the benefit of historical hindsight can. Leaders have embarked on wars with a series of carefully planned opening moves, often brilliant tactical successes, without having considered "What next?" or "How does it end?" Several examples are provided in the Japanese attack on Pearl Harbor, Hitler's invasion of the Soviet Union in 1941, and the continuation of fighting in World War I after initial expectations for rapid victory were disappointed.[24]

The Japanese attack on Pearl Harbor surprised U.S. leaders, who had expected war but not an attack on the U.S. Pacific Fleet in Hawaii. The tactical success of this attack was spectacular. The U.S. fleet was severely crippled, and the simultaneous Japanese offensives against the Philippines also produced temporary victory. However, this attack did not succeed if success is measured by long-term political, as opposed to immediate tactical, accomplishments. The U.S. entered World War II, and Japan had no hope of defeating the mobilized American and allied forces in a protracted war. Japanese military planners even acknowledged the likelihood of their eventual defeat if the war against the United States was not terminated rapidly. Japanese leaders hoped that a stunning blow at the outset of war would induce President Roosevelt and his military advisers to settle for a half-loaf of Japanese predominance in the Asian Pacific. Planners in Tokyo had no end game for what to do if the Americans decided not to accept a modus vivendi in the Pacific but chose to fight on.

Hitler surprised his Soviet adversaries with his attack of June 22, 1941, and German victories in 1941 against the USSR armed forces were stunning.

23. The point is emphasized in Smoke, *War: Controlling Escalation*, passim.
24. Fred Charles Iklé, *Every War Must End* (New York: Columbia University Press, 1971); Geoffrey Blainey, *The Causes of Wars* (New York: Free Press, 1973). Blainey's discussion of the causes of longer and shorter wars is especially pertinent (pp. 186–227).

However, German intelligence had underestimated the mobilization potential and combat power of the Soviet Union. This misestimation was all the
more unfortunate for Hitler in light of his gratuitous declaration of war
against the United States immediately after being informed of the Japanese
attack on Pearl Harbor. Thus, the führer assured himself a multifront war
against a coalition having a total military and industrial potential greater
than Germany's. Given Hitler's psychology and ideology, this overreach was
perhaps to be expected, but his military advisers had more misgivings about
the gap between German aspirations and capabilities. Those members of the
German General Staff who were not automatons held in thrall by the führer's
style, or gripped by fear of his retribution, were outspoken among themselves
(and in their subsequently published diaries) about the foolishness of Operation Barbarossa. The most skeptical among Hitler's commanders had been
forced to resign or were neutered by the apparent success of German blitzkrieg tactics in France and the rapid defeat of Poland by Germany even earlier.[25]

World War I represents a case in which, on the issue of escalation control,
the twentieth-century democracies managed to look every bit as incompetent as their authoritarian counterparts. Both the Triple Alliance and the
Triple Entente came about because their members could see war coming. But
they expected any war in Europe to be on the periphery, say the Balkans,
and to be contained there by a clever combination of military threats and
diplomatic maneuverings.[26] After all, Bismarck in the preceding century had
enabled Germany to take on several opponents in succession, but for limited
aims, and to arrange a postwar rebalancing of power that left Germany in an
even better position. But Bismarck was no longer at the helm of Prussia or

25. Albert Seaton, *The Russo-German War, 1941–1945* (New York: Praeger, 1970), 23–
42, discusses the development of the German command structure and Hitler's relationships
with military leaders; on Germany's plans for attacking the Soviet Union, see pp. 50–64.
There is a great deal of Soviet historical research on the conditions surrounding the "initial
period of war" and Germany's plans for accomplishing its decisive aims in that period. See, for
example, V. Mernov, "O soderzhanii nachal'nogo perioda mirovykh voyn" [On the Contents
of the Initial Period of World War], *Voenno-istoricheskii zhurnal*, no. 9 (September 1960): 31–
41, esp. 39, and P. Korkodinov, "Fakti i mysli o nachal'nom periode Belikoy Otechestvennoy
voyny" [Facts and Theory on the Initial Period of the Great Patriotic War], *Voenno-istoricheskii
zhurnal*, no. 10 (October 1965), 26–34, esp. 29ff.
26. Hypotheses on the sources of "balancing" and "bandwagoning" alliance behavior are
developed in Stephen M. Walt, *The Origins of Alliances* (Ithaca, N.Y.: Cornell University Press,
1987), ch. 5. Walt places balancing (allying with others against a prevailing threat) and bandwagoning (aligning with the source of threat) within the general explanatory framework of
"alliances as a response to threat." Other causes for alliance formation are developed in ch. 2
of the same work, pp. 33–49.

Germany, and Kaiser Wilhelm II and Chief of the General Staff Helmuth von Moltke (the younger) inherited a war plan (the "Schlieffen Plan," subsequently modified by Moltke) predicated on a rapid and decisive victory in the west, after which the Russians would be summarily dealt with.[27]

One self-destructive response by leaders during the July crisis of 1914, according to the arguments of some historians and political scientists, was to reinforce a shared paranoia about getting in the first decisive military blow.[28] This led to a race among Austria-Hungary, Germany, and Russia to mobilize their armed forces, beating the opponent who is about to attack before he can land an initial, perhaps decisive, strike. Mutual fears and expectations of preemption were also based on an expectation held by political leaders that a war could not last long. Predictions by political, economic, and literary figures in Europe during the years immediately prior to the outbreak of World War I often included an assumption that no great power's economy could stand the strain of a prolonged war. Therefore, any war would have to be short; combatants might not run out of martial spirit, but they would certainly run out of money and resources. In worst-case economic scenarios, continuation of the fighting for several years could bankrupt the treasuries of Europe.[29] There was also a substantial amount of wishful thinking on the part of leaders about the effectiveness of first strikes and preemptive attacks. The Schlieffen Plan was predicated on optimism of this sort, as well as on pessimism about the alternative: a two-front war, which Germany was almost certain to lose.

Political objectives can change during war. A government that has not thought through its objectives prior to war may find that it is under some pressure to invent them during it. In World War II, important factions within the Japanese cabinet resisted surrender even after the bombings of Hiroshima and Nagasaki and the entry of the Soviet Union into the war. The personal intervention of Emperor Hirohito on behalf of honorable surrender was necessary in order to persuade diehards to lay down their arms. Even then there was rearguard military resistance to the decision.[30] It had

27. Turner, *Origins of the First World War*, 103–15, and Corelli Barnett, *The Swordbearers: Supreme Command in the First World War* (New York: William Morrow & Co., 1964), ch. 1, esp. pp. 3–4.

28. Barbara W. Tuchman, *The Guns of August* (New York: Dell Publishing Co., 1962); Paul Bracken, *The Command and Control of Nuclear Forces* (New Haven, Conn.: Yale University Press, 1983), 2, 65, 240; Lebow, *Nuclear Crisis Management*, 24–25, 32–33, et pass.

29. Blainey, *The Causes of War*, 18–35 et pass.

30. Paul Kecskemeti, *Strategic Surrender: The Politics of Victory and Defeat* (Stanford, Calif.: Stanford University Press, 1958), 155–214.

become an important, indeed fundamental, objective of the Japanese not to lose the symbol of their civilization and statehood: the imperial throne. Assuming the preservation of the emperor's person and honorific status in a postwar Japan, Japanese political and military leaders were able to assuage their feelings of defeat and so to accept surrender.

The character of the international system also influences the definition of war aims and expectations about political and military objectives. Thus, there may be a direct connection between types of international systems and propensities to contain, or to amplify, escalation once war has started. In the classic balance-of-power system of the seventeenth century, limited wars were fought in order to sort out the basic distribution of territory and resources among the major European actors. This frequent use of limited war to restore the balance of power became less productive of system stability during the eighteenth and nineteenth centuries, when dynastic regimes felt the heat of nationalism applied to the sword of revolution. The Napoleonic Wars are well known for having marked a turning point in military strategy (the "nation in arms") but are less appreciated for their perturbation of the very idea of system stability.[31]

When systems are unstable, it is because powerful actors have antisystemic objectives: they would like to rearrange the existing rank order of military or economic power, not just shoot up the battlefield. Napoleon threatened to destroy an international order predicated on dynastic legitimacy. Thus he forced the states of Europe to choose between two unenviable statuses: either Napoleon's adversaries or Napoleon's vassals. Few are so ambitious. But international systems are always arenas in which jockeying for power and position go on. Theorists are not certain whether the most stable systems are unipolar, bipolar, or multipolar. Unipolar systems have one dominant actor, as in the system dominated by the Roman Empire. Bipolar systems and multipolar systems involve competition between two or more roughly equivalent military and/or economic powers. Historians and political scientists have spent much ink over the issue of whether bipolar or multipolar systems are more war-aversive. Less thought has been given to which kind of system may make escalation, once war among major actors has begun, more probable.

There is an abundant need for better information about the relationship between international system structure and "propensity for escalation" or some equivalent dependent variable. Containment of conflicts to the small-

31. Michael Mandelbaum, *The Nuclear Revolution* (Cambridge: Cambridge University Press, 1981), 57–58.

est possible number of states, and to the potentially lowest level of violence, might be one measure of success or failure for different kinds of international systems. Of particular interest would be two questions relative to systemic propensities for escalation. First, do systems that have a *collective security* approach to crisis and conflict containment perform more successfully than systems that have an *alliance-balancing* approach? Collective security, as it was implemented between the two world wars, failed to prevent escalation of regional wars into global war. However, alliance balancing did no better prior to World War I.

A second issue relative to the relationship between systemic structure and escalatory potential is whether regional hegemons contribute to escalation or deescalation of wars. One might offer either of two hypotheses here. First, regional hegemons might contribute to stability by the suppression of internecine warfare within their domains of dominance; the Warsaw Pact and NATO can be said to have performed this function, the latter less deliberately than the former, from World War II until 1989. Related to this is the point that if war nonetheless breaks out, a regional hegemon might help to localize it and prevent its spread to the system as a whole. An alternative hypothesis would be that regional hegemons, especially if there exists more than one in the same system, create a competitive atmosphere that is more likely to result in war. Their intraregional stabilizing influence is contrary to their destabilizing international impacts. Minor police forces may prevent local disturbances, but in the international system the regional police departments of today may become the international terrorists of the future.

The tendency of policymakers to postpone discussion of their objectives for war termination also conceals some of the costs and risks attendant to escalation. Military estimates are often subject to wishful thinking and distortion if hard questions about how the war can end are not posed. Fred C. Iklé discusses the illustrative example of the German unrestricted submarine warfare campaign of World War I. German Chancellor Bethmann-Hollweg was among those who were skeptical that the campaign could induce British capitulation, and who feared that unrestricted undersea warfare would bring the United States into the war, perhaps decisively, against Germany. Careful military estimates were made by the Germans on this issue. They seemed to show a very convincing case for going ahead with unrestricted submarine warfare, despite the risks of escalation. This "convincing" case, however, was based on an unexamined assumption: a certain tonnage of shipping losses would place inordinate burdens on the British economy, and the British would therefore sue for peace before U.S. entry into the war could make any difference.[32]

When the United States and its allied coalition partners attacked Iraq on January 16, 1991, President Bush stated U.S. objectives as limited: to drive Iraqi forces from Kuwait and to restore the legitimate government of that country. However, Pentagon officials spoke of neutralizing all of Iraq's offensive military capability, and President Bush alluded to the possibility of putting Iraqi President Saddam Hussein on trial for war crimes (because of the treatment of U.S. prisoners). The scale of U.S. air operations during the first weeks of war was more consistent with total than with partial destruction of Iraq's modern armed forces. Pentagon officials in off-the-record briefings in late January admitted that the U.S. military leadership was bombing Saddam's command-and-control headquarters, though not specifically targeting him deliberately. As one official explained, "There is not a directed effort under way to get him, but everybody around here believes the fastest way to end the war is if Saddam Hussein walks under a Tomahawk missile."[33] The official response was somewhat disingenuous: U.S. target planning included numerous installations or residences where it was thought that Saddam might be found. Another Pentagon official was more direct: "What we're trying to do is eliminate their command and control centers, knowing that he might get hit in the course of our going after those targets. So, while we're not specifically targeting him, we are well aware that there could be a side benefit to these attacks."[34]

The Pentagon's assumption seemed to be that the war could be concluded more rapidly if Saddam were eliminated. However, there was no reliable information as to what arrangements, if any, Saddam had made for governmental succession. His death could have resulted in a devolution of command and control to widely separated military commanders. If so, the problem of war termination would become more difficult. It was unclear whether Saddam's likely successors would be any more willing to surrender than he was. His strategy, which might be passed along to his successors, was described by Secretary of Defense Richard Cheney and Chairman of the Joint Chiefs of Staff Colin Powell in press briefings on January 23, 1991, as one of "hunkering down" and withholding military forces for a protracted conflict. According to some U.S. analysts, Iraq's political strategy was to wear out the

32. Iklé, Every War Must End, 42–50.
33. Philadelphia Inquirer, January 24, 1991.
34. Ibid. Sensitivity on this point reflected U.S. presidential guidance, in place for fourteen years, banning assassination attempts on foreign government officials.

patience of the U.S. government and public by engaging American forces in a protracted and frustrating ground campaign, once the air war had been concluded. A prolonged war might also allow more time to accomplish "horizontal escalation" by dragging Israeli forces into battle.

Intentional and Unintentional Escalation

Another aspect of escalation control is whether the states in conflict can make escalation happen according to their designs. It is sometimes the case that crisis or war expands beyond the reach of those who seek to control it. This is the risk inherent in the tactic of "brinkmanship," in which the opponent is meant to believe that you are more resolute about going to the "brink" of war than he is. Should the opponent decide to be as resolute as you, deterrence will fail and war will result. There are actually two models of risk implicit in U.S. deterrence literature. The first model stresses the deliberate risks of escalation, the manipulation of threats that have attached to them some ambiguity about what happens subsequently. In this model, the threatener expects to maintain control over events, more or less, and to use the fear of escalation on the part of the threatenee as a bargaining tool.[35] A second model of escalation that can be found in the literature places the emphasis on the autonomous instead of the deliberate risks of escalation.

The distinction is subtle and can be missed by theorists as well as by political leaders. When the emphasis is placed on autonomous rather than deliberate escalation, there remains an element of uncertainty and a shared danger that one side might miscalculate the capabilities or resolve of its adversary. Despite these apparent similarities, differences in the center of gravity between deliberate and inadvertent escalation require further discussion. Inadvertent escalation is not calculated to influence the opponent—it just happens. Inadvertent escalation frightens the opponent precisely because it appears that the government of the other state has lost the ability to control its own forces or decisionmaking. Inadvertent escalation is more likely to result from "accidental" causes, but these are not accidents in the common sense of the term. The "accidental" aspect refers to the precise timing of a mishap, not its occurrence. Charles Perrow comes close to the idea of autonomous escalation when he discusses "normal accidents" that occur in nuclear power plants and other complex organizations.[36] According

35. Schelling, Arms and Influence, 99ff.
36. Perrow, Normal Accidents: Living with High-Risk Technologies (New York: Basic Books, 1984).

to Perrow, accidents are to be expected in complex, high-technology organizations: the organizational environment for decisionmaking will determine what kind of accidents and how frequently they occur.

Inadvertent escalation might have more to do, then, with the command-and-control systems of military organizations than with the failure of individual weapon platforms or components. And this is just what researchers have noted. Desmond Ball, Bruce Blair, Paul Bracken, and John Steinbruner have contributed great insight to the subject of autonomous risks of escalation by noting the potential fallibilities of nuclear command organizations.[37] Nuclear command-and-control organizations are forced to optimize between the responsibility for negative control, against unauthorized or accidental launch and detonation of weapons, and positive control, assuring responsive delivery of forces to target once authorized.[38] Measures that make negative control easier, such as the compartmentation of information about nuclear release and the addition of electronic locks to warheads, may make rapid response more difficult.

Nuclear alerts create heightened levels of tension in military command organizations on account of this two-sided, and somewhat contradictory, responsibility to prevent accidents and guarantee authorized responsiveness. During an increased level of Cold War alert above normal peacetime conditions, the United States or NATO might have wanted to disperse theater nuclear weapons from their storage sites to their field destinations. This protective measure would be designed to ensure that the weapons would not be destroyed in a surprise attack, should the Soviet Union contemplate one. However, the very fact of dispersal of those weapons from their storage areas

37. Desmond Ball, "Nuclear War at Sea," *International Security* (Winter 1985–86): 3–31; Bruce G. Blair, *Strategic Command and Control: Redefining the Nuclear Threat* (Washington, D.C.: Brookings Institution, 1985); Bracken, *The Command and Control of Nuclear Forces*; John Steinbruner, "Choices and Trade-offs," ch. 16 in *Managing Nuclear Operations*, ed. Carter, Steinbruner, and Zraket, 535–54.

38. One of the major differences between prenuclear and nuclear command organizations is that nuclear weapons have forced military planners, political leaders, and theorists to acknowledge this uncomfortable trade-off: between reliable performance and military effectiveness, on one side, and capacity for restraint in threatening and using force, on the other. Much of the disagreement about the causes of World War I, in the historical and political science literature, revolves around the extent to which historians and political scientists acknowledge that such a trade-off existed for leaders in July 1914 and the extent to which the record shows that global leaders were, or were not, aware of it. See Trachtenberg, "The Meaning of Mobilization in 1914," esp. 137–50, and Fritz Fischer, *War of Illusions: German Policies from 1911 to 1914*, trans. Marian Jackson (New York: W. W. Norton, 1975), esp. chs. 18–19, 22. See also Levy, "The Causes of War," 1:209–333, and Levy, "Preferences, Constraints, and Choices in July 1914," 151–86.

might send a different message from that intended by NATO. It might have suggested to the Soviet Union, especially during a tense crisis, that NATO was dispersing the weapons prior to launching a preemptive nuclear strike.[39]

Reagan administration maritime strategy sought to use the coercive threat of destroying Soviet nuclear attack and ballistic missile submarines in the early stages of a war in Europe to bring about deescalation and conflict termination on terms favorable to NATO.[40] However, the destruction of Soviet ballistic missile submarines by U.S. attack submarines might not have been interpreted as a tactical event only, but as a direct strike against survivable Soviet strategic nuclear power.[41] At that point, Soviet leaders might have reacted in one of several ways. They might have accepted this destruction of their SSBNs if the rate of loss was thought not to be significant and if a conventional war in Europe were otherwise going well. Or they might have counterescalated by destroying U.S. and allied shipping with tactical nuclear weapons, leaving open the issue of escalation on land. Or they might have launched a large nuclear strike against a comprehensive target set in Europe. Or, worse still, they might have struck preemptively against targets in the continental United States, on the assumption that the United States was preparing a preemptive attack of its own.[42] Admittedly, a war that would force these kinds of choices on Washington or Moscow seemed improbable, if not impossible. Nevertheless, the Reagan doctrine for sea warfare illustrated the point that a neat tactical move might be an ultimately deadly one. A move designed to impress the opponent with one's willingness to deliberately risk expansion of the fighting might cause the opponent to conclude that one is reckless or insensitive to inadvertent risk.

Organizational Rigidity

Another issue pertinent to escalation control is whether policymakers fully understand the large and complex military organizations they must operate

---

39. On the management of U.S. nuclear alerts, see Scott D. Sagan, "Nuclear Alerts and Crisis Management," *International Security* (Spring 1985), in *Nuclear Diplomacy and Crisis Management*, ed. Sean M. Lynn-Jones, Steven E. Miller, and Stephen Van Evera (Cambridge, Mass.: MIT Press, 1990), 159–99.

40. An official statement of Reagan maritime strategy appears in Adm. James D. Watkins, USN, "The Maritime Strategy," *Proceedings of the U.S. Naval Institute* (January 1986): 2–15.

41. See Ball, "Nuclear War at Sea"; Barry R. Posen, "Inadvertent Nuclear War? Escalation and NATO's Northern Flank," *International Security* (Fall 1982), in *Strategy and Nuclear Deterrence*, ed. Steven E. Miller (Princeton, N.J.: Princeton University Press, 1984), 85–112.

42. For background on strategic ASW, see Donald C. Daniel, *Anti-Submarine Warfare and Superpower Strategic Stability* (Urbana: University of Illinois Press, 1986).

in crisis and wartime. Large and complex bureaucratic organizations, includ-ing military ones, are dependent on the day-to-day flow of operating proce-dures and routines. Within a stable environment, such routines are the sources of organizational efficiency and effectiveness. Under conditions of rapid environmental change requiring adaptive decisionmaking, bureau-cratic organizations may be subjected to severe stresses. Military command-and-control organizations are no exception to this problem.

Bureaucratic organizations cope with their environments by adapting to certain repetitive, limited changes in the state of familiar variables. If new conditions are assigned to familiar variables, or if totally unfamiliar variables are introduced into the system, it may respond inadequately or not at all. This bureaucratic dependency on familiar stimuli and response programs is made even more necessary in nuclear command-and-control organizations by the extremely short times available for reaction to warning of attack. Since submarine-launched ballistic missiles off the U.S. Atlantic and Pacific coasts could strike at important military and command targets, including Washington, D.C., in fifteen minutes or less, responses are preprogrammed and packaged for different types of warning stimuli. The U.S. president, faced with such a contingency, would be making a "decision" only to verify that the warning was authentic and that the most appropriate option from the U.S. Single Integrated Operational Plan (SIOP) was being imple-mented. The president could not retool the plan at the last minute, creating options that planners had not anticipated, no matter how insistently he might feel that the existing warning called for a nonprogrammed response.[43]

Organizational rigidity is compounded by the problem of complexity and specialization. More specialized parts of an organization require that more complicated systems of command, control, and communications be devised to coordinate activities. This, in turn, creates additional layers of bureau-crats and middle managers, multiplying the "action channels" through which information must flow.[44] Added to the problem of "compartmenta-

43. Bush administration improvements to command and control were intended to provide leaders under nuclear war conditions with more options for reprogramming missions, based on damage assessments and other intelligence information. Bush's efforts continued a trend begun in the latter 1970s, under the U.S. "countervailing" strategy, to improve the flexibility of postattack command-and-control systems. The problem of making the transition from peace to war within the short warning time provided by missile attack remains largely unaffected by these improvements in retargeting, however. See Desmond Ball and Robert C. Toth, "Revising the SIOP: Taking War-Fighting to Dangerous Extremes," *International Security* (Spring 1990): 65–92.

44. This is very well addressed in Martin Van Creveld, *Command in War* (Cambridge, Mass.: Harvard University Press, 1985).

tion" of information (i.e., restricting categories of information on a "need to know" basis for reasons of security), complexity and specialization can contribute to decision pathologies in military command and other organizations. Thus, the U.S. military command system worldwide has failed to send apparently simple messages to correct destinations on account of compartmentation, incorrect distribution of traffic, and inability to recognize an atypical situation calling for adaptive responses. For example, when the ill-fated intelligence ship USS *Liberty* was unable to receive messages from Washington during the 1967 Six-Day War, it was attacked accidentally by Israel. An equally serious communications failure occurred in January 1968 when the USS *Pueblo*, collecting intelligence off the coast of North Korea, was captured by North Koreans. One year was required to free the surviving members of the crew, and the entire fleet of AGER (Auxiliary General-Environmental Research) surveillance craft was decommissioned shortly thereafter.[45]

Nuclear command organizations share some of these vulnerabilities to complexity and compartmentation with other military organizations. False warnings of attack were recorded frequently during 1979 and 1980 at the headquarters of North American Aerospace Defense Command (NORAD) in Cheyenne Mountain, Colorado. These warnings were almost all discounted immediately as misjudgments or as artificially induced phenomena. However, one incident in 1979 and one in 1980 were more serious. In 1979, a training tape was played at the wrong console and simulated all too realistically a Soviet attack; and in 1980 a faulty computer chip caused another simulation which resulted in the launching of alternate command post aircraft and other procedures that, during a real crisis, might have been provocative to leaders of another state.[46] These incidents and many others resulted in no political alarms because they could be isolated from any other incident that might have aroused leaders' fears, and because they took place within a low-threat international environment in which no expectation of imminent attack was plausible.

A more ominous possibility is that simultaneous and alarming incidents could take place during an international crisis. Such incidents could reinforce one another to create dangerous anxiety on the part of policymakers and military commanders. This anxiety-producing effect of multiple stimuli

45. Jeffrey Richelson, *American Espionage and the Soviet Target* (New York: William Morrow & Co., 1987), 158–59.
46. Peter Pringle and William Arkin, *SIOP: The Secret U.S. Plan for Nuclear War* (New York: W. W. Norton, 1983), 130–34.

could occur through a process termed "malevolent redundancy."[47] Malevolent, or malign, redundancy is the result of interactions between parts of a system, interactions not anticipated in the design of the system. A disturbance of one part of a complex system causes failure in another part; because the disturbance was not anticipated by the system designers, the failure goes undiagnosed until too late. Sometimes operators, not understanding the unexpected relationship between X and Y, make the situation worse in their misguided attempts to correct X in isolation. An error of this kind took place at the Three Mile Island nuclear power plant in Pennsylvania, when unexpected interaction effects between otherwise unrelated components of the system led to misdiagnosis and initially erroneous remedies.

In the case of U.S. and Soviet nuclear command organizations during the Cold War, malevolent redundancy could have resulted from the unintended "wiring together" of these command systems in ways that were not fault-tolerant. Each side's intelligence-and-warning systems are vertically integrated with its strategic retaliatory forces in order to preclude a surprise attack. Those intelligence-and-warning systems are also constantly monitoring the opponent's forces and intelligence indicators. During a crisis confrontation or conventional war, the warning-and-intelligence systems of each side might reinforce the tendency of the opposite number to exaggerate threats, or misperceptions of threat.[48]

The United States had not had the experience of managing simultaneous Soviet and American nuclear alerts. The Soviet Union did place a number of airborne divisions on alert status during the Arab-Israeli war of October 1973. Some U.S. commentators regarded this as a substitute for actual willingness to intervene with force; others took it as a more ominous signal.[49] Accompanied by a Soviet threat of unilateral military intervention if Israel did not observe the cease-fire agreement sponsored by the superpowers through the United Nations, the Soviet military maneuvers did have reciprocal effects within the U.S. government. The United States raised its alert level to DEFCON 3 worldwide to signal that the crisis had taken a new and dangerous turn, and U.S. officials used language that alluded to the possibility of nuclear escalation if the crisis was not contained.[50] U.S. officials in-

47. Paul Bracken, "Accidental Nuclear War," ch. 2 in *Hawks, Doves, and Owls*, ed. Allison, Carnesale, and Nye, 25–43, esp. 36.

48. Bracken, *The Command and Control of Nuclear Forces*, passim, discusses this problem at length. See also Lebow, *Nuclear Crisis Management*, 75–103.

49. On the U.S. alert during the Arab-Israeli war of 1973, see Barry M. Blechman and Douglas M. Hart, "The Political Utility of Nuclear Weapons: The 1973 Middle East Crisis," *International Security* (Summer 1982), in *Strategy and Nuclear Deterrence*, ed. Miller, 273–97.

50. Ibid. See also Sagan, "Nuclear Alerts and Crisis Management," 182–90.

cluding Nixon and Kissinger may have been convinced that these escalatory steps, including the global military alert, helped to resolve the crisis favorably from a U.S. standpoint. One could argue with equal justification, however, that the alert was unnecessary, inexpedient, and possibly provocative of escalation over which both sides might have lost control. (I offer related arguments about this crisis in Chapter 2, above.)

The superpowers' interests in resolving the October 1973 crisis and in terminating the Arab-Israeli war were not identical, but they were partly convergent. U.S. intelligence did detect Soviet troop movements that could have been interpreted as preparatory steps for military intervention in Egypt. However, even if the Soviets had so intervened, they would have been hardpressed to accomplish much in the way of direct military gain through the use of rapidly deployable forces only (such as their crack airborne divisions, which were observed by U.S. intelligence being made ready for deployment). Soviet airborne divisions without further reinforcement, which could not have arrived for days, would have been destroyed by Israeli forces if the Soviet troops attempted to take the offensive to rescue the Third Army Corps. Necessary reinforcements would have allowed time for U.S. and Israeli countermeasures. The enforcement of the U.N. cease-fire resolutions offered more hope to Egypt than a direct Soviet intervention that might be opposed by the United States and its NATO allies.

The "manipulation of risk" argument for the U.S. alert is also deficient in assuming that the risks of further escalation could have been controlled subsequent to any Soviet military intervention and U.S. military response. If the Soviets had opted for confrontation in Egypt, the United States would have found itself without some credible, intermediate rungs on the ladder of escalation between coercive diplomacy and all-out war. Deployment of significant numbers of U.S. fighting forces to Egypt in 1973 would have required a major effort by the Pentagon (which during the 1973 crisis struggled to supply Israel with equipment to replace its losses). The U.S. post-Vietnam military establishment was in no mood for a major conventional war outside of Europe. The real danger of the U.S. *nuclear* aspect of the global alert is that it might have alarmed Soviet leaders sufficiently to get them involved in *conventional* military operations in the Middle East, much to the disadvantage of the United States.

In the Cuban missile crisis, President Kennedy adopted a contrasting approach to that adopted by Kissinger on behalf of Nixon in October 1973. Kennedy sought de-escalation by allowing Khrushchev room to backpedal from a position that was obviously untenable once the United States had discovered the Soviet missiles in Cuba before those missiles could be mated with warheads and made fully operational. Recently declassified documents pertinent to the deliberations of "ExComm" reveal that Kennedy had not foreclosed the option of trading U.S. Jupiter medium-range ballistic missiles in Turkey for the Soviet SS-4s and SS-5s in Cuba. Earlier accounts of the crisis, including first-person accounts by Kennedy advisers, had stated that Kennedy absolutely refused to consider any such "trade."[51] This revelation suggests that Kennedy was more willing to make a politically obnoxious deal, from the standpoint of U.S. allies in NATO Europe, in order to avoid a military confrontation with the Soviet Union over Cuba. As it happened, the United States was able to avoid having to make such an arrangement in order to compel Khrushchev to remove the missiles.

Kennedy's apparent willingness to consider a missile trade as an alternative to war shows the impact of nuclear weapons on crisis management. Soviet strategic nuclear forces were grossly inferior to American ones at the time of the Cuban missile crisis: roughly a seventeen-to-one superiority in deliverable warheads favored the United States. Nevertheless, the U.S. president was apparently willing to consider seriously an option that would have had serious political costs within the Western alliance, rather than run additional risks of escalation to war between the superpowers.

The arguments about whether nuclear weapons made any difference in resolving the Cuban missile crisis have been evaluated by the historian Marc Trachtenberg.[52] Trachtenberg evaluates three genres of argument about the role of nuclear weapons in the crisis. The first set of arguments treats nuclear weapons as essentially irrelevant, other than to deter the nuclear first use of another side. The second contends that nuclear weapons were relevant to the crisis outcomes, but nuclear superiority was not. What was most important was the sense of shared risk between Kennedy and Khrushchev and their advisers. A third set of arguments contends that U.S. nuclear superiority made a great deal of difference in resolving the crisis favorably from the standpoint of U.S. objectives. We might summarize these arguments as "nuclear irrelevance," "risk significance," and "nuclear superiority."

According to Trachtenberg, the "nuclear irrelevance" arguments could not be sustained for either the U.S. or the Soviet leadership. He notes that

51. See McGeorge Bundy, "October 27, 1962: Transcripts of the Meetings of the Ex-Comm," ed. James G. Blight, *International Security* (Winter 1987–88): 30–92.

52. Marc Trachtenberg, "The Influence of Nuclear Weapons in the Cuban Missile Crisis," *International Security* (Summer 1985), in *Nuclear Diplomacy and Crisis Management*, ed. Lynn-Jones, Miller, and Van Evera, 256–82.

"the fear of nuclear war affected both Soviet and American behavior in the crisis; and, indeed, these fears were consciously manipulated, most notably by the American strategic alert."[53] The "risk significance" arguments are more persuasive than either the "irrelevance" or the "superiority" argument. However, risk calculations were not the same on both sides and, according to Trachtenberg, the balance of resolve favorable to the United States was an important factor contributing to the relatively favorable outcome for Kennedy. U.S. force superiority was not irrelevant to the Soviet and U.S. leaderships, according to Trachtenberg, but it mattered a great deal more to the Kremlin than to Washington. Most important for our discussion of escalation, ExComm's fear of escalation "substantially cancelled out, in its own mind, whatever benefits it might have theoretically been able to derive from its 'strategic superiority.' "[54]

From the Cuban missile crisis, then, we do not get a picture of one side manipulating the risk of escalation with temerity and optimism based on the conviction that further expansion of hostilities is controllable toward outcomes in its favor. The point is significant, for it distinguishes between those escalations into which policymakers plunge despite their preferences not to and those escalations which they embark upon in the expectation that favorable outcomes, even victory, are probable. In October 1962 the asymmetrical balance of strategic nuclear force favorable to the Americans mattered little to Kennedy and his advisers compared to the absolute damage that any Soviet first or second strike could do to a few U.S. cities. This did not make nuclear superiority totally irrelevant, but it did make calculations of *relative loss and gain* take second place to the expectation of *absolutely* unacceptable damage for both sides.

Based on the Cuban missile crisis and other incidents discussed here, one might posit two conditions favorable to de-escalation when nuclear-armed states engage in crisis management. First, leaders might fear loss of control over military operations. Organizations carrying out standard procedures under nonstandard conditions might cause inadvertent escalation or war. Second, leaders might be so conscious of the unacceptable damage attendant even to small nuclear exchanges that they are unwilling to push brinkmanship very far. In the Cuban missile crisis, fear of loss of control and fear of possible consequences both operated to favor de-escalation. In the October 1973 Middle East crisis, there were no apparent lapses of political control

53. Ibid., 280–81.
54. Ibid., 281.

over military *operations* (at least for the U.S. side; little evidence is available about Soviet decisionmaking). Instead, there were, in the U.S. case, decisions made hastily and perhaps on the basis of misjudgment about the probable motives of the Soviet leadership. U.S. leaders reached for a quick way to send a message of resolve and determination to the Soviet Union, assuming that Soviet leaders in 1973 harbored aggressive military ambitions for intervention. The choice of a military alert ruled out other steps to clarify ambiguities in Soviet messages and Soviet troop movements.

The problem of nuclear-alert management poses dilemmas for policymakers, but there is some experience in Moscow and Washington in dealing with such problems. More stressful conditions might be created by the initial military engagements of a conventional war between nuclear-armed states. Leaders would want to continue the kinds of control over their own military operations, and to communicate reliably with their counterparts in other national capitals, but they might not be able to. The general-purpose forces of the Soviet Union and the United States contain thousands of nuclear weapons, which are scattered among geographically dispersed armies, fleets, and air forces. Therefore, in a crisis or at the outset of conventional war, the difficulty of establishing and maintaining thresholds on the periphery of conflict might subvert the best intentions of those at the center. Soviet leaders in January 1991, for example, claimed to have lost control over the "committees of national salvation" and "black beret" Ministry of the Interior troops who fired on unarmed Latvian and Lithuanian citizens.[55] In recognition of this problem of peripheral control as it might apply to nuclear forces, Soviet leaders in 1990 moved to reorganize the command and control of nuclear forces so that the likelihood of unauthorized use by separatist nationalities within the armed forces was diminished.[56]

Incremental or Drastic Escalation?

A third feature of escalation control is whether escalation takes place in slow stages of relatively equal duration and severity, or whether it jumps spasmod-

---

55. An article in the controversial Soviet journal *Argumenty i fakty* [Arguments and Facts] in January 1991, attributed to Col. Alksnis, spokesman for the Soyuz bloc in the Congress of People's Deputies, made the claim that Gorbachev established the committees of national salvation in Lithuania and in Latvia. According to Viktor Alksnis, Gorbachev disclaimed any connection after Interior Ministry (MVD) troops shot unarmed civilians in the aftermath of coups declared by the committees. U.S. press accounts include *Philadelphia Inquirer*, January 28, 1991.

56. Bracken, "War Termination," 197–216, discusses the issue of peripheral control in the context of U.S.-Soviet crisis and possible wartime operations.

ically across many rungs of the escalation ladder at once. If one side has a doctrine of graduated escalation but its opponent does not, the side with the expectation of large jumps may interpret small escalations by its opponent as large changes in the status quo.

The problem of incremental escalation was for many years inherent in the NATO "flexible response" doctrine. That doctrine, as is well known, called for a graduated progression of conventional, theater nuclear, and strategic nuclear responses to a Soviet attack on Western Europe. The NATO decisionmaking process required an estimated twenty-four hours from the time that corps commanders asked for nuclear release until authorization for release made its way back down the chain of command. It was expected that initial uses by NATO of tactical nuclear weapons would be selective and carefully controlled, according to carefully drafted guidelines for selection of weapons, targets, and collateral damage.[57] Further decisions to use nuclear weapons would have required additional consultation among high-level alliance political and military leaders. The objective of this selective and somewhat demonstrative use of nuclear weapons on the battlefield was primarily to signal the resolve of the alliance to continue its resistance even at a higher cost.

Soviet military doctrine expressed a less apparent interest in employing nuclear weapons in a graduated way for signaling or coercive bargaining. But Soviet military writers did not rule out the selective use of nuclear or conventional weapons, according to the mission priorities of army and front commanders. A Rand Corporation study which compared Soviet and U.S. doctrine on escalation noted that "there is little doubt that Soviet military thinkers *approach* the issue of escalation from a fundamentally different direction than do most of their Western counterparts. The roots of this asymmetry run deep and involve issues of culture, geography, and historical experiences."[58] The Soviet notion of intrawar deterrence during the Cold War years was almost certainly very different from the American or NATO one prevalent until the INF and CFE agreements drove NATO into rethinking its basic military strategy for the defense of Europe. Only the Soviet political leadership could have authorized the release of codes to enable nuclear weapons, and interlocking connections between the armed forces and Party organizations were designed to ensure against any unauthorized use. But once

57. Catherine McArdle Kelleher, "NATO Nuclear Operations," ch. 14 in *Managing Nuclear Operations*, ed. Carter, Steinbruner, and Zraket, 445–69.

58. Paul K. Davis and Peter J. E. Stan, *Concepts and Models of Escalation* (Santa Monica, Calif.: Rand Corp., May 1984), 15.

release had been granted, Soviet commanders might have been less restricted *during wartime operations* than their U.S. or NATO counterparts as to the timing and execution of retaliatory strikes.[59] The expectation on the part of some U.S. nuclear strategists—that the Soviet command-and-control system could have distinguished between "limited" counterforce attacks on Soviet territory and a massive attack on a wide variety of counterforce and other targets—was doubted by other expert analysts.[60]

NATO's assumption that nuclear escalation could be graduated remained in some tension with NATO's requirement for credibly coupling the U.S. strategic nuclear deterrent to nuclear and conventional forces based in Europe. The conflict between the logic of "coupling" and the logic of "firebreaks" was built into NATO for two unavoidable reasons: 1) asymmetry of power among the member states and 2) inequality of risk if war actually broke out. The U.S. interpretation of flexible response (MC-14/3) was that it allowed additional time for bargaining and conciliation to take place between superpower adversaries, even after conventional war had begun or nuclear first use had occurred. NATO Europeans, though not properly typecast of one mind, in general had good reasons for skepticism that such a fighting-while-negotiating posture would be sufficiently deterring to a Soviet leader poised for war. Behind these nominal arguments about coupling and firebreaks, of course, were dissimilarities in interest. For example, détente with Soviet Union was a higher-priority item for continental Europeans in the 1970s and early 1980s than it was for the Americans. Then, too, different perspectives of shared risk were inevitable, including the shared risks of escalation from conventional into nuclear war, as between the nuclear-armed and nonnuclear members of the alliance.[61]

59. Until the mid-1960s, the KGB was assigned responsibility for custody and transport of nuclear charges, and the military was assigned responsibility for custody and transport of delivery vehicles. There is some evidence that a Soviet equivalent of U.S. permissive-action links (PALs), or electronic locks, were installed on some components of the Soviet strategic nuclear forces. See Stephen M. Meyer, "Soviet Nuclear Operations," ch. 15 in Ashton B. Carter, John D. Steinbruner, and Charles A. Zraket, eds., *Managing Nuclear Operations* (Washington, D.C.: Brookings Institution, 1987), 470–534, for discussion of pertinent points on Soviet nuclear command and control.

60. Desmond Ball, *Soviet Strategic Planning and the Control of Nuclear War*, Reference Paper no. 109 (Canberra: Research School of Pacific Studies, Australian National University, November 1983).

61. For additional background, see Gregory F. Treverton, *Making the Alliance Work: The United States and Western Europe* (Ithaca, N.Y.: Cornell University Press, 1985), chs. 2 and 3, and Josef Joffe, *The Limited Partnership: Europe, the United States, and the Burdens of Alliance* (Cambridge, Mass.: Ballinger Publishing Co., 1987), chs. 2 and 5.

NATO's typology of graduated escalation also lacked credibility in light of that alliance's fragile command-and-control system. Even conventional war in Europe, any time from the 1960s through the 1980s, would have placed great stresses on NATO's ability to maintain cohesion in its multinational fighting forces. Armies deployed in NATO's corps sectors along the inter-German and West German–Czech borders operated and trained according to different national doctrines. Communication among the various national units deployed in Europe was subject to breakdown even during crisis. NATO's cumbersome procedures for obtaining nuclear release via the "bottom up" process, from corps commanders to the highest political and military levels, were more effective at preventing unauthorized use than they were at providing for wartime needs. The likelihood was strong that NATO could not in fact take a decision to use nuclear weapons in a timely manner, and that the United States or some other nuclear-armed member state would have to do so unilaterally.

Soviet leaders gave no evidence of making a distinction between "NATO" nuclear weapons launched into their territory and "U.S." nuclear weapons having the same destination. In either instance, the Soviet General Staff would almost certainly have concluded that general nuclear war was about to begin. Preemption in the last resort could have been an admissible option in the face of clear evidence that the United States was willing to authorize attacks on the Soviet homeland from Europe. The U.S. view of INF (intermediate nuclear force) weapons, as having modernized an "intermediate" rung of the ladder of escalation in order to add to NATO's wartime options, implied a separation between the categories of "theater" and "strategic" war not duplicated in Soviet terminology. The first use of any nuclear weapons in Europe would almost certainly have taken U.S., allied NATO, and Soviet leaders into a vast unknown, in which the interest of political leaders in gradual escalation could easily have been overtaken by the momentum of military operations.

COERCIVE DIPLOMACY

The third principal component of the concept of war termination is coercive diplomacy. This aspect of war termination has been alluded to, by example and by approximation, in the preceding discussions of escalation control and agreed battle. One objective of coercive diplomacy is controlling escalation while maximizing one's gains or minimizing one's losses in other respects.[62] Both escalation control and coercive diplomacy, in turn, assume that the possibility of an agreed battle is not excluded by the combatants. Despite these interrelationships among the various components of war termination, coercive diplomacy demands appreciation in its own right.

The term "coercive diplomacy" includes an apparent contradiction, from the standpoint of intelligent lay readers outside the field of political science. It implies fighting and negotiating at the same time. War is not first fought to a successful conclusion, followed by the helpless capitulation of the vanquished to the victors. Instead, states fight while negotiating, and in many cases they attempt to prevail in a crisis or war at the lowest possible domestic political cost. In the nuclear age, the use of coercive diplomacy is more relevant to crisis management than to nuclear warfighting. Even nuclear warfighting, however disastrous it might be, would maintain aspects of coercive diplomacy so long as the opponents sought some end to the fighting short of total societal destruction.

The successful use of coercive diplomacy requires that certain environmental conditions be present, and these cannot be guaranteed.[63] An erroneous appreciation of the environment for decision is likely to lead to misplaced signals or disregarded messages. In general, the environment permissive of coercive diplomacy must provide the following: 1) the party employing coercive diplomacy must threaten to do something to its opponent within a time frame that is meaningful to the latter; 2) the threatener should have the capability to carry out the threat and be so perceived by the opponent; 3) the threatener should have the willingness to execute the threat and be so perceived; 4) the time between a threat and its execution must not be so long that environmental conditions change, making the threat irrelevant; and 5) the offering of "carrots" must be included along with the threatened use of "sticks," which is to say that some reward for compliance must be apparent to the threatened party.

An example of unsuccessful coercive diplomacy was the escalation of U.S.

62. Alexander L. George, Stanford University, is most responsible for development of the concept of coercive diplomacy. See Alexander L. George, David K. Hall, and William E. Simons, The Limits of Coercive Diplomacy: Laos, Cuba, Vietnam (Boston: Little, Brown, 1971); Phil Williams, Crisis Management: Confrontation and Diplomacy in the Nuclear Age (New York: John Wiley & Sons, 1976), 135–91; and Schelling, Arms and Influence, 1–34.

63. Alexander George, "The Development of Doctrine and Strategy," in The Limits of Coercive Diplomacy, ed. George, Hall, and Simons, 1–35.

involvement in Vietnam. The idea was that North Vietnam would be made to pay an increasingly more costly price for its aggression against South Vietnam. This was a simplified application of a deterrence model for conventional war or nuclear crisis to a far more complex reality, in which unconventional and conventional war were mixed together. The United States assumed that the environmental conditions conducive to coercion of North Vietnam and its Viet Cong ally were present when, in fact, they were absent. The U.S. bombing of North Vietnam could not stop the flow of supplies into the South; nor could the politico-military infrastructure of North Vietnam be subjected to blows that would disrupt effective management of its war effort. It was difficult to influence the morale of the North Vietnamese leadership because few U.S. officials had any insight into the Politburo's cost–benefit calculus. As to the war in South Vietnam, it was a collage of American and South Vietnamese efforts to secure certain areas from further revolutionary activity while expanding the defense perimeter to include as much of the rural countryside as forces and strategy permitted. But reform of the government of South Vietnam, a prerequisite to the mobilization of popular support for the government and against the insurgents, never materialized. A weak South Vietnamese government meant that the United States was standing on a weak pedestal from which to make threats against North Vietnam: the Hanoi Politburo knew that the government of South Vietnam could not withstand a protracted civil war supported from outside sanctuaries.[64]

Coercive strategies have also been tried more recently by U.S. planners. (An interpretation of U.S. strategy in the 1991 Gulf War as a coercive strategy appears in the preceding chapter.) In 1987 the United States and allied navies were assigned to patrol the Persian Gulf in order to protect reflagged Kuwaiti tankers against Iranian gunboats and missiles. President Reagan appeared in this instance to be engaging in coercive diplomacy without knowing it, much in the fashion of Molière's prose-speaking bourgeois gentlemen. Iranian attacks on Gulf shipping grew out of the Iran-Iraq War. The U.S. did not want to take sides in that conflict officially, although unofficially it supported Iraq. The U.S. position was that the shipping lanes should be free for commercial and other maritime uses unimpeded by military obstruction. That position, however admirable from a "law of the sea" standpoint, was

---

64. For perspective on unconventional war, see Sam C. Sarkesian, "U.S. Strategy and Unconventional Conflicts," ch. 10 in *The U.S. Army in a New Security Era*, ed. Sam C. Sarkesian and John Allen Williams (Boulder, Colo.: Lynne Rienner, 1990), 195–216.

more consistent with Iraqi objectives than with those of Iran. It was a weaker form of coercion, and thus less risky to U.S. prestige, than the involvement of U.S. forces in Lebanon during Reagan's first term. In the case of the U.S. commitment to the multinational peacekeeping force deployed in Lebanon, U.S. leaders were unable to devise a military objective that supported effectively their political objective. The major problem in Lebanon was not deterrence of external aggression but the termination of internal sectarian strife. Having arrived in Lebanon in the guise of peacekeeping forces, American troops became highly visible surrogate targets for disgruntled factions in the Lebanese civil war. The United States could neither impose a settlement upon the disputants nor make its own role appear to be that of an honest broker. U.S. forces were caught between a mission that was part "coercive diplomacy" and part "preventive diplomacy," of the kind engineered by former U.N. Secretary-General Dag Hammarskjöld and applied by the United Nations in the Congo in 1960.

Coercive diplomacy can be confused with preventive diplomacy, as the preceding discussion argues. It might also be confused with military escalation or used as a diplomatic backdrop for a military strategy that is essentially based on escalation dominance. Escalation dominance is the capability to prevail militarily in any foreseeable threshold engagement. U.S. maritime strategy during the Reagan administration used coercive diplomacy in this fashion, in support of a warfighting doctrine that called for prompt escalation to attacks on Soviet ballistic missile submarines at the outset of conventional war in Europe.

One assumption behind the Reagan maritime strategy, not an illogical one, was that the outbreak of war in Europe would be the first, and perhaps decisive, phase of a world war. The U.S. Navy would have to act preemptively to establish control of the seas, including denial to the Soviet Union of any ability to interfere with sea lanes of communication from North America to Western Europe. More controversial among academic strategists, the U.S. Navy strategy of the Reagan years also called for prompt attacks on Soviet submarine and naval air bases along with the preemptive offensive strikes against Soviet attack submarines and ballistic missile submarines. U.S. Navy strategists argued that Soviet planners expected us to attack their ballistic missile submarines at the outset of war, and that the reason for the U.S. attacks would not be escalation but war termination. By reducing the expected size of the Soviet strategic nuclear force available for postwar bargaining and war termination, the United States would be more likely, according to navy strategists, to obtain a favorable political outcome.

The risks of the Reagan maritime strategy in crossing the threshold from conventional to nuclear war have been noted by critics of that strategy.[65] This aspect of the U.S. maritime strategy was not necessarily inadvertent. The United States wished to pose to the Soviet Union the "threat that leaves something to chance" when U.S. and Soviet forces were engaged in direct conflict. As Thomas C. Schelling has noted, there are two separate issues here: the danger of escalation and the role such a danger plays in a nation's strategy.[66] A strategy may deliberately pose a credible risk of inadvertent escalation because it is more persuasive to the adversary than threatening to start a general nuclear war. Forces at sea, as a result of permissive interpretation of crisis or wartime rules of engagement, might stumble into the decision for escalation.

On the other hand, the "threat that leaves something to chance" is a two-sided proposition.[67] In the application of the Reagan maritime strategy to the early stages of any conflict in Europe, for example, the Soviet Union might have anticipated that the United States would lose effective control of its own operations. American forces might have sent this message without intending to. If the sinking of Soviet attack and ballistic missile submarines had been accompanied by other indicators that Moscow interpreted as a loss of U.S. peripheral control over military operations, Soviet expectations of winning or losing a competitive bargaining process would no longer be the issue. The same problem applies to U.S. and NATO plans for nuclear escalation subsequent to first use on land in Europe. Would Moscow have assumed that a careful and deliberate set of nuclear signals was being sent? Or would Soviet leaders have concluded that desperate NATO policymakers had delegated to commanders the authority for additional use at their discretion? Once the destruction of NATO and Soviet command, control, and communications systems had proceeded to the point at which significant degradation of assessment had taken place, as might have happened during the conventional phase of a war in Europe, reliable knowledge about the political meaning attached to nuclear attacks, demonstrative or otherwise, would have been difficult to obtain.

Drawing the line between coercive persuasion and provocation was one of

65. John J. Mearsheimer, "A Strategic Misstep: The Maritime Strategy and Deterrence in Europe," *International Security* (Fall 1986): 3–57. For a rejoinder, see Capt. Linton F. Brooks, USN, "Naval Power and National Security: The Case for a Maritime Strategy," *International Security* (Fall 1986): 58–88.
66. Schelling, *Arms and Influence*, 109.
67. Schelling, *The Strategy of Conflict*, 187–204.

the problems facing President Kennedy and his ExComm advisers during the Cuban missile crisis. An air strike against the Soviet surface-to-air missile sites in Cuba could provoke Soviet retaliation against Berlin or other Western assets vulnerable to "horizontal escalation." The alternative of invading Cuba, deposing Castro, and expelling the missiles thereafter also posed risks of widening the war and losing sight of the premier issue at stake as framed by the president: removal of the Soviet missiles from Cuba.

The line between coercion and provocation of the Soviet Union also had to be drawn when the implementation of the "quarantine" was discussed. A blockade that was too restrictive risked provoking the very war that President Kennedy was seeking to avoid. The U.S. objective was to get the Soviet Union to withdraw the missiles without war, even local, conventional war, if possible. However, the milder form of coercion—deterrence—could only prevent the shipment of additional missiles to Cuba. The stronger form—compellence—was necessary in order to induce the Soviet leadership to remove the missiles. The blockade included aspects of both deterrence and compellence, but additional compellence was necessary in the form of preparations for air strikes, for invasion of Cuba, and for nuclear war if need be. These preparations were made visible and apparent to Soviet warning and assessment.[68]

The transparency of the line between coercion and provocation in the 1962 Cuban crisis has become more apparent as time has passed and as new archives, including Soviet ones, have been opened to scholars. We now know that there was apparent division within the Soviet leadership over whether to acquiesce in U.S. demands for prompt removal of the missiles. Khrushchev has testified that his decision to remove the missiles was opposed by Soviet military and other leaders, and by Castro. Soviet military opponents of Khrushchev's decision, according to Khrushchev, were sufficiently

68. Without the knowledge of, or authorization by, the president, secretary of defense, or the chairman of the U.S. Joint Chiefs of Staff, SAC Commander-in-Chief Thomas S. Power, having been ordered to go on full alert, decided to announce the fact "in the clear" instead of using the normal means of encoded messages. This unusual procedure was apparently chosen by Power to reinforce a message implicit in SAC's DEFCON 2 alert procedures, which included an increase in the airborne alert component of the B-52 force. See Garthoff, *Reflections on the Cuban Missile Crisis*, 60–61, on Power's procedures, and 73–74 on the U.S. military buildup for a possible invasion of Cuba. Garthoff, who prepared intelligence estimates for decision-makers during the Cuban missile crisis, elsewhere comments with regard to U.S. military preparations for the possible invasion of Cuba prior to the discovery of the Soviet missiles: "there was no intention to invade Cuba, although in addition to covert operations there were many military contingency plans prepared before the crisis, which were dusted off and available once the Soviet missiles came in." See his comments in Blight and Welch, *On the Brink*, 250.

insistent on holding firm that he was forced to ask if they (the military hard-liners) could guarantee that firmness would not result in nuclear war.[69] There is some evidence that Khrushchev's first decision about the U.S. blockade was to ignore it, and at least one Soviet writer has claimed that Khrushchev issued orders to ship captains to proceed despite the blockade. If so, the orders were subsequently reconsidered by the Soviet leadership.[70]

During a conference held in Cambridge, Massachusetts, in October 1987, a group of American and Soviet experts on the Cuban missile crisis, includ-ing members of the Kennedy ExComm and at least one adviser to Khru-shchev, discussed the perceptions of the two leaderships in Washington and Moscow as the crisis unfolded.[71] Some of the discussions raised questions about command and control of Soviet forces and its implications for crisis management and escalation control during the U.S. exercise of coercive diplomacy.

Former U.S. Secretary of Defense Robert S. McNamara asked Soviet par-ticipants whether, during the Cuban missile crisis, their warheads were equipped with permissive-action links, those electronic or mechanical locks which prevent accidental or unauthorized firing of the weapon. McNamara pointed out that the Kennedy administration introduced PALs on most nu-clear weapons in order "to reduce the risks of inadvertent war" because "it was the conventional wisdom among our military that, even though our forces were highly disciplined, it was not unlikely that, in the event of war, some troops would use the nuclear weapons under their control rather than allow them to be overrun."[72] McNamara then added that during the Cuban missile crisis he was concerned that Soviet or Cuban troops might choose to

69. Norman Cousins, "The Cuban Missile Crisis: An Anniversary," *Saturday Review*, Oc-tober 15, 1977, cited in Garthoff, *Reflections on the Cuban Missile Crisis*, 77.

70. For a discussion of this, see Garthoff, *Reflections on the Cuban Missile Crisis*, 66, n. 106.

71. The conference was sponsored and hosted by Harvard University, and included U.S. participants and former ExComm members McGeorge Bundy, Robert McNamara, and Theo-dore Sorenson and Soviet participants Fyodor Burlatsky, Sergo Mikoyan, and Georgi Shakna-zarov, together with academic participants. Burlatsky is a well-known Soviet political com-mentator who wrote a much-feted play for Moscow audiences about U.S. decisionmaking in Cuba. Sergo Mikoyan is the son of Anastas Mikoyan, who served under Khrushchev as first deputy premier; he accompanied his father to Cuba on a diplomatic mission after the Cuban missile crisis and was familiar with many details of Soviet decisionmaking at the time. Georgi Shaknazarov was an aide to Mikhail Gorbachev in 1987 and has participated in other U.S.-Soviet discussions of arms control and related topics. See Blight and Welch, *On the Brink*, 225–90.

72. Ibid., 274–75.

"use" instead of "lose" if they came under attack, and he asked the Soviet officials if this was a matter of concern to the Soviet government. Sergo Mikoyan, son of First Deputy Premier (under Khrushchev) Anastas Mikoyan and privy to high-level Soviet decisionmaking as a result of his father's position in 1962, said: "I agree that such a possibility existed."[73]

Participants then queried whether Soviet nuclear warheads had actually arrived in Cuba at any time during the crisis, and if so, when. The Soviet representatives reached no consensus on this. Harvard Professor Joseph Nye noted that U.S. intelligence had never confirmed the presence of Soviet nuclear warheads in Cuba, although obviously U.S. decisionmaking proceeded on the assumption that warheads had been deployed along with the missiles.[74]

Fyodor Burlatsky, now a prominent Soviet literary writer and in 1962 a speechwriter for Khrushchev, and Sergo Mikoyan offered opposite reactions to Nye's question as to whether Soviet warheads were ever actually in Cuba during the Cuban missile crisis. Mikoyan stated that in his opinion "warheads were in Cuba, surely," adding that this judgment was based on logical deduction: "it would be senseless to have the missiles there but no warheads."[75] Burlatsky disagreed, noting that he was sure there were never any Soviet warheads in Cuba. Burlatsky confidently asserted that Khrushchev's plan was to ship the warheads to Cuba as a *second step*, provided the U.S. acquiesced in the presence of missiles.[76]

Colonel General Dmitri A. Volkogonov, head of the Institute of Military History of the USSR, researched the Cuban missile crisis ("Caribbean crisis" in Soviet terminology) using materials from the central archives of the Ministry of Defense (TsAMO). Volkogonov claimed on the basis of his research that nuclear warheads *were* shipped to Cuba, and he estimated that twenty of the forty nuclear warheads were planned for immediate deployment with the first contingent of missiles (forty-eight planned R-12 or SS-4 MRBMs, of which forty-two actually arrived in Cuba; thirty-two R-14 or SS-5 IRBMs,

73. Ibid., 274.
74. Ibid. According to Raymond Garthoff, a U.S. Special National Intelligence Estimate on October 20, 1962, noted that "the construction of at least one probable nuclear storage facility is a strong indication of the Soviet intent to provide nuclear warheads. In any case, it is prudent to assume that when the missiles are otherwise operational, nuclear warheads will be available." Later, other such facilities were identified by U.S. intelligence. SNIE 11-19-62, October 20, 1962, cited in Garthoff, *Reflections on the Cuban Missile Crisis*, 38.
75. Blight and Welch, *On the Brink*, 274.
76. Ibid., 274–75.

of which none had arrived by the time the U.S. discovered the missile deployments).[77]

The issue of Soviet warheads in Cuba prior to October 16, 1962, is obviously related to one aspect of the problem of reconciling coercive diplomacy with escalation control. The connection is between the "Were warheads actually present?" question and the "What were prevailing Soviet protocols for launch control?" issue. McNamara pressed this point on Soviet participants more than once at the Cambridge conference in 1987, noting that U.S. field commanders *at that time* "could have started a nuclear war if they wanted to, because we didn't have PALs."[78] He received no direct response from Soviet participants, whose subsequent discussion expressed more concern about what might have happened following a U.S. air strike or invasion. The consensus was that the Soviet Union would have had to respond in some way, though not necessarily with nuclear strikes against the United States or its allies. McNamara's attempt to get Soviet principals to speculate about the possibility of inadvertent escalation, through accidental or unauthorized launch of a missile from Cuba, was not very successful.

Although the questions about launch protocols and availability of warheads in Cuba for MRBMs and IRBMs are not fully resolved, apparently tactical nuclear warheads accompanied Soviet ground forces deployed in Cuba. The tactical warheads, deployed as a matter of standard operating procedure with Soviet short-range tactical rocket launchers in Europe, followed their mates to their destinations in Cuba. At a Havana conference on the Cuban missile crisis in January 1992, General of the Soviet Army Anatoly Gribkov said that nine tactical nuclear warheads had been shipped to Cuba to accompany six short-range tactical rocket launchers (presumably FROG-7s).[79] General Gribkov, who had important planning responsibilities for the Soviet missile buildup in Cuba, also provided significant and disturbing information about Soviet command-and-control arrangements for the tactical nuclear warheads shipped there and available by October 1962. According to Gribkov, the Soviet military commander in Cuba, General of the Soviet Army Issa A. Pliyev, had been given discretionary authority to use

77. Volkogonov's estimates appear in Garthoff, *Reflections on the Cuban Missile Crisis*, 39. Garthoff regards these estimates as consistent with the best U.S. intelligence estimates.

78. Blight and Welch, *On the Brink*, 275.

79. Raymond Garthoff, *The Havana Conference on the Cuban Missile Crisis*, Cold War International History Project Bulletin no. 1 (Washington, D.C.: Woodrow Wilson International Center for Scholars, Spring 1992), 2–3.

these short-range nuclear weapons in the event of any U.S. invasion of Cuba.[80] Pliyev was not required to seek further authorization from Moscow before doing so. Subsequent to the Havana Conference, well-informed Russian sources have contradicted Gribkov's account. More recent discussions between U.S. and Russian scholars have revealed that as many as 98–104 tactical warheads may have been shipped to Cuba and arrived prior to the outbreak of crisis. These warheads included: eighty warheads for coastal defense cruise missiles; twelve for Luna surface-to-surface rockets; six for IL-28 bombers; and (perhaps) additional naval land mines. These *tactical* warheads were, of course, in addition to the sixty force loadings for SS-4 and SS-5 medium- and intermediate-range missiles capable of attacking North America from Cuba.[81]

The contrast between the "fail safe" command-and-control arrangements for Soviet strategic nuclear weapons and the "fail deadly" arrangements for Soviet tactical warheads is a striking illustration of the contrast in the perspective of the operational commanders and providers of military logistics with that of the upper-level leadership. Operational commanders are concerned with "how to fight" questions, and they desire maximum readiness for the day deterrence actually fails. Political leaders are concerned with the control of inadvertent escalation which might force them into an otherwise avoidable shooting war, or into a wider war than the one in which they are presently engaged. The case of Soviet command-and-control diversity in the missile crisis of 1962 also broadens our understanding of the difference between political leaders' lack of knowledge about the *details* of military operations, on one hand, and their lack of awareness about the *interface* between higher-level expectations concerning the role of force and lower-level views that force is an end in itself, on the other. Khrushchev was not ignorant about Soviet ground forces or about their arms and equipment. Their available nuclear weapons did not seem to matter until the priority of escalation control and conflict termination took precedence over efforts to deceive and to bluff the Americans in Cuba. It then became necessary to make clear to U.S. leaders that Khrushchev did not want a shooting war in the Caribbean between U.S. and Soviet forces, especially a *nuclear* war.

The question of the interface between leaders' and commanders' expecta-

80. Ibid.
81. The author gratefully acknowledges insights and information from Raymond Garthoff, Brookings Institution.

tions remains important because of an incident that occurred on October 27 as the crisis built toward its climax. An American U-2 reconnaissance aircraft was shot down over Cuba, and U.S. policymakers wondered whether this was a Soviet signal that war was on. Members of the ExComm were without valid information about who gave the orders to fire the Soviet SAM that downed the U.S. plane. Speculation at the time in Washington included the various possibilities that Khrushchev himself had ordered the U-2 shootdown, that hard-liners in the Politburo had prevailed over Khrushchev's objections and done so, that standing orders and rules of engagement for Soviet air-defense commanders in Cuba had been implemented according to plan, or that the Cubans had somehow got control of a Soviet SAM site and fired the weapon. In fact, two Soviet air-defense commanders in Cuba had taken the decision to shoot down the U-2, even though no authorization for such a firing had been given from Moscow and despite standing orders that would have suggested caution.[82]

Another incident, which also occurred on October 27, is likewise related to the problematic connection between coercive diplomacy and escalation control, in the context of nuclear-crisis management and crisis termination. This incident, already noted above in the section on "agreed battle" but pertinent here also, was the U-2 "stray" that ended up in Soviet airspace as a result of navigational errors. Among the dangers inherent in this incident, according to Scott Sagan, was the possibility that Soviet nuclear and other forces not yet placed on alert could have been alerted as a result of this incident.[83] Sagan notes that it was fortunate that this incident occurred at a time which, "despite Khrushchev's claims to the contrary, Soviet strategic nuclear forces had *not*, in fact, been placed on a high-alert status."[84] U.S. experts on Soviet military policy Arnold Horelick and Raymond Garthoff concur that the Soviets did not conduct a major alert of their armed forces during the Cuban missile crisis. Horelick suggests that the Soviets "were just too scared to issue a general alert, for fear of provoking an American attack."[85] Garthoff states that the United States never observed any Soviet alerts, although Soviet leaders took low-level measures such as cancellation of leaves and troop rotations.[86]

---

82. Garthoff, *Reflections on the Cuban Missile Crisis*, 84.
83. Sagan, *Moving Targets*, 147–48.
84. Ibid., 148.
85. Arnold Horelick, remarks at Hawk's Cay Conference, March 5–8, 1987, cited in Blight and Welch, *On the Brink*, 90.
86. Ibid., 91.

On the other hand, the Soviet forces had alerted *already*, the U-2 "stray incident" might have been more complicated and provocative of inadvertent escalation that it was. Soviet strategic-nuclear force commanders at the highest levels of combat-readiness (*boevoy gotovnosti*) could have interpreted the U-2 stray as a reconnaissance flight immediately prior to a U.S. first strike. This would have been a worst-case reading; but one consequence of shifting alert levels from lower to higher categories, at least in the case of U.S. nuclear and other forces, is that command-and-control systems become more sensitive. They do so in at least two ways. First, they are increasingly sensitive to indicators that might point toward hostile intent on the part of potential opponents seeking surprise attack opportunities; indicators that might be ignored in low-alert conditions now become meaningful.

A second kind of sensitivity that takes hold as alert levels rise is an increased sensitivity to the vulnerability of the command system itself. The physical destruction of the command system is one issue here, but by no means the most important. Equally of concern is the fear on the part of those responsible for command-and-control systems that a partial failure will disrupt the execution of any coherent war plan, should that become necessary. Planners thrive on a well-prepared set of options whose components have been put into place in peacetime and which, in the event of war, can be activated almost automatically, according to preestablished instructions. Deviations from this preestablished repertoire, which the partial destruction or disorientation of the command system would certainly invite, could not be improvised with ease, and perhaps not at all.

One irony of this, with regard to nuclear-crisis management and the control of escalation during crisis-time coercive diplomacy, is that planners might fear the results of a total attack less than they fear the results of a partial one. The results of a total attack are, from the standpoint of social consequences, much worse than the outcomes of a limited nuclear strike. But from the standpoint of planners, a massive attack creates less stress on the response system, for the response is foreordained: an equally massive retaliatory strike against a large target set. A limited attack requires the U.S. or Soviet nuclear command system to *characterize* the attack with some precision, to *distinguish* the target set intended for destruction by the attacker, and to *select* an appropriate response which may, or may not, be available within the scope of SIOP or its Soviet equivalent.[87]

87. For more extensive discussion of these points, see Ashton B. Carter, "Assessing Command System Vulnerability," ch. 17 in *Managing Nuclear Operations*, ed. Carter, Steinbruner, and Zraket, 555–610. A critique of prevalent U.S. defense community concepts of escalation

In short, the U.S. nuclear command system of the Cold War was unlikely to be able to do what it had not rehearsed, and there have been no two-way U.S.-Soviet alerts documented in the open literature. Therefore, the case of *nuclear crisis* management and the role of coercive diplomacy in confrontations between nuclear powers stands apart from other episodes of crisis management. In the case of nuclear-armed adversaries, the control of escalation once a two-sided general alert is under way will almost certainly demand of policymakers a willingness to select, at least initially, the *least coercive* measures available. The role of intimidation in nuclear strategy, including crisis management between nuclear armed states, becomes less important compared to the role of accommodation in dampening crisis interactions and in perceiving correctly the motivations of the opponent. In crisis between powers not armed with nuclear weapons, it is also sometimes advisable to enhance the role of accommodation compared to that of intimidation, but the difference between the nuclear and nonnuclear cases is profound. The shared danger of unknown consequences is what drives escalation upward *and* de-escalation downward in the case of nuclear-armed disputants. This makes risk manipulation and threats that leave something to chance both potentially fruitful and potentially self-destructive for nuclear-crisis managers. They can never know in advance where the "flat of the curve" is, beyond which an intentionally coercive move drives the opponent into desperate calculations instead of prudent ones.

SURRENDER AND WAR TERMINATION

Past strategies are prologue to an uncertain future. The relative certainty of a biopolar world is giving way to the indeterminacy of a new constellation of political alignments, in Europe and globally. The probability of war between the United States and the Russian Federation or the Commonwealth of Independent States now located on the territory of the former Soviet Union is zero or close to it. The fate of the Soviet Union as a sovereign, centrally managed political entity was sealed by the abortive coup of August 19–21,

---

control and crisis management, pertinent to the preceding discussion, appears in Colin S. Gray, *Nuclear Strategy and National Style* (Lanham, Md.: Hamilton Press, 1986), ch. 6.

1991. The idea of war in Europe seems quaint, if not obsolete. Outside of Europe, on the other hand, pots boil, with implications for the member states of NATO, for the former Soviet Union, and for the former allies of the Soviet Union in Eastern Europe. The outbreak of war in the Persian Gulf in 1991 involved twenty-nine combatants, including a coalition operating under the charter of the United Nations. It was not a war between the two nuclear giants, but it was a war involving an aspiring nuclear power and a putative regional hegemon, Iraq, against a coalition led by the United States. The Gulf War was certainly entitled to the appellation "major coalition war."[88]

Despite the geographic diversity of the involved states, the regional containment of the 1991 Gulf War was almost guaranteed by the obvious military superiority of the U.N. coalition. However, creative minds could write "counterfactual" scenarios in which the Gulf War expanded into a global war, with the possibility of nuclear escalation from an Iraqi use of biological or chemical weapons against Israel, for example. Even without nuclear escalation, the involvement of Israel as a combatant could have led to geographic or horizontal escalation of the fighting. It could also have prolonged the war by dividing the membership of the anti-Iraq coalition, especially the Arab members from the others.

Therefore, the Gulf War of 1991 presented the hypothetical possibilities of vertical, horizontal, or temporal escalation and the possibility that these kinds of escalation could be combined. The potential for regional wars to grow into major coalition wars, obviously demonstrated in the Gulf War, proves that post–Cold War complacency about war termination or war avoidance is not warranted. There was significant irony in the U.S. deployment of some five hundred thousand troops to the Gulf theater of operations by the end of January 1991. Those forces were greater in number than those deployed by the United States in Europe at any time during the Cold War.

The run-up to the outbreak of the Gulf War on January 16, 1991, showed that coercive diplomacy is ineffective when the targeted political leadership refuses to be coerced (see the more extensive discussion of the Gulf crisis and war in Chapter 4, above). It also shows that the "gradual escalation" model is misapplied if the opponent's incentive structure cannot be influenced by the perceived difference between incremental escalation and something stronger. Pentagon memory banks relating to Vietnam disparage grad-

---

88. See Gregory F. Treverton, "Ending Major Coalition Wars," ch. 6 in *Conflict Termination and Military Strategy: Coercion, Persuasion, and War,* ed. Stephen J. Cimbala and Keith A. Dunn (Boulder, Colo.: Westview Press, 1987), 89–108.

uated escalation as a matter of institutional honor and self-preservation, but neither Vietnam nor the Gulf War proved that graduated escalation *never* works. Each case shows that the applicability of graduated escalation is contingent on the perceptions and expectations of the opponent.

U.S. efforts from August 1990 to January 1991 to coerce Saddam Hussein into withdrawing Iraqi forces from Kuwait also failed because, having deployed them there, Saddam saw it as a matter of personal honor and prestige to leave them there. The Iraqi leader gambled that Bush would not have the domestic and international political support to launch a war; he played for time and sought to wait out the U.N. coalition and the U.S. president. Saddam's cost–benefit ratio was lopsided from the standpoint of any influence structure that could be affected by coercive diplomacy. It had cost him virtually nothing to occupy Kuwait, and it would cost the United States and its allies a great deal to get him out.

The outbreak of a war immediately creates for policymakers the question of war termination, including the conditions for a cease-fire and subsequent peace settlement (not necessarily the same). The problem of strategic surrender is more inclusive than the accomplishment of dominance over the battlefield. One side may dominate the fighting to the point at which the adversary has few remaining assets, yet those assets can represent "bargaining chips" for the defeated. Forces and resources not yet destroyed can be offered in voluntary capitulation to the eventual victor by the eventual loser, in order to spare the loser gratuitous destruction. Paul Kecskemeti's study of surrenders in World War II shows that some of the losing states had more incentives than others to bargain for surrender terms.[89]

According to Kecskemeti, strategic surrender is both the final act of a war and the first act of a new postwar relationship between former belligerents. "Strategic surrender" must not be confused with "tactical surrender." In tactical surrender troops stop fighting but a formal state of belligerency remains. Various Arab-Israeli wars have had this outcome. Strategic surrender, on the other hand, is a political as well as a military act. In strategic surrender, the defeated government gives up the status of belligerency.[90] In strategic surrender, all of the loser's forces are surrendered to the winner, not just part of them. From the standpoint of military theory, the interesting surrenders are those which take place even though the defeated state could still fight and impose significant costs on the eventual victors. If the losing state is without

89. Kecskemeti, *Strategic Surrender*.
90. Ibid., 11–12.

the means to continue fighting, the terms of surrender can be imposed by the victor without bargaining. A bargained strategic surrender was the outcome for war termination between the Allies and Japan in World War II. On the other hand, the strategic surrender of Nazi Germany was imposed by the total and complete disarmament of its fighting forces.

The difference between a tactical and a strategic surrender is the distance between discouraged and defeated field armies and a head of state who is willing to acknowledge that the military outcome is a foregone conclusion. In Imperial Japan in 1945, it took considerable intervention by the emperor to overcome the opposition of military die-hards to a surrender on terms. The Japanese forces retained significant residual fighting power if the Allies were to invade the home islands. The use of the atomic bomb may have contributed to shortening the war, but the tactical defeat of Japan's armies and fleets had already been accomplished. Remaining forces would have fought in futility, though at significant cost to the Allies. Thus, the surrender terms that Japan finally accepted allowed for continuation of the imperial throne as a national symbol, legitimating the willingness of Japan's armed forces to lay down their arms despite formidable instincts against doing so.[91]

With regard to the U.S. experience in obtaining surrender from Germany, Japan, and Italy, Kecskemeti observes that two components of the Allied "unconditional surrender" formula might have interfered with the attainment of a more rapid strategic surrender. The first component was a "no negotiation" rule; the second, a "vacuum" or "no recognition" approach.[92] In practice, the Allies were forced to modify these rules, as they proved impractical to apply to each of the belligerents. Reluctantly, the Allies were forced to recognize the Italian government as a cobelligerent after it quit the war, in order not to impede the subsequent conduct of military operations against the Germans in Italy. The Japanese government was willing to sign terms of surrender, and might so have done earlier, after reassurance about the status of the imperial throne and the personal safety of the emperor was obtained. Only the German government's behavior suited exactly the Allied rules of unconditionality. No alternative government was in the wings with which to negotiate; the Allies had to destroy Hitler's military power entirely before the nominal successors would capitulate.

The cases from World War II illustrate that even "total war" involves in-

91. Ibid., 156–211. See also Herbert Feis, *The Atomic Bomb and the End of World War II* (Princeton, N.J.: Princeton University Press, 1961).
92. Kecskemeti, *Strategic Surrender*, 218–19. He refers to these rules of the unconditional surrender principle as "rules of unconditionality."

trawar deterrence and escalation control at either of two prominent thresholds. The first of these is when tactical defeat has not yet become tactical surrender: one side has effectively routed the forces of the other, but the remaining forces have regrouped and continue to fight on. Often the motive for perseverance among the remainder is simply survival, as it was for the retreating French who crossed the Berezina after Napoleon in 1812. The second threshold, once tactical defeat has been acknowledged in tactical surrender by the giving up of military resistance, involves the movement from tactical to strategic surrender. We may outline these stages as follows:

1. Tactical defeat: the forces of the loser are effectively routed, but components fight on for survival, to minimize losses, for the sake of honor and prestige, or for other causes not listed here.
2. Tactical surrender: the forces of the loser cease to offer resistance, most obviously by laying down weapons and offering themselves to their captors.
3. Strategic surrender: the government or legally constituted authority responsible for authorizing continued military action by the loser declares that the state of belligerency has ended.

The most fundamental question provoked by the above construction is, What makes a war a war? As Peter H. Vigor has explained, from the Soviet standpoint and consistent also with the logic of Clausewitz, a war is a policy conflict between states. The war is not ended until the political issues over which states are in contention have been fully resolved.[93] Thus, one might argue that Prussia/Germany and France fought not three wars between 1870 and 1945, but one war with three intermissions. Similarly, it might be said that the Arab-Israeli war has been continued from 1948 to the present on account of the official state of belligerency against Israel that various Arab states still maintain.[94] We have already observed that cessation of battle is not tantamount to strategic surrender: Kecskemeti's concept of "strategic surrender" (an end to the status of belligerency on the part of the loser) is therefore very consistent with that of Clausewitz, who emphasized that the purpose of war ought to be its controlling element.[95]

Kecskemeti follows the tradition of Clausewitz in holding that, despite the

93. P. H. Vigor, Soviet Blitzkrieg Theory (New York: St. Martin's Press, 1983).
94. Ibid.
95. Carl von Clausewitz, On War, ed. and trans. Michael Howard and Peter Paret (Princeton, N.J.: Princeton University Press, 1976).

propagandistic claims made for total war and unconditional surrender, it is not always advantageous in practice for policymakers and commanders to adhere to rigid and expansive definitions of war aims. Kecskemeti noted that three parameters define the scope of a war: 1) the asymmetry of the military outcome; 2) the degree to which belligerents have had to mobilize their resources and personnel; and 3) the asymmetry of the political outcome.[96] Clausewitz noted that, in theory, war followed the laws of logical necessity; in practice, the laws of probability. Therefore, war does not "always require to be fought out until one party is overthrown."[97] According to Clausewitz, wars in which one side cannot completely disarm the other give rise to variation in the "motives to peace." Motives to peace will rise or fall for each side on the basis of two variables: 1) probability of future success if fighting continues and 2) the required costs of that fighting.[98]

Considering how to influence the opponent's expectation of future success, Clausewitz notes that the traditional and obvious suggestions would be to destroy the enemy's army and to conquer his provinces. However, it is not always necessary to destroy the opponent's armed forces in their entirety in order to accomplish our political or military objective: "If we attack the enemy's Army, it is a very different thing whether we intend to follow up the first blow with a succession of others, until the whole force is destroyed, or whether we mean to content ourselves with a victory to shake the enemy's feeling of superiority, and to instil into him a feeling of apprehension about the future. If this is our object, we only go so far in the destruction of his forces as is sufficient."[99] The opponent's expected probability of success may also be influenced, according to Clausewitz, by the use of political means, including measures to break up his alliance or to gain new allies for ourselves.

Equally as important as influencing the opponent's expected probability of success or failure, in Clausewitz's view, was raising the price of continued fighting for the enemy. Clausewitz referred to this price as the opponent's "outlay in strength."[100] A state's outlay in strength includes the punishment and destruction of its forces in combat action and the conquest of provinces that can no longer support the war effort. Increasing the waste of the opponent's forces can be accomplished in several ways. One of these is the gradual

96. Kecskemeti, *Strategic Surrender*, 17–18.
97. Gen. Carl von Clausewitz, *On War*, trans. Col. J. J. Graham (London: Routledge & Kegan Paul, 1966), 30.
98. Ibid.
99. Ibid., 31.
100. Ibid., 32.

"wearing out" of the enemy, or a "gradual exhaustion of the physical powers and of the will by the long continuation of exertion."[101] Clausewitz noted, in book 1, chapter 2, of On War, that war is dominated by the political object for which states fight; therefore, "the value of that object determines the measure of the sacrifices by which it is to be purchased."[102]

Recall that these comments of Clausewitz on the expected probability of success in war, and on the expected futility of continued fighting, are offered in the discussion of conflicts in which it is either inexpedient or impossible for one side to destroy completely the opposed military forces. Therefore, the intensity with which the combatants' political objects are held is an important component of their willingness to continue fighting and to absorb the attendant costs. One of the reasons why Clausewitz felt that the defensive strategy was the superior form of warfare was that it required less exertion of the part of armed forces which were defending familiar and prepared territory. But another reason for the inherent superiority of the defensive form of battle was that it was likely to have been motivated by defensive political aims: the state having been attacked, the immediate defensive aim was to expel the invader. The struggle between attacker and defender is one that favors the latter, provided the defender can use to advantage the wearing out of the attacker's forces. Writes Clausewitz: "this negative intention, which constitutes the principle of the pure defensive, is also the natural means of overcoming the enemy by the duration of the combat, that is of wearing him out."[103]

Elsewhere in On War, Clausewitz also discusses the culminating point at which an attacker's thrust has spent itself, creating the most opportune moment for the defender to assume the offensive and to drive the invader back from the defender's territory. A putative attacker must sooner or later overrun supply lines, expose vulnerable flanks, and otherwise create opportunities for the defender to reestablish battlefield equilibrium. Time is on the side of the strategic defensive, according to Clausewitz: the process of "wear and tear" on forces will exact costs on the attacker faster than it will on the defender. We know from much historical experience, however, that this is not always true. Attackers can minimize losses by moving faster, by surprising the defender, by striking into the operational and strategic depth early in combat, and by the use of strategic deception to mislead otherwise well prepared defenders.[104]

101. Ibid., 33.
102. Ibid.; 30.
103. Ibid., 34.
104. These points are extensively documented by Soviet historians, on the basis of their

De-escalation of a crisis is similar in form to ending a war on terms, although the substantial costs of war are obviously worse than those of a crisis. Ending a war on terms acceptable to combatants that are still capable of fighting asks leaders to accept less than they might get from all-out exertion of their armies and societies. The assumption behind discussions of de-escalation is that leaders retain their rationality, or their sense of a balance between wartime benefits and costs, even after their armed forces have accepted battle and their societies have suffered terribly. The historical record is clear that leaders have frequently done just that, perhaps against their own and their people's instincts. When they have failed to do so, they have ensured a passage from limited into total war, or toward Clausewitz's ideal type of absolute war, without political or military constraint. The choice between the costs of limited and total war seems obvious from the perspective of observers looking backward through history. But to leaders engaged in decisionmaking, mixing hopeful anticipation of favorable outcomes with fearful dread of unfavorable ones, the temptation to push on has intoxicating power. Unless the opposed states can send credible wartime signals that gratuitous provocation of further escalation can be avoided, provided acceptable terms for ending war can be arranged, simple inertia can continue the fighting to no apparent purpose.

Although it might seem that deterrence has failed altogether once war begins, the outbreak of a war changes only the form of deterrence, not its substance. Deterrence continues into war in the form of objectives, means, and communications between adversaries by means of tacit and explicit bargaining. Ending wars on terms presupposes that leaders operate with some notion of an agreed battle, of escalation control, and of coercive diplomacy, although these concepts may be more intuitive than substantive for leaders coping with stressful crisis and wartime conditions. Sooner or later even the most ferocious wars, including those motivated by national hatreds and collective war psychology, must resolve themselves into apolitical or political endings. Apolitical endings interest us little; one-sided destruction for its own sake is not war, but victimization.[105] Political endings require that sig-

---

World War II experience, among others. See, for example, M. M. Kir'yan, *Vnezapnost' v nastupatel'nykh operatsiyakh Velikoy Otechestvennoy voyny* [Surprise in Offensive Operations of the Great Patriotic War] (Moscow: "Nauka," 1986); A. I. Radziyevskiy, *Tankovyy udar: Tankovaya armiya v nastupatel'noy operatsii fronta po opytu Velikoy Otechestvennoy voyny* [Tank Attack: The Tank Army in a Frontal Offensive Operation from the Experience of the Great Fatherland War] (Moscow: Voyenizdat, 1977); and V. I. Matsulenko, *Operatsii i boy na okruzhenii'ye* [Encirclement Operations and Combat] (Moscow: Voyenizdat, 1983).

105. For pertinent arguments on noncombatant immunity and military necessity, see Mi-

nals of a willingness to bargain, even though the sides may not retain equal military or other assets for wartime negotiation, be mixed carefully with signals of resolve to continue fighting if need be.

Crisis management has in common with conflict termination the need to mix carrots and sticks to obtain an acceptable outcome somewhere between total victory and abject surrender. During the Cuban missile crisis, President Kennedy and Premier Khrushchev each sought to end the conflict on terms that would allow both Washington and Moscow to avoid the appearance of humiliation. U.S. signals of nonprovocation were made loud and clear despite the strong deterrent effect of U.S. military superiority, in nuclear and in conventional military power, applicable to the Caribbean theater of operations. Although some have retrospectively chided Kennedy for not "winning," by using a strong military hand to push Castro out of Cuba and to publicize Soviet military impotence, the U.S. president correctly emphasized the need to avoid provocation of the Soviet leadership as a necessary condition for crisis resolution without war.

---

chael Walzer, *Just and Unjust Wars: A Moral Argument with Historical Illustrations* (New York: Harper Colophon/Basic Books, 1977), 138–59.

CONCLUSION

This chapter presents a brief summary of my major conclusions, followed by an expansion of those major points and their implications. The conclusions from this study are listed immediately below.

1. Deterrence is most often discussed in the academic and policy literature as the successful manipulation of threats or threat systems to obtain desired objectives. Developed as an interim notion to account for the way in which nuclear weapons might be useful to policymakers without actually being used in warfighting, deterrence theory took on a life of its own during the Cold War. In so doing, it became a substitute for policymaking and for more complex explanations for the outbreak of war. Deterrence justified all things. As a result, only the negative side of deterrence, the threats directed at potential opponents, received emphasis in many studies and discussions. Comparative neglect of the positive aspects of military persuasion, the avoidance of unnecessary provocation of potential or actual opponents during time of peace, crisis, and even war, was the result.

2. The avoidance of unnecessary provocation of other states is, of course, desirable in peacetime, but it may be even more important during crisis, in the early stages of a war, and in bringing wars to an end. The notion that the positive as well as the negative aspects of military persuasion can be extended into wartime flies in the face of military-professional traditionalism. It also contradicts public expectations in mass democracies. Nevertheless, in order that crisis may be managed successfully or that wars may be brought to a conclusion consistent with policy objectives and with the minimum loss of life and other values, crisis and wartime signals of threat must be balanced with messages of conciliation, limitation, and nonprovocation.

The case studies of the crisis of July 1914 and the Gulf War of 1991, outlined earlier in this study and recapped briefly below, demonstrate how complicated this balancing process can be.

3. There is more to the issue of combining deterrence with the avoidance of unnecessary provocation in peacetime, crisis, and war than the obvious point about using both carrots and sticks in any influence process. When to use carrots, and when sticks, is the issue with which policymakers and military planners must grapple. The "when" depends upon the character of the international system, the attributes of states and their systems of decision-making, and the individual characteristics of leaders and military planners. It mattered, for example, that the July 1914 crisis took place in a European balance-of-power system, that autocratic leaders sought to displace domestic social and political problems onto foreign policy, and that the kaiser and the tsar had decisive influence over the decision for war. It mattered equally in January 1991 that the Cold War had ended, that one cause for which U.S. public and congressional support could be rallied was a threat to oil supplies, and that George Bush was president.

4. Multipolar and bipolar systems both have drawbacks for policymakers who want to exploit the most effective mixture of positive and negative inducements. Multipolar power systems open the door to buck passing or chain ganging: to buck passing if defensive military doctrines are predominant, to chain ganging if offensive doctrines are preeminent. Multipolar systems offer more indeterminacy for planners about perceived objectives and about shared responsibilities of states for preserving order and stability in the system. Bipolar systems, on the other hand, project the competition between two leading states throughout the entire system of state relations. Bipolar systems also lead to a sphere of influence demarcation between "ours" and "theirs" that results in repeated challenges over those values which are judged to be marginal or in-between. Cold War crises over Berlin and Cuba illustrate the propensity for bipolar systems to induce competition in the manipulation of threat systems in order to "interrogate" concerning the tenacity of each side with regard to its goals and commitments, which might be subject to erosion at the margin.

5. If we understand "deterrence" to include the avoidance of unnecessary provocation, then deterrence does not fail all at once. The July crisis of 1914, the Gulf crisis of 1990–91, and the Cuban missile crisis of 1962 did not result from failures of immediate deterrence only. These episodes were the culmination of many factors, including a preceding context covering many months or years in which negative messages drowned out more hopeful

ones. The crisis of July 1914 and the Cuban missile crisis of 1962, in terms of the behavior of leaders immediately prior to and during those crises, involved large elements of misperception and the misattribution of worst-case motives to the other side. In the Gulf crisis of 1990–91, Iraq misperceived the U.S. and allied determination to wage war in lieu of an Iraqi diplomatic accommodation to U.S. and U.N. demands. The United States misperceived Iraq's determination to hold onto Kuwait in the face of all sanctions other than military ones. U.S. compellence, a more active form of deterrence, failed in the Persian Gulf without the use of force, and compellence in the form of coercive air war failed again to change Iraq's policy objectives without a ground war.

THEORIES OF DETERRENCE AND THE IMPORTANCE OF NONPROVOCATION

Deterrence is the process by which a state establishes in the minds of its potential opponents that they cannot obtain a military victory at an acceptable cost.[1] This can be accomplished by threatening potential attackers with guaranteed retaliation that will inflict unacceptable costs, or it can be done by physically denying to potential attackers the capacity for victory in battle. As Patrick Morgan has noted about the concept of deterrence as it has developed in the U.S. literature, deterrence usually assumes a threat of military retaliation to forestall a military attack. Deterrence is normally discussed in relation to war, and the concept has been applied most frequently to nuclear war.[2] Morgan also makes the important point that deterrence can also operate in war as well as prior to the start of a war.[3] The operation of deterrence in war is for the purpose of limitation on the scope of violence, or the containment of political objectives, or both.

Although U.S. and other Western theorists of deterrence have denied that

1. There is a large literature on deterrence theory. For an insightful discussion of the concept, see Patrick M. Morgan, *Deterrence: A Conceptual Analysis* (Beverly Hills, Calif.: Sage Publications, 1983), 19–26.
2. Ibid., 29.
3. Ibid. See also Paul Bracken, "War Termination," ch. 6 in *Managing Nuclear Operations*, ed. Ashton B. Carter, John D. Steinbruner, and Charles A. Zraket (Washington, D.C.: Brookings Institution, 1987), 197–216.

they intended deterrence theory to substitute for the study of war prevention or avoidance altogether, in practice much analysis was pulled in this direction by the exigency of policy requirements.[4] U.S. leaders felt they were in a Cold War with the Soviet Union which might at any moment explode into actual violence. Following the schematic of problems defined in government, analysts produced studies of deterrence as if the process of deterrence were abstracted from a larger political and social whole. Eventually a significant literature critiquing deterrence theory appeared, and the critics served to divest deterrence of much of its mystique.[5] At one or another time, deterrence represented for U.S. policymakers a method for avoiding a major war, an approach to the containment of the Soviet Union by coercion, a method for determining military requirements, and other concepts or definitions as needed. Most important and unfortunately, deterrence substituted the identification of the threat to U.S. security for a coherent definition of U.S. policy objectives. A derivative of this point about the substitution of threat assessment for definition of objectives was the preoccupation of planners and analysts with technical analyses of capabilities, to the relative detriment of politico-strategic insight into the intentions and cultures of states.[6]

As the notion of deterrence began to be subjected to additional academic scrutiny as well as testing in the real world of policy, it became the concern of many scholars that deterrence was limited to the situation in which threats made by one state could be clearly seen to have influenced the expected utility calculations of prospective attackers. These situations offered a distorted sample of all international events. By the time states were making explicit threats to one another, the vast array of options available to states for the avoidance of war under the "security dilemma" of international legal anarchy had been reduced to those which emphasized military means. In addition, deterrence theory became associated with nuclear weapons in a way that was to complicate the lives of both. Even the making of plausible threats for the use of nuclear weapons seemed inappropriate for all but the

---

4. This point is well argued in Raymond L. Garthoff, *Deterrence and the Revolution in Soviet Military Doctrine* (Washington, D.C.: Brookings Institution, 1990), 6–15 et pass.
5. For recent debates on this, see Christopher H. Achen and Duncan Snidal, "Rational Deterrence Theory and Comparative Case Studies," *World Politics* (January 1989): 143–69, and, in the same issue: Alexander L. George and Richard Smoke, "Deterrence and Foreign Policy," 170–82; Robert Jervis, "Rational Deterrence: Theory and Evidence," 183–207; Richard Ned Lebow and Janice Gross Stein, "Rational Deterrence Theory: I Think, Therefore I Deter," 208–25; and George W. Downs, "The Rational Deterrence Debate," 225–34.
6. Garthoff, *Deterrence and the Revolution in Soviet Military Doctrine*, 8–9.

most drastic of circumstances. Threat assessment driven by capabilities analysis could posit massive preemptive or selective nuclear strikes against unsuspecting opponents. Real policymakers received no answer to their doubts about whether meaningful definitions of military victory would follow any such adventurism.

The extension of U.S. nuclear deterrence to Western Europe became part and parcel of Cold War politics. Although a logcial case can be made for the nuclearization of U.S. strategy for the defense of Europe, the driving forces were political and economic, not strategic.[7] Budgets drove U.S. and West European policymakers under the nuclear umbrella as an alternative to the maintenance of prohibitively expensive conventional forces adequate to defeat a Warsaw Pact offensive. NATO's conventional forces were not insubstantial for most of the Cold War period, however, and some Kennedy administration defense experts argued that NATO could have fielded an affordable conventional defense if Soviet ground forces' strength had been estimated correctly. Moreover, there were costs to the nuclearization of NATO strategy in the form of Soviet misperceptions of U.S. strategy. U.S. leaders saw their efforts to extend nuclear deterrence to Western Europe as defensive deterrence, but Soviet military planners and political leaders feared that the U.S. nuclear umbrella was an instrument of strategic compellence designed to overturn the political status quo in Europe.[8]

There was a significant gap between the views of deterrence, including nuclear deterrence, held by U.S. and West European policymakers and the views propounded by leading nuclear strategists. Although strategists could conceive of scenarios in which nuclear weapons were used in a selective and timely way, planners in NATO found it difficult to formulate these in ways that would be appealing to crisis-bound political leaders. NATO exercises from the 1950s through the 1980s were on more than one occasion marked by tension generated by the nuclear undercurrent of NATO defense planning. The West German government was constantly reminded by antinuclear groups and other peace advocates that to defend Germany with nuclear

7. For this argument, see Trachtenberg, *History and Strategy* (Princeton, N.J.: Princeton University Press, 1991), 153–68.
8. Garthoff, *Deterrence and the Revolution in Soviet Military Doctrine*, ch. 1. See also Garthoff, "Soviet Perceptions of Western Strategic Thought and Doctrine," ch. 4 in *Soviet Military Doctrine and Western Policy*, ed. Gregory Flynn (London: Routledge, 1989), 197–328, specifically on Soviet perceptions of U.S. countervailing strategy under Carter and Reagan (p. 243). Also see David Holloway, *The Soviet Union and the Arms Race* (New Haven, Conn.: Yale University Press, 1983), ch. 3.

weapons was to destroy it, and it would require comparatively few nuclear weapons exploded on West German soil to disconnect war from policy.[9] U.S. extended nuclear deterrence was also affected in unpredictable ways by the French insistence on nuclear unilateralism within the NATO political alliance and by the withdrawal of France from NATO's integrated military command structure in 1966. Extended nuclear deterrence required centralized command and control, according to U.S. policymakers and strategic analysts in the Kennedy-Johnson years, and the United States pushed this point to the extent of the ill-fated Multilateral Force (MLF) until the concept for mixed-nationality, nuclear-armed ships died of natural causes.[10]

It appeared that, in the case of nuclear weapons, deterrence operated not so much as a formula by which leaders could calculate expected utility, but as an expectation that shared disutilities of nuclear fighting would cancel each other out. It was certainly clear in the aftermath of the Cuban missile crisis that neither Kennedy nor Khrushchev preferred to push matters even to the point of conventional war between U.S. and Soviet forces, given the possibility of nuclear escalation. However, each leader was prepared to run some unknown risk that the crisis might get out of hand in order to uphold his preferred policy position. Kennedy and Khrushchev sought for different purposes to manipulate the risk of escalation and war for deterrence, but once trapped into this vortex each quickly reached for signals of nonprovocation in order to escape inadvertent escalation. Both feared nuclear war more than they feared a conscious decision to engage in nuclear war. This "existential" quality of nuclear deterrence did not necessarily protect against erosion of the nuclear threshold once conventional warfighting had begun. Therefore, the knowledge that nuclear escalation was a logically possible outcome from conventional warfighting between nuclear-armed states imposed a *pax atomica* on conventional as well as nuclear deterrence in Europe.

As a number of crises in the Cold War era also showed, the reluctance of the U.S. and Soviet nuclear superpowers to provoke one another into actual war was balanced against the desire to assert diplomatic and strategic positions. In the latter 1970s and early 1980s, for example, U.S. and Soviet

9. The development of U.S. and NATO strategy is discussed in Lawrence Freedman, *The Evolution of Nuclear Strategy* (New York: St. Martin's Press, 1981).
10. The MLF proposal called for crews of several nations, including West Germany, to man nuclear-armed surface ships under NATO command. The proposal was intended by the United States to support its extended deterrence concepts without diminishing American control over NATO's nuclear decision. For U.S. planners it offered a safe way to give the Germans a finger on the nuclear trigger, but such a decision if taken would have invited further Soviet interpretation of U.S. defensive deterrence as offensive compellence.

positions on a variety of Cold War issues diverged, and the period from the Soviet invasion of Afghanistan in 1979 through the onset of NATO's Pershing II and ground-launched cruise missile (GLCM) deployments in December 1983 offered many opportunities for U.S.-Soviet collision on major policy issues. The confrontation between Moscow and Washington over NATO's "572" Pershing II and cruise missile deployments showed the unavoidably two-sided nature of deterrence and provocation in attempted military persuasion through force modernization. NATO sought to induce Soviet limitation on the numbers of their modernized SS-20 intermediate-range ballistic missiles in return for a postponement of NATO's Pershing II and GLCM deployments. The Soviet Union described its SS-20s, which Moscow began deploying in 1977, as modernized versions of older and obsolete systems, denying that the SS-20s (though MIRVed and mobile) represented a qualitatively new nuclear threat to Western Europe.

There was significant evidence available to NATO that the Soviet consideration of its SS-20 force as an evolutionary modernization of formerly deployed and now obsolete systems was genuine. The Soviet Union had not sought to provoke NATO into a new round of theater nuclear force modernization, and Soviet leaders were genuinely surprised by the vehemence of NATO's reaction. NATO's Pershing II and GLCM deployments represented to Soviet military planners an attempt at political intimidation, and the Pershing II was thought to provide options for prompt attacks against vital military targets in the western Soviet Union. Each side saw the other's attempt to reinforce deterrence as an attempted provocation. As in previous episodes of Cold War diplomacy supported by military modernization, each saw the other as engaged in extended compellence for the purpose of overturning the political and military status quo.[11] The Soviet view of NATO's modernization and NATO's view of the SS-20 deployments were undoubtedly also affected by the deterioration in U.S.-Soviet relations from 1980 to 1983.

The situation of generalized threat perception between Washington and Moscow was a precarious one in the early years of the Reagan administration. The Reagan administration during its first term called for a "full-court press"

11. Raymond L. Garthoff, Detente and Confrontation: American-Soviet Relations from Nixon to Reagan (Washington, D.C.: Brookings Institution, 1985), 870–86. Garthoff argues that the Soviet SS-20 modernization was not intended, despite NATO misperceptions, as a measure to promote the decoupling of Europe from its U.S. nuclear guarantee. If it had been so intended, the Soviets would not have been so insistent on the point that no nuclear war in Europe could remain limited. See Garthoff, Deterrence and the Revolution in Soviet Military Doctrine, 19.

against the Soviet Union, including a revision and an updating of plans for protracted nuclear war inherited from the Carter administration. U.S. nuclear and conventional force modernizations were presented to the Soviet Union not as an affirmation of the strategic parity that Washington and Moscow had both come to accept, but as an attempt to restore U.S. military superiority for the purpose of strategic compellence. This meant that there was now a greater likelihood of general deterrence breaking down into crisis than there had been for approximately a decade. Also factored into this by Moscow was undoubtedly the Reagan Strategic Defense Initiative (SDI), which was charged by the president with the mission of making ballistic missiles obsolete. Although the Soviet Union had the world's only deployed strategic ballistic-missile defense system, it was an ABM Treaty–constrained system limited to ground-based defenses and was not capable of providing comprehensive protection for Soviet national territory.

Later, during Reagan's second term, the administration would revert to more traditional, parity-affirming assumptions about nuclear force modernization and the role of defenses in a system of mutual deterrence. However, the cumulative impact of theater nuclear force modernization and the declaratory challenge to mutual deterrence created a temporary period of uncertainty in U.S.-Soviet relations in which general deterrence was potentially vulnerable. In retrospect, we can see that some potential crises were avoided only because of economic weaknesses and political turbulence within the Soviet Union that U.S. leaders did not then know about. Crises avoided are hard to measure, but one can identify certain early-1980s trends in military exercises and in messages sent through action channels during periods of high political tension. Soviet and NATO military channels were on the alert for any indicators of imminent threat, and the operating tempos of U.S. and allied NATO forces in areas contiguous to the Soviet Union were notably different from those of the middle to latter 1970s. The higher levels of military tension between the two sides were apparent to the public in only a general way, although occasional incidents, such as the shootdown of KAL 007 in September 1983, made the public and the news media aware of some of the more unfortunate side-effects of political tension on military readiness and warning.

There was little doubt in U.S. official circles that the Soviet Union shot down the airline deliberately, but some U.S. intelligence experts acknowledged the possibility that the Soviet leadership might have acted against a presumed spy plane, on the basis of standing instructions.[12] Whatever the

---

12. For assessments of U.S. and Soviet performances in this episode, see Seymour M.

facts, the Reagan administration used selectively assembled intelligence data to argue that the airliner was shot down despite Soviet knowledge that it was a civilian plane. The administration's rush to judgment, and the angry Soviet response and denial that a civilian aircraft had been knowingly attacked, illustrated the state of political suspicions and military susceptibility to provocation on the two sides.[13] The incident was reminiscent of the U-2 shootdown over Cuba on October 27, 1962, during a very critical stage of the missile crisis. Although the United States and the Soviet Union were already in a state of crisis in October 1962, there are interesting similarities in the U.S. efforts to interpret both incidents. In both the U-2 shootdown during the Cuban missile crisis and the KAL 007 shootdown of September 1983, uncertain analysts and policymakers ranged over a wide variety of speculative assessments, and some policymakers wanted to drive the decisionmaking process on the basis of worst-case assumptions about the reasons for the Soviet actions.

The KAL 007 incident and misperceptions attendant to NATO and Soviet theater nuclear force modernization were dangerous because nuclear weapons make the possibility of transition from a condition of general deterrence to a collapse of immediate deterrence so rapid. What makes nuclear weapons dangerous for crisis stability is not only the speed with which nuclear weapons can strike targets, but the speed with which they can cause leaders to move their military organizations from a condition of low readiness to a condition of higher readiness. Many students of nuclear history have missed this point, assuming that an ultrastable political environment has been guaranteed by mutual deterrence, or, in the U.S. version, "mutual assured destruction." But mutual deterrence is a static descriptor that leaves out many of the dynamics of crisis interaction, as the crisis of July 1914 indicates. In terms of alliances rather than individual states, the Europe of July 1914 was bipolar, not multipolar. And, in contrast to historiography that depicts the leaders of Germany, Russia, Austria-Hungary, and other powers as hapless victims of circumstance or fools who blundered into war, other evidence suggests that many of those responsible for foreign policies of the great powers of Europe in July 1914 feared the costs of major war as much

---

Hersh, *"The Target Is Destroyed": What Really Happened to Flight 007 and What America Knew About It* (New York: Random House, 1986), and Alexander Dallin, *Black Box: KAL 007 and the Superpowers* (Berkeley: University of California Press, 1985).

13. The Soviet Union was at first noncommittal, but eventually the government called a press conference at which a major presentation in defense of the Soviet position was made by a military man, then Chief of the Soviet General Staff, Marshal N. V. Ogarkov.

as they expected to accomplish any significant gains from war. Despite essentially bipolar alliance systems and more realistic fears of war than are customarily supposed, the leaders of 1914 found themselves in a conflict that destroyed their regimes and societies. Their decisions can be explained in part, as can the NATO nuclear-force modernization decisions discussed above, by the unavoidable and inherent tension in military persuasion between the requirements for deterrence and those for the avoidance of unnecessary provocation. Such tension is not equally acute in all kinds of international political or military deterrent systems, however. For example, Robert Jervis has outlined ideal types for four possible worlds, based on two sets of variables: 1) whether offense or defense has the advantage and 2) whether offensive and defensive force postures can be distinguished from one another.[14] When defense has the advantage and when defensive force postures can be readily distinguished from offensive ones, preservation of the status quo is much easier than overturning it. In the other extreme, when offense has the advantage and the two kinds of force postures cannot be distinguished, states are constantly fearful of attack and motivated to consider preemption as a normal way of doing business. In between are the intermediate conditions: 1) defensive advantage in warfighting, but no clear or consistent distinction between offensive and defensive force postures; 2) offensive advantage in war, but a clear distinction between offensive and defensive postures.[15] The international political and military system immediately prior to World War I might be described as a system that heightened the security dilemma by emphasizing offensive technologies and doctrines for waging war over defensive ones, while the distinction at that time between offensive and defensive force mobilization and war-preparedness was not very clear to leaders or to military planners.[16]

Nuclear weapons have the potential either to diminish or to increase the security dilemma of states, depending on the numbers of weapons deployed and on such characteristics as vulnerability and accuracy. Nuclear forces that are survivably based and that cannot fulfill the requirements for a first strike against forces of their opponents are considered less threatening to stability

14. Robert Jervis, "Cooperation Under the Security Dilemma," *World Politics* (January 1978): 186–214, reprinted with revisions in *International Politics: Anarchy, Force, Political Economy, and Decision Making*, ed. Robert J. Art and Robert Jervis (New York: Harper Collins, 1985), 86–100 and 185–207, esp. 202–5.

15. Ibid., 203.

16. Jack Snyder, *The Ideology of the Offensive: Military Decision Making and the Disasters of 1914* (Ithaca, N.Y.: Cornell University Press, 1984).

than those which are vulnerable to preemptive attack and can pose threats of first-strike vulnerability to other states' forces. In these respects nuclear weapons, though more destructive than prenuclear ones, have a similar status in force structures with respect to the balance between deterrence and provocation. Even before the nuclear age, forces that could strike quickly and annihilate the forces of their opponents created an unstable atmosphere of imminent threat and a perilous security dilemma for those countries whose forces were slower to react or were less capable of massive offensives.

Friction and Nuclear-Crisis Management

With respect to the relationship of deterrence and provocation in military persuasion, on the other hand, a very important difference lies in the role of nuclear weapons in crisis management, compared to the role of conventional forces in actual combat. To see this we need to recall the concept of "friction" developed by the Prussian military strategist, Carl von Clausewitz. Friction, according to Clausewitz, was the sum total of all those things which would disrupt a commander's plans and expectations about the course of battle. Friction, by analogy with the concept known in physics, acted to slow down the military machine and to complicate the expected or desired relationship among its various parts.[17] Supplies are late or insufficient, forces cannot move on a muddy or snow-covered battlefield, communications break down unexpectedly: all these are staples of real war, as opposed to war on paper, as Clausewitz noted.

By analogy, friction may also influence the ability of leaders to control the outcome of a crisis between nuclear-armed states. Its effects on crisis management in the nuclear age may follow the historical precedents set in prenuclear crises, but not necessarily. Anticipation of the damage that nuclear weapons can do and of the speed with which that destruction can be accomplished has forced U.S. and Soviet leaders to build large command-and-control systems that are primed for immediate retaliation in response to warning. Although each state has taken steps to ensure that neither accidental nor inadvertent nuclear launches would start a war, nuclear command organizations primed for retaliation depend upon standard operating procedures and stable menus of strike plans. Leaders in a crisis who might want to

17. Carl von Clausewitz, *On War*, ed. and trans. Michael Howard and Peter Paret (Princeton, N.J.: Princeton University Press, 1976), 119ff.

modify these plans could find, like the kaiser in 1914, in response to his last-minute request to Moltke to turn German mobilization eastward against Russia instead of westward against France, that such a change is "impossible."[18]

Military leaders, as the preceding example suggests, can use friction as an excuse or as a genuine reason to resist changes in war plans desired by others. Tampering with the workings of the military machine may, in fact as well as in the worst fears of planners, be detrimental to the accomplishment of mobilization in good time. Another way in which friction might be important in nuclear-crisis management is that command-and-control systems are delicate composites of people, organizational procedures, and expensive technology. Uncertainty about what is happening in a crisis, or a set of threat stimuli for which organizations are not prepared, could cause technology to fail, procedures to be ill-suited to the new situation, and people to work in confusion until the appropriate time for decision has passed.[19]

The inability or unwillingness to change previously set plans and the uncertainties and confusion attendant to unexpected events are kinds of friction that could take place in nuclear-crisis management, and the evidence presented in Chapter 1 shows that such symptoms appeared in the July crisis of 1914. But a third form of friction in a nuclear crisis might be very different from the kind expected by Clausewitz in battle, and even somewhat different from the friction experienced by leaders during their futile effort at crisis management in July 1914. This third form of friction is created by an unfavorable combination of systemic supports for aggression, offensively primed military machines and military doctrines, and an immediate deterrence situation in which preemption pays. This sort of friction speeds up the process of turning a crisis into a war, instead of slowing down the machinery of decisionmaking when one might wish to do so.[20] If this supposition is correct, it suggests for future research agendas a need to combine general systems theories of state behavior, middle-range theories of organizational and group decisionmaking, and case studies of individual crises in which the trade-off between deterrence and provocation was an important aspect of crisis decisionmaking.

18. Corelli Barnett, *The Swordbearers: Supreme Command in the First World War* (New York: William Morrow, 1964), 6.

19. See Richard Ned Lebow, *Nuclear Crisis Management: A Dangerous Illusion* (Ithaca, N.Y.: Cornell University Press, 1987), for elaboration on this and other possible dysfunctions of nuclear-crisis decisionmaking.

20. I am grateful to Ned Lebow for suggesting the idea of friction speeding up, rather than slowing down, a process of taking or implementing decisions; he is not responsible for its application here, of course.

Bipolar and Multipolar Systems

Among my other findings are some indications about the character of the deterrence/provocation trade-off in a multipolar system compared to a bipolar system. A bipolar system such as the Cold War system from 1945 to 1985 allowed for no "buck passing" of responsibility for peace and security to other states; that responsibility lay in Washington and in Moscow, and other actors, however influential on the margin, remained constrained by U.S. and Soviet strategic primacy. A multipolar system into which the world may now be headed offers more flexibility of alignment, compared to its Cold War predecessor. But it also offers the opportunity for each of the leading powers to bypass responsibility for international peace and security. The Gulf War of 1991 was a favorable omen for the potential of leading states in a multipolar system to take collective initiative against threats to the peace. However, the Gulf precedent is not necessarily a binding one. Much depends on the continuation of détente diplomacy, military deconstruction in the former Soviet Union and elsewhere in Europe, and the success of *perestroika* in rebuilding a shattered economy. The United States and its Western allies of the Cold War years are now in the ambiguous position that the victors at the Congress of Vienna held with regard to the defeated French after Waterloo. The Concert of Europe sought to provide a forum under which a France without Napoleonic armies and revolutionary fervor could be restored to a stable international system based on dynastic legitimacy. Similarly, the United States and NATO will welcome a suitably capitalist former Soviet Union to the table of the great powers, for a capitalist former Soviet Union will not threaten to turn the table over.

In the aftermath of the failed Soviet coup of August 19–21, 1991, few of the architects of the "new world order" had firm answers as to how a twentieth or twenty-first century Concert of Europe could be reconstructed without a stable Soviet or Russian partner. In the immediate aftermath of the coup, various republics of the former Soviet Union declared their independence from any central authority. The case of Ukraine was especially vital for the eventual autonomy and stability of any central "Soviet" or post-Soviet governing authority. On December 1, 1991, the hopes of Mikhail Gorbachev, and the hopes of those Western politicians who had bet on Gorbachev to dispel the forces of anarchy, were dashed by Ukraine's referendum in favor of independence. If any single date following the abortive coup of 1991 could be taken to mark the demise of the idea of voluntary "union" within the territory of the former USSR, then the Ukrainian declaration of independence was it. Ukrainian independence was greeted with immediate recognition by various Western governments and by Russian Federation President Boris Yeltsin.

Yeltsin's reasons for recognition of Ukrainian independence were pragmatic, following from his own decision in favor of independence from the center and his need for republic-to-republic cooperation with Ukraine on issues including trade, economic development, and the command and control of nuclear weapons. The cheering of Ukrainian independence and of the death of any Soviet "center" by Western audiences was less a pragmatic than an ideological reflex. The geopolitics of post–Cold War stability in Europe seemed to matter less to the advocate of "democracy at any price" than the opportunity for still another session of Soviet-bashing. Self-determination in nineteenth- and twentieth-century history, from the standpoint of its relationship to peace and international stability, has been a mixed blessing.

If national self-determination occurs within a preexisting framework of civil society, and if it can be contained without spillover into international strife, so much the better. But if the potential side-effects of national self-determination include civil war—which could bring down not only Russia and its fraternal republicans on the territory of the former Soviet Union, but also the post–Cold War security community being forged in Eastern and Central Europe—then the risks of national self-assertion outrank the benefits of Soviet disintegration.

When the risks of nationalist self-assertion spilling over into international war are acknowledged by scholars and politicians, they usually refer to the First World War and its aftermath. However, one has to imagine a Thirty Years' War fought with nuclear weapons to obtain a clearer picture of what could happen in the aftermath of a "Soviet" civil war that divides loyalties of the former Soviet armed forces and spreads across the borders of the former Soviet Union into Eastern and Central Europe. If we dismiss as unlikely this admittedly worst-case scenario, it is still not obvious to political leaders or scholars how we are to get from the "risky but responsible" bipolarity of the Cold War years to the "promising but irresponsible" future multipolarity in Europe and globally.

The trade-off between deterrence and provocation becomes obviously more complex within a multipolar as opposed to a bipolar alignment, but additional complexity in managing the deterrence/provocation trade-off does not necessarily lead to a higher probability of war among major powers. The kinds of military doctrines that states hold, and by which they prepare their armed forces for war, are also important in estimating the effects of any system transformation. This trade-off becomes more difficult for states to manage successfully when offensive military doctrines are emphasized by planners. The emphasis on offensive doctrines skews the details of mobilization planning and, more improtant, distorts the expectations that leaders have about what other states will do under crisis conditions of high threat and maximum uncertainty.

The impact of offensive military doctrines and multipolar power systems on the probability of crisis and war depends on several less-obvious factors, too. A situation of general deterrence, prior to the breaking out of a crisis, hides from leaders the potential for the system to break down. Leaders assume that the system is more stable than it actually is. Thus, leaders prior to the outbreak of World War I in July 1914 became complacent about avoiding war because they had avoided it during the Bosnian annexation (1908–9), Agadir (1911), the First Balkan War (1912–13), and other crises. Although they lacked a concept of crisis management, they had great confidence in their ability to manage crises. A condition of general deterrence had broken down before and reestablished itself. In July of 1914, however, the system had worn out its shock absorbers.

The most direct explanation for the outbreak of war in August 1914, according to this reasoning, is that the cumulative incapacity of the system to withstand stress was less than its ability to cope with individual cases of crisis instability. This finding is supported by the evidence, but it is not complete. Leaders of the great powers of Europe in 1914 were not rats in a maze, doomed to fail after so many trials in a cosmic experiment. The evidence from the July crisis is clear: war could have been avoided, but choices made by the leaders and their war planners closed off war-avoiding options in favor of war-provoking ones.

In addition to the impact of cumulative stress on system stability, the powers of Europe in July 1914 were burdened by the continuation of behavior acceptable under a condition of general deterrence into a condition of immediate deterrence, where the same patterns of behavior proved to be dysfunctional. The philosopher J.G.A. Pocock, in his study *The Machiavellian Moment*, notes that an important moment in historical time has two kinds of significance.[21] The first and more obvious kind of significance is that an event actually occurred at a certain time and place and under the immediate

21. J.G.A. Pocock, *The Machiavellian Moment: Florentine Political Thought and the Atlantic Republican Tradition* (Princeton, N.J.: Princeton University Press, 1975).

historical circumstances of the moment. It matters that the American Revolution happened in 1776, for example, and not a century earlier or later. The second meaning of a "moment" is more subtle than the first. It is the moment at which political leaders and others become conscious of the opportunity to reshape their historical destinies through political choices. In the language of social science, they shift from a more deterministic view of possibility to a probabilistic one in which they become more self-conscious and assertive with regard to their control over their environment.

Leaders on the cusp of war in July 1914 abdicated this responsibility to seize their "Machiavellian moment" and to assert the priority of not provoking war over and against that of deterring it. Instead, leaders of Germany, Russia, and Austria-Hungary clung to past programs and doctrines that had seemed to work in the management of earlier crises. The context within which they had to work had changed, however. First, as noted earlier, the system was less shock-resistant to disruption after escaping entrapment in several earlier crises. Second, as noted in Chapter 1, above, the system was undergoing a structural transformation. It was being transformed in the decade preceding the outbreak of World War I from a loosely coupled multipolar system, based on state actors as decision units, to a tightly coupled bipolar system with antagonistic alliances as decision units. The impact of alliances on all the powers was not equal in 1914, but the commitment of France and Russia to prompt attacks on Germany in the event that Germany should attack either of them, and the support until very late in the July crisis given by Germany for Austria's coercion of Serbia, contributed obviously and significantly to a new context for decisionmaking.

This new context, or "Machiavellian moment," for the leaders in July 1914 appeared when Russia began to mobilize, under the rubric of "measures preparatory to war," on July 25 and in response to the Austrian ultimatum to Serbia. Germany at this point had to act to restrain Austria, for German military planners assumed that the success of the Schlieffen Plan depended on Germany's mobilization not lagging too far behind that of Russia (assumed to progress at a slower rate). Germany waffled; and Austria, believing that it had secured the kaiser's blessing for the suppression of Serbian nationalism, began the bombardment of Belgrade several days later. This awoke the kaiser from his complacency, but too late. Austria was not to be deterred from attacking Serbia; Austria could have been restrained only by Germany, and Germany did not consider this option in time.

The Russian mobilization measures "preparatory to war" also presented a Machiavellian moment to Great Britain. Britain had to signal its possible involvement in any war growing out of an uncontained Balkan crisis, especially a war that included fighting between Germany and France. The "excuse" for doing so was readily at hand. The Serbian response to the Austrian ultimatum was to fulfill almost all the conditions stipulated. The Serbian response was so unexpectedly forthcoming that the kaiser was to remark that there was no longer any reason for war. Unfortunately, he did not impress this notion on the Austrians. Nor did Britain, seeing that any war between Austria and Serbia might involve Russia, and therefore Germany, take prompt action to head off the escalation of the crisis into a European and global war.

However, France bears the greatest responsibility for encouraging Russia to mobilize promptly in response to any perceived threat from Austria or Germany. Prewar consultations between the French and Russian general staffs infected Russian planners with French overconfidence about the decisive impact of timely blows against Germany, provided they were simultaneously struck against Germany's eastern and western flanks. Prewar plans called for Russia to attack Austria in Galicia as well as Germany in East Prussia, and the timetable for Russian mobilization would have to be accelerated in order to make this possible. Russian planning for two prompt offensives against Germany and Austria-Hungary led to overcommitted force employment that contributed to the early military disaster at Tannenberg. More important for our study, Russia's expectation that it would have to mobilize rapidly in a situation of immediate deterrence helped to turn crisis instability into war.

It might be argued that England's situation in July 1914 contradicts my hypothesis that, in a situation of immediate as opposed to general deterrence, nonprovocation is more important than deterrence. A case can be made that from July 24 to 28 England should have acted firmly to deter Germany from supporting any Austrian action against Serbia. Had the British done so, however, it is not obvious that the German reaction would have been compliant. Germany had great confidence in the ability of its armed forces to score a quick and decisive victory in a six-week campaign against France (exactly forty-two days, according to Schlieffen's plan of 1905) and then to defeat Russia at its leisure. Germany feared Britain's navy, but not Britain's ability to make a prompt continental commitment of ground forces.

Against the argument that Britain should have acted promptly in July 1914 to deter Germany, one could argue with equal cogency that Britain and France should have acted on behalf of nonprovocation instead of deterrence and halted Russia's headlong rush to mobilize. There was arguably no need for Russia to mobilize rapidly in July 1914. A slower mobilization would have allowed the tsar's forces to go into battle in August 1914 with an improved state of readiness that could have improved their ultimate performance on the battlefield. A delayed Russian mobilization could also have taken advantage of Austria's strategic predicament and Germany's clear intention to attack France first. Austria's strategic predicament was that once war began against Serbia, Austria would have seven of its divisions tied down in the Balkans which could not immediately be used against Russia. One of Austria's greatest prewar fears was that Russia would delay its attack until Austria was committed into battle against Serbia, for Belgrade's forces were thought to be not inconsiderable by all the powers. An Austria stuck in Serbia would be vulnerable to Russian offensives against Galicia into Hungary and perhaps through Romania, depending on the ultimate loyalties of the Romanian government.

Russia's hasty mobilization also failed to take advantage of Germany's well-known (by 1912, if not earlier) commitment to attack France first and to fight a defensive, holding operation in East Prussia. Instead of using this as an excuse for prompt mobilization and attacks into German territory, Russia could have used the German plan to attack France first as a rationale for a defensive posture in the first stage of any war. A strategically defensive posture against Germany combined with an offensive posture against Austria would have deterred Austria without provoking Germany and could possibly have disconnected the two Alliance partners. There were opportunities for Russia to bring about such a diplomatic and strategic configuration. As late in the game as the autumn of 1910, the two governments were cautiously moving toward accommodation on a number of issues. On December 10 of that year, the German chancellor declared in the Reichstag, following a meeting between the kaiser and the tsar at Potsdam, that Germany and Russia had agreed not to take part in hostile alliances.[22] Only a minority of influential persons favored improved relations between the two states, however; sympathy among Russia's ruling elites remained with the French, whose own strategic predicament imposed specific constraints on Russia as France's ally.

The fact that Russia might choose to follow a course of strategic defensivism against Germany led to fears of abandonment on the part of France. The

22. I. V. Bestuzhev, "Bor'ba v rossii po voprosam vneshnei politiki nakanune pervoi mirovoi voiny" [The Struggle in Russia over Questions of Foreign Policy on the Eve of the First World War], *Istoricheski zapiski* 75 (1965): 44–85, esp. 45.

French, therefore, especially after the accession of Poincaré to the presidency, pushed hard on St. Petersburg for a commitment to a prompt offensive against Germany on the fifteenth day of mobilization. Russia's attempt to do this was not only a military disaster but a political one. The Russian perception that measures "preparatory to war" had to be in place before German mobilization began was interpreted in Berlin and in Vienna as a Russian threat to deny Austria its opportunity for revenge against Serbia. This is confirmed by the interpretation given to the actions of Foreign Minister Sazonov by Friedrich Graf Szapary, Austria-Hungary's ambassador to St. Petersburg, after meeting with Sazonov on July 29. Szapary attributed to Sazonov the following strategy: "The Minister (Sazonov), like his Imperial master, fights shy of war and, without reacting immediately to our Serbian campaign, hopes to be able to contest the fruits of it, if possible without war, and should war come, to enter it better prepared than now."[23]

Sazonov's attempt to walk both sides of the divide between deterrence and nonprovocation was at the mercy of the accuracy of his information about the details of military planning and the suitability of plans for supporting his stand in negotiations. His proposal for partial mobilization of the military districts facing Austria-Hungary while delaying mobilization in those districts facing Germany was not the preferred option of the Russian General Staff. But, with the advantage of hindsight, historians are not agreed on its feasibility. Luigi Albertini argues that Russia had no plans for a partial mobilization and that, even if it had, it would have been a "blunder."[24] In this he supports the views of Russian Quartermaster General Iurii Danilov. Danilov, completely skeptical about the feasibility of any plan for partial mobilization, was absent from St. Petersburg at the time of the Austrian ultimatum to Serbia and for several days thereafter. It was during this interval that Sazonov had proposed, with the consent of General Ianushkevich, chief of the General Staff, the plan for partial mobilization against Austria.[25]

Danilov returned to find General Staff headquarters in turmoil (probably on July 26) over the issue of partial mobilization, and he immediately asked that Ianushkevich call together the latter's staff for a conference on the issue of mobilization.[26] The conference held on July 27 was an important turning

23. Luigi Albertini, The Origins of the War of 1914, trans. and ed. Isabella M. Massey (London: Oxford University Press, 1953), 2:552, n. 2.

24. Ibid., 2:543.

25. Iurii Danilov, La Russie dans la Guerre Mondiale (Paris: Payot, 1927), 32–33. See also Albertini, The Origins of the War of 1914, 2:542–43.

26. Albertini, The Origins of the War of 1914, 2:543; Danilov, La Russie dans la Guerre Mondiale, 32–33.

point; for until that moment Ianushkevich had gone along with Sazonov's proposed partial mobilization, despite the apparent fact that no such plan was in the organizational repertoire of the General Staff. The meeting was attended by Danilov, Ianushkevich, General Dobrorolsky (chief of the mobilization section), and General Ronzhin (chief of military transport) and resulted in a decision that two drafts, one for partial and one for general mobilization, should be submitted to the tsar simultaneously.[27] Dobrorolsky attributed the change of mind on the part of the chief of the General Staff to Ianushkevich's initially "slight knowledge of strategic questions," as he had been in office for only five months.[28] However, Ianushkevich, according to Dobrorolsky, was subsequently "convinced by the representations of his subordinates" and "began to regard the problem of mobilization no longer from the political but from the strategic point of view."[29]

The assumption that partial mobilization was not a viable option was based on two strands of thinking in the Russian General Staff: 1) those who regarded mobilization as tantamount to war and 2) those closely allied who considered mobilization, if distinct from war, as an exercise in defensive realism based on worst-case scenarios. However, this conclusion, which some but not all historians endorse, is based on the narrow judgments made by Russian military planners *subsequent* to the taking of measures "preparatory to war" on the 25th and 26th of July. These measures, which included putting border and fortified military areas on a war footing as well as other steps significantly removed from normal peacetime preparedness, were logically preparatory to general mobilization but functionally equivalent to partial mobilization. Russia could have stopped with the measures "preparatory to war" and not further mobilized forces in the Moscow, Kiev, Kazan, and Odessa military districts, relying upon diplomacy to defuse the July crisis.

For the purpose of sending signals of resolution with a minimum of "noise" (deterrence without provocation), Russia in fact had options less provocative to Germany than a mobilization of thirteen army corps against Austria. Of course, Germany's Foreign Minister Gottlieb von Jagow had indicated (undoubtedly without having thought the matter through) that a partial Russian mobilization against Austria would be acceptable to Germany. The advice given to Sazonov by the German ambassador to St. Petersburg, Count Portalès, during their 11:00 A.M. meeting on July 29 was more fully appreciative

27. Albertini, *The Origins of the War of 1914*, 2:543.
28. Ibid., 2:544, n. 1.
29. Ibid.

of the risks of escalation. Having been informed by Sazonov that Russia was that very day to mobilize the military districts bordering Austria, Portalès responded that "the danger of all military measures lies in the counter-measures of the other side. It is to be expected that the General Staffs of eventual enemies of Russia would not want to sacrifice the trump card of their great lead over Russia in mobilization and would press for counter-measures. I urgently beg you to consider this danger."[30] This expressed fear of a conflict spiral over which both sides would lose control, as the nonprovocation component of deterrent messages receded into the background of diplomatic exchanges, was very prescient.

The historian L.C.F. Turner has argued against the claim that Russia could not have conducted a partial mobilization in July 1914. Turner also disputes Albertini on the notion that the plan for a partial mobilization was basically Sazonov's. According to Turner, Sazonov was "pathetically ignorant of military affairs" and was merely revisiting a scheme for partial mobilization already formulated by the War Ministry during the crisis surrounding the First Balkan War in 1912.[31] Turner's reference note on this point is to himself, however, and his claim that Minister of War Sukhomlinov had already worked out a partial mobilization plan on the basis of events in 1912 is suspect, owing to the location of mobilization planning within the General Staff and not the War Ministry (the separation of the two was brought about by the military reforms of 1909).

Turner makes a stronger argument for the possibility of a partial mobilization by Russia during the July crisis in his claim that it was to Russia's advantage to delay any mobilization until Austria had committed forces to combat against Serbia. This was a source of considerable concern to Austrian war planners, and a French appreciation of the advantages of a Russian delaying strategy of this type was noted in a military memorandum sent to President Poincaré on September 2, 1912, which claimed that large operations by Austria in the Balkans would put Austria *and Germany* "at the mercy of the Entente."[32] The point has force only if Russia truly sought to isolate any Austro-Serbian conflict from expansion; Germany's fear was that Russia would use its involvement on behalf of Serbia as a pretext for wider war. Russia's dilemma in this regard was an acute one. By allowing Austria to get bogged down in a war against Serbia, Russia could intervene against weak-

---

30. Ibid., 2:549.
31. L.C.F. Turner, *Origins of the First World War* (New York: W. W. Norton, 1970), 91.
32. Ibid., 93.

ened and tied-down Austrian forces with a larger chance for a rapid and decisive military victory over Vienna. However, if the likelihood of Russian success was as good as that, then Germany could be motivated much more strongly to take prompt action against Russia, or France, in anticipation of war with Russia. Germany feared Austrian weakness as much as it did Russian and French strength. Germany's leaders were somewhat paradoxically more concerned about abandonment of Germany by its weaker ally, and they were not as aware as they should have been about Foreign Minister, Count Berchtold's strategems for involving Germany at great risk in a Balkan war.

D.C.B. Lieven does not support Turner's contention that Russia could successfully have conducted a partial mobilization against Austria without also mobilizing against Germany.[33] According to Lieven, Russian military planners did not foresee the strong performance given by the Serbian army in World War I and assumed that it would be up to Russia to cause Austria to divide its forces between Serbia and Russia. In order to focus the attention of Vienna's planners in two directions, Russia would have to be able to present a plausible, prompt threat to Austria's frontier in Galicia. In addition, the Russian General Staff was horrified when it discovered that, in the winter of 1912, Austria had gradually mobilized its forces in Galicia without Russia's knowledge.[34] Lieven is more noncommittal on the subject of whether the physical and geographic conditions of Russia at that time, together with its military manpower system, would have permitted or precluded a partial mobilization. Lieven does acknowledge, however, that it would have been very difficult for a partial mobilization to sort out the distribution of reserves, since regiments did not draw their reserves from a single military district.[35]

One cannot dispute the view of Danilov and Albertini that, given the context for military planning within which Russia entered the July 1914 crisis, partial mobilization had not been effectively planned for. Ironically, the tsar *thought* that Russia had a plan for partial mobilization, and he was quite disconcerted to discover that no such plan existed. Nicholas summoned the head of mobilization for the General Staff, General Dobrorolsky,

---

33. D.C.B. Lieven, *Russia and the Origins of the First World War* (New York: St. Martin's Press, 1983), 148–49. See also Trachtenberg, *History and Strategy*, 80–87, for interesting arguments about Russian partial mobilization. Trachtenberg suggests that the decision by Russia for partial mobilization may have contributed to a temporary softening of the German stance on the evening of July 29/30.

34. Lieven, *Russia and the Origins of the First World War*, 149.

35. Ibid., 150.

during the later stages of the crisis and issued a command to "inform Chief of Mobilization Section . . . of my wish that, *at the end of the present tense crisis*, the mobilization plan shall be so revised that it affords the possibility of carrying out the mobilization of the separate military districts independently of one another."[36] Given the geographical and logistical constraints against fulfilling this mandate, and the disinclination of his military planners to provide it, the tsar's insistence on a future partial-mobilization option sounds familiar to those who followed the evolution of U.S. nuclear strategy from massive retaliation to limited nuclear options and counterforce, city-avoidance proposals of various kinds.

This skepticism about Russian partial mobilization in 1914 and about limited nuclear options in the Cold War years must be tempered by an acknowledgment about the quality of the international system within which this kind of military planning takes place. Multipolar systems create incentives for states to commit two kinds of errors, in opposite directions: chain ganging and buck passing. Those who chain gang may be reluctantly dragged into wars along with allies; those who pass the buck to others may find themselves isolated against an aspiring hegemon at a later date once the others have been defeated, or after they have refused to accept the passed buck.[37] Bipolar systems, in contrast, should induce neither kind of behavior: responsibility for system security is more clearly fixed on two powerful rivals instead of dispersed among many powers, avoiding the necessity for chain ganging and removing the incentive for buck passing. Multipolar systems have the potential to create more confusion, compared with bipolar systems, in military planning: in bipolar systems, each side knows with reasonable certainty who the potential enemy is. Thus, Imperial Russia needed flexibility in its mobilization plans, although planners found it hard to bring about, because it might have had to fight Austria or Germany alone, or both together. In contrast, the putative flexibility of U.S. strategic planning for limited nuclear war was not driven by any uncertainty about the identity of the most probable adversary but, rather, by the frustrating character of a situation that precluded victory even through the more rapid generation and launching of a massive surprise strike.

36. Dobrorolsky letter cited in Albertini, *The Origins of the War of 1914*, 544, n. 1 (emphasis added).
37. See Thomas J. Christensen and Jack Snyder, "Chain Gangs and Passed Bucks: Predicting Alliance Patterns in Multipolarity," *International Organization* (Spring 1990): 137–68. See also Kenneth Waltz, *Theory of International Politics* (Reading, Mass.: Addison-Wesley, 1979).

LEADERS, ORGANIZATIONS, AND WAR PLANS

The tsar's "discovery" that he lacked plans for partial mobilization should not be any more surprising than the lack of familiarity with the details of war plans characteristic of U.S. military leaders in the nuclear age. For example, few presidents, perhaps none until Jimmy Carter, actually reviewed nuclear war plans and personally interested themselves in the command post exercises that would be activated in the event of nuclear attack on the United States. Command post exercises are the equivalent of mobilization exercises for top echelons of civil and military command in the United States. Most presidents have preferred not to bother. In addition, the process of conducting U.S. nuclear alerts is often one that catches leaders by surprise. Events take place that were not expected, and leaders' reactions to them are unpredictable. Some alerts have been called for reasons that were dubious under the circumstances. A U.S. secretary of defense in the Eisenhower administration, without forewarning his senior military commanders, decided to call an alert just to see if people were on their toes. In 1973, the Washington Special Action Group (WSAG), chaired by National Security Adviser to the President Henry Kissinger, ordered a DEFCON 3 alert for U.S. global forces, including nuclear forces, to deter unilateral Soviet intervention in the Mideast fighting between Israel and Egypt. The alert was ordered by WSAG in the absence of President Nixon, who was not available when the WSAG deliberations were taking place (but who nonetheless recalled in his memoirs that he had authorized the alert).[38]

The United States claimed that the worldwide alert was necessary to put Soviet President Leonid Brezhnev on notice that any military intervention by his forces in the 1973 Arab-Israeli war would meet with a U.S. military response. However, the Soviet threat was to intervene unless Israel observed a cease-fire that prevented the enclosure and destruction by Israel of the Egyptian Third Army Corps. Having suffered heavy losses in the initial period of fighting, which broke out on October 6, Israel mobilized and coun-

---

38. For examples and background with regard to the alerting of U.S. nuclear forces, see Scott D. Sagan, "Nuclear Alerts and Crisis Management," *International Security* (Spring 1985): 99–139; Bruce G. Blair, "Alerting in Crisis and Conventional War," ch. 3 in *Managing Nuclear Operations*, ed. Carter, Steinbruner, and Zraket, 75–120; Scott D. Sagan, *Moving Targets: Nuclear Strategy and National Security* (Princeton, N.J.: Princeton University Press, 1989), 166–73; Barry M. Blechman and Douglas Hart, "The Political Utility of Nuclear Weapons: The 1973 Middle East Crisis," in *Strategy and Nuclear Deterrence*, ed. Steven E. Miller (Princeton, N.J.: Princeton University Press, 1986), 273–97; and Lebow, *Nuclear Crisis Management*.

Conclusion 279

terattacked, gradually establishing military superiority over the Egyptians and the Syrians in their respective operational theaters. On October 20 Kissinger went to Moscow, and on October 22 the United Nations, based on U.S.-Soviet consultations, announced a cease-fire. Israel had not expected a cease-fire to be called for by the superpowers so soon. Israeli Defense Force (IDF) commanders and their government leaders, knowing of previous cease-fire rejections by Arab governments, did not plan their counteroffensive operations on the assumption that hasty attacks were necessary. IDF commanders assumed that more methodical and carefully prepared battles would ultimately pay dividends. When the cease-fire broke on October 22, Israeli commanders moved quickly to make last-minute grabs of territory, but these operations were costly (as the IDF had anticipated) because they were ill-prepared, with insufficient air preparation and inadequate concentrations of infantry forces. IDF Southern Command planning for Operation Abirei-Lev 2 had allotted thirty-six hours for the task of crossing the Suez Canal from the east to the west bank and encircling the Egyptian Third Army; the operation in fact required six days and would not have been accomplished if fighting had actually stopped on October 22.[39]

The Soviet threat to intervene unilaterally in the October War was communicated by Brezhnev, according to U.S. officials, on October 23. By October 24, Israeli forces would have cut off water supplies to the Egyptian Third Army Corps and would have completed their encirclement of it; Israel's military position on the ground was dominant. What the Soviet plan for intervention would have been in operational terms is not clear. U.S. intelligence claimed that the Soviet Union has alerted and relocated some of its elite airborne divisions to locations in the southern USSR, from which they could have been moved rapidly to Egypt.

Israel's dominant military position on the ground makes it unlikely that the Soviets could have intervened unilaterally in a timely manner to thwart Israeli destruction of the Egyptian armed forces, had Tel Aviv so decided. Soviet paratroopers would have provided target practice for Israeli armored divisions, and larger-than-airborne interventions by the USSR could certainly have met with U.S. *conventional* military escalation. After all, the United States and its NATO allies ought to have been able to establish maritime superiority in the Mediterranean in a very short time (though not

39. Gen. Abraham (Bren) Adan, *On the Banks of the Suez* (Novato, Calif.: Presidio Press, 1980, 1991), 426–34. The battle for Suez City was especially costly and discouraging for Israeli commanders, who had been tasked to complete that mission by October 24 and to mop up remaining resistance on the southern west bank.

uncontested superiority, and not without some danger of nuclear escalation if the crisis continued). The truth is that the U.S. military did not have a prepared *contingency plan* for a rapid Israeli crushing of Egyptian forces in the face of Soviet objections and willingness to issue threats. So a plan was improvised: namely, reaching for the alert mechanism and risking a superpower confrontation on the confident assumption that Brezhnev would have to back down. This "alert overkill" could have had disastrous consequences: it could have turned an Arab-Israeli war into a U.S.-Soviet military confrontation. U.S. officials sought deliberately to manipulate this risk of *nuclear* escalation as a tool of crisis management, without giving sufficient attention to the difference between deliberate and inadvertent escalation. The unknown risks of a U.S.-Soviet nuclear confrontation at sea or other unintended superpower confrontations, not the known ones of Soviet paratroops colliding with Israeli armored and infantry brigades, were the more important issues once the alert had been authorized.[40]

Given his actual military options, Brezhnev's threat of unilateral military intervention was an obvious bargaining chip to obtain cooperative U.S.-Soviet enforcement of a cease-fire against Israel. Israel's alleged "violations" of the cease-fire amounted to last-ditch attacks in order to solidify a position of military superiority, an understandable temptation for a country that had, after all, been subjected to surprise attack on October 6. Brezhnev had jeopardized U.S.-Soviet détente already by not tipping U.S. officials to Egyptian and Syrian plans for launching a war. Soviet leaders surely had guessed at or were privy to those plans, for they organized a massive evacuation of Soviet dependents in the days preceding the outbreak of war. Unilateral intervention by the Soviet Union in the October War would have brought the entire détente process of the Nixon-Ford years crashing down on the heads of Brezhnev and his colleagues, perhaps reopening the strategic nuclear arms race that had preceded parity. Brezhnev's threat of intervention was a dangerous overplaying of his hand, and the U.S. response was an overreaction that could have led to inadvertent escalation of the crisis or to actual war.

Brezhnev's threat of intervention was not unlike the pledge given by Kaiser Wilhelm II to Austrian representatives on July 5, 1914, when he gave Austria an open-ended promise of German support for any measures Austria would care to take against Serbia. Wilhelm would live to regret this pledge,

---

40. For additional details on this crisis, see Blechman and Hart, "The Political Utility of Nuclear Weapons," passim. Blechman and Hart offer a sympathetic appraisal of the decision; my analysis is more critical and skeptical of the U.S. rationale.

and the frantic exchanges of telegrams with cousin "Nicky" (Tsar Nicholas of Russia) at the end of July reveal that both kaiser and tsar now sought a way out of war but lacked an effective diplomatic mechanism for reversing the momentum of escalation. That momentum came not from previously laid down military plans per se, although they did contribute something to the atmosphere of hasty decisions and closed options that troubled the leaders of Europe in July 1914; the major source of the momentum toward war was a strategic fatalism that threats previously made and pledges committed had to be made good, even in changed circumstances and with greater risks of escalation. Following the assassination of the archduke on June 28, and especially after the Austrian ultimatum to Serbia on July 23, the context was no longer one of general deterrence but rather one of immediate deterrence. Threats that would be more deterring than provoking under the conditions of general deterrence, prior to the onset of actual crisis, were now more provoking than deterring to their intended audiences.

The alerting of U.S. military forces during the 1962 Cuban missile crisis produced several inexplicable or confusing incidents that troubled policymakers at the time and that, even today, defy satisfactory explanation. Several of these incidents had the potential for increasing the level of political provocation between heads of state, based on each leadership's less than complete knowledge of the details or timing of standard military operations. One was the apparent test-firing of a U.S. ICBM (fortunately not carrying an active warhead) on October 26 from Vandenberg Air Force Base in California in accordance with standard procedures for ICBM test-firings already scheduled prior to the crisis. In a more widely reported incident, on October 27, as the crisis reached its most sensitive and dangerous peak, a U.S. U-2 reconnaissance plane strayed into Soviet airspace above the Chukhotsk peninsula, causing Soviet air-defense forces to scramble fighter-interceptors in an attempt to chase the U-2 out of Soviet airspace or, if necessary, to shoot it down.[41]

Neither of these incidents has received a satisfactory explanation; and the second and more important, the U-2 "stray" incident, could have provoked a Soviet response in the form of military action taken against U.S. forces. For example, the United States, having received the U-2 pilot's distress signal for help, sent fighter aircraft from Alaska to escort the distressed U-2 safely home. These U.S. defense interceptors carried air-to-air missiles that were nuclear-armed. Confrontations between these U.S. aircraft and their

41. Sagan, *Moving Targets*, 146–47.

Soviet counterparts could have led to an air war over the polar regions at a time of great tension between the two nuclear superpowers.

The U.S. explanation, not contested in any subsequent first-person memoirs of crisis participants, was that the U-2 aircraft had lost its way when its celestial navigation failed owing to interference from aurora borealis, the "northern lights" phenomenon.[42] This leaves unanswered the question of why these "routine" reconnaissance flights were not canceled during the tensest moments of a U.S.-Soviet crisis. It took no military expert to be aware of the Soviets' declared sensitivity about intrusion into their airspace, even under normal peacetime conditions during the Cold War. That sensitivity was on display again in September 1983 when Korean Air Lines 007 was shot down by Soviet interceptors in the Far East. Khrushchev immediately protested the intrusion to Kennedy by asking, "What is this, a provocation? One of your planes violates our frontier during this anxious time we are both experiencing, when everything has been put into combat readiness. Is it not a fact that an intruding American plane could be easily taken for a nuclear bomber, which might push us to a fateful step?"[43]

Khrushchev, on the other hand, was no more able to account for another incident with strong potential for inadvertent escalation which had alarmed the U.S. leadership on the same day. A U-2 over Cuba was shot down by a Soviet SA-2 surface-to-air missile, and U.S. leaders wondered whether this meant that Khrushchev had now made a decision to move from crisis into war. Alternative explanations given at the time were 1) that Khrushchev had been pressured into escalation by hard-liners in the Kremlin leadership, 2) that Soviet standing orders to field commanders in Cuba had called for attacks on aircraft under such circumstances, or 3) that the Cubans had acted on their own, after illegal seizure or authorized acquisition of Soviet air-defense sites.[44] U.S. Soviet expert Raymond Garthoff first revealed the correct explanation in an article in the journal *Foreign Policy* in fall 1988; subsequently he included it in his book on the crisis, just cited. The decision to shoot down the U.S. reconnaissance plane was taken by two Soviet air-defense commanders in Cuba who misconstrued their standing orders to authorize just such an action. Whereas standing orders had authorized firing on U.S. aircraft in the event of an American invasion of Cuba, Soviet air-

42. Ibid., 147.
43. Ibid., 148.
44. Raymond L. Garthoff, *Reflections on the Cuban Missile Crisis*, rev. ed. (Washington, D.C.: Brookings Institution, 1989), 82–84.

defense commanders interpreted this to include hostile U.S. aerial *reconnaissance* that was not part of any invasion.[45]

One incident that did *not* go wrong in the Cuban missile crisis was prevented from causing greater trouble because midlevel CIA personnel worked *on the assumption that policymakers would misconstrue* reports received directly from the field. This incident was the episode in which a U.S. and British agent in the Soviet GRU (Military Intelligence Directorate of the Soviet General Staff), Colonel Oleg Penkovskiy, used coded telephonic signals given to him by his handlers to communicate with U.S. officials while he was being arrested during the crisis. Penkovskiy had been given a special signal to be used if he was being arrested, another if he believed that war was imminent. As he was being placed under arrest, he signaled from his apartment using the code that meant imminent war.[46] Penkovskiy's motive for taking such a drastic step was not clear, but its meaning on October 22 or 23 in Washington and Moscow was ominous. Penkovskiy's Western intelligence contacts who received this communication blamed it on his self-important and unpredictable personality, however, and chose not to give the signal any credibility. Nor did they forward the information that Penkovskiy had signaled "imminent war" to higher CIA headquarters.[47]

One could go on indefinitely with examples of political leaders whose unfamiliarity with the details of military operations caused them to misestimate the impact of those operations on adversaries and allies. It is not necessarily surprising, given the bureaucratic compartmentalism of modern governments and the intelligence and security restrictions placed on national security information, that islands of expertise and authority should exist within the larger civil and military-defense establishments of modern countries. The more important issue is under what conditions it matters that political leaders who order up military options find that they cannot be ordered "cafeteria style" but must be taken more or less in the form provided by the "caterers." Further to this analogy, the caterers are more interested in culinary delights, or war-planning masterpieces in which the schedules move on time and the equipment is polished and ready, than they are with the signals leaders intend to send through their use of military forces.

45. Ibid., 84.
46. Ibid., 64. The incident was revealed for the first time by Garthoff in the first edition of his book.
47. Ibid., 65. Garthoff has subsequently indicated that the Penkovskiy message incident should not be taken at face value, based on additional information from Russian sources after the Soviet demise.

The point that policymakers are often unable to improvise options to their taste, on account of military and bureaucratic constraints on their freedom of action, has led some academics and government officials into unnecessary pessimism about having to choose between "no war" and "total war." One of the unfortunate artifacts of most civil and military bureaucratic understanding of the U.S. intervention in Vietnam and in the Persian Gulf during 1991 is a contempt for the use of military forces in gradual installments for the purpose of coercion or limited war. Coercive diplomacy is judged to have failed in Vietnam, although closer analysis reveals that the use of force in Vietnam was thwarted not by misguided military "gradualism" but by an unclear specification of U.S. political objectives, by an incompetent allied government, and by the relentless pressure of North Vietnam, whose staying power was (to put in mildly) underestimated. However, the midlevel U.S. military leadership, those who held the rank of colonel at the time of Vietnam, vowed never again to be stuck in a limited war in which their resort to force was fettered by seemingly irrelevant political constraints. They wanted total war or no war, the choice that previous generations had in World War I and World War II; for only that choice allowed for U.S. public support, without which armed forces personnel felt abandoned and rejected.

Along with favorable developments in military thought stimulated by the military's self-study of past doctrine, new technology that was only imagined or in development during the 1970s or early 1980s began to come on-line in the middle to latter 1980s.[48] This new technology affected all arms of service, but its most immediate impact was on the possibility of conducting "AirLand battle" as the U.S. Army referred to it. AirLand battle was designed to use a combination of firepower, maneuver, and new communications and electronics technologies for conventional deep strike against the second strategic echelon of the Soviet Union and its Warsaw Pact allies. Disconnecting the head of the attacking formations from its reinforcements would, according to U.S. Army and NATO doctrine (in the form of "follow-on forces attack" subconcepts, or FOFA) allow NATO, presumed to be fighting outnumbered and on the defensive in Europe, to withstand an attack without depending on immediate nuclear escalation.

The last point was all but forgotten in the aftermath of Gorbachev's ac-

48. Among those contributing to the institutionalization of new U.S. army doctrine were the "Jedi Knights" who had graduated from Command and General Staff College in the years since Vietnam and who found themselves in key planning or operational positions in 1990. These officers were able to exploit the revised army doctrine for "AirLand battle" which had been developed at the Training and Doctrine Command (TRADOC) during the 1980s.

cession to power and the gradual withering away of the Soviet threat between 1985 and 1990. The reason for developing AirLand battle and conventional deep strike was to raise the nuclear threshold in Europe. Some argued that improved conventional warfighting capabilities would actually improve deterrence, because a delayed nuclear escalation was a more believable threat than an immediate resort to nuclear first use. Other supporters of conventional deep strike were less concerned with deterrence than they were with the question of what to do if deterrence failed. Both views were oriented to the development of improved deterrence and defense options for a major war on the continent of Europe.

As a result of the political transformation of Eastern Europe into a socialist graveyard and the reformulation of Soviet global objectives under Gorbachev, major war in Europe could no longer serve as a baseline for planning guidance after 1989. However, the new technologies and strategies for fighting a major conventional war below the nuclear threshold were conveniently available to the United States and its NATO allies in January 1991 when U.S. and coalition forces struck at Iraq. The United States applied against Iraq the template for operations and logistics that had been developed for AirLand battle in Europe. Fortunately for U.S. planners, five months were available in order to build up the necessary stock and equipment in Saudi Arabia. Early knockout blows delivered against Iraq's command and control, air defense, and other important communications-and-control targets ensured the United States and its allies early and total control of the skies. The military engagements seemed to go entirely according to the wishes of the allied coalition, and pundits applauded the apparent fact that the United States had waged unlimited war and emerged victorious in a short time. The Gulf was the antithesis of Vietnam, at least for formerly frustrated officers and for many other interpreters of events in the Middle East.

THE REAL GULF WAR: RESTRAINT, DETERRENCE, AND PROVOCATION

From the standpoint of the relationship between credible deterrence and the avoidance of unnecessary escalation or provocation, appearances were deceiving. Public euphoria over the U.S.-led victory in the Gulf War obscured some of the more important aspects of that war. In fact if not in appearance, the war was not fought as a total war in political or in military terms. President Bush had set forth, and the United Nations had authorized, only the specific political objective of expelling Iraqi forces from Kuwait. The conquest of Iraq, the removal of its government, and the reconstruction of its society were not objectives. President Bush stuck to this very strict definition of U.S. objectives for political reasons: anything more ambitious risked disruption of the coalition that had supported the war effort and alienation of U.N. backing for postwar pacific settlement. The United States was fighting a limited war in Iraq, not a total war, although the large amounts of firepower used, the speed of U.S. and allied victory, and the publicity given to high technology created a completely different impression. In fact, it was the president's decision to keep the war limited in its political objectives that made possible the seemingly unrestrained use of firepower appropriate to those objectives. The United States was able to fight with a clearer sense of its military mission in the Gulf because it had a more explicit and specific definition of its political mission, compared with its experience in Vietnam.

In sum, the war in the Gulf was a limited war, and it was fought with considerable restraint. Had Saddam Hussein succeeded in getting Israel into the war, or used chemical weapons against allied forces, other options might have been considered. But even then, it was clear that neither allied chemical weaponry nor Israeli participation was necessary for victory over Iraq. The Gulf War was a success because the coalition was able to win it with a comparatively small proportion of its total firepower and to accomplish its military mission according to guidelines that imposed much political restraint. First, Saddam Hussein was left with significant parts of his army intact, albeit with most of his modern air force destroyed or parked in Iran. Second, Saddam survived in power, albeit with revolutions brewing in the northern and southern parts of his country. Third, neither the United States nor its allies took military revenge against Jordan, which had allied its fortunes, perhaps out of necessity, with Iraq during the crisis preceding the war and after the shooting started. Fourth, the U.S. political leadership never seriously considered using nuclear weapons in Iraq, even if Saddam used chemical weapons to attack allied forces.[49] Fifth, and most important for allied cohesion and for the Arab states who joined the anti-Iraqi coalition,

49. Misleading press reports notwithstanding. Confusion is sometimes prompted by the fact that all kinds of "contingency plans" involving nuclear weapons are available and continually updated, but their availability in case of need is not tantamount to a serious presidential or National Security Council consideration of such an option.

Israel remained a nonbelligerent despite deliberately provocative efforts by Iraq to involve Israel.

The most important example of political constraint, apart from the non-involvement of Israel in military operations against Iraq, was the Soviet Union's lack of support for its major client and former ally Iraq. Iraq's willingness to play at brinkmanship with the United States without a guarantee of Soviet support proved to be a decisive military—and political—error. The latter was much the more significant. If the Soviet Union had supported Iraq in 1991 to the extent that the Soviet Union had supported Arab states in earlier wars against Israel (with U.S. support), a very different political and military situation would have obtained. First, no U.N. Security Council resolutions in favor of military action would have passed. Second, NATO allies would have had additional second thoughts about participating, as would other members of the coalition. Third, the possibility of escalation into a very different war with enormous consequences for the region and for world peace might well have stayed the U.S. military hand for unilateral intervention. In fact, it is quite likely that, with diplomatic and military deterrent support from the Soviet Union, Saddam Hussein could have continued his attack on Kuwait into Saudi Arabia and acquired significant territory there before being halted by any rapidly deployable U.S. or other allied forces.

Keeping the Soviet Union in its diplomatic corner required that the United States limit its political objectives to the restoration of the government of Kuwait and its territory, plus whatever compensation the United Nations would demand of Saddam for damages inflicted on Kuwait. The Soviet Union would face diplomatic humiliation if it stood for Saddam's replacement and overthrow by coalition forces in February 1991. Given the condition of the Soviet economy and armed forces at that time, the United States could have imposed its will on Moscow by ignoring Soviet concerns, occupying Baghdad, and chasing Saddam out of the country. The United States and its allies could have gone further still: after ousting Saddam Hussein, they could have installed a new government in Baghdad to their liking, or they could have deliberately divided the country into a northern enclave called the People's Democratic Republic of Kurdistan and into other regional enclaves based on religion, ethnicity, or other primordial values. In terms of sheer power, even without Soviet cooperation the victorious coalition could have installed a military proconsul in Baghdad (as was done with Douglas MacArthur in Japan) with the mandate to exchange the Iraqi constitution for a democratic political system. In terms of raw power, the allies could have created a Capitalist Republic of Iraq on the territory of a state that had drawn the larger share of its modern arms from its erstwhile fraternal socialist ally in Moscow.

Although the Soviet Union could not have interposed a military presence to prevent the coalition from deposing Saddam in February of 1991, Moscow could have presented a plausible threat of political or military escalation elsewhere. Therefore, relations with the Soviet Union had to be handled with sensitivity to its perceived status as a great power with significant interests in the region. Any contemplated Soviet support for Saddam had to be deterred, but the Soviet Union could not be provoked into military support for Iraq or into backing away from impending arms control agreements in Europe. Further, the Soviet Union held hostage those states of Eastern Europe whose complete liberation depended on the final and total withdrawal of Soviet forces, especially the newly reunited Germans from whose territory some three hundred eighty thousand Soviet troops would have to be withdrawn. If the United States wanted continued Soviet cooperation for winding down the Cold War, it had to limit its political objectives in the Gulf War to those which saved face for Moscow and saved for Saddam Hussein his regime.

Not only the Gulf War but the prewar buildup also was conducted with a sensitivity to the trade-off between deterrence and provocation. President Bush probably made up his mind in late November that war was inevitable, and his announcement on November 29, 1990, of U.S. intent to double forces programmed for the Gulf region was a coercive signal to Saddam as well as a measure of military mobilization. During the entire five-month period of U.S. mobilization for war, public diplomacy was used to isolate Iraq from potential allies and to emphasize the precise and limited nature of U.S. and allied war aims. The fact that Saddam Hussein could enlist almost no sympathy among Arab governments (although public opinion in those countries was less unanimous) created a political vacuum into which his military strategy dropped dead. Saddam's deterrence strategy depended on not provoking an overwhelming coalition of fellow Arabs against himself, thus legitimating U.S. and U.N. action on behalf of world order and stability. Saddam's diplomatic ineptitude was not just diplomatically fatal: it set the stage for military disaster.

The image of unrestrained U.S. military power in the Gulf is the result of confusion in the news media and elsewhere between two kinds of polarities: limited versus total war, and conventional versus unconventional war. The U.S. difficulties in Vietnam were not so much the result of fighting a limited war as they were the outcome of lack of preparedness for unconventional war. In unconventional war, the military actions are only part of a broader and intrastate revolutionary war, in which the political allegiance of the popular masses and the legitimacy of the form of government are the very reasons for belligerency. In Kuwait, there was no controversy over what was the legitimate form of government, and among Kuwaiti citizens there were few who preferred to live under the domain of Saddam Hussein. Therefore, the issue of political legitimacy was already resolved for the Kuwaitis. The military aspects of the war then reduced themselves to the expulsion of Iraq's armies from hostile territory.

The coalition war against Iraq demonstrated a variant of collective security in which many states favoring the status quo temporarily join together in order to defeat the aspirations of a rising hegemon. U.S. and allied military success in the Gulf War of 1991 temporarily distracted attention from the more problematic aspects of the political crisis that had preceded Iraq's attack on Kuwait. Although Iraq had not issued specific threats of military invasion against Kuwait, Saddam's anxious statements about falling oil revenues had been combined with diplomatic demarches to intimidate his OPEC partners for many months. Kuwait's vulnerability to sudden assault from Iraq was obvious to U.S. and other military planners; since defense was no real option, they counted on deterrence. But the United States and its oil-dependent allies made no real effort to extend deterrence to Kuwait prior to the crisis. Although charges that U.S. Ambassador April Glaspie, in a meeting shortly before war started, had inadvertently given Saddam Hussein a green light were ultimately and successfully disputed by her, it remained the case that the U.S. and allied governments had not sufficiently communicated to Iraq that their sense of strategic commitment to Kuwait required a military response.

Hindsight breeds intrepid scholarship, but it took no hindsight to look at a map of the Middle East and see that Kuwait in the hands of Iraq threatened the oil lifeline on which Europe and Japan were even more dependent than the United States. It was a case of extended deterrence in two directions: to protect Kuwait against invasion and to guarantee to Europe and Japan adequate supplies of petroleum. Efforts to deter Iraq's military adventurism were perhaps compromised by U.S. and other powers' undisguised sympathy and support for Iraq in its eight-year, indecisive, and costly war against Iran during the 1980s. Iraq's armed forces had been modernized with the aid of NATO countries and their commercial arms dealers, and the full story of Western contributions to the modernization of Iraq's military command-and-control system during the 1980s will probably remain out of print for some time.[50]

Although the reasons why are speculative, the outcome was that Saddam Hussein got the provocative message that neither his Arab OPEC confederates nor the oil-consuming countries would do anything to relieve his financial crisis. At the same time, he missed any deterrent messages that the United States or other countries might have intended to send. One reason why signals were not clearly understood is that the Iraqi invasion of Kuwait occurred during a period of transformation in the international system, away from Cold War bipolarity and toward a new configuration not yet fully foreseeable.

Financially desperate Iraq might have calculated that a more fluid international system offered opportunities for regional hegemons outside the reach or interest of the redefined policy agendas of Washington and Moscow. The extent to which Iraq gambled on Soviet extended deterrence against U.S. military intervention is unknown, but there is no evidence to suggest that Saddam counted on military help from Moscow. He probably counted more on historical Arab antipathy to Western military presence in the region, and on the likelihood that any war would involve Israel and quickly change the war's political character in a direction favorable to his interests.

Faced with Iraq's invasion of Kuwait, the Bush administration and its allies marshaled over a period of five months an anti-Iraqi coalition of overwhelming military superiority. Still, Bush's demand that Iraq comply with all the

50. Iraq's command-and-control components designed or fabricated by Western technology firms, with the relevant governments' approval, included a network of heavily fortified command bunkers, fiber-optic cables for communication, and automated information-processing systems that were near to state of the art. Of course, the disadvantage for Iraq in this set of arrangements was that, in a war against the United States and its Western allies, among others, the characteristics and locations of its command-and-control infrastructure would be better known to its enemies, and thus more easily destroyed. Some press reports also indicated that Soviet military intelligence may have passed along to the United States very useful information about Iraqi air defenses and electronic warfare systems, built under the direction of Soviet advisers and operated according to Soviet practices. See Tim Weiner and Mark Thompson, "Soviets Give U.S. Significant Intelligence Help," *Philadelphia Inquirer*, August 26, 1991. On the other hand, leading Soviet military officers in the aftermath of the war lamented the poor performance of Soviet equipment in Iraqi hands, and some demanded a reassessment of Soviet military doctrine per se. Those calling for a complete postmortem on the Gulf War included Soviet Defense Minister Dmitri T. Yazov, who told Soviet legislators that "what happened in Kuwait necessitates a review of the attitude to army air defense and the country's [Soviet Union's] entire air-defense system." Fen Montaigne, "For the Soviets, a Military Muddle," *Philadelphia Inquirer*, March 2, 1991.

united resolutions and withdraw from Kuwait by January 15, 1991, was not complied with. Saddam's resistance, even though diplomatically isolated and militarily outgunned, illustrates the problem that compellence is harder than deterrence, or a harder form of deterrence than passive deterrence.[51] Compellence requires that a state be made to undo an action already under way or completed; the more passive form of deterrence requires that the target state not take the action which is forbidden by the threatener. Once conquered and assimilated into Iraq's definition of its own state and territory, Kuwait was not yielded up without a costly battle for the Iraqi armed forces and society.

The Bush administration, from August 2 until January 16, sought to compel (a form of deterrence) Iraqi withdrawal from Kuwait without provoking Saddam Hussein into extending his war into other contiguous or nearby states. This might seem to be an exercise in deterrence only, but it was not, and the administration took pains to reassure allies in the coalition that it would not suddenly strike at Iraq in advance of the U.N. deadline of January 15. For diplomatic as well as military reasons the United States wanted to delay any attack, if war could not be avoided, until the necessary military preparations could be made on the ground in Saudi Arabia. The U.S. government also wanted to give the clear impression that Saddam would have one last clear chance to avoid war before U.S. and allied forces struck at Baghdad. Thus, the United States continued its diplomatic dialogue with Iraq's foreign minister in January even after the president and his National Security Council had decided that war was inevitable.

Even the conduct of the air war against Iraq in January and February can be said to have combined the attributes of deterrence and the avoidance of unnecessary provocation. It was a coercive air campaign as well as a destructive one. Although some officials and observers held out the hope that the air war alone could compel Iraqi withdrawal from Kuwait, the U.S. Central Command Commander-in-Chief (CINC CENTCOM) General Norman Schwarzkopf prepared a ground campaign on the assumption that enemy troops would not surrender until coalition ground forces physically occupied their territory.[52] Since the coalition had effective air superiority within days of the outbreak of war, it could strike at will against counterforce and countervalue targets. The United States could in theory have laid waste to Iraq's

51. I am grateful to Prof. David Tarr, University of Wisconsin, for insights pertinent to this discussion; he bears no responsibility for my arguments.
52. Norman Friedman, *Desert Victory: The War for Kuwait* (Annapolis, Md.: Naval Institute Press, 1991), 217.

major cities and social infrastructure in addition to attacking its military machine. Surgical precision, despite the advertised sophistication of modern technology, is never really possible in bombing compaigns. Some collateral damage to civilians and their livelihoods is inevitable, even in the most precisely orchestrated bombing campaign. The point, nonetheless, is that the United States and its allies did a lot less damage to nonmilitary targets than they could have. The reason was that those targets not yet attacked could always be attacked later unless compliance with U.N. demands was forthcoming, as it eventually was.

The distinction between counterforce and countervalue (i.e., military and nonmilitary) targets is too simple in this context, however, for it implies that coercive air war is tantamount to a city-avoidance strategy. The distinction is misleading in two respects. First, in air war against any modern state, important military and war-supporting targets will be found in or near urban areas: air-defense installations, command-and-control centers, communications and transportation nodes, electrical power plants, and so forth. Second, precision aiming of all or even most weapons in the U.S. arsenal is precluded by the fact that only a small proportion of munitions can be delivered by "smart" bombs or delivery vehicles. The vast majority of U.S. munitions used in the Gulf air war of 1991 were "dumb bombs" that operate by massive doses against area targets, such as those deposited by U.S. B-52s on Iraqi fortified areas in Kuwait, or those depleted-uranium pellets which shot up columns of Iraqi tanks.[53] Misdescription of all successful weapons in the Gulf War as "smart" weapons helped to create confusion in the public mind between the "smartness" of weapons and the relative frequency of their use. A good example was the Patriot air-defense missile, which was confused by many observers with Star Wars technology although it in fact represented an older generation of traditional missile defenses against air-breathing weapons.[54]

53. Ibid., 216–17 and plates.
54. The Patriot surface-to-air missile was developed to improve NATO theater defenses in Europe against what were expected to be deep strikes by raiding Soviet aircraft in the early stages of a war. It is not really an antimissile missile or ABM (antiballistic missile) system, although in the Gulf War it was adapted for that purpose against Iraq's comparatively slow-flying Scud short-range ballistic missiles. There is considerable controversy among analysts about how effectively Patriot performed its antimissile role in the Gulf and about how effective the smart bombs really were. Some analysts testified before Congress that smart bombs were far less accurate than touted in Department of Defense after-action reports, and one analyst claimed that the Scuds did more damage to civilian areas in Israel after Patriots were deployed there than before those missiles were made available to Israel. Thus, although U.S. Army figures stated that forty-five of forty-seven Scuds launched at Israel were successfully intercepted, defense analyst Pierre Sprey said Israeli casualties per Scud fired increased by some 80

Because only some weapons can be aimed with precision and because some important targets in a war against a modern state will be located in or near cities, the idea of coercive air warfare does not imply that nonmilitary targets are off-limits. Nonmilitary targets are either irrelevant to the prosecution of the war or they are relevant, but *temporarily excluded* from the target list, in order to give the enemy an *incentive* to settle on terms. Irrelevant targets include schools, churches, historical monuments, and other features of the economic and social infrastructure that it would seem militarily pointless and politically gratuitous to attack.[55] Relevant targets that are excluded temporarily from the initial attacks in a coercive air war can include national political or military command-and-control centers, certain categories of the enemy's military forces which are required for postwar internal security, and other economic or social assets the immediate destruction of which is less significant than the threat of subsequent attack at the discretion of the victor.

These "withholds," as they are sometimes referred to by targeteers, did not include the national military or political command centers in the war against Iraq during January and February 1991. Pentagon and other sources made it clear that if Saddam Hussein walked under a Tomahawk missile or a laser-guided bomb, no one would be disciplined for inaccurate shooting. However, the political problem was this: if Saddam were *certain* that his own headquarters would be targeted and destroyed in the early stages of a war, he would have fewer incentives to terminate the war even under conditions highly favorable to the United States and its allies.[56] There were, in addition, practical difficulties in ascertaining the exact location of Saddam's "headquarters" at any particular time. He was quite obviously moved about in a clandestine manner throughout the air and ground war, and his survival attested to the success of his strategy for preserving self-protective command

percent after the Patriots were deployed. Former Undersecretary of Defense for Research and Development William Perry, also giving testimony to the House Armed Services Committee, said that the Patriot was not capable of dealing with countermeasures or unforeseen complications, such as the breaking up of Scuds in flight (Perry returned to the Department of Defense in January 1993 as deputy secretary). MIT Prof. Theodore Postol noted that after a Patriot successfully intercepted a Scud, falling pieces of both missiles inflicted "tremendous levels of damage" on residential areas. See Donna Cassata, "Weapons Star Role Is Doubted," *Philadelphia Inquirer*, April 23, 1991.

55. Discussion of these and other issues related to the just conduct of war is provided in Michael Walzer, *Just and Unjust Wars: A Moral Argument with Historical Illustrations* (New York: Harper Colophon/Basic Books, 1977).

56. Options for war termination are discussed in Paul Pillar, *Negotiating Peace: War Termination as a Bargaining Process* (Princeton, N.J.: Princeton University Press, 1983), 14–22.

and control. Thus, although a very efficient way to end a war might be to strike specifically against the enemy's political leadership, and although it might be especially tempting to strike against dictators who impose a war on their own people, it is a mission not always accomplished easily. Nor is military decapitation a necessary component of political decapitation. The U.S. strategy did not explicitly call for the destruction of Iraq's political command and control, for the objective was not to destroy the cohesion of the entire state or society. Instead, the U.S. and allied policy objective was the destruction of military command and control pertinent to the further prosecution of an offensive war. This objective called for destruction of less than all of Saddam's war machine and left open the matter of his personal and political survival. The United States accepted that a more ambiguous postwar situation would result from this restraint than from a policy of total war which automatically mandated the destruction or removal of Iraq's regime from power.

Cynics who say that wars are limited only by the power available to the victors, and that states who have the option to annihilate defeated opponents will always do so, can look to the Gulf War of 1991 as an example of deliberate political and military restraint. On the other hand, optimists concerning the autolimitation of U.S. and allied means of destruction in the Gulf War must remember that Iraq's attack on Kuwait remains as a candidate case for deterrence failure. In addition, the coalition effort to compel Iraq's withdrawal from Kuwait by means other than force also failed. The failure of compellence was all the more remarkable given the forces aggregated against Iraq, and given the nonsupport of Iraqi resistance from its former Soviet patron following the end of the Cold War and systemic bipolarity. Saddam's tenacity was undoubtedly owing in part to his insufficient appreciation of the historic system transformation that had taken place in 1989 and 1990 — a transformation that permitted the United Nations of 1990 to act temporarily as a revived Concert of Europe, perhaps for the last time in the region.

Postwar arguments that American "unipolar" dominance of the post–Cold War international system had been established missed the point that the Gulf War was successful because of its limited aims, limited means, allied support, and Soviet acquiescence. No longer was it possible for any single state to wage unilateral war or diplomacy on behalf of system stability with any favorable probability of success. The demise of bipolarity would not mean international hegemony but, rather, some new form of multilateralism that would institutionalize regional security communities (e.g., in Europe) based on structures other than military alliances. In Europe these new pillars of security community might be built on the foundations of the Conference on Security and Cooperation in Europe and the West European Union, but the newer structures of security would have to reach further into states' decisions about military budgets, military doctrine, and military exercises or management of alerts. In the Middle East, the construction of new pillars of security community would be even harder than the admittedly challenging task facing those who are reordering European security agendas. If the arguments made in this book are correct, the new security arrangements will be only as durable as their appreciation is subtle concerning the inevitable relationship between deterrence and nonprovocation in the management of crisis and the avoidance of war.

INDEX

Able Archer exercise, 107
Acheson, Dean, 167n.1, 201
"action channels," escalation control and,
225–26
Adan, Abraham (Bren), 279n.39
AGER (Auxiliary General-Environmental
Research), 226
agreed battle strategy, 13, 200–215, 244;
nuclear weapons and, 211–15
agreed crisis management theory, 206–10
air campaigns: agreed battle strategy and,
204–5; as coercive warfare, 191–92; effectiveness of, in World War II, 178–80; nuclear weapons crisis management and, 76–
77; role of, in Gulf War, 177–82, 291–92
AirLand battle concept, 284–85
Albertini, Luigi, on Russian partial mobilization, 57n.86, 61n.93, 62, 273, 275
Alexeev, Aleksandr, 110
Alksnis, Viktor, 231n.55
Allenby, Edmund (General), 138n.58
alliance diplomacy, 19–20, 220
Allison, Graham T., 29n.21
American Civil War, 159
annihilation, war of: German military strategy based on, 28–29; theories regarding,
156–61
Arab coalition, role of, in Gulf War, 290–91
Arab-Israeli War, worldwide nuclear alert
during, 278–80. See also October War of
1973
Argumenty i fakty, 231n.55

armed forces, post-Soviet restructuring of,
144–63
Arms and Influence, 169–70
Art, Robert J., 104n.63, 105–6
ASAT antisatellite system (Soviet), inadvertency vs. deliberateness regarding, 64–65
ASW (anti-submarine warfare), command-
and-control systems and, 85, 110–11
Atomic Energy Commission, 76
attrition, war of: crisis management through,
68–69; theories regarding, 156–61
Austria-Hungary: dissolution of, 47; German
alliance with, 46, 61–62; mobilization
strategies in, 70–71, 275–76; Russian influence in, 50–51, 60–62; war of attrition
against, 156–57

Baker, James (Secretary of State), 175,
196n.52, 205
balance-of-power concept: limited warfare
models and, 185–87; nuclear weapons development and, 189–91
Balkan Crisis of 1912, 32; crisis management
theory and, 3; Schlieffen Plan and, 29
Ball, Desmond, 223
ballistic missiles: impact of, on nuclear
weapons policy, 84–86, 89–90; limited
warfare and, 189–91; preventive war strategy and, 79–80; role of, in Cuban missile
crisis, 239–44; role of, in Gulf War, 292–
93

nationalization and, 152–63; preferred
strategies for, 91–99; prenuclear threat-
coercion systems and, 1–2; preventive war
concept and, 77–80; punishment vs. denial capabilities of, 193–97; Schlieffen
Plan influence on, 49–72, 119–20; SIOP-
62 plan, 80–83; stockpiling philosophy,
75–77; targeting strategies with, 180–81;
U.S. interservice rivalry regarding, 88–89;
weapons technology and, 5–7, 9–10, 74–
77
Nye, Joseph, 241

October War of 1973, 116–18, 227–28,
230–31
offensive operations, military risks of, 44–49
Ogarkov, N. V. (Marshal), 90n.39, 263n.13
oil dependency, Gulf War and, 289–95
On War, 252
Operation Abirei-Lev 2, 279
Operation Barbarossa, 7, 125–26, 129–31,
148, 155, 164, 216–18
"operational arms control" agreements, 10
organizational theory: command-and-control
vulnerability and, 115–18; German mobilization and, 29n.21; impact of, on deterrence, 278–85; mobilization strategy and,
44–49; nuclear crisis decisionmaking patterns and, 103–8; rigidity of as factor in
escalation control, 224–31
Osgood, Robert, 183–85
Ottoman empire, dissolution of, 47

Patriot air-defense missile system, 292–93
"peaceful coexistence" theory, 9
Pearl Harbor, Japanese attack on, 216–17
Penkovskiy, Oleg, 283
People's Democratic Republic of Kurdistan,
287
permissive-action links (PALs), 102,
233n.59, 240n.71, 242
Perrow, Charles, 115, 222–23
Perry, William, 293n.54
Pershing II missile system, 261
Plan 19: mobilization model based on, 56;
1910 version, 32; 1912 variations to, 33–
35, 50n.67, 158–59
Pliyev, Issa A., 242–43
Poincaré, Raymond, 66, 272
Poland, Russian territories in, 32–33
polarity of power, crisis management and

mobilization, 24. See also bipolar systems;
multipolarity
political objectives: escalation control and,
218–19; impact of, on crisis management,
278–85; role of, in Gulf War, 286–95. See
also bureaucratic politics
Powell, Colin (General), 221–22
Powell, Robert, 94n.45
Power, Thomas S. (General), 239n.68
Powers, Francis Gary, 112–13
preemption: crisis instability and, 103; preventive war strategy and, 78
preferred strategies for nuclear crisis management, 91–99
prenuclear threats and coercion, nuclear crisis management and, 1–2
Presidential Succession Act, 103
preventive diplomacy, 77–80, 237
"prisoner's dilemma," crisis management
and, 66–67
process-oriented strategies, nuclear weapons
policies and, 93–94
provocation: coercion and, 238–44; role of,
in Gulf War, 285–95. See also nonprovocation strategy
Prussia, limited warfare models and, 184–85
punitive retaliation strategy, 91n.40

Qaddafi, Muammar, 178
"quarantine" strategy, in Cuban missile crisis, 239

Reagan, Ronald: coercive diplomacy strategy
of, 236–38; "direct confrontation" strategy of, 90n.39; maritime strategy under,
224, 237–38; nuclear weapons buildup under, 114, 261–62
"Regulation Concerning the Period Preparatory to War," 58
Rennenkampf, Paul (General), 33
retaliation strategies, defined, 91
Ribbentrop-Molotov Pact, 7, 125
Rice, Condoleezza, 109–10
"risk significance" concept, 230
Rosenberg, David Alan, 78
Rostunov, I. I., 50n.67
Russia: decisionmaking system of, 30n.23;
dynamics of threat and, 63–67; French alliance with, 29–30; partial vs. general
mobilization policies, 30–44, 49–51, 55–
59, 70–71, 270–77; pre–World War I mili-

tary policy, 4–5, 47–49. See also Commonwealth of Independent States (CIS); Soviet Union
Russian Federation. See Commonwealth of Independent States (CIS)
Russian Imperial Council, 37, 40
Russo-Japanese War, 31

Sadat, Anwar, 116
Saddam Hussein: coercive diplomacy toward, 177–82, 191–97, 247–48; Gulf War and, 166–68, 221–22, 286–95; invasion of Kuwait, 166–68; military strategies of, 10–13; reaction to deterrence and compellence, 165–66
Sagan, Scott, 114–15, 244
saliency, agreed battle strategy and, 214–15
Salin, I. V., 126
Samsonov, Alexander (General), 33
Sazonov, Sergei: crisis management strategies, 51–55, 60–62; dynamics of threat and, 63; "flexible response" message of, 57; mobilization strategies of, 30, 31n.24, 37, 40–41, 43–44, 50–51, 56–58, 273–75
Schelling, Thomas C., 55, 110–11, 169, 204–5, 238
Schlesinger Doctrine, 92n.42, 93
Schlieffen, Alfred von, 28, 46–47
Schlieffen Plan: command-and-control failures in, 95n.47; crisis management theory and, 4; escalation control and, 218; German reliance on, 28–30; July crisis and, 36–37; nuclear bargaining strategies compared with, 83–91, 95–96, 98–99, 119–20; preventive war strategy based on, 78
Schwarzkopf, Norman (General), 106, 291–92
second-strike counterforce policies, 86n.32
security dilemma, 103; deterrence theory and, 258–59
self-destruct devices, 112–13
self-determination, deterrence theory and, 268
Shaknazarov, Georgi, 240n.71
Shaposhnikov, B. N., 126–27
Shaposhnikov, Yevgeny, 152–53
Showalter, Dennis, 28n.19, 160
Single Integrated Operational Plan (SIOP-62): escalation control and, 225–31; nu-

clear weapons crisis management and, 80–83
Six-Day War, 226
"slow squeeze" diplomacy, in Gulf War, 174
"smart bombs," 13, 292
Snyder, Jack, 24–25, 30n.22, 32n.28, 44–45
Sokolovskiy, V. D., 127
"Solarium" study, 78
Sorenson, Theodore, 240n.71
South Korea, 167, 171
Soviet Union: agreed crisis management with U.S., 207–14; antisubmarine warfare (ASW), 85, 111; Arab-Israeli war airborne alert incident, 116–18, 227–28; command-and-control systems in, 107–19, 124–31; counterforce strategy and, 82–83; Cuban missile crisis and, 6–7, 14–15, 105–6, 170, 172, 195, 239–44, 256–57; deterrence theory in, 257–58; failed coup of 1991, 267–68; Gulf War and, 167–77, 287–95; incremental vs. drastic escalation control in, 232–34; initial wartime preparations in, 122–33, 217n.25; Korean Air Lines 007 jet incident, 114; Korean War and, 167; Kwantung Army, strategic operations against, 140–44; military policy in, 9–10, 124–31, 133–44, 188n.38; nuclear weapons development in, 5–7, 75–77, 90–91, 97–99; political disintegration of, 151–63; stability of bipolarity with U.S. and, 99–119; World War II crisis management, 7–8, 16–17. See also Commonwealth of Independent States (CIS); Russia
Spanish Civil War, 124
special-purpose organizations, development of, 101–2
Sprague, Robert, 78
SSBNs (ballistic-missile-firing submarines), 80, 85
Stalin, Joseph: command-and-control systems under, 124–31; crisis management theory of, 7–8; intelligence operations under, 147–48
Stalingrad, Battle of, 136–39
Steinbruner, John D., 63, 223
Strategic Air Command (SAC): bomber force strategies and, 87–88; creation of, 101–2; Cuban missile crisis and, 239n.68;

preventive war strategy and, 78–80; target sets of, 75n.3, 80–81
Strategic Arms Limitation Talks (SALT), 100
Strategic Defense Initiative (SDI), 262; inadvertency vs. deliberateness regarding, 64–65
structural arms control agreements, 10
submarine-launched ballistic missile (SLBM): nuclear weapons policy regarding, 84–86
Sukhomlinov, V. A. (War Minister), 31–35, 41n.47, 50–55, 57, 275
surprise attacks: preparation times for, 132–33; Soviet defensive military strategies and, 135–36, 142n.67. See also first-strike capabilities
surface-to-air missile (SAM), 112–13
"surge mobilization," 36n.38
"surgical" air strikes, 13
surrender terms: escalation control and, 218–19; strategic vs. tactical surrender, 248–54; termination of war and, 246–54; "unconditional surrender" formula, 249–50
Svechin, A. A., 43, 156, 159
Szapary, Friedrich Graf, 273

targeting strategies: coercive diplomacy and, 177–82; Gulf War escalation control and, 221–22, 291–95. See also bombing strategies
"tantamount to war" concept of mobilization, 57–59
Taube, Baron M. de, 54n.80, 60
Technological Capabilities Panel, 76
technology: intelligence gathering and, 148–50; in Iraq command-and-control system, 290n.50; role of, in military policy, 284–85
termination of war: agreed battle strategy and, 200–15; vs. "conflict termination," 205–6; coercive diplomacy and, 234–46; crisis management theory and, 13–17, 199–200; escalation control and, 215–34; surrender terms and, 246–54
threat perception: coercive diplomacy and, 235–46; deterrence theory and, 21–27, 258–59, 261–62; dynamics of, in mobilization strategy, 63–67; Gulf War and, 165–66

Three Mile Island nuclear power plant, 227
threshold concept, agreed battle strategy and, 214–15
"timetable war," 94–95
Timoshenko, S. K., 126–27
"total war for limited objectives," 28n.19, 99n.52
Trachtenberg, Marc, 98–99, 229–30
trade embargoes, impact on Gulf War, 168
Trident SLBM systems, 85–86
Triple Alliance, 24–25, 71–72, 157, 217–18
Triple Entente, 24–25, 71–72, 217–18
Trotsky, Leon, 145–46
Truman, Harry S.: Korean War and, 166–67, 201–2; nuclear crisis management under, 74–77
"try and see" approach to coercive diplomacy, 172
Turner, L. C. F., 30n.24, 275–76
Twenty-fifth Constitutional Amendment, 103

U-2 incident, 108, 112–15, 209–10; as failure of command-and-control systems, 244–46; Korean Air Lines 007 incident compared with, 263; leadership characteristics during, 281–83
Ukraine: arms nationalization in, 152–63; independence referendum of, 267–68
ultimatums: coercive diplomacy and, 172, 175–77; role of, in July 1914 crisis, 280–81
United Nations, 9; Gulf War and, 12–13, 168–69, 171–72, 174–77, 287–95
Unterberger, General, 32n.26
USS Liberty, 226
USS Pueblo, 226

Vasilevskii, A. M., 140
Vietnam War: agreed battle strategy and, 202–3; impact on military decisionmaking, 107; influence of, on Gulf War, 288–89; as unsuccessful coercive diplomacy, 195, 235–36, 248
Vigor, Peter H., 250
Viviani, René Raphaël, 66
Volkogonov, Dmitri A., 241–42
Voroshilov, K. Ye, 126–27

Walt, Stephen, 25, 217n.26
Waltz, Kenneth, 24–25